Searching for
Jane Austen

This book was published with the generous support of the University Book Store, Madison, Wisconsin, and the Anonymous Fund for the Humanities of the University of Wisconsin.

Searching for Jane Austen

Emily Auerbach

The University of Wisconsin Press

The University of Wisconsin Press
1930 Monroe Street
Madison, Wisconsin 53711

www.wisc.edu/wisconsinpress/

3 Henrietta Street
London WC2E 8LU, England

Library of Congress Cataloging-in-Publication Data
Auerbach, Emily, 1956–
    Searching for Jane Austen / Emily Auerbach.
    p. cm.
    Includes bibliographical references and index.
    ISBN 0-299-20180-5 (alk. paper)
    ISBN 0-299-20184-8 (pbk. : alk. paper)
    1. Austen, Jane, 1775–1817–Criticism and interpretation. 2. Women and
literature–England–History–19th century. 3. Love stories, English–History and
criticism. I. Title.
PR4037.A93   2004
823'.7–dc22   2004005252

Appendix A is reprinted from *The Virginia Quarterly Review* 75 (Winter 1999) 1:
109–20. "Jane Austen" by Mark Twain, which is quoted in its entirety in Appendix B, is copyright © 1999 by Richard A. Watson and Chase Manhattan Bank as
Trustees of the Mark Twain Foundation, which reserves all reproduction or
dramatization rights in every medium; it is published here with the permission of
the University of California Press and Robert H. Hirst, General Editor of the
Mark Twain Project. Lines from *The Poems of Emily Dickinson,* ed. Thomas H.
Johnson (Cambridge, Mass.: The Belknap Press of Harvard University Press,
copyright © 1951, 1955, 1979 by the President and Fellows of Harvard College)
are reprinted by permission of the publishers and the Trustees of Amherst
College.

Book design: Alcorn Publication Design

*Anybody who has had the temerity to write about Jane Austen
is aware . . . that of all great writers she is the most difficult
to catch in the act of greatness.*

—Virginia Woolf

Contents

Illustrations

Acknowledgments

"Thank ye."
> —*Northanger Abbey*

"She thanked . . . with brief, though fervent gratitude."
> —*Sense & Sensibility*

"Let me thank you again and again."
> —*Pride & Prejudice*

"How shall I ever thank you as I ought?"
> —*Mansfield Park*

"A thousand and a thousand thanks."
> —*Emma*

"Thank you, thank you."
> —*Persuasion*

Searching for Jane Austen would not exist were it not for the encouragement, help, and inspiration of many people. First and foremost, I must thank my mother, Wanda Auerbach, who taught me to love literature and encouraged my career every step of the way. I will always treasure the days spent in her company as we read aloud my manuscript and pondered the merit of each word and idea.

I had originally planned to use the following witty dedication for my book: "To my mother, who has read Jane Austen, and to my father and husband, who have not." Little did I suspect that my book would take so long to complete that by the time it reached publication, both men would have read Jane Austen and numbered themselves among her fans! I thank both Robert Auerbach and Keith Meyer for the many ways they have contributed to my life and to this book. I also am thankful to my children, David, Beth, and Melanie, for their willingness to share me with Jane Austen and other courageous women writers.

One colleague at the University of Wisconsin–Madison, Professor Emeritus of English Joseph Wiesenfarth, played a highly instrumental role both by offering specific suggestions on this manuscript in its earlier, unwieldy state and by pioneering an approach to Austen's craftsmanship in his own book, *An Errand of Form: An Assay of Jane Austen's Art.* I am convinced that Jane Austen had Joe Wiesenfarth in mind when she described the sensible and generous Mr. Knightley in *Emma.* In addition, I wish to thank Professor Juliet McMaster of the University of Alberta for her gracious comments on my manuscript, the ideas she gave me during our radio interviews, and her inspiring work on Austen's writings, particularly the juvenilia.

As part of my public radio series *The Courage to Write,* I have had the pleasure of interviewing a wide variety of Austen scholars in addition to Joseph Wiesenfarth and Juliet McMaster. Many of their ideas no doubt are incorporated into this study. In other instances, I have drawn so heavily on the carefully documented works of other Austen scholars that I feel immensely grateful to them, even if we have never spoken. Members of the Jane Austen Society of North America and the Jane Austen Society of Australia have generously offered their advice and help. Let me thank (in alphabetical order) the following Austen scholars and aficionados: Joan Austen-Leigh, Elaine Bander, Stephanie Barron, Garnet Bass, Andrew Davies, Margaret Anne Doody, Margaret Drabble, Jan Fergus, Susannah Fullerton, John Halperin, Reginald Hill, Thomas Hoberg, Park Honan, Claudia Johnson, Deborah Kaplan, Kuldip Kuwahara, Deirdre Le Faye, Joan Ray, Catherine Rasmussen, Jacqueline Reid-Walsh, Carol Shields, Brian Southam, Tony Tanner, Fay Weldon, and Laurel Yourke. A dozen of these scholars joined me in Madison for a festival in 2001 entitled "Jane Austen in the Twenty-first Century" sponsored by the Center for the Humanities and coordinated by Joan Strasbaugh.

I am grateful to both of my University of Wisconsin Departments—Liberal Studies and the Arts in the Division of Continuing Studies and English in the College of Letters and Sciences—for granting me time and research support to work on this book. The staff at the University of Wisconsin Press has been extremely helpful in helping me transform a manuscript into a book.

Finally, I must thank my students of all ages who force me through their questions to think and rethink the deeper meaning of every line Jane Austen wrote. I hope that some of my former students will become teachers, writers, and filmmakers who do ample justice to the *real* Jane Austen we uncovered together in our search for her.

Abbreviations

All references to Jane Austen's writings are taken from R. W. Chapman's standard Oxford University Press edition of *The Novels of Jane Austen* (vols. 1–5, 3rd edition, 1933) and *Minor Works* (vol. 6, 1954). Page numbers are inserted directly into the text, with the following abbreviations used if needed for clarity:

Sense and Sensibility (SS)

Pride and Prejudice (PP)

Mansfield Park (MP)

Emma (E)

Northanger Abbey (NA)

Persuasion (P)

Minor Works (MW)

Those readers with other editions of Austen's novels who wish to locate a quotation by volume and chapter number may do so easily through one of the many electronic searching methods, such as http://www.pemberley .com/janeinfo/novlsrch.html.

References to Jane Austen's letters are indicated parenthetically by date and, unless otherwise indicated, are taken from Deirdre Le Faye's edition of *Jane Austen's Letters* (Oxford: Oxford University Press, 1995).

Searching for
Jane Austen

❦

1

Dear Aunt Jane
Putting Her Down and Touching Her Up

It is the twenty-first century. Forty undergraduates sit poised in their seats for the first day of English 467, a Jane Austen seminar at the University of Wisconsin–Madison. As I walk to the front of the class, I notice a striking fact: only one of my students is male. "My mother made me take this class," he apologetically explains. "Well, really I'm here because Colin Firth makes me swoon," admits a starry-eyed student who says she and her roommates have watched the 1996 BBC/A&E version of *Pride and Prejudice* twenty times. "I want to learn more about Jane," says another. I sigh and take out my notes. It suddenly seems appealing to teach Milton to a class filled equally with males and females, none thinking of him as John or having seen film versions of *Paradise Lost* starring Hollywood's leading heartthrobs as Adam and Satan.

In a recent radio interview, acclaimed film director Ang Lee *(Sense and Sensibility; Crouching Tiger, Hidden Dragon)* admitted that he had never read Austen's novels because he saw them as "girlie books."[1] Newspaper articles about contemporary Austen conferences boast headlines such as "All About Jane."[2] Book jackets of new Austen studies sport prettified images of her face surrounded with flowers and lace, and comedians joke about men dragged to Austen movies against their wills. Old attitudes die hard.

Old texts die hard, too, particularly when they are cheap and free from copyright protection. Internet users priding themselves on their state-of-the-art technology unknowingly download not only distorted representations of Austen's face but also incomplete or altered versions of her writing. As we will see, Austen's relatives and early editors would be pleased to know this: they worked hard to sweeten her image, weaken her words, and soften her bite. Paradoxically, Jane Austen nowadays seems everywhere yet still hard to find. Hence my title: *Searching for Jane Austen*.

Like many other early women writers, Austen published anonymously and presented her ideas indirectly. After all, the Poet Laureate of England would insist two decades after Austen's death that women had no business writing literature.[3] Austen did what Emily Dickinson later advised in a poem: "Tell all the truth—but tell it slant."[4] Parallels between Dickinson and Austen prove illuminating in other ways. Early biographers and editors spoke pityingly of the unmarried and therefore small lives of both women, had the nerve to tamper with their manuscripts and add ruffles and ringlets to their portraits, and thus laid the groundwork for disparaging attitudes still with us today.

Jane Austen's own elusiveness compounds the problem of finding her. I agree with Virginia Woolf that anyone "who has had the temerity to write about Jane Austen" knows that "of all great writers she is the most difficult to catch in the act of greatness."[5] While working on *Searching for Jane Austen,* I have felt myself growing closer and closer to the *real* Jane Austen, a profoundly different woman from the one I thought I knew before beginn2ing this book. Of course I have not caught Jane Austen, but I know I will never read or teach her again in the same way.

When Jane Austen died in 1817 at the age of forty-one, she was at work on *Sanditon,* a novel she would never complete. She had already published four novels anonymously (*Sense and Sensibility* [1811], *Pride and Prejudice* [1813], *Mansfield Park* [1814], *Emma* [1815]), completed two others (*Northanger Abbey, Persuasion*), penned a variety of letters, light verses, and fragments, and recopied into a three-volume set some of her youthful sketches, later called *the juvenilia*. Although she had successfully avoided the public eye, Austen died knowing that she had earned some money from sales of her books and that her admirers had included Sir Walter Scott and the Prince Regent. Like the character in one of Austen's adolescent stories who smiles and whispers to herself, "This is a day well spent," Austen herself might have concluded on 18 July 1817, this is a life well spent.[6]

Or *was* it a life? From the time of her death to the present, there has been a steady stream of biographers who have expressed the notion that Jane Austen had no real life at all, that she was a sweet spinster whose span of time was without significant event.

The first in this stream was Jane Austen's brother Henry. When *Northanger Abbey* and *Persuasion* were published posthumously in 1818, Henry Austen added a brief Biographical Notice.[7] "Short and easy must be the task of the mere biographer," rued Henry Austen, concluding that nothing much happened to his sister. He shared with readers an account of Jane Austen's height, graceful carriage, proper deportment, pleasing features, and modest cheeks; he stressed her piety and emphasized her humility. He failed to mention, however, that she wrote saucy adolescent burlesques filled with outrageous heroines who murder their parents and poison their rivals. He also chose not to say that his sister acted in private family theatricals, negotiated with publishers, alluded in her novels to the slave trade and the rebellious Americans, and wrote acerbic letters to her sister, such as one suggesting of a critic of *Pride and Prejudice*, "Kill poor Mrs Sclater if you like it" (9 February 1813).

Poor Mrs. Sclater was indeed killed—by relatives who omitted that sentence from biographical accounts and from early editions of Austen's letters, just one of many examples of whitewashing. Austen's remark about some neighbors—"I was as civil to them as their bad breath would allow me"—became "I was as civil to them as *circumstances* would allow me" when it was first printed for the public.[8] Neither letter appeared in Henry Austen's Biographical Notice, presumably because such comments would have undermined his claim that Jane Austen "never spoke an unkind word to anybody or had anything but sweet thoughts."

To present a kinder, gentler Jane to the world, Henry Austen carefully quoted from only two letters. In one, Austen seems to apologize for the small scale of her feminine writing, referring to it as "a little bit of ivory, two inches wide, on which I work with a brush so fine as to produce little effect after much labour" (16 December 1816). In the other, a dying Austen praises her sister Cassandra's tender nursing and prays God to bless her family (28 May 1817). Henry Austen admitted that he had removed from this final letter some "gentle animadversion" of no concern to those outside the family. One wonders just how gentle this hostile criticism was and what dying remark about offensive neighbors or obtuse critics may have been lost to us forever. Together Henry and Cassandra Austen carefully destroyed or sprayed verbal perfume on portions of their sister's letters deemed too offensive for outsiders.

A clergyman, Henry Austen was determined to present his sister's qualifications as a devout Christian who led a blameless life. He conveniently ignored the fact that many clergymen in her novels appear riddled with foibles and that one juvenile sketch introduces a young woman who confesses, "I have changed my religion so often that at present I have not an idea of any left" ("A Letter from a Young Lady," *MW*, 175). He insisted that his amiable sister never sought a public, so of course he omitted letters showing Austen's keen interest in sales: "You will be glad to hear that every Copy of S.&S. [*Sense and Sensibility*] is sold & that it has brought me £140—besides the Copyright, if that sh^d ever be of any value.—I have now therefore written myself into £250.—which only makes me long for more.—I have something in hand [*Mansfield Park*]—which I hope on the credit of P.&P. [*Pride and Prejudice*] will sell well, tho' not half so entertaining" (6 July 1813). This gives the lie to Henry Austen's insistence in his Biographical Notice that his sister was never motivated by hope of profit. As Jan Fergus has documented so incontrovertibly, Austen sprinkles references to money and readers throughout her letters.[9] Austen "shall . . . try to make all the Money" and "make People . . . pay" for *Pride and Prejudice*, hopes "that *many* will feel themselves obliged to buy" the second edition of *Sense and Sensibility*, admits of *Mansfield Park*, "I am very greedy & want to make the most of it," and comments about readers who borrow rather than buy her books, "tho' I like praise as well as anybody, I like what Edward calls *Pewter* too" (25 September 1813, 6 November 1813, 20 November 1814, 30 November 1814).

Although proud of his sister's writing, Henry Austen labored in his Biographical Notice to present a modest, delicate, saintly woman unconcerned with her artistic reputation. He favored adjectives such as sweet, kind, happy, and tranquil. For example, we learn that his sister had an "extremely sweet" voice and endowments that "sweetened every hour" of her relatives' lives. Henry Austen credited his ever-saccharine sister with a "perfect placidity of temper" and flawlessness, ignoring the fact that she wrote in a letter, "pictures of perfection as you know make me sick and wicked" (23 March 1817).

In keeping with the tone of that Biographical Notice, Austen's relatives chose a sweet and humble inscription for her gravestone. No mention was made of Austen's writings or her feistiness: "The benevolence of her heart, the sweetness of her temper, and the extraordinary endowments of her mind obtained the regard of all who knew her, and the warmest love of her intimate connections. . . . In their deepest affliction they are consoled by a firm though humble hope that her charity, devotion, faith and purity, have rendered her soul acceptable in the sight of her redeemer." Half a century passed before the family added a second tablet referring to "Jane Austen known to many by her writings."

Like his brother Henry, James Austen emphasized his sister's mild and traditional feminine nature. His verse elegy praised her "Temper, even, calm & sweet" and her readiness "to share / The labours of domestic care."[10] His sister did not let her writing inflame her vanity and pride or distract her from completing useful chores, James insisted. James's son, James Edward Austen-Leigh, continued this verbal softening in his 1870 *Memoir*. As the first full-scale biography of Austen, Austen-Leigh's *Memoir* exercised a powerful influence on later Austen biographies, critical studies, and encyclopedia entries. We are still feeling the effects of the Jane Austen myth constructed in 1870 for public consumption.

In the very first sentence of his *Memoir*, Austen-Leigh refers to his "dear Aunt Jane." Noting that her nephews and nieces "did not think of her as being clever" but valued her "as one always kind, sympathetic, and amusing," Austen-Leigh praises his maiden aunt's charming, delightful personality, "sweet temper and loving heart," "cheerful contented disposition," "humble mind," and "modest simplicity."[11] Austen-Leigh emphasizes those qualities considered ladylike, such as Aunt Jane's enjoyment of the piano or her devotion to nursing the sick. Like his Uncle Henry, Austen-Leigh liberally sprinkles the word "sweet" throughout his biographical account. Reading Austen-Leigh's comment that Aunt Jane's "sweetness of temper never failed," detective novelist P. D. James begs to differ: "On the contrary, it failed frequently, and if it hadn't we would not have had the six great novels."[12]

Austen-Leigh accurately presents the skeletal facts of Austen's biography: she was a clergyman's daughter born in rural Hampshire in 1775, had a lifelong companionship with her sister Cassandra, treasured her relationship with her many brothers, including two in the navy, changed residence a few times, never married, lived rather unremarkably, yet somehow produced six remarkable novels before her untimely death in 1817 from some sort of lingering illness.

Absent from Austen-Leigh's biography is any sense of pizzazz. He acknowledges that Austen's mother "expressed herself . . . with epigrammatic force," but he gives no examples of the blunt doggerel she wrote, such as Mrs. Austen's account of people attending a ball:

> Next, Squire Hicks and his fair spouse—
> They came from Mr. Bramston's house.
> With Madam, and her maiden Sister,
> (Had she been absent, who'd have missed her?)

Although visitors to the Austen home reported encountering "the flow of native homebred wit, with all the fun and nonsense of a clever family," Austen-Leigh instead presents a blandly idealized and thus unbelievable family life "never troubled by disagreements even in little matters."[13]

Austen-Leigh does spend considerable time relating an anecdote about Austen's secrecy: "She was careful that her occupation should not be suspected by servants, or visitors, or any persons beyond her own family party. She wrote upon small sheets of paper which could easily be put away, or covered with a piece of blotting paper. There was, between the front door and the offices, a swing door which creaked when it was opened; but she objected to having this little inconvenience remedied, because it gave her notice when anyone was coming."[14] This presents Austen in an appropriately feminine and diminutive role: writing on small paper and enduring a little inconvenience in order to hide her work from view.

Austen-Leigh presents his modest aunt's occupation as a little hobby for her own amusement and claims that she felt no mortification about her lack of early success. If so, why did Austen negotiate to buy back the manuscript of a novel publishers had purchased but failed to print? Why did she sign her correspondence Mrs. Ashton Dennis, or M.A.D.? If it is true that "so lowly did she esteem her own claims," why did Austen include in *Northanger Abbey* a ringing defense of novels and novelists?[15]

Austen-Leigh must have broken out in a sweat about what to do with his supposedly docile aunt's iconoclastic minor writings. As we will see in the next chapter (Beware of Swoons: Jane Austen's Early Writings), Austen began writing at an early age for the amusement of her family. As an adolescent, she penned rowdy spoofs mocking literary and social conventions of the day. Margaret Drabble calls these juvenile works "an excellent antidote to the conventional view of Jane Austen as a calm, well-mannered novelist."[16] Austen never fully outgrew this early taste in satire and wrote sarcastic fragments and witty doggerel until the end of her life. No one who reads Austen's uncensored early writings and satiric fragments can ever return to the image of dear Aunt Jane.

Relatives knew this. How could they reconcile their biographical presentation of Saint Jane with her adolescent stories about young women who toss rivals out the window, raise armies, and get "dead Drunk"? In his 1870 *Memoir,* Austen-Leigh praises the family decision not to publish these puerile, nonsensical early stories. Austen-Leigh prints just *one* example: an early sketch called "The Mystery." Only a page long, this incomplete comedy features mostly male characters speaking in acceptable ways ("Are you convinced of its propriety?"). This fragment gives no hint of the outrageous heroines and audacious scenes contained in most other youthful pieces. In some ways, it might have been better for Austen-Leigh to include *no* early piece than to give one misleading example to support the family's decision not to publish the whole. As Juliet McMaster observed, Austen-Leigh made a "misguided and eccentric choice" in publishing only "The Mystery" from the three-volume collection of youthful effusions.[17]

Austen-Leigh faced further difficulties when he came to his aunt's letters. Cassandra had burned many, but apparently not enough. As cousin Caroline warned, "There is nothing in these letters which I have seen that would be acceptable to the public."[18] Austen-Leigh carefully deletes unacceptable letters and parts of letters and prefaces this section of his *Memoir* with a patronizing apology for his aunt's triviality: "A wish has sometimes been expressed that some of Jane Austen's letters should be published. Some entire letters, and many extracts, will be given in this memoir; but the reader must be warned not to expect too much from them. . . . There is in them no notice of politics or public events; scarcely any discussions on literature. . . . They may be said to resemble the nest which some little bird builds of the materials nearest at hand, of the twigs and mosses supplied by the tree in which it is placed; curiously constructed out of the simplest matters."[19] This image of a little nest supports his earlier claim in the *Memoir* that his simple aunt "never touched upon politics, law, or medicine" and only concerned herself with "the performance of home duties, and the cultivation of domestic affections."[20]

The first Aunt Jane letter Austen-Leigh shares contains no ellipsis dots, tricking readers into thinking they are encountering it in its entirety. But compare the beginning of Austen-Leigh's version with the uncensored letter:

> My dear Cassandra,
> I thank you for so speedy a return to my last two, and particularly thank you for your anecdote of Charlotte Graham and her cousin, Harriet Bailey, which has very much amused both my mother and myself.[21]

> My dear Cassandra,
> Having just finished the first volume of les Veillees du Chateau, I think it a good opportunity for beginning a

9

letter to you while my mind is stored with Ideas worth transmitting.—I thank you for so speedy a return to my last two, and particularly thank you for your anecdote of Charlotte Graham & her cousin Harriot Bailey, which has very much amused both my mother & myself. (8 November 1800)

How else do we explain Austen-Leigh's deletion of the first sentence than to say he did not want Aunt Jane to allude to literary works (*Tales of the Castle* by Madame du Genlis) or to be caught boasting of her intellect ("my mind is stored with Ideas")? Better to open with a harmless aunt thanking her sister and enjoying sharing anecdotes with her mother. Austen-Leigh also omits from this first letter sharp comments such as "the party . . . was in general a very ungenteel one, and there was hardly a pretty girl in the room." Gone is a boast ("I said two or three amusing things"). Also deleted are references to a Turkish ship, the French, and Cyprus. In effect, Austen-Leigh creates a brilliant Catch-22. After removing references to politics and literature from the letters, he then observes that his songbird-like aunt takes "no notice of politics or public events" and avoids "discussions of literature."

This pattern continues throughout the *Memoir*. "The politics of the day occupied very little of her attention," Austen-Leigh concludes, but he fails to tell readers that he has carefully excised her remarks about sloops and frigates, the East Indies, Nova Scotia, and a 44-gun ship called the *Expedition*. Austen-Leigh claims that the reason his aunt refers to the American wilderness, Niagara Falls, and Lake Ontario in a verse sent to a niece is just that she needed a rhyme: "I believe that all this nonsense was nearly extempore, and that the fancy of drawing the images from America arose at the moment from the obvious rhyme in the first stanza [Anna/savannah]." Austen-Leigh would have been appalled to discover a recent feminist rereading of the poem calling his interpretation "dismissive" and "pejorative" and suggesting that Austen skillfully chose New World imagery to capture a female mind yearning for vaster, "unfurled" worlds.[22]

Austen-Leigh also needed to support his claim that his aunt knew nothing of medicine, so he cuts sentences referring to bones, fractures, bile, and emetics. To keep his aunt from sounding too intellectual or bookish, he takes the razor to her allusions to Laurence Sterne's *Tristram Shandy*, Samuel Richardson's *Sir Charles Grandison*, Daniel Defoe's *Robinson Crusoe*, and other literary works. Better a reference to a petticoat than a novel, apparently.

Better blandness than wit. Austen-Leigh includes his cousin's remark that their Aunt Jane "was as far as possible from being censorious or satirical . . . nor did she ever turn individuals into ridicule."[23] To bolster this claim, he of course had to withhold astringent comments from the letters such as the following:

> Mrs Hall of Sherborn was brought to bed yesterday of a dead child, some weeks before she was expected, oweing [sic] to a fright.—I suppose she happened unawares to look at her husband.

> I expect a very stupid Ball, there will be nobody worth dancing with, & nobody worth talking to.

> Mr Waller is dead, I see;—I cannot greive [sic] about it, nor perhaps can his Widow very much.[24]

Just how sweet is a woman who can joke about a stillborn child? As Virginia Woolf noted, Austen must have been "alarming to find at home."[25]

Almost every page of the *Memoir* contains an omission or alteration, usually without any indication that this is occurring. Austen-Leigh leaves in references to sacred crosses but not to secular fireworks. He suppresses sentences in which his aunt calls a rector "a wretch," attacks "the ignorant class of school mistresses," and describes a house as possessing "all the comforts of little Children, dirt, and litter." Austen's competitive quip about novelist Sir Walter Scott ("I do not like him, & do not mean to like Waverley") becomes lobotomized into "I do not mean to like Waverley." Readers of the *Memoir* also miss hearing her snipe about an unwelcome visitor, "Wyndham Knatchbull is to be asked for Sunday, & if he is cruel enough to consent, somebody must be contrived to meet him." Victorian sensibilities perhaps explain why Austen-Leigh deleted his aunt's reference to "some naked Cupids over the Mantlepeice, which must be a fine study for Girls" or altered a letter to a niece who had visited:

> Give my love to little Cassandra, I hope she found my Bed comfortable last night & has not filled it with fleas. (Austen's original)

> Give my Love to little Cass. I hope she found my bed comfortable last night. (Austen-Leigh's sanitized version)

How Austen-Leigh's hatchet job robs Austen of her sparkle.[26]

"Make the doors upon a woman's wit, and it will out at the casement; shut that, and 'twill out at the key-hole," Rosalind observes in *As You Like It* (4.1.161). Austen's keen sense of the absurd comes through, even in the *Memoir*. Perhaps because he considered his aunt's pose appropriately modest and self-deprecatory, Austen-Leigh includes in near entirety Austen's correspondence with James Stanier Clarke, the librarian for the Prince Regent. Reading between the lines, we discover a woman far more self-confident than Austen-Leigh expected us to find.

When the self-important, rather obtuse James Stanier Clarke writes to Austen to express his admiration of her novels, he suggests that she consider writing a biography of a clergyman rather like himself: "I also dear Madam wished to be allowed to ask you, to delineate in some future Work the Habits of Life and Character and enthusiasm of a Clergyman—who should pass his time between the metropolis & the Country— . . . Neither Goldsmith—nor La Fontaine . . . have in my mind quite delineated an English Clergyman, at least of the present day—Fond of, & entirely engaged in Literature—no man's Enemy but his own" (16 November 1815). As if to show just how "entirely engaged in Literature" a clergyman could be, Clarke quotes in the same letter some lines from Beattie's *Minstrel:* "Silent when glad, affectionate tho' shy. . . . / & now he laughed aloud yet none knew why."

Austen-Leigh labels Clarke's letter "gracious" and insists that it left his aunt feeling inadequate. Readers today, however, note Austen's unfeminine boldness as she thanks Clarke for praising her novels ("I am too vain to wish to convince you that you have praised them beyond their Merit"). The final paragraph of Austen's letter stands as a masterpiece of creative tact and shrewd self-deprecation:

> I am quite honoured by your thinking me capable of drawing such a Clergyman as you gave the sketch of in your note of Nov: 16. But I assure you I am *not*. The comic part of the Character I might be equal to, but not the Good, the Enthusiastic, the Literary. Such a Man's Conversation must at times be on subjects of Science & Philosophy of which I know nothing—or at least be occasionally abundant in quotations & allusions which a Woman, who like me, knows only her own Mother-tongue & has read very little in that, would be totally without the power of giving.—A Classical Education, or at any rate, a very extensive acquaintance with English Literature, Ancient & Modern, appears to me

quite Indispensable for the person who w^d do any justice to your Clergyman—And I think I may boast myself to be, with all possible Vanity, the most unlearned, & uninformed Female who ever dared to be an Authoress. Beleive me, dear Sir, Your oblig^d & faith^l Hum. Servt. J. A. (11 December 1815)

One suspects that Clarke took Austen's feminine-sounding apology ("A Woman . . . like me") at face value, probably assuming she was right that only a highly educated, classically trained Man could do justice to such a highly-educated, literate being as himself. As he includes the letter in his *Memoir* of 1870, Austen-Leigh wants readers to take it as a straightforward apology from a modest woman. He observes, "How unequal the author of 'Pride and Prejudice' felt herself to delineating an enthusiastic clergyman."[27]

Unequal, or unwilling? Do we not hear the sound of Austen's laughter behind this letter? By pronouncing herself "equal" to the *comic* part of a clergyman's character, she suggests that even men of God may be ridiculous. She displays her wit by ironically *boasting* with all possible *Vanity* of her unlearned, uninformed state.

James Stanier Clarke had extraordinary persistence, continuing to suggest that she write about a clergyman ("describe him burying his own mother—as I did"). When he receives a new appointment as "Chaplain and Private English Secretary to the Prince of Cobourg," he writes to suggest that Austen might wish to pen a "Historical Romance illustrative of the History of the august house of Cobourg" (27 March 1816).

Maybe Jane Austen was beginning by now to feel like Elizabeth Bennet in conversation with the Reverend Mr. Collins in *Pride and Prejudice:* the more Elizabeth declines Mr. Collins's proposal of marriage, the more he finds her so charming that he must renew the offer. Jane Austen's letter to James Stanier Clarke a few days later again closes with a masterful apologia:

You are very, very kind in your hints as to the sort of Composition which might recommend me at present, & I am fully sensible that an Historical Romance, founded on the House of Saxe Cobourg might be much more to the purpose of Profit or Popularity, than such pictures of domestic Life in Country Villages as I deal in—but I could no more write a Romance than an Epic Poem.—I could not sit seriously down to write a serious Romance under any other motive than to save my Life, & if it were indispensable for me to keep it up & never relax into laughing at myself or other people, I am sure I should be hung before I had finished the first Chapter.—No—I must keep to my own style & go on in my own Way; And though I may never succeed again in that, I am convinced that I should totally fail in any other. (1 April 1816)

This letter captures Jane Austen's undaunted belief in herself and her skill at masking such confidence with irony. On the surface she calls Clarke "very, very kind" and pleads incapacity ("I could no more" . . . "I could not" . . . "I should totally fail") as her excuse. How could he take offense? Yet she makes it clear in the letter that she is perceptive and aware ("I am fully sensible"), has artistic integrity rather than a desire to pursue "Profit or Popularity," finds wit a welcome relief from the Reverend Clarkes of the world, and is determined to stick defiantly ("No—") to her own voice no matter how many very, very kind hints she receives. She immodestly emphasizes herself ("I," "my," "own") and conveys a sense of necessity ("must") in her triumphant sentence, "I must keep to my own style & go on in my own Way." While modestly admitting that she may "totally fail" in a serious literary production, she claims previous success by writing in the final sentence, "I may never succeed *again*" (my italics). This is the letter of a brilliant, self-assured woman who knew how to pretend to play the feminine game while remaining true to herself and her distinctive literary voice.

Austen-Leigh acknowledges in his *Memoir* that Austen found Clarke's suggestions ludicrous, but he suggests that this is because Clarke expected too *much*, not too little, of her. The analogy Austen-Leigh offers reinforces this: for Clarke to have proposed for Austen to write about the House of Cobourg "was much as if Sir William Ross had been set to paint a great battle piece."[28] Ross was a miniaturist, so Austen-Leigh's reference to him reinforces the notion of Austen as a "little" writer. In addition, Ross had, by the time Austen-Leigh published his *Memoir*, given up his art altogether because photography made his work obsolete. Austen-Leigh's analogy thus makes Austen seem not only small but also quaint. It gives no hint that Austen determinedly stuck to her own style, tackled human problems on a grand scale, and radically transformed the novel genre through her innovations.

His aunt found Clarke's suggestions so amusing, Austen-Leigh reports, that she incorporated some of them into her paper entitled

"Plan of a Novel, according to hints from various quarters," written just a year before her death. This 1816 satire-dripping essay must have served as an outlet for Austen's annoyance with Clarke and others. In margin notes to this mock plot summary of the ideal novel, she documents which relatives, reviewers, or acquaintances (including Clarke) are responsible for various suggestions she pretends to take. According to various quarters, novels should bear little resemblance to real life. Italics indicate those portions of this essay that Austen-Leigh chose to alter for his *Memoir:*

> Scene to be in the Country, Heroine the Daughter of a Clergyman, one who after having lived much in the World had retired from it, & settled in a Curacy, with a very small fortune of his own.–He, the most excellent Man that can be imagined, perfect in Character, Temper & Manners–without the smallest drawback or peculiarity to prevent his being the most delightful companion to his Daughter from one year's end to the other.–*Heroine a faultless Character herself–, perfectly good, with much tenderness & sentiment, & not the least Wit–very highly accomplished, understanding modern Languages & (generally speaking) everything that the most accomplished young Women learn, but particularly excelling in Music–her favourite pursuit–& playing equally well on the Piano Forte & Harp–& singing in the first stile. Her Person, quite beautiful–dark eyes & plum cheeks.*–Book to open with the description of Father & Daughter–who are to converse in long speeches, elegant Language–& a tone of high-serious sentiment. (*MW,* 428–29)

Instead of Austen's lengthy sentence describing the ideal heroine, Austen-Leigh includes only this twelve-word abridgement: "Heroine faultless in character, beautiful in person, and possessing every possible accomplishment."[29] This chopped version censors the fact that Austen describes her era's ideal heroine as having "not the least Wit." Later, Austen describes the heroine as rejecting the acquaintance of a talented, shrewd young woman because this antiheroine has "a considerable degree of Wit"; this, too, Austen-Leigh chose to delete from his published version of the Plan. An aunt who *liked* wit? How dreadful.

As we read "Plan of a Novel, according to hints from various quarters" we can almost hear Austen chuckling as she transformed James Stanier Clarke's actual suggestions into parody. For the private amusement of herself and her family, she makes her mock-heroine's father into Clarke's ideal clergyman. Austen-Leigh apparently felt his aunt's parody was *too* mean-spirited because he censored her direct echoing of Clarke's remarks about burying his mother and her verbatim use of Clarke's idea that the affectedly literary clergyman was "nobody's enemy but his own." Note below how closely Clarke's hints (left) are parodied in Austen's original Plan (right). Italics show how Austen-Leigh deleted the sharpest portions of his aunt's satire from the version of the Plan he published in his 1870 *Memoir*:

Clarke	Austen
Pray continue to write, & make all your friends send Sketches to help you– . . . Do let us have an English Clergyman . . . shew dear Madam what good would be done if Tythes were taken away entirely, and describe him burying his own mother . . . because the High Priest of the Parish in which she died–did not pay her remains the respect he ought to do . . . Carry your Clergyman to Sea as the Friend of some distinguished Naval Character about a Court–you can then bring forward . . . many interesting Scenes of Character & Interest. . . . Delineate . . . the Habits of Life & Character & enthusiasm of a Clergyman . . . Fond of, & entirely engaged in literature– no man's Enemy but his own. (21 December 1815)	It will comprehend his going to sea as Chaplain to a distinguished Naval Character about the Court, his going afterwards to Court himself, which introduced him to a great variety of Characters & involved him in many interesting situations, concluding with his opinion of the Benefits to result from Tythes being done away, *& his having buried his own Mother (Heroine's lamented Grandmother) in consequence of the High Priest of the Parish in which she died, refusing to pay her Remains the respect due to them. The Father to be of a very literary turn, an Enthusiast in Literature, nobody's Enemy but his own–* (MW, 429)

The Austen who wrote this sarcastic plan–the full version, not the censored one omitting the direct parody of Clarke's "helpful" suggestions–is not a placid cherub but, as novelist Carol Shields calls her, an "ironic, spiky" woman writer with tremendous confidence in her own art.[30]

The *Memoir* works hard to contain Austen's genius–to put it in its place. Austen-Leigh thus paves the way for generations of critics to locate Austen in a respectably ladylike literary nook, not in the pantheon of the world's greatest writers. She is "not indeed amongst the higher orders of genius," he concludes, nor do her works make any conscious attempt "to raise the standard of human life" or "inculcate any particular moral." Austen-Leigh's Jane Austen writes harmless domestic novels for her own amusement "without any self-seeking or craving after applause," and she accepts obscurity because "so lowly did she esteem her own claims."[31] Not surprisingly, he does not include lines from letters such as her quip, "I write only for Fame" (14 January 1796).

Austen-Leigh may have meant well but he clearly had an agenda: he wanted posterity to regard his aunt as feminine and angelic—one too refined to have mentioned naked bodies and fleas; too otherworldly to have thought of money; too modest to have felt superior to others. To create this image, he and other relatives censored her spark—her vivacious bite and self-confident dash—and presented a drab, humble paragon of propriety. Since the *Memoir* has been called a book that "can never be superseded," "the basis of all subsequent biographies of Jane Austen," and "still the place to begin" in the twenty-first century, these changes are important.[32] Books, articles, and newsletter columns about Austen in our own time (including some I wrote a few years ago!) continue to misquote her letters because they use Austen-Leigh's *Memoir* as a reputable source or overlook subtle and therefore insidious changes in wording. Austen-Leigh's portrayal of an inoffensive and uninteresting maiden aunt became gospel: "Might we not borrow from Miss Austen's biography the title which the nephew bestows upon her, and recognize her officially as 'dear Aunt Jane'?" writes Victorian critic Richard Simpson.[33]

Niece Caroline Austen helped to carry "dear Aunt Jane" even further into feminine Elysium, praising her "great sweetness of manner" and insisting that "her sweetness of temper never failed her."[34] Caroline Austen emphasizes her aunt's "home virtues," such as serving breakfast, nursing others with tender devotion, and behaving at all times with becoming modesty: "She was a humble and beleiving Christian; her life had passed in the cheerful performance of all home duties, and with *no* aiming at applause, she had sought, as if by instinct to promote the happiness of all those who came within her influence." Caroline Austen discouraged her cousin James from publishing their aunt's wild adolescent works and occasionally acerbic letters. How else could she maintain that Aunt Jane was never censorious or satirical? As Victorian novelist Margaret Oliphant observed, "The family were half-ashamed to have it known that she was not just a young lady like the others, doing her embroidery."[35]

Cassandra Austen's 1802 sketch of Jane Austen from the back

If a picture speaks a thousand words, then we can learn voluminous tomes from the many touch up jobs given to Jane Austen's portrait. The one signed and dated portrait of Jane Austen is an 1802 watercolor Cassandra made of her sister from the back as she sits on a bank, her face obscured by her bonnet. The other portrait deemed authentic is an unsigned and undated pencil and watercolor sketch of Jane Austen sitting in a chair, which relatives claimed Cassandra made in approximately 1811; Cassandra had both portraits with her at her final home. Cassandra Austen's tiny second sketch (only $4^1/_2$-by-$3^1/_8$ inches) shows a young woman with penetrating eyes, a small unsmiling mouth, simple clothes, and tightly folded arms. She sits stiffly on a plain chair and seems to be looking at the world with a sharp, uncompromising gaze. Brian Southam describes this portrait as "a face sharp and watchful, with large unmelting eyes and pursed lips," and Park Honan notes Austen's "defiant, slightly aloof expression" as the eyes "look calmly and with a certain sparkle at an upward angle at the world."[36]

Defiance and sparkle apparently troubled Austen's relatives. When Austen-Leigh prepared to publish his *Memoir,* he commissioned a watercolor miniature and a steel engraving derived from Cassandra Austen's second sketch. The resulting portrait appearing in the 1870 *Memoir* presents an Austen with a fuller mouth, her lips slightly upturned as if she is almost smiling. Her eyes are made softer, more doelike, and her gaze has been lowered. Her face is rounder, neck longer, figure less sturdy, and hair less wispy. Ruffles deck both the rim of the bonnet and the neckline of the dress. The chair curves gracefully, and Austen's arms now hang loosely so she does not appear to grip herself so tightly or confidently. As Helen Denman notes in her study of the portrait, "It is a charming watercolor, but it is Cassandra's impression beautified for Victorian eyes and Victorian sensibilities, a pious imaginary delineation of 'dear Aunt Jane'."[37] Austen's features have blurred, her posture is rounded rather than rigid, and she has sprouted more noticeably feminine breasts. A prettified chair matches the prettified young woman who looks softly at us with a serene expression in her gentle eyes.

The response of family members to this doctored-up portrait suggests we no longer are looking at Jane Austen. Niece Cassy Austen viewed the portrait as an improvement, not a faithful rendering: "I think the portrait is very much superior to any thing that could have been expected from the sketch it was taken from—It is a very pleasing, sweet face,—tho', I confess, to not thinking it *much* like the

Cassandra Austen's sketch of Jane Austen (c. 1811) (Reproduced by permission of National Portrait Gallery, London)

Engraved version for 1870 *Memoir*

original;—but *that*, the public will not be able to detect."[38] Niece Caroline Austen noted "the general resemblance is *not* strong," observing in particular that the eyes had been made "larger than *the truth:* that is, rounder, and more open"; a neighbor commented that the portrait lacked the original's "sparkling Eyes," which were "not large but joyous and intelligent" and discerned that the cap had been made more womanly.[39]

Several supposed Jane Austen portraits emerged in the nineteenth century, but not one has been proven authentic. Austen's waist (emphasized by a sash) shrinks, her shoulders become more petite, her arms open up into a more casual pose, and her finger boasts a wedding ring. When Lord Brabourne issued an edition of Jane Austen's letters in 1884, he chose a different picture for his frontispiece: an undated, unsigned oil painting showing a young girl holding a parasol, one foot demurely uplifted, one hand awkwardly tucked away, a billowing, cloud-like dress of white proclaiming her innocence. Better a smiling girl holding a parasol than a woman boasting a penetrating gaze. Although some scholars (Claudia Johnson, Margaret Anne Doody, and others) think this painting may be authentic, Deirdre Le Faye concludes in her article about the ongoing controversy, "this attractive little girl is not Jane Austen."[40] In any case, why put a painting of a girl on the frontispiece of a woman's collection of letters?

Later image of Austen with an added wedding ring

Image of a young "Austen" with parasol used in the frontispiece of Lord Brabourne's bowdlerized edition of Austen's letters

Throughout the twentieth century, most biographers chose to reprint the altered renditions or to create brand new ones rather than reproduce Cassandra's sketch. For example, a 1931 *World Book Encyclopedia* presents a supposed Jane Austen looking straight ahead, wearing a seductive dress and sporting a new hairdo. Two decades later a book called *Presenting Miss Jane Austen* emphasizes Austen's unmarried status in its title and trumpets on its frontispiece a new sketch of the artist as a young woman.[41] This "conjectural portrait" shows Jane Austen with her hair piled high with ringlets, her eyes gently reflective. Our eyes are drawn immediately to the center, where a cross piously encircles Austen's elongated neck. Another variation on the theme of a sweet-faced, elegantly coiffured Austen appears in a 1981 publication of her early writings. Who is this woman?

Even today, it is difficult to find Cassandra's original sketch: we are more apt to see the beribboned later versions. Many biographers continue to seem uncomfortable with what Claudia Johnson calls the "unsmiling austerity" of Cassandra's sketch.[42] As if to support her

Clockwise from top left: Image of "Austen" from 1931 *World Book Encyclopedia*; "Conjectural Portrait" of a pious Austen in 1952 *Presenting Miss Jane Austen*; Image of Austen on cover of 1981 *Love and Freindship* (© 1977, 1978 by Suzanne Perkins, used by permission of Harmony Books, a division of Random House, Inc.)

Writers of sense and sensibility.

New York Times Book Review image of Austen with a wedding ring

judgment that Austen was emotionally unfulfilled because she never married, Valerie Myer describes the Jane Austen of Cassandra's sketch in unflattering terms: "Cassandra's drawing shows a woman more sharp-featured than appealing. . . . Her curls escape charmingly from the cap, but there are lines of disappointment running from nose to mouth, and the mouth itself looks small and mean. She looks like a peevish hamster."[43] Perhaps in part because they are readily available on the Internet and freed from copyright restrictions and expensive permissions, prettified versions of Austen's face continue to appear on book jackets. The *New York Times Book Review* calls for readers with sense and sensibility by printing an image of a beruffled Jane Austen with limpid pools for eyes and, yes, a wedding ring. I miss the *sharp* Jane Austen of Cassandra's sketch. Could it be those lines by her mouth are lines of determination, not disappointment?

What does the continual repicturing of Austen say to us? Why gussy her up with ruffles and a fake Mona Lisa smile? Just as Edith Wharton's husband remarked to a visitor as he pointed to his wife's hourglass figure, "Look at that small waist. No one would ever guess that she had written a line of poetry," so perhaps Austen's relatives wanted to assure the public that a woman writer need not be monstrous or masculine.[44]

This softening appears over and over again in the presentation of women writers. For example, in the preface to the first volume of poetry published by an American woman, Anne Bradstreet's brother-in-law assures readers of the poet's piety and femininity: "It is the work of a woman honoured, and esteemed where she lives, for her gracious demeanour, her eminent parts, her pious conversation, her courteous disposition, her exact diligence in her place, and discreet managing of her family occasions, and these Poems are the fruit but of some few hours, curtailed from her sleep and other refreshments."[45] Margaret Fuller's brother tries to soften the revolutionary *Woman in the Nineteenth Century* by insisting in his preface that his sister (in her role as the married Mrs. Osseli) was "preeminently a Christian" who was "the angel of the sick-chamber . . . eminent in that sphere of womanly duty" and faithful "to all home duties."[46] When Harriet Beecher Stowe spoke out in public before mixed audiences, her husband got up on the stage before her to assure the audiences that his submissive wife was properly "meek, humble, and pious."[47]

Jane Austen's relatives might have been pleased to read this 1882 response to the "dear Aunt Jane" they had helped create: "We see only a sweet, modest woman. . . . She began authorship almost without knowing what the dignity of authorship meant. . . . for writing had been, for her, so much like singing is for the song-bird. She has left to all time, not only her books, but a picture of what a female author and artist should be: true to home duties, while she is true to her genius; delicate and brilliant in her work, yet without a word having ever dropt from her pen that can offend the blush of modesty."[48] Perhaps the desire to project precisely this sort of little songbird image led relatives and publishers to dull sharp edges, blur severity, soften a sardonic gaze, and add fragility to a self-confident stance. Apparently it was just too disquieting to consider Austen as a woman who enjoyed her chosen vocation as the author of satiric novels and seemed, despite or perhaps because of her singleness, to blossom rather than to pine away.

In a startlingly similar way, early editors of Emily Dickinson softened the one authentic daguerreotype of her by bedecking her with harlequin-like ruffles and girlish ringlets for the frontispiece of *The Complete Poems of Emily Dickinson*. Underneath the superficial changes made to the visual image of Emily Dickinson lies a far deeper, more insidious problem of distortion. Although this is a book about Jane Austen, bear with me as we venture into Emily Dickinson territory: the story of what happened to Dickinson's poetry and biography parallels and thus elucidates what had already happened to Jane Austen.

The Complete Poems of Emily Dickinson published in 1924 was hardly complete: not even one third of her poems were included. Omitted were many poems dealing with writing ("I dwell in possibility," "Tell all the Truth but tell it slant," "I reckon when I count at all / First poets") or using violent imagery ("My life had stood a loaded gun," "Rearrange a wife's affection / when they dislocate my brain"). Those poems

Emily Dickinson daguerreotype
(Reproduced by permission of Amherst
College)

Emily Dickinson with ringlets and ruffles
for 1924 edition of her *Complete Poems*
(Reproduced by permission of the
Houghton Library, Harvard University)

that were included were *not* printed as Dickinson wrote them, but rather with the "improvements" that *Atlantic Monthly* editor Thomas Wentworth Higginson made when he first published Dickinson's poems in the late 1800s. Because Higginson viewed Dickinson as an "eccentric poetess" whose verse was "*too delicate*–not strong enough to publish," he felt compelled to correct her strange punctuation, smooth rhymes, add titles, and delete the most disturbing stanzas.[49]

To take one example, Emily Dickinson's poem "A solemn thing– it was–I said" appeared in a dramatically different form. The early editions printed only the first two stanzas of the four-stanza poem and drastically changed the two surviving stanzas:

(no title)	"Wedded"
A solemn thing–it was–I said–	A solemn thing it was, I said,
A woman–white–to be–	A woman white to be,
And wear–if God should count me fit–	And wear, if God should count me fit,
Her blameless mystery–	Her **hallowed** mystery.
A hallowed thing–to drop a life	A **timid** thing to drop a life
Into the purple well–	Into a purple well,
Too plummetless–that it return–	Too plummetless that it **come back**
Eternity–until–	Eternity until.

I pondered how the bliss would look—	(nothing for stanza 3)
And would it feel as big—	
When I could take it in my hand—	
As hovering—seen—through fog—	
And then—the size of this "small" life—	(nothing for stanza 4)
The Sages—call it small—	
Swelled—like Horizons—in my vest—	
And I sneered—softly—"small"!	
(Dickinson's original poem, J. 271)	*(Editors' "improved" version)*

In its original form, the poem brilliantly contradicts any biographer, critic, or other "sage" who dismisses as "small" the profound, "plummetless" life of a philosophic or artistic woman—be that Emily Dickinson or Jane Austen. How ironic it is that editors truncated a poem about sages belittling women! Are we to dismiss as coincidence the fact that editors just happened to omit Dickinson's triumphant affirmation of her life's joy and scope ("bliss," "big," "horizons") as well as her vehement scorn of the Sages ("I sneered—softly—'small'!")? How do we explain the substitution of "timid" for "hallowed" as anything other than a radical editorial change?

Though the poem never mentions a bride and had no title, Dickinson's first editors (Thomas Wentworth Higginson and Mabel Loomis Todd) entitled it "Wedded" and placed it in an artificial grouping of her poetry that they labeled "Love." When this poem was reprinted in the 1924 edition, editors dropped the title "Wedded" but continued to place the poem in a section called "Love" and with only its first two (altered) stanzas. Love became the theme of early biographies of Dickinson that portrayed her as a childlike, rather pitiable woman who wrote poetry because of her "broken heart." In a preface, Martha Bianchi Dickinson described her aunt in a tone of romantic bathos: "Certainly in that first witchery of an undreamed Southern springtime Emily was overtaken—doomed once and forever by her own heart."[50] Distorted versions are difficult to eradicate: in 2003 one of my students appeared in class with a 1985 Dickinson collection she had just bought in a used book store: it had the amputated, distorted, "timid" Higginson version of "A solemn thing," still entitled "Wedded." What do readers find if they purchase a cheap (because inaccurate) Barnes & Noble edition of "Dickinson's Collected Poems"? Without any editorial comment, this recent version continues to print the curly-haired image of Dickinson, Bianchi's problematic introduction, and censored versions of Dickinson's poems.

Corrected editions of Emily Dickinson's poetry as well as uncensored versions of Jane Austen's juvenilia and letters have been available to us since the 1950s. Scores of stellar feminist biographies and critical studies of both women writers have been on library shelves for decades. Yet we have not escaped the past, with its faulty images, texts, myths, and judgments.

For nearly two centuries, few have challenged Henry Austen's 1818 verdict that his sister's biography was "not by any means a life of events" (*NA*, 3). James Edward Austen-Leigh agreed: "Of events her life was singularly barren; few changes and no great crisis ever broke the smooth current of its course."[51] Austen-Leigh's daughter remarked of his stance toward Aunt Jane, "as there was so little to tell, it appeared to him impossible to write anything that could be called a 'life'."[52] A 1912 survey of literature listed Austen as a "good-looking, sociable maiden aunt" utterly removed from current events: "For her there existed no French Revolution, no public abuses, no history."[53] Calling her life "as quiet as her work," John Bailey concluded in 1931 that even Jane Austen herself could not have made her "small . . . tiny" life interesting: "Whether she could have written an autobiography is doubtful. . . . Jane's life was very uneventful; as unexciting, and indeed, except for her writings, unimportant, as it was pleasant to herself and her little world. Nothing of interest ever happened to her. . . . Jane's life [had] no events of importance. . . . The heights and depths of life she did not, and could not, touch."[54] Her apologetic biographers all seem to exclaim, "Get a life, Jane Austen!"

Most encyclopedias throughout the first half of the twentieth century reflected this initial assessment—and even the placid, devoid-of-event wording of Austen's brother and nephew:

> AUSTEN, Jane (1775–1817) . . . The life of no woman of genius could have been more uneventful than Miss Austen's. She did not marry. During her placid life Miss Austen never allowed her literary work to interfere with her domestic duties: sewing much and admirably, keeping house. (*The Encyclopedia Britannica*, 1910)

> No startling events disturbed the placid current of her life. (*World Book Encyclopedia*, 1936)

Because encyclopedias often recycle an entry for decades, have a God-like tone, and reach millions, one can only suppose that they have had a far greater impact on Austen's image than generations of biographies and critical works.

On one level, Jane Austen's life was indeed "barren of events": she never married or had children, never traveled to another country or went to college (none were open to women), and never moved in a public sphere or involved herself openly in political and social movements of her time. Though she had brothers in the navy, a cousin whose husband was guillotined in France, and an aunt accused falsely of shoplifting, her own life seems devoid of dramatic adventure. The current *Reader's Encyclopedia* states with utter authority of Austen, "The only dramatic event of her life was an attachment to a clergyman who died before they could become engaged."[55] But if an *event* is a happening, something of significance, is it not eventful that Austen revolutionized literature and became the first woman to earn repeated comparisons to Shakespeare? As Juliet McMaster comments, "Because a woman doesn't marry, it is thought to be uneventful; because she doesn't enter the market place, it is thought to be uneventful. But this is a woman who in the quiet of a Hampshire village produced six stunning novels."[56]

Reactions to Austen also reflect attitudes toward feminine activities. E. V. Lucas, the man responsible for Austen entries included in the *Encyclopedia Britannica* for over a century, not only perpetuated the notion of Austen's barren life but also damned with praise the "divine chit-chat of this little lady."[57] Why did he call Austen *little* and observe that her fiction addresses "life's *little* perplexities of emotion and conduct"? Cardinal John Henry Newman claimed that Austen "frittered" away her time on "over-little things," Adolphus Jack called Austen "the mistress of a pretty school . . . not a master to whom anyone would turn to learn about life," and Leslie Stephen insisted that Austen should not be ranked "with the great authors" but rather with those "amusing themselves with the humours of a country tea-table."[58] If Blake tells us we can see the world in a grain of sand, why not in a cup of tea? Eudora Welty reminds us in the final sentences of her autobiography, "A sheltered life can be a daring life as well. For all serious daring starts from within."[59] Captain Ahab's maritime struggle with Moby Dick may be no more significant than Elizabeth Bennet's domestic battle with Lady Catherine in *Pride and Prejudice*.

What if Michelangelo had been confined to tiny canvases and a palette consisting only of soft shades of pink? What if Shakespeare had been denied the chance to act on stage and had been told to spend his days playing charades and completing "carpet work"? Chances are that even under such restrictive circumstances their genius would have come out, though perhaps in a genre or medium dismissed as lacking in profundity. Biographers might have deemed them sheltered and little.

Just as Austen mocked those who insisted that interesting books had to have heroines escaping from dungeons or swashbuckling villains wielding daggers, so she might have laughed at those "sages" who felt that an unmarried woman who read widely and observed the comings and goings of neighbors and relatives could not lead an interesting life. How could this "most decorous of maiden ladies" (Thomas Wentworth Higginson), this "frail, diffident little spinster who saw little in this world beyond the hedgerows of her own countryside" (Alexander Woolcott) and had "a certain ineluctable faded charm. Like some of the loveliest butterflies—with no guts at all" (H. G. Wells), this "mean . . . old maid" and "narrow-gutted spinster" (D. H. Lawrence) who lived a wretchedly "pinched and narrow" life (Ralph Waldo Emerson) create profound novels?[60] Ezra Pound put it bluntly: "No one expects Jane Austen to be as interesting as Stendhal. A book about a dull, stupid, hemmed-in sort of life, by a person who has lived it, will never be as interesting as the work of some author who has comprehended many men's manners and seen many grades and conditions of existence."[61] How could a limited woman write great literature?

But *was* she so limited—or are the limitations in us? To appreciate Jane Austen, we must put aside our long-standing assumptions about what is important and what is not—in life and in literature. Perhaps Virginia Woolf said it best: "It is obvious that the values of women differ very often from the values which have been made by the other sex; . . . Yet it is the masculine values that prevail. Speaking crudely, football and sport are 'important'; the worship of fashion, the buying of clothes 'trivial.' And these values are inevitably transferred from life to fiction. This is an important book, the critic assumes, because it deals with war. This is an insignificant book because it deals with the feelings of women in a drawing-room. A scene in a battlefield is more important than a scene in a shop—everywhere and much more subtly the difference of value persists."[62] No wonder Thomas Carlyle labeled Austen's novels featuring sisters talking in drawing rooms mere "dishwashings," a kind of trivial women's art.[63] After all, Jane Austen did not serve as a dragoon (Stendhal and Coleridge), hold political office (Disraeli or Wordsworth), or write works entitled *The Pirate* and *Castle Dangerous* (Sir Walter Scott), *Going to a Fight* and *Life of Napoleon* (William Hazlitt), or *The French Revolution* (William Blake, Edmund Burke, Thomas Carlyle).

In 1920 one critic called Jane Austen "a neat, natty, little artist."[64] Reading these and other put-downs of Austen, Virginia Woolf noted, "The people who talk of her as if she were a niminy priminy spinster always annoy me."[65] Woolf's words ring true if we listen to these twentieth-century comments about the non-life of Jane Austen:

> Jane Austen is the feminine Peter Pan of letters. She never grew up. In her world there is . . . just the make-believe mating of dolls. (George Sampson, 1924)

> I like Jane. I have read several Janes. . . . She was a great little novelist. . . . But her world is a tiny one. . . . She did not know enough of the world to be a great novelist. She had not the ambition to be a great novelist. She knew her place. (Arnold Bennett, 1927)

> It is the most striking fact discovered by her life history—she did not take her work very seriously. Hers was no career of solemn and solitary self-dedication. Neat, elegant, and sociable, she spent most of her day sitting in the drawing-room of the parsonage which was her home, sewing and gossiping. . . . There are no adventures in her books, no abstract ideas. (Lord David Cecil, 1935)

> Jane Austen's art [is] domestic, provincial, feminine and prosaic, placidly realist, strictly within the author's very limited experience. . . . Jane Austen's life is almost devoid of incident. . . . Jane never left home except on short visits, never married, was domesticated, and until 1811 wrote without encouragement for her own amusement. . . . It was a life spent largely in a routine of trivial occupations among people the most ordinary and most useless. (Richard Aldington, 1948)

> See Jane sit . . . not much bothering her pretty head about . . . slave labor . . . a veritable Aunt Jane—naïve, complacent, and demurely without overt political opinions. (John Leonard's paraphrase of Edward Said, 1993)[66]

Why do so many biographers and scholars refer to a grown woman writer as "Jane"?

The phrase "never married" appears over and over again in commentary about Jane Austen. The very first sentence of *Jane Austen: Facts and Problems* by key Austen editor R. W. Chapman is "Jane Austen never married."[67] Chapman's emphasis is one of the "problems" I see, as is his presumptuous editing of her innovative punctuation. Two years before his death in 1969, Leonard Woolf called the happy marriages in Austen's novels "a kind of compensation daydream for her failure in real life," a remark perhaps suggesting that he needed to reread his wife's *A Room of One's Own*.[68] Benét's *Reader's Encyclopedia* includes as part of its one-paragraph entry on Jane Austen the sentence, "She never married," while no comment that "He never married" appears in its much lengthier discussion of Henry David Thoreau.

Why, to pursue this further, do readers of *The Ancient Mariner*, *The Christmas Carol*, and *Moby-Dick* give little thought to the marital status of Samuel Taylor Coleridge, Charles Dickens, and Herman Melville (or should we call them Samuel, Charles, and Herman)? When we think of Milton's *Paradise Lost*, do we wonder about John's marriages (he had three)? Was there a Mrs. Chaucer?

Rudyard Kipling (did he marry? do we care?) felt moved to write a verse tribute in 1926 called not "Austen's Writing" but "Jane's Marriage," beginning with Jane Austen ascending into heaven:

> Jane went to Paradise:
> That was only fair.
> Good Sir Walter met her first,
> And led her up the stair.

As Jane Austen stands at the top of the stair next to Shakespeare, three archangels ask her to name "Anything in Heaven's gift / That she might command." She answers, "Love." Obliging Seraphim circle the heavens searching for someone willing to love Jane. Finally Captain Wentworth, hero of *Persuasion*, expresses willingness, so "Entered into Paradise / The man Jane loved!"[69] Finally "Jane" finds every woman's *true* reward: not immortality or pride in her own craft, but Mr. Right.

Kipling *liked* Austen's works. Yet like so many other readers—then and now—he simply could not imagine that heaven for a woman could be a life as an unmarried professional writer. Imagine the tables turned: what if Jane Austen (had she lived in the right era) penned a ditty called "Rudyard's Marriage" envisioning Kipling united for eternity to the woman of his fictional dreams?

For the most part, biographies, critical studies, and encyclopedia entries today regard Jane Austen as a serious artist and afford her the dignity she deserves. Yet unsupported assumptions about Austen's emotional life as a single woman continue to emerge now and then in our own times:

Hers was a life of disappointment and frustration. . . . Her obstinate heart prevented her from marrying except for love. . . . All Jane Austen's novels follow the romance pattern of happy marriages achieved after difficulties have been overcome. Her own life was very different, emotionally unfulfilled.

Probably Jane herself did not see life as being happy, or ending happily, most of the time—and in all likelihood not ending happily for her. Could she have been jealous and resentful of the happiness she was forced to provide her own characters? . . . Jane Austen's "peace" was surely on the brink of destruction . . . as a result of loneliness, of sexual longing.

Elizabeth Bennet is Jane Austen with added spirit, with subversive passion, and, above all, looks. . . . The dull fact of Jane Austen's spinsterhood—her plainness, her childlessness, her virgin death—invests her comedies with disappointment, and with a sense of thwarted homing.[70]

The problem is not limited to a few critics cited as straw men and women to knock down. This widespread cultural bias remains with us today. Many of my students continue to adopt pitying tones when describing "old maid" writers like Austen and Dickinson, assuming they must be unfulfilled and sex-starved, yet they readily accept unmarried male writers as pioneering bachelors of thought. Despite the admirable efforts of Harold Bloom, Joseph Wiesenfarth, Tony Tanner, and a host of other critics who write of Austen, not Jane, she remains for many readers a little lady writing little books for other little ladies. As we will see in the final chapter (Behold Me Immortal: Finding Jane Austen Today), movie and stage versions of Austen's novels may at times perpetuate this stereotype, reducing Austen's profound, complex novels into "chick flicks" filled with gushing romance. "Bachelors Beware! Five Gorgeous Beauties on a Madcap Hunt!" promised one Hollywood poster for *Pride and Prejudice*.[71]

"Show us how absurd we'd seem to you," Anne Stevenson asks Austen in her 1983 poem "Re-Reading Jane."[72] Despite decades of excellent twentieth-century studies determined to wrest her away from condescending critics, the real Jane Austen remains difficult to find. Coffee table books claim that Austen preferred being known as a loving aunt than as a famous author, but only offer as proof the testimony of those nephews and nieces who worked so hard to whitewash her.[73]

Recent biographer David Nokes (2000) does an excellent job of exposing this family snow job, yet he chooses to call his subject "Jane," as does M. C. Hammond in *Relating to Jane* (1998) and Audrey Hawkbridge in *Jane and Her Gentlemen* (2000), with its sections entitled "Jane" and "In Search of Love."[74] A useful reference guide to terms like "negus" and "vicar" has the unfortunate title *What Jane Austen ATE and Charles Dickens KNEW*. The book jacket shows Charles Dickens reading dramatically from one of his books while Jane Austen serves a cake dotted with rosebuds and topped with a Cupid.

Cover illustration for *What Jane Austen Ate and Charles Dickens Knew*

Although the sketch of Dickens resembles ones actually existing of him, the Austen image looks like a cross between Martha Stewart and Scarlett O'Hara, with curly, blond hair, dangling earrings, and a frilly dress. Demure and elegant, she looks supremely pleased to be serving up such a charming cake. A 1999 biography opens with the sentence, "People who knew Jane Austen described her as pretty."[75] Does *any* biography of *any* male author from *any* century open with the sentence, "People who knew John Smith described him as handsome"? *The Friendly Jane Austen* (1999) sports a cover illustration of a doofy-looking Austen that adds a small floral print to her dress, even more lace and curls, and a smile apparently designed to suggest friendliness. Its book jacket treats the author as sex-starved Jane: "Learn about the man who almost won Jane's hand. . . . Discover how Jane felt about weddings." I long for *The Unfriendly Jane Austen, The Obstinate Intellect*, and *What Jane Austen Knew and Charles Dickens Wore!*

"Discover how Austen felt about her writing" might be more to the point. Not a heartbroken Cinderella, a girlish wisp, a gossipy hausfrau, an ethereal saint, or a puritanical maiden aunt, Jane Austen was a complex woman whose lively mind, keen wit, deep moral sense, and professional devotion to her craft allowed her to transform daily incidents of domestic life into remarkable literature. Thinking of Austen's detractors carping that she never raised children or visited foreign places, author Katherine Mansfield observed, "Mightn't her reply have been, 'Ah, but what about my novels?'"[76]

Craftsmanship may be the one aspect of a woman's writing that relatives, biographers, and critics seem to honor least. As late as 1935, John Middleton Murry called his famous wife, Katherine Mansfield, "a tiny artist," suppressed and distorted her work, and depicted her as a simple and childlike being: "A perfectly exquisite, perfectly simple human being. As soon as possible after her death, I made it my duty to gather together and to publish her Journal and Letters. It seemed to me a matter of cardinal importance that the world should know what manner of woman—or girl (for she wasn't much more when she died)—Katherine Mansfield was. Her art was not really distinct from her life; she was never what we understand by a professional writer; she was distinguished by the peculiar gift of spontaneity."[77] Never mind that Mansfield wrote over eighty intricately constructed short stories that revolutionized fiction, or that she traveled throughout Europe and supported herself through her writing! Never mind that she wrote while dying of tuberculosis, musing as she coughed

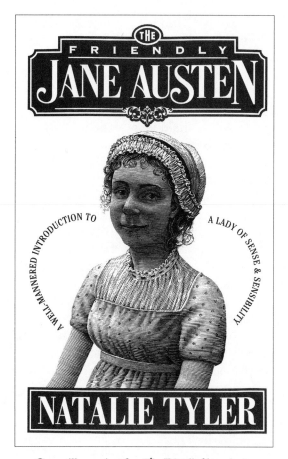

Cover illustration for *The Friendly Jane Austen*
(Reproduced by permission of Scott McKowen)

blood, "I really only ask for time to write it all—time to write my books—I live to write." As she informed Murry, "I'm a writer first and a woman after—More even than talking or laughing or being happy I want to write."[78]

Katherine Anne Porter could have been writing about Jane Austen when she defended Katherine Mansfield from charges of being a simple, girlish writer: "Katherine Mansfield's work is the important fact about her, and she is in danger of the worst fate that an artist can suffer—to be overwhelmed by her own legend, to have her work neglected for an interest in her 'personality.' Mr. Murry writes that 'her art was of a peculiarly instinctive kind.' I confess I cannot understand the use of this word. I judge her work to have been to a great degree a matter of intelligent use of her faculties, a conscious practice of a hard-won craftsmanship."[79] Indeed, Katherine Mansfield's journals show that throughout her short life (she died at thirty-four), she diligently practiced her craft: "I chose not only the length of every sentence, but even the sound of every sentence. . . . If a thing has really come off it seems to me there mustn't be one single word out of place, or one word that could be taken out. That's how I AIM at writing."[80] As Porter concluded, Mansfield was "deliberate in her choice of material and in her methods of using it . . . such mastership is not gained by letting the instincts have it all their own way."[81]

In the same year that Murry described Mansfield as childlike and instinctual, Lord David Cecil wrote in his study of Jane Austen that the most striking fact about her was that she did not dedicate herself to her work or approach it seriously.[82] G. K. Chesterton noted that she wrote fiction "as domestic as a diary in the intervals of pies and puddings, without so much as looking out of the window to notice the French Revolution."[83] Other nineteenth- and twentieth-century critics referred to Austen's craft as a nice little hobby, a pleasant pastime, a private amusement, or a secondary matter.[84] The scholar who wrote the introduction to the 1906 edition of Austen's novels and letters claimed she never worked at the material but "found it all on the sensitive plates of her own delicate mind."[85] Calling her "instinctive and charming," Henry James concluded that "our dear, everybody's dear, Jane" constructed novels unconsciously, like "the brown thrush who tells his story from the garden bough."[86] Would anyone argue that Charles Dickens chirped out his fiction with simple instinct and pleasant charm?

Jane Austen was a dedicated writer who cared deeply about her work and spent much of her life perfecting her manuscripts. "An artist cannot do anything slovenly," she observed as early as 17 November 1798, and before any of her novels appeared in print she had already referred to herself as a self-conscious writer: "I begin already to weigh my words & sentences more than I did, & am looking about for a sentiment, an illustration or a metaphor in every corner of the room" (24 January 1809). She "lop't & crop't" her works (29 January 1813), carefully noted changes in editions, recorded reactions to her novels, and continued to write until just days before her death. But, as we will see in the concluding chapter, relatives suppressed even her final literary production: an irreverent poem about an angry saint. We must search for Jane Austen.

Despite probable disappointments in love, sadness within the family circle, chronic shortage of cash, and occasional frustrations with publishers, Jane Austen seems to have enjoyed much of her life. Those who picture Austen bemoaning her barren womb, bewailing her single state, and pining away should read her letter to a niece (not included in Austen-Leigh's Memoir):

> My Dear Fanny,
>
> You are inimitable, irresistable. You are the delight of my Life. Such Letters, such entertaining Letters as you have lately sent!– . . . Such a lovely display of what Imagination does. . . . –Oh! what a loss it will be, when you are married. You are too agreable in your single state, too agreable as a Neice. I shall hate you when your delicious play of Mind is all settled down into conjugal & maternal affections. . . . Do not imagine that I have any real objection, I have rather taken a fancy to him than not, & I like Chilham Castle for you;–I only do not like you s^{hd} marry anybody. And yet I do wish you to marry very much, because I know you will never be happy till you are; but the loss of a Fanny Knight will be never made up to me. (20 February 1817)

Although jokingly exaggerated ("I shall hate you"), this ambivalent letter nevertheless conveys Austen's sense that "conjugal and maternal duties" could be viewed as burdens, not rewards. Twentieth-century poet Helen Bevinton wryly describes Austen's choice to remain single:

> Marriage is a great improver
> Wrote Miss Jane Austen, who was moved
> By the connubial bliss about her
> To stay forever unimproved.[87]

Perhaps Austen centers all six of her novels on young women hovering between girlhood and womanhood—between their roles as daughters and wives—precisely to celebrate that fleeting time of independence when they, like Fanny, display a "delicious play of mind."

Though single and childless, Jane Austen seems to have found abundant recompense in her life. She refers to her books as her children and to her heroines as "my Elinor," "my Emma," and "my Fanny." As P. D. James observes, "Her books were her children and they were sufficient."[88] Even before her first novel found a publisher, Austen writes with a sense of contentment to her sister Cassandra after revisiting a ballroom: "It was the same room in which we danced 15 years ago!–I thought it all over–& inspite of the shame of being so much older, felt with thankfulness that I was quite as happy now as then" (9 December 1808). On her own at a London art museum, she certainly does not seem to feel lonely: "I liked my solitary elegance very much, & was ready to laugh all the time, at my being where I was" (24 May 1813).

Just as Emily Dickinson writes in a letter that she hopes God will keep her "from what they call households" so she can pursue her "golden dream" as a writer, so Jane Austen sensed that a woman's traditional duties might preclude authorship.[89] After company leaves, Austen writes to Cassandra about the joys of having time to herself: "When you receive this our guests will be all gone or going; and I shall be left to the comfortable disposal of my time, to ease my mind from the torments of rice puddings & apple dumplings . . . I enjoyed Edward's company very much.–& yet I was not sorry when Friday came. It had been a busy week & I wanted a few days quiet, & exemption from the Thought & contrivance which any sort of company gives." As the letter continues, Austen muses on the situation of a married woman: "I often wonder how *you* can find time for what you do, in addition to the care of the House;–And how good Mrs West c^d have written such Books & collected so many hard words, with all her family cares, is still more a matter of astonishment! Composition seems to me Impossible, with a head full of Joints of Mutton and doses of rhubarb" (8 September 1816). One wonders if the reason Jane Austen accepted a marriage proposal, slept on the idea, but turned it down the next morning is in part because she wished to avoid "conjugal and maternal" duties that inevitably would have hindered her freedom to write.

Composition and publication seem to have brought Austen great pleasure. Just months before the publication of her first novel, she writes her sister about her work on the proofs, her brother Henry's help, and her awareness of the monetary side of publishing: "No indeed, I am never too busy to think of S&S. I can no more forget it, than a mother can forget her sucking child; & I am much obliged to you for your enquiries. I have had two sheets to correct . . . I have scarcely a hope of its being out in June.–Henry does not neglect it; he *has* hurried the Printer, & says he will see him again today.–It will not stand still during his absence . . . The *Incomes* remain as they were, but I will get them altered if I can" (25 April 1811). How different this professional, ambitious, busy woman writer is from her relatives' manufactured image of a "dear Aunt Jane" who scribbled humbly as a recreation with no thought of earning money.

In fact, Aunt Jane loved discussing her writing and dispensing professional advice. To niece Anna Lefroy, an aspiring author, Austen writes happily, "You are now collecting your People delightfully, getting them exactly into such a spot as is the delight of my life;—3 or 4 Families in a Country Village is the very thing to work on" (9 September 1814). Do not write about Ireland if you have never been there, she warns Anna, and do not create unbelievable, one-dimensional characters: "Henry Mellish I am afraid will be too much in the common Novel style—a handsome, amiable, unexceptionable Young Man (such as do not much abound in real Life)" (28 September 1814). In the same letter, Austen also complains to her niece about the artificial, trite expressions in too many novels, advising her to delete the phrase "vortex of Dissipation": "I do not object to the Thing, but I cannot bear the expression;—it is such thorough novel slang—and so old, that I dare say Adam met with it in the first novel he opened." Plots can be as trite as expressions, Austen notes, mockingly informing Anna that she will conform to publishers' expectations in her next novel: "My Heroine shall not merely be wafted down an American river in a boat by herself, she shall cross the Atlantic in the same way, & never stop till she reaches Gravesent" (24 November 1814). This is the voice of a woman who believed in the superiority of her art.

In an essay entitled "Jane Austen and the Geese" (the Geese are critics), Virginia Woolf observes, "We remember that Jane Austen wrote novels. It might be worthwhile for her critics to read them."[90] How remarkable, Woolf marvels in *A Room of One's Own*, that despite the attitudes of her time, Jane Austen never lost sight of her own way: "What genius, what integrity it must have required in face of all that criticism, in the midst of that purely patriarchal society, to hold fast to the thing as [she] saw it without shrinking, to [ignore] that persistent voice, now grumbling, now patronising, now domineering, now grieved, now shocked, now avuncular, that voice cannot let women alone, but must be at them . . . admonishing them . . . to keep within certain limits."[91] A literary titan working amid the teacups and satin stitches of her daily life, Jane Austen transformed domestic details into six masterpieces. With extraordinary courage she held steadfastly to her own vision. By the time her heroine argues in *Persuasion* that "Men have had every advantage of us in telling their own story . . . the pen has been in their hands," Austen already had taken pen in hand to tell a story all her own (*P*, 234). To do so, she ignored all the very, very kind hints. Instead, she kept to her own style and went on in her own indomitable way.

In our search for Jane Austen, we must break free of dear Aunt Jane—and of two centuries of putdowns and touchups. We must strip off those ruffles and ringlets, restore those deleted fleas and bowels, and meet Jane Austen's sharp, uncompromising gaze head on.

2

Beware of Swoons
Jane Austen's Early Writings

"We had the best of educations. . . . The Drawling-master
. . . used to come once a week: He taught us Drawling,
Stretching, and Fainting in Coils."

"What was THAT like?" said Alice.

"Well, I can't show it you myself," the Mock Turtle said:
"I'm too stiff. And the Gryphon never learnt it."

"Hadn't time," said the Gryphon: "I went to the Classics
master, though. He was an old crab, HE was."

"I never went to him," the Mock Turtle said with a sigh,
"he taught Laughing and Grief, they used to say."
   —Lewis Carroll, *Alice in Wonderland*

I would not sell my daily swoon
For all the rubies in Rangoon.
What! sell my swoon? My lovely swoon? . . .
It's not for sale, my swoon's immune.
         —Ogden Nash, "Cat Naps Are Too Good for Cats"

"One fatal swoon has cost me my Life. . . . Beware of swoons
Dear Laura. Run mad as often as you chuse; but do not
faint—."
   —Jane Austen, "Love and Freindship"

To those who wrinkle their noses in distaste and insist, without
reading her, that Jane Austen is prim, proper, and priggish, I
recommend sampling her flamboyant, risqué adolescent works.
Sketches Austen wrote in her teens (called *juvenilia* by scholars)
parody sentimental fiction, reverse gender roles, and reject every
precept in conduct books for girls, presenting heroines who get
drunk, lie, steal, and murder: "Her sister the perfidious Sukey, was
likewise shortly after exalted in a manner she truly deserved. . . .

Her barbarous Murder was discovered & in spite of every interceding freind she was speedily raised to the Gallows—" ("Jack and Alice," written when Austen was twelve or thirteen, *MW,* 29). Once having encountered *this* Jane Austen—an uninhibited, rebellious, exuberant young woman with a piercing wit—readers shed the false image of the staid maiden aunt and can discover far more layers of meaning in her six masterpieces.

Jane Austen must have remained fond of her early skits, sketches, and mock-novels because later in life she transcribed many of them into three notebooks she grandiosely entitled *Volume the First, Volume the Second,* and *Volume the Third.* Brian Southam notes that the twenty-nine surviving pieces included in these three volumes (nearly ninety thousand words) allow readers to encounter Jane Austen in training to be a novelist. In these sketches, mini-novels, skits, letters, and scraps we see her rejection of formulaic eighteenth-century literature, her growing ability to transform the scenes around her into fiction, and "the prelude of trial and experiment that lay behind the accomplishment of the six novels." [1]

To the subtitle of my first chapter (Putting Her Down and Touching Her Up) I perhaps should have added "Shutting Her Up" to acknowledge relatives' successful suppression of the juvenilia. Though written in the 1780s to early 1790s when Austen was about age eleven to eighteen, these early writings did not reach the public until the twentieth century: *Volume the First* and *Volume the Second* were not published in full until 1933 and 1922, respectively, while readers had to wait until 1951 for publication of *Volume the Third.* [2] Margaret Drabble concludes after reading all three volumes, "Austen's burlesques, her *History*, and her tales and proto-novels constitute one of the most remarkable collections ever discovered from so young a pen." [3]

Other famous novelists have cut their literary teeth at an early age. For example, the precocious Brontë siblings penned more words as adolescents than as adults, writing melodramas featuring their toy wooden soldiers as romantic heroes and villains inhabiting imaginary kingdoms. Unlike the Brontës, the Austens wrote primarily to make each other laugh. Jane Austen dedicates one early tale about a violent, naughty girl named Cassandra to the refined, noble, virtuous, lovely, elegant, rational, "magestic" Cassandra Austen in hopes that "the following Tale will afford one moment's amusement" ("The Beautifull Cassandra," *MW,* 44). Austen dedicates other youthful sketches to her parents, friends, or her brothers, including those away at sea. For example, she labels one farcical three-paragraph story "a short, but interesting Tale . . . with all imaginable Respect inscribed to Mr Francis William Austen Midshipman on board his Majestys Ship the Perseverance by his Obedient Servant THE AUTHOR" ("The Adventures of Mr. Harley," *MW,* 40). Reading aloud and laughing over young Jane Austen's outrageous skits, mock dedications, and spoofs must have enlivened evenings at Steventon.

Burlesques make the most sense if one knows the target of the satire. One butt of Austen's jokes was the sentimental romance of the day with its plot coincidences, stock characters, unbelievable adventures, and trite expressions. For example, note this overblown description from an actual novel of 1789:

> I beheld the poor desolate dying Agnes; her hair torn and disheveled, hanging in loose ringlets; her head-clothes and neck covering, lying in tatters on the ground; her beautiful arms bare; and all the symptoms of wild distraction glaring round the lovely ruin.
>
> She was just then changing from a fit of raving, to melancholy madness; and was sitting on the ground by the dead body of our lost Edward; his head, swollen and disfigured, was on her lap; with one hand she held a smelling bottle to his nose, the other with her eyes were lifted to heaven, in a supplicating attitude.[4]

This novel would have appeared when Austen was a teenager. Even then she sensed the ludicrousness of such emotionally overwrought, pulsating works of pulp fiction—the Harlequin romances of her day—and she delighted in sharing crass imitations of them with her family and friends. Although she was born in the same decade as William Wordsworth and technically could be called Romantic, she makes the nature poets' pastoral imagery, emotional effusions, and classical allusions another verbal target. A comparison of William Collins's "Ode to Pity" (below left) considered a good poem of the day, and Jane Austen's "Ode to Pity" (below right; written when she was about seventeen years old) shows just how well Austen knew her subject before parodying it:

Collins	Austen
O THOU, the Friend of Man assign'd,	Ever musing I delight to tread
With balmy Hands his Wounds to bind,	The Paths of honour and the Myrtle Grove
And charm his frantic Woe:	Whilst the pale Moon her beams doth shed
When first *Distress,* with Dagger keen,	On disappointed Love.
Broke forth to waste his destin'd Scene,	While Philomel on airy hawthorn Bush
His wild unsated Foe!	Sings sweet and Melancholy, And the thrush
	Converses with the Dove.

By *Pella's* Bard, a magic Name,
By all the Griefs his Thought could
　frame,
　Receive my humble Rite:
Long, *Pity,* let the Nations view
Thy sky-worn Robes of tend'rest Blue,
　And Eyes of dewy Light! [5]

Gently brawling down the turnpike road,
　Sweetly noisy falls the Silent Stream
The Moon emerges from behind a Cloud
　And darts upon the Myrtle Grove her
　beam.
Ah! then what Lovely Scenes appear,
　The hut, the Cot, the Grot, and Chapel
　queer,
And eke the Abbey too a mouldering heap,
　Conceal'd by aged pines her head doth rear
And quite invisible doth take a peep.
(*MW,* 74–75)

Jane Austen could have written serious pastoral poetry, one senses in her parody, just as she could have written sentimental epistolary novels or gothic romances. But she was too much of a realist to write such verse about myrtle groves, moonlight, and songbirds without puncturing the mood with ridiculous oxymorons ("gentle brawling," "noisy . . . silent stream") and attention-getting word play ("the hut, the Cot, the Grot"). She laughingly dedicates her "Ode to Pity" to her sister "from a thorough knowledge of her pitiful Nature."

Another chief object of her derision was the standard conduct book for girls. As Deborah Kaplan observes, such instructional guides were at their heyday in Austen's time and advised in an avuncular tone that young women evince modesty and meekness.[6] For example, Dr. Gregory's *A Father's Legacy to His Daughters*, a sort of Emily Post etiquette book of the eighteenth century that was well known to Austen, suggested that young ladies avoid displaying health, wit, and learning and recommended that they cultivate their delicacy and hide any strength. A few edifying samples from Dr. Gregory:

> One of the chief beauties in a female character, is that modest *reserve*, that retiring *delicacy*, which avoids the public eye. . . . When a girl ceases to *blush*, she has lost the most powerful charm of beauty. That extreme sensibility which it indicates, may be a weakness and encumbrance in *our* sex, as I have too often felt; but in *yours* it is particularly engaging. . . . This modesty, which I think so essential in your sex, will naturally dispose you to be rather silent in company.
>
> *Wit* is the most dangerous talent you can possess. . . . Wit is so flattering to vanity, that they who possess it become

intoxicated and lose self-command. . . . Be even cautious in displaying your *good sense*. It will be thought you assume a superiority over the rest of the company. But if you happen to have any learning, keep it a profound secret, especially from the men who generally look with a jealous and malignant eye on a woman of great parts and a cultivated understanding. . . . Do not be anxious to share the full extent of your knowledge.

I do not wish you to *affect* delicacy, I wish you to *possess* it.

When a woman speaks of her great strength, her extraordinary appetite, her ability to bear excessive fatigue, we recoil at the description.

Never allow yourself to be so far transported with mirth as to forget the delicacy of your sex.[7]

The witty Austen must have been "transported with mirth" when she read such passages by the well-meaning Dr. Gregory!

Other conduct book authors iterated the importance of a woman knowing her place and controlling her "inclinations":

The utmost of a woman's character is contained in domestic life; first, her piety towards God; and next in the duties of a daughter, a wife, a mother, and a sister. Nothing can atone for the want of modesty and innocence. (*Wisdom in Miniature*, 1795)

The business of the wife is to controul her own inclinations, instead of projecting how she may gratify them. . . . [I hope] women will not join in a conspiracy to annihilate the small degree of knightly courtesy which yet exists, by themselves assuming the deportment of amazonian boldness, or affecting amazonian independence. (Jane West, *Letters to a Young Lady in which the Duties and Character of Women Are Considered*, 1806)

An enraged woman is one of the most disgusting sights in nature. . . . [Cultivate] gentleness, meekness, patience. (Hester Chapone, "On the Government of Temper" in *Letters on the Improvement of the Mind*, 1773)

I wish you ever to possess . . . meekness and modesty, by soft attraction and virtuous love. Your business chiefly is to

read men, in order to make yourselves agreeable and useful.
(James Fordyce, *Sermons to Young Women*, 1766)

Delicacy of manners and purity of speech are so much expected from an amiable, modest female. (Chase Amos, *The
Excellent Female*, 1791)

Whatever be the influence which the amiable virtues of a
wife may obtain over her husband, let not the consciousness of it ever lead her to seek opportunities of displaying
it, nor to cherish a wish to intrude into those departments
which belong not to her jurisdiction. . . . Remember your
domestic duties . . . advance in piety; be not snatched into
the vortex of amusements. (Thomas Gisborne, *An Enquiry
into the Duties of the Female Sex*, 1797) [8]

Even the titles and chapters of these books ("On the Government of
Temper," "Company, Conversation, and Deportment," "The Excellent Female," "The Polite Lady," "A Letter of Genteel and Moral
Advice to a Young Lady," "Letters on the Improvement of the Female Sex: With Observations of Their Manners") invite laughter.

Or perhaps they invite interruption. The rebellious, man-crazy
Lydia Bennet in *Pride and Prejudice* finds it insufferable to listen to
the Reverend Mr. Collins read from John Fordyce's *Sermons for Young
Women:*

Mr. Collins . . . chose Fordyce's Sermons. Lydia gaped as
he opened the volume, and before he had, with very monotonous solemnity, read three pages, she interrupted him
with,

"Do you know, mama, that my uncle Philips talks of
turning away Richard, and if he does, Colonel Forster will
hire him. . . . I will walk to Meryton to hear more about
it, and to ask when Mr. Denny comes back from town."

Lydia was bid by her two eldest sisters to hold her
tongue; but Mr. Collins, much offended, laid aside his
book, and said,

"I have often observed how little young ladies are interested by books of a serious stamp, though written solely
for their benefit. It amazes me, I confess;—for certainly,
there can be nothing so advantageous to them as instruction." (*PP*, 68–69)

Jane Austen aims her adolescent arrows precisely at those "books of a serious stamp" written for the benefit of gaping young ladies and presented to them "with very monotonous solemnity."

Austen's youthful sketches remind me of Mark Twain's literary fascination a century later with bad boys who break every rule. The ambition of Jacob in Twain's "The Good Little Boy" is "to be put in a Sunday-school book" though "he knew it was more fatal than consumption to be so supernaturally good as the boys in the books were."[9] In contrast, Jim in "The Bad Little Boy" has a rip-roaring time violating all preachy Sunday-school book rules:

> Once there was a bad little boy whose name was Jim—though, if you will notice, you will find that bad little boys are nearly always called James in your Sunday-school books. . . . Once this little bad boy stole the key of the pantry, and slipped in there and helped himself to some jam, and filled up the vessel with tar, so that his mother would never know the difference; but all at once a terrible feeling didn't come over him, and something didn't seem to whisper to him "Is it right to disobey my mother? Isn't it sinful to do this? Where do bad little boys go who gobble up their good kind mother's jam?" and then he didn't kneel down all alone and promise never to be wicked any more, and rise up with a light, happy heart, and go and tell his mother all about it, and beg her forgiveness, and be blessed by her with tears of pride and thankfulness in her eyes. No; that is the way with all other bad boys in the books; but it happened otherwise with this Jim, strangely enough. He ate that jam, and said it was bully, in his sinful, vulgar way . . . and observed "that the old woman would get up and snort" when she found it out.

Twain notes that Jim hated moral boys and bore a charmed life: "And he grew up and married, and raised a large family, and brained them all with an ax one night, and got wealthy by all manner of cheating and rascality and now he is the infernalest wickedest scoundrel in his native village, and is universally respected and belongs to the legislature." He does not, Twain tells us in mock surprise, find "the vine-embowered home of his boyhood tumbled down and gone to decay" nor "his loved ones sleeping in the quiet churchyard."[10]

I include the Twain because I think his purpose was similar to Austen's in her adolescent fiction: to use comic exaggeration and parody to show that conduct books and popular literature had "no life-likeness" or "seeming of reality."[11] While Twain attacks the milk sop boys of Sunday-school books and adventure stories for boys featuring manly heroes, such as *The Deerslayer,* Austen goes after the dull domestic angels of conduct books and the sentimental romances for young women featuring fainting damsels in distress. (See the Appendix for more on Twain and Austen, including a reprint of Twain's unpublished and incomplete essay called "Jane Austen.")

Both targets are clear in Jane Austen's earliest extant sketch, written when she was about age eleven or twelve. Austen calls this first piece "Frederic and Elfrida: A Novel," though its five chapters, song, and epitaph together only comprise ten printed pages. Even in this earliest "novel" Austen mocks artificial literary language: "Charlotte was received with the greatest Joy by Frederic & Elfrida, who, after pressing her alternately to their Bosoms, proposed to her to take a walk in a Grove of Poplars which led from the Parsonage to a verdant Lawn enamelled with a variety of variegated flowers & watered by a purling Stream, brought from the Valley of Tempé by a passage under ground." After remaining in the grove "scarcely . . . above 9 hours," they hear a "delightfull voice" warble a song about Damon, a stock name for a swain (*MW,* 5).

Elevated language ("ornamented with festoons," "shone resplendent") takes a fall into the mud when Austen begins juxtaposing praise and insult, the ideal and the real. Frederic, Elfrida, and Charlotte meet a young woman named Rebecca and all cry out *in unison,* "Lovely & too charming Fair one, notwithstanding your forbidding Squint, your greasy tresses & your swelling Back, which are more frightfull than imagination can paint or pen describe, I cannot refrain from expressing my raptures, at the engaging Qualities of your Mind, which so amply atone for the Horror, with which your first appearance must ever inspire the unwary visitor." The youthful Austen delights in ending an elegant sentence with a violent surprise: "From this period, the intimacy between the Families . . . daily increased till at length it grew to such a pitch, that they did not scruple to kick one another out of the window on the slightest provocation" (*MW,* 6). As John Halperin notes, "She must have been a disconcerting teenager."[12]

She must have been a well-read teenager, too, unlike a character she describes as possessing "an Understanding unimproved by reading & a Mind totally devoid of Taste or Judgment" ("Catharine, or the Bower," *MW,* 198). Austen delights in playing with the sound of words, noting in her first sketch that Rebecca is "surrounded by Patches, Powder, Pomatum & Paint" ("Frederic and Elfrida," *MW,* 7). With similar alliterative flourish, she dedicates a later juvenile work to her cousin Miss Cooper, "Conscious of the Charming Character which in every Country, & every Clime in Christendom is Cried Concerning you, with Caution & Care I Commend to your Charitable Criticism this Clever Collection of Curious Comments, which have been Carefully Culled, Collected, & Classed by your Comical Cousin" ("A Collection of Letters," *MW,* 149).

The comical young Austen plays not only with contrived language but also with conventional plots, such as the one where an older character forbids young lovers to marry. In "Frederic and Elfrida," Mrs. Fitzroy objects to a marriage between Rebecca ("being but 36") and Captain Roger ("little more than 63") because of their "tender years," so she proposes as a remedy "that they should wait a little while till they were a good deal older" (*MW,* 7). The plot becomes even more absurd. Charlotte leaves her friends "with a heavy heart and streaming Eyes" and rapidly accepts marriage proposals from two different men before sitting down to an amazing supper of "a young Leveret, a brace of Partridges, a leash of Pheasants, and a Dozen of Pigeons." Perhaps indigestion helps explain why the next morning, remembering that she is engaged to two men, Charlotte drowns herself in a deep (probably still purling) stream. Austen interrupts her narrative to note in mock seriousness that readers are unworthy if they fail to shed tears when they pass the "pathetic . . . beautiful" epitaph for Charlotte: "Here lies our friend who having promis-ed / That unto two she would be marri-ed" (*MW,* 9). Instead, readers laugh at the foreshadowing of Twain's Emmeline Grangerford, the girl in *Huckleberry Finn* who welcomes deaths so she can write lugubrious poems about them or paint sorrowful pictures with captions such as "And Art Thou Gone Yes Thou Art Gone Alas."[13]

Even in this first sketch Austen reverses gender roles, as if to thumb her elegant nose at the shelves full of conduct books for girls. Rather than having Frederic seek the hand of a shy, sweet Elfrida in a series of tender love scenes, Austen has the brazen, aggressive Elfrida propose that Frederic marry her immediately:

> She flew to Frederic and in a manner truly heroick spluttered out to him her intention of being married the next Day.
>
> To one in his predicament who possessed less personal Courage than Frederic was master of, such a speech would

have been Death; but he not being the least terrified boldly replied.

"Damme Elfrida *you* may be married tomorrow but *I* won't."

This answer distressed her too much for her delicate Constitution. She accordingly fainted and was in such a hurry to have a succession of fainting fits, that she had scarcely patience enough to recover from one before she fell into another.

Tho', in any threatening Danger to his Life or Liberty, Frederic was as bold as brass yet in other respects his heart was as soft as cotton and immediately on hearing of the dangerous way Elfrida was in, he flew to her and finding her better than he had been taught to expect, was united to her Forever.

Finis (*MW,* 11–12)

A masterpiece? No. But the ending of "Frederic and Elfrida" foreshadows Austen's more subtle descriptions in later novels of heroines who fall in love first. In *Northanger Abbey* Henry Tilney marries Catherine Morland mostly because he feels gratitude for her affection for him, "a new circumstance in romance . . . and dreadfully derogatory of an heroine's dignity" (*NA,* 243). Similarly, in *Mansfield Park* Fanny Price falls in love with Edmund Bertram several hundred pages before he thinks of her in that way. Austen's youthful experiments pave the way for unconventional approaches to young women in her six mature novels.

Heroines are not supposed to pursue men, time their fainting fits, or get dead drunk, like Alice of "Jack and Alice: A Novel." As the wealthy widow Lady Williams informs us of Alice, "She has many rare & charming qualities, but Sobriety is not one of them" (*MW,* 23). Here Austen uses a form of irony she will choose again and again: understatement, or *litotes.* By telling us that Sobriety is *not* one of Alice's qualities rather than directly stating that she is a drunk, Austen invites the reader to figure it out—to be in on the joke.

Perhaps Austen also chooses this method as a way of mocking her own era's euphemistic approach to women's lives. To the saying "Horses sweat, gentlemen perspire, and ladies feel the heat," one should perhaps add Austen's delightfully overrefined comment in an early letter: "What dreadful Hot weather we have!—It keeps one in a continual state of Inelegance" (18 September 1796). In another early letter she refers to "pigstyes of a most elegant construction" (2 December

1798). Similarly, in her adolescent works Austen delights in juxtaposing ornate diction and warty real life. Sometimes she just gives us the warts: in "Jack and Alice" we meet sweaty ladies with ruddy faces. Flushed with wine and "nearly dead drunk," Alice reddens with anger while insisting to Lady Williams that a woman can never have too much color (*MW,* 19).

In addition to teasing her readers by presenting a grossly unfeminine heroine, Austen also gives them a "hero" who never appears in the "novel." The leading man of "Jack and Alice" is definitely *not* Jack:

> It may be proper to return to the Hero of this Novel, the brother of Alice, of whom I beleive I have scarcely ever had occasion to speak; which may perhaps be partly oweing to his unfortunate propensity to Liquor, which so compleatly deprived him of the use of those faculties Nature had endowed him with, that he never did anything worth mentioning. His Death . . . was the natural Consequence of this pernicious practice. By his decease, his sister became the sole inheritress of a very large fortune, which as it gave her fresh Hopes of rendering herself acceptable as a wife to Charles Adams could not fail of being most pleasing to her— & and as the effect was Joyfull the Cause could scarcely be lamented. (*MW,* 24–25)

The leading man of "Jack and Alice" is Charles Adams, whom Austen presents as a vain man possessing the accomplishments and dazzling beauty usually reserved for literary heroines. Austen writes hyperbolically that Charles is "an amiable, accomplished, and bewitching young Man; of so dazzling a Beauty that none but Eagles could look him in the Face" (*MW,* 13).

When Alice sends her father to propose to Charles Adams that he marry her, Charles rejects the offer by cataloguing all his own perfections—perfections normally used to describe women:

> Sir, I may perhaps be expected to appeared pleased at & gratefull for the offer you have made me: but let me tell you that I consider it as an affront. I look upon myself to be Sir a perfect Beauty—where would you see a finer figure or a more charming face. Then, sir I imagine my Manners and Address to be of the most polished kind; there is a certain elegance a peculiar sweetness in them that I never saw equalled & cannot describe—Partiality aside, I am certainly

more accomplished in every Language, every Science, every Art and every thing than any other person in Europe. My temper is even, my virtues innumerable, my self unparalelled. Since such Sir is my character, what do you mean by wishing me to marry your Daughter? (*MW*, 24)

Austen gives Charles a heroine's qualities of "perfect beauty," "finer figure," "charming face," "polished" and sweet, elegant manners and accomplishments, a comic exaggeration of the traits Richardson gave Sir Charles Grandison.[14] By describing Charles in such traditionally feminine terms, Austen asks readers to imagine what it would be like if men were judged by their superficial appearances and tinkling accomplishments. Would they be as vain and spiteful as women were accused of being? Charles ends his rejection of Alice with a flourish of self-praise: "Your daughter sir, is neither sufficiently beautifull, sufficiently amiable, sufficiently witty, nor sufficiently rich for me—. I expect nothing more in my wife than my wife will find in me—Perfection. These sir, are my sentiments & I honour myself for having such" (*MW*, 26).

Just as in "Frederick and Elfrida" Austen presents a predatory heroine proposing to a trepid hero, so in "Jack and Alice" women overtly pursue Charles. Some wind up pinioned in the steel woman-traps Charles sets on his property to protect himself from the constant onslaught of marriage-obsessed women. At a time when no women were allowed to be doctors, Austen imagines a female surgeon capable of instant miracles: "Lady Williams now interposed & observed that the young Lady's leg ought to be set without farther delay. After examining the fracture therefore, she immediately began & performed the operation with great skill which was the more wonderfull on account of her having never performed such a one before. Lucy, then arose from the ground . . . finding that she could walk with the greatest ease" (*MW*, 22–23). A woman performs an operation on a woman caught pursuing a man. Throughout the juvenilia, we find additional examples of characters experimenting with the roles of the opposite sex, whether it be men serving as chaperones or women commanding armies. Austen even plays around with the idea of a male widow and a female uncle.

At the end of "Jack and Alice," Charles marries Lady Williams, a "sufficiently rich . . . widow with a handsome Jointure & the remains of a very handsome face" (*MW*, 13). Alice, the supposed heroine of this farcical "novel," takes refuge in her bottle and forgets her problems. Where else in literature *before* Austen do we find a story in which hero and heroine (Jack and Alice presumably should be the stars of "Jack and Alice") end up so ignominiously?

Some heroines in the juvenilia militantly pursue men not for their beauty but for their possessions. For example, Mary Stanhope in "The Three Sisters" launches into a page of materialistic demands ("you *must*") before agreeing to marry Mr. Watts, a man she hates:

> "Remember I am to have a new Carriage hung as high as the Duttons', and blue spotted with silver; and I shall expect a new saddle horse, a suit of fine lace, and an infinite number of the most valuable Jewels. Diamonds such as never twere seen! and Pearls, Rubies, Emeralds, and Beads out of number. You must set up your Phaeton which must be cream coloured with a wreath of silver flowers round it, You must buy 4 of the finest Bays in the Kingdom and you must drive me in it every day. This is not all; You must entirely new furnish your House after my Taste, You must hire two more Footmen to attend me, two Women to wait on me, must always let me do just as I please and make a very good husband. . . ."
>
> "And pray Miss Stanhope" (said Mr Watts) "What am I to expect from you in return for all this?"
>
> "Expect? why you may expect to have me pleased." (*MW*, 65)

Like Lydia Bennet in *Pride and Prejudice* focusing on her wedding clothes and lording it over her sisters by parading her married status, so Mary in "The Three Sisters" accepts Mr. Watts primarily because she does not want one of her sisters to be married before her. Mary worries that her husband "has a large fortune and will make great Settlements on me; but then he is very healthy. . . . What's the use of a great Jointure if Men live forever?" (*MW*, 58, 64).

The heroines of Austen's juvenilia just do *not* seem to have read those conduct books advising young women to be pious, modest, silent in company, and self-effacing, ignoring their own inclinations in deference to the needs and wishes of their husbands. They seem not necessarily to have "a disposition that can yield to the desires of others" (Jane West, *Letters to a Young Lady in Which the Duties and Character of Women are Considered*) but instead display the very "amazonian boldness" they were warned to eschew.[15] They poison and threaten to slash the throats of their rivals ("Jack and Alice") or they steal desserts, refuse to pay for them, and knock over the cook ("Beautifull Cassandra").

One blatant rule violator is the heroine of "Henry and Eliza." Eliza steals from her parents, elopes, sails a man-of-war with fifty-five guns, escapes from a dungeon, and walks thirty miles without stopping. As Karen Hartnick notes, "Eliza lives out the traditional male adventure—she leaves her family, travels, faces danger, demonstrates cunning and bravery, and defeats her enemies in armed battle."[16] Yet throughout "Henry and Eliza" Austen describes her ruthless heroine as enchanting, noble, and exalted. Eliza sings about her Innocent Heart after robbing her parents and vows not to swerve from "virtue's dear boundaries" after stealing another woman's lover. Rather than displaying feminine humility, Eliza is "happy in the conscious knowledge of her own Excellence" and rewarded at the end by "the applause of her own Heart" (*MW,* 34, 39).

In "Henry and Eliza" Austen not only presents a brash heroine but also mocks the "foundling child" plot common in novels of the day. Eliza is found in a haystack and adopted by the Harcourts, but at the end of the story it turns out Lady Harcourt actually is Eliza's mother: she has put her in the haystack and forgotten about her. Why abandon her to begin with? She explains to her husband that in his absence "dreading your just resentment at her not proving the Boy you wished, I took her to a Haycock and laid her down" (*MW,* 39).

As if to strike back at a world granting boys opportunities while requiring utter placidity of its girls, the heroines of Austen's juvenilia defiantly commit every crime imaginable. "I murdered my father at a very early period of my Life, I have since murdered my Mother, and I am now going to murder my Sister. I have changed my religion so often that at present I have not an idea of any left. I have been a perjured witness in every public tryal for these last twelve Years; and I have forged my own Will. In short there is scarcely a crime that I have not committed" ("A Letter from a Young Lady, whose feelings being too Strong for her Judgement led her into the commission of Errors which her Heart disapproved," *MW,* 175). Though the title indicates the young lady disapproves of her actions and she vows "I am now going to reform," the letter ends with her announcement, "I am now going to murder my Sister." This occurs even after she has completed "a close examination of [her] conduct." What would Dr. Gregory say?

By enclosing this list of crimes within a letter from one young lady to another, Austen mocks her era's penchant for epistolary novels consisting of a heartfelt, sentimental exchange between unbelievably virtuous and affectionate young women who seem to have nothing else to do but write lengthy letters detailing the events of their whole lives. "Lesley Castle" is composed *entirely* as a novel of letters between young women signing themselves as "your affectionate friend," "yours ever after," and "your dear sincere friend." The savage content of these letters, however, shatters the polite format. We meet vain characters like the Miss Lesleys ("We are very handsome and the greatest of our Perfections is, that we are entirely insensible of them ourselves") and callous women whose only worry when a bridegroom falls and breaks his skull is that there will be leftover food from the canceled wedding. Austen exposes the jealousy and spite of women who regard each other as rivals: Margaret describes Lady Lesley as "so extremely unmajestic in her little diminutive figure, as to render her in comparison with the elegant height of Matilda & Myself, an insignificant Dwarf," while Lady Lesley describes Margaret and her sister as "two great, tall, out of the way, over-grown Girls . . . Scotch Giants." Such insults often are masked by smarmy pseudopoliteness: "My dear Charlotte . . . Ah! my dear friend. . . . How often have I wished that I possessed as little personal Beauty as you do; that my figure were as inelegant; my face as unlovely; and my Appearance as unpleasing as yours! . . . Adieu my dear Charlotte" (*MW,* 111, 122, 123, 135–36, 138).

Similarly, Arabella in "The female philosopher–A Letter" tells her "dear Louisa" that when speaking about Louisa to others, she did "ample Justice" to her "Merits":

> "Louisa Clark (said I) is in general a very pleasant Girl, yet sometimes her good humour is clouded by Peevishness, Envy & Spite. She neither wants Understanding nor is without some pretensions to Beauty, but these are so very trifling, that the value she sets on her personal charms, & the adoration she expects them to be offered are at once a striking example of her vanity, her pride, & her folly." So said I, & to my opinion everyone added weight by the concurrence of their own.
>
>
>
> your affe:te
> Arabella Smythe (*MW,* 172)
>
>

This sort of young woman who skewers her rivals while pretending affection will appear in virtually all of Austen's later novels.

Austen adds an extra ironic twist to "The Female Philosopher"–with its devastating portrait of vicious females–by *pretending* it is a conduct book dedicated to her infant niece: "My Dear Neice," reads the inscription, "I think it my particular Duty to prevent your feeling as much as possible the want of my personal instructions, by

addressing to You on paper my Opinions & Admonitions on the conduct of Young Women, which you will find expressed in the following
pages" (*MW,* 170). Another niece receives as a mock-instructional
present a short, nonsensical piece called "A Beautiful Description of
the Different Effects of Sensibility on Different Minds." In this fragment, Austen undercuts the pathos of Sir William's grief for the ill
Melissa ("Oh! Melissa, Ah! Melissa!") with the entrance of a punning
doctor: "How is she? Very weak. Aye, indeed it is a very week since
you have taken to your bed" (*MW,* 72). The doctor also puns on the
effect spirits (cordials) will have on her spirits. Mrs. Burnaby times
her sentiment, deciding to sigh once a week. Austen's dedication of
"A Beautiful Description" boasts a highly edifying guide to life for
her niece: "I dedicate to You the following Miscellanious Morsels,
convinced that if you seriously attend to them, You will derive from
them very important Instructions, with regard to your Conduct in
Life" (*MW,* 71).

A general sense of hilarity pervades Austen's early writings as
she has her characters' words and situations reveal the opposite of
what they are asserting. For example, Margaret Lesley describes herself as "retired from almost all the World, (for we visit no one but
the M'Leods, the M'Kenzies, the M'Phersons, the M'Cartneys, the
M'donalds, the M'Kinnons, the M'lellens, the M'Kays, the Macbeths
and the Macduffs)," and Susan Lesley is "remarkably good-tempered
when she has her own way, and very lively when she is not out of
humour" ("Lesley's Castle," *MW,* 111, 119). After encountering marriage partners who hate each other, readers are told that all ends "with
great Harmony & Cordiality" ("The Three Sisters," *MW,* 71). When
Lady Percival leaves, Sir William's "Affliction was considerably lessened by his Joy," and he promptly shoots a rival for the hand of another woman so that "the lady has then no reason to refuse him"
("Sir William Mountague," *MW,* 41, 42). Murders, robberies, and
animosities are all cavalierly glossed over by graceful sentence structures and elegant diction.

Jane Austen's precocity shows in her extraordinary vocabulary
and her ability to mock conventional syntax. For example, she parodies the balanced antithesis in so many of Dr. Johnson's sentences:
"Tho' Benevolent and Candid, she was Generous and sincere; Tho'
Pious and Good, she was Religious and amiable, and Tho' Elegant
and Agreable, she was Polished and Entertaining" ("Jack and Alice,"
MW, 13). Austen also saw right through adult hypocrisy and affectation. As Virginia Woolf noted of the adolescent Austen, she "had few

illusions about other people and none about herself."[17] Austen will puncture a maudlin announcement of a young woman's death with the wry comment that the duke "mourned her loss with unshaken constancy for the next fortnight" ("Jack and Alice," *MW,* 28). Irony allows Austen to expose the discrepancy between what people say and what they mean, what they proscribe for others and what they practice themselves, what they pretend and what they know to be true. As Caroline notes in "Jack and Alice," "Oh . . . I wish I was really what I pretend to be" (*MW,* 14). Like modern real estate ads that call a small dump a "cozy abode," Austen cites in "A Tale" an advertisement for a cottage that is "ready furnished except two rooms & a Closet" (*MW,* 177). The catch? It turns out the house only *has* two rooms and a closet!

Could Austen's irony have a political bite to it? Does she imply that the upper classes *pose* as benevolent while engaging in cruelty to those beneath them on the social ladder? Austen opens one sketch with the startling sentence, "Sir George and Lady Harcourt were superintending the Labours of their Haymakers, rewarding the industry of some by smiles of approbation, and punishing the idleness of others, by a cudgel" ("Henry and Eliza," *MW,* 33). In "A Fragment written to inculcate the practise of Virtue" (which Chapman notes was "erased in MS"), Austen takes an understated stab at the heartlessness of the fortunate toward the unfortunate: "We all know that many are unfortunate in their progress through the world, but we do not know all that are so. To seek them out to study their wants, & to leave them unsupplied is the duty, and ought to be the Business of Man. But few have time, fewer still have inclination, and no one has either the one or the other for such employments. Who amidst those that perspire away their Evenings in crouded assemblies can have leisure to bestow a thought on such as sweat under the fatigue of their daily Labour" (*MW,* 71). This reads more like Jonathan Swift than Jane Austen. Members of the leisured class lack the time and inclination to concern themselves with tired, perspiring laborers, so they leave their needs "unsupplied." Like the narrator of Swift's "Modest Proposal" who pretends to approve of boiling the children of poor people for food, the narrator of Austen's fragment labels it the "duty" and "business" of the upper class to ignore the plight of workers. Did Austen abandon this fragment—erase it, in fact—because it was moving in a more radical direction than she felt comfortable pursuing, or did an Austen relative later erase it? Whichever the case, it remains fascinating that Austen wrote it at all.

In "A Collection of Letters" the haughty Lady Greville tells Maria, "It is not my way to find fault with people because they are poor, for I always think that they are more to be despised & pitied than blamed for it" (*MW,* 156). This foreshadows Lady Catherine de Bourgh of *Pride and Prejudice,* whose approach to the poor is to sally forth into the village "to scold them into harmony and plenty" (*PP,* 169). Because Maria's grandfather was a wine merchant, Lady Greville has Maria stand outside her carriage when they talk, noting "some sort of people have no feelings either of cold or Delicacy"; she then criticizes Maria's chapped face for being "ruddy and coarse" (*MW,* 159). In another juvenile sketch included in "A Collection of Letters," the materialistic Henrietta boasts with no awareness of her ridiculousness, "I *am* very Charitable every now and then" (*MW,* 169; italics in Chapman corrected by Juliet McMaster to match manuscript). This anticipates Emma Woodhouse, who follows "a charitable visit . . . to a poor sick family" by forgetting all about them within minutes, distracted by her own matchmaking plans (*E,* 83, 87).

An adolescent Austen also mocks those who pride themselves on their connections rather than merit. She satirizes the Dudleys, a family "famed for their Pride," and observes that the mother is "an ill-educated, untaught woman of ancient family" who "was proud of that family almost without knowing why" ("Catharine, or the Bower," *MW,* 195). Throughout the juvenilia, Austen irreverently presents duchesses, countesses, and other titled characters who feel smug but behave ignobly.

Austen challenges the entire notion of politics in her brief "The History of England," written by a "partial, prejudiced, and ignorant Historian" with "very few Dates" (*MW,* 138). She makes Mary Queen of Scots, not Elizabeth, her heroine, and notes murders and dynastic struggles with calm understatement: "Henry the 4th ascended the throne of England much to his own satisfaction in the year 1399, after having prevailed on his cousin & predecessor Richard the 2d, to resign it to him, & to retire for the rest of his Life to Pomfret Castle, where he happened to be murdered" (*MW,* 139). By tossing out disparaging remarks about rulers ("I cannot say much for this Monarch's Sense"), events ("Lord Cobham was burnt alive, but I forget what for"), and martyrs ("Joan of Arc made such a *row.* . . . They should not have burnt her but they did"), Austen displays a surprising irreverence toward authority (*MW,* 139–40). Cassandra provided caricature-like illustrations of the monarchs to accompany her sister's mock-history.

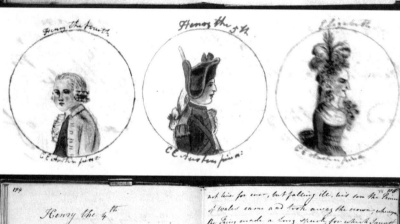

Details from Jane Austen's juvenile *History of England,* with Cassandra Austen's caricatures of kings and queens (Reproduced by permission of the British Library)

The comic exaggeration and cartoonish illustrations may fool us into thinking "History of England" has no purpose beyond amusement. Devoney Looser convincingly argues that Austen registers important truths about the inventive and biased nature of schoolroom history and the need for herstory.[18] Current debates about the blurred line between history and fiction suggest that Jane Austen was way ahead of her time.

Most of Austen's early satire concerns itself not with historical figures but with relationships within a family. Her adolescent fiction takes apart—corsage by carriage—every step a couple makes on its way to the altar. Bride and groom are nothing more than selfish schemers. Instead of a man wooing a woman with unselfish devotion, we find Benjamin leaving love letters for Sally one mile from his house and seven miles from hers, explaining to her that he chose this discrepancy in distance "as I considered that the walk would be of benefit to you in your weak & uncertain state of Health" ("Amelia Webster," *MW,* 48). In another sketch Miss Fitzgerald proposes marriage to Willoughby (who has spoken only of herrings and the bottle, not of marriage) simply because they are the only ones left in the room without partners: "Since you Willoughby are the only one left, I cannot refuse your earnest solicitations—There is my Hand" ("The Visit," *MW,* 54).

Readers of *Sense and Sensibility* will recognize the name "Willoughby": indeed, Austen's adolescent works are filled with names she will return to in her novels. We also see foreshadowing of scenes and themes that will appear in far subtler form in the novels. For example, in *Sense and Sensibility* Austen will write with genuine feeling about the grief-stricken Marianne in danger of losing her life unless she quits wallowing in grief and finds the strength to survive the disappointment of Willoughby's rejection. In the juvenilia, such scenes appear only for their comic effect. For example, when Emma learns Edgar is away, she succumbs to her feelings: "it was with difficulty that Emma could refrain from tears on hearing of the absence of Edgar; she remained however tolerably composed till the Wilmot's were gone when having no check to the over flowings of her greif, she gave free vent to them, & retiring to her own room, continued in tears the remainder of her Life" ("Edgar & Emma," *MW,* 33). Even a man's departure from home for an errand can prove fatal to the woman he leaves behind, for "Maria had been so much grieved at his departure that she died of a broken heart about three hours after his departure" ("Evelyn," *MW,* 189).

Just as Twain made Jacob in "The Good Little Boy" "so honest that he was simply ridiculous" and so good that he could not survive, so Austen made some of her heroines so "feminine"—that is, overly emotional and vulnerable—that they cannot face reality. If women are taught they must marry to be complete ("women unquestionably were created to be the wedded mates of man," writes Jane West), how can they survive solitude?[19]

Austen's adolescent sketches make us think, question, and laugh, but they do *not* make us feel sympathy for any character: we simply stay at too great a distance from them, as when watching slapstick Laurel and Hardy comedies. Characters can be thrown out of windows, drowned in purling streams, rejected in love, and starved to death and we feel nothing because the satire is so heavy handed. For example, Austen writes that one stricken heroine "began to find herself rather hungry, & had reason to think, by their biting off two of her fingers, that her Children were much in the same situation" ("Henry and Eliza," *MW,* 37).

Pathos becomes bathos in "Love and Freindship," another "novel in a series of letters" pillorying every literary convention Austen could find. After praising her own beauty, virtues, and accomplishments, a heroine named Laura admits her only fault was "a sensibility too tremblingly alive to every affliction of my Friends, my Acquaintance and particularly to every affliction of my own." Indeed she is so tremblingly sensible that she faints and swoons her way into difficulties. Laura places so high a value on "Delicate feeling, tender Sentiments, and refined Sensibility" that she rejects the acquaintance of sensible women and welcomes (instantaneously, of course) a friendship with the equally sappy Sophia: "Sophia was . . . most elegantly formed. A soft Languor spread over her lovely features, but increased their Beauty−. It was the Charectarestic of her Mind−. She was all Sensibility and Feeling. We flew into each others arms & after having exchanged vows of mutual Friendship for the rest of our Lives, instantly unfolded to each other the most inward Secrets of our Hearts−." Moved by various affecting scenes that were "too pathetic for the feelings of Sophia and myself," Laura explains, "We fainted Alternately on a Sofa" (*MW,* 78, 84, 85, 86).

The two women faint rather than function. They are so bent on indulging in "overpowering Effusions of . . . Grief" that they cannot come to the aid of their two stricken husbands. When their husbands' carriage overturns and leaves the two men "most elegantly attired but weltering in their blood," Sophia "shreiked & fainted on the Ground" while Laura "screamed & instantly ran mad." Rather than administering CPR or at least getting their husbands out of the road, Laura and Sophia remain deprived of their senses for over an hour, by which time both are widows. Sophia spends so much time fainting on the damp ground that she contracts "a galloping Consumption," dying after uttering these affecting words to her partner in emotion: "One fatal swoon has cost me my Life. . . . Beware of swoons dear Laura . . . Run mad as often as you chuse; but do not faint—."

In addition to exposing the absurdity of hyperventilating heroines and their affected sensibility, Austen scoffs at improbable plots. Austen mocks love at first sight by having Laura attach herself to Lindsay the minute he enters the room: "no sooner did I first behold him, than I felt that on him the happiness or Misery of my future Life must depend." When Laura enters a stagecoach after the death of her swooning friend, she meets her father-in-law, sister-in-law, and many friends: "Oh! Heavens, (exclaimed I) is it possible that I should so unexpectedly be surrounded by my nearest Relations & Connections?" Possible, Austen demonstrates, only in impossible fiction. She closes her "novel of letters" with Laura ensconced in a "romantic Village" where she can indulge in "melancholy solitude" and apparently have plenty of time for writing letters narrating a lifetime full of affecting scenes and tender moments (*MW*, 88, 99, 102, 80, 103, 108–9). After reading "Love and Freindship" Virginia Woolf asked, "What is this note which never merges in the rest, which sounds distinctly and penetratingly all through the volume? It is the sound of laughter. The girl of fifteen [or thereabouts] is laughing, in her corner, at the world."[20]

Austen laughed at the dialogue she read in the fiction and drama of her day because she knew it failed to capture the way human beings actually spoke to each other. In "The First Act of a Comedy" Austen parodies those playwrights who clumsily use dialogue as a way to reveal plot. When the daughter asks, "Pray papa, how far is it to London?" her father replies, "My girl, my Darling, my favourite of all my Children, who art the picture of thy poor Mother, who died 2 months ago, with whom I am going to Town to marry to Strephon, and to whom I mean to bequeath my whole Estate, it wants seven miles" (*MW*, 173). What a wonderful sentence to diagram! Throughout her youthful writing Austen presents characters speaking in contorted sentences, using polysyllabic expression, arcane literary allusions, and a superabundance of exclamations. As Rachel Brownstein notes, "Conventional sentiments and conventional sentences are mocked at once."[21]

Love scenes in particular cry out for burlesque. In "A Collection of Letters" Austen mixes passionate declarations of love with financial ruminations, as in this letter from Thomas Musgrove to Henrietta: "Adorable Henrietta how beautiful you are! I declare you are quite divine! You are more than Mortal. You are an angel. You are Venus herself. . . . And Ah! Angelic Miss Henrietta Heaven is my Witness how ardently I do hope for the death of your villanous Uncle & his Abandoned Wife, Since my fair one will not consent to be mine till their decease has placed her affluence above what my fortune can procure–. Though it is an improvable Estate–. . . . Amiable princess of my Heart farewell." Henrietta labels this "a pattern for a Love-letter" and "such a masterpeice of Writing" because it displays "Such sentiment, Such purity of Thought, Such flow of Language & such unfeigned Love in one Sheet." She responds to Musgrove that she is so much in love with him that she impatiently awaits the death of her aunt and uncle: "If they will not die soon, I beleive I shall run mad." Fearing he may not win Henrietta, Musgrove lugubriously remarks, "When I am dead . . . Let me be carried & lain at her feet, & perhaps she may not disdain to drop a pitying tear on my poor remains." While all the characters in the letters praise the lovers' "sweet sensibility" and "noble behaviour," readers see their mercenary, selfish natures as they propose that the laws of England be changed so that uncles and aunts cannot possess their estates if wanted by their nephews and nieces (*MW,* 163, 164, 167).

Perhaps the older generation should just give up *everything,* Austen helpfully suggests in "Evelyn." A young man named Mr. Gower successfully convinces the Webbs to give him not only food and money but also their house, grounds, and daughter. Mr. Gower "generously" allows the Webbs to remain an additional half hour in the home they are vacating, so the Webbs "burst forth into raptures of Admiration at his politeness, which they agreed served only to make their Conduct appear more inexcusable in trespassing on his time" (*MW,* 183). Even when Mr. Gower remarries (after the death of Maria Gower), the Webbs send him more money and express delight at his well-deserved happiness.

Yet in "Catharine, or the Bower" Austen turns her satiric gaze on *both* the degenerate younger generation and on a conservative older generation too quick to complain about how much worse the world has become: "After Supper, the Conversation turning on the state of Affairs in the political World, Mrs P, who was firmly of opinion that the whole race of Mankind were degenerating, said that for her part,

Everything she beleived was going to rack and ruin, all order was destroyed over the face of the World . . . and Depravity never was so general before; concluding with a wish that she might live to see the Manners of the People in Queen Elizabeth's reign, restored again." Throughout "Catharine, or the Bower" Mrs. Percival asserts like Jeremiah that the world is going to ruin. London, she argues, has become "the hot house of Vice where virtue had long been banished from Society & wickedness of every description was daily gaining ground." She launches into "a long harangue on the shocking behaviour of modern young Men" contrasting it with "many instructive anecdotes of the Decorum & Modesty which had marked the Characters of those whom she had known, when she had been young" (*MW,* 200, 239, 230). Indeed, Austen shows good-old-days nostalgia to be a form of vanity.

Mrs. Percival, however, could certainly find plenty of evidence for the degeneracy of mankind and womankind by examining the behavior and remarks of other characters in "Catharine, or the Bower." Some are "Splendidly, yet unhappily married." Rather than acquiring "useful knowledge & Mental Improvement," young women learn a smattering of superficial husband-catching accomplishments "which were now to be displayed & in a few years entirely neglected." Camilla is an ornamental idiot: "All her Ideas were towards the Elegance of her appearance, the fashion of her dress, & the Admiration she wished them to excite. She professed a love of Books without Reading, was lively without Wit, & generally good humoured without Merit." Camilla's elegant exterior masks a heartless interior, as she wishes of the rival Dudley family that her father "would propose knocking all their Brains out" and of her "friend" Kitty at the ball that "I hope she may fall down & break her neck, or sprain her Ancle" (*MW,* 194, 198, 204, 224).

Kitty has good reason in "Catharine, or the Bower" for concluding in self-reproach, "what a silly Thing is Woman! How vain, how unreasonable!" but men appear equally contemptible. Stanley is as vain about his personal appearance as any woman, taking so long to dress that he and Kitty are late to the ball. Which is worse, to have no interest in politics (like Camilla, who says "Oh! dear . . . I know nothing of Politics, & cannot bear to hear them mentioned") or to be a willing waffler, like Stanley, who is "so far from being really of any party, that he had scarcely a fixed opinion on the Subject" and "could therefore always take either side, & always argue with temper"? If Mrs. Percival is right that "the welfare of every Nation depends upon the virtue of it's individuals," the nation is in deep trouble (*MW,* 236, 201, 231, 232).

And perhaps it is a good thing that Mrs. Percival never met Lady Susan, the "heroine" of Austen's late juvenile work, or she would have fretted even more about the state of the world. Devoted to the "delicious gratification of making a whole family miserable," Lady Susan flirts, lies, schemes, and manipulates her way among others, using her "bewitching powers" and "captivating Deceit" to ruin marriages and lives (*MW,* 248–49).

John Halperin labels Austen's role in these early writings as that of "literary demolition-expert" and calls these early sketches "the surest guide to her–to Jane Austen herself."[22] Claudia Johnson pronounces the sketches "the fruit of unparalleled self-assurance."[23] To read the sketches is to encounter characters poisoning each other, dying of grief, and hurling elegantly devastating insults at each other. One might ask, why read such verbal slapstick, such caricatures? These early verses, sketches, and fragments not only have value in their own right–for their sheer vibrancy and verbal precocity–but also are essential to any search for Austen. They offer a unique glimpse into what Jane Austen rejected: literary conventions that were divorced from real life; social customs that were absurdly affected and hypocritical; ideas about womanhood that were insincere, confining, or degrading.

Through her youthful sketches, Austen also staked out a place for herself within her family. There are striking links between Austen's early pieces and the witty periodical two of her brothers simultaneously were editing at Oxford. In sixty issues of the *Loiterer* (1789–90) James and Henry Austen and their friends offered "a regular succession of moral lectures, critical remarks, and elegant humour" about alcohol, politics, fashion, marriage, boxing, and other topics of the day. Some suspect that a fourteen-year-old Jane Austen wrote the entry of 28 March 1789 attributed to "Sophia Sentiment" complaining that the *Loiterer* should feature more stories about the female sex. "Get a new set of correspondents, from among the young of both sexes, but particularly ours," Sophia Sentiment advises the editors, and then perhaps she will no longer deem the *Loiterer* "the stupidest work" of its kind. The melodramatic plot Sophia Sentiment suggests for a story bears a striking resemblance to those Jane Austen was parodying in her juvenilia: "Let the lover be killed in a duel . . . and as for his mistress, she will of course go mad; only remember whatever you do, that your hero and heroine must possess a great deal of feeling, and have pretty names."[24] In addition, I suspect that Jane Austen also wrote the letter of 21 November 1790, said to be by "Margaret Mitten," to the *Loiterer*'s editors. In language reminiscent of the boastful characters in Austen's juvenilia, a supremely self-confident Margaret Mitten praises herself: "I have preserved my figure in the unbending Majesty of prim perpendicularity. . . . Such is my person, nor is my mind unworthy of it, for except for an unfortunate propensity for tittle tattle, and a hereditary love of the bottle, I have few failings, and am wanting in no virtue except Candour, Generosity, and Truth."[25] Like the brazen heroines of Austen's adolescent spoofs urging men to marry them immediately, Margaret Mitten suggests becoming "Mrs. Loiterer" because of her many perfections. One suspects that as a teenager, Jane Austen would have relished becoming part of her witty brothers' first effort at publication and penning her own burlesques as well. She knows no women can attend Oxford, yet she has the utmost confidence in her own literary powers.

As Margaret Doody observes after studying the meticulous textual changes Austen made in the manuscripts of her youthful sketches, these are not mere childlike "Effusions of Fancy," as Austen's father called them, but startling pieces that "bear all the signs of careful workmanship, and of reworking."[26] Jane Austen remained interested in these pieces long after she had written them, so it would be a mistake to see the juvenilia as presenting an approach that a mature Jane Austen completely abandoned. Just a year before her death, Austen jotted down the satiric "Plan of a Novel" showing her continued distaste for the stock conventions and improbable characters of contemporary literature. In addition to the portions of the "Plan" quoted in the first chapter, consider this excerpt: "The scene will be for ever shifting from one Set of People to another—but All the Good will be unexceptionable in every respect—and there will be no foibles or weaknesses but with the Wicked, who will be completely depraved and infamous, hardly a resemblance of Humanity left in them.—Early in her career, in the progress of her first removals, Heroine must meet with the Hero—all perfection of course—and only prevented from paying his addresses to her, by some excess of refinement. . . . [Heroine] often carried away by the anti-hero, but rescued either by her Father or the Hero . . . continually cheated and defrauded of her hire, worn down to a Skeleton, and now and then starved to death" (*MW*, 429–30). This mature Austen seems surprisingly similar to her adolescent self.

Juliet McMaster observes that as we read the adolescent works of Jane Austen we see her "writing with her hair down and breaking every rule."[27] Later that hair—both literally and symbolically—would be restrained: "My long hair is always plaited up out of sight," Austen writes to her sister (1 December 1798). But once having encountered a wild-haired Austen who speaks in the unabashedly bold, impish voice of the juvenilia, we never can go back to that old image of Jane Austen—the one her relatives wanted us to accept. Now note how ridiculous seem those sweetened comments of her relatives. Nephew James Edward Austen-Leigh and niece Caroline Austen do not fool us when they insist that Aunt Jane uttered only honeyed words, never turned her neighbors into ridicule, and was "as far as possible from being censorious or satirical."[28] Henry Austen fails to convince us that his sister was a flawless saint: "Faultless herself, as nearly as human nature can be, she always sought, in the faults of others, something to excuse, to forgive or forget. . . . She never uttered either a hasty, a silly, or a severe expression. . . . [She was] fearful of giving offence to God, and incapable of feeling it towards any fellow creature" (*NA*, 6, 8). As readers of the complete juvenilia, we know that Jane Austen was an irreverent, impudent, caustic, and funny rebel, as satirical as they come, delighting in silly and severe expressions ridiculing the faults of others.

After sampling Jane Austen's rakish adolescent works, readers of her more subtle, mature novels know to look between the lines of her seemingly acceptable prose for glimpses of that irrepressible originality and courage to be witty.[29] At the same time, they sense how far she has come. Something profound must have happened—some period of tremendous artistic and personal growth—to transform Jane Austen from a slapstick writer to a mature novelist. Frederick and Elfrida are caricatures; Elizabeth Bennet and Mr. Darcy of *Pride and Prejudice* are not. If we imagine movie versions of the juvenilia as opposed to the novels, it would be like comparing *The Three Stooges* to a *Masterpiece Theatre* drama. Both have validity (the first, for sheer *fun*), but they are *different.*

Perhaps Jane Austen's extensive reading—we know as a young woman she read Shakespeare, Swift, Richardson, Fielding, Cowper, Crabbe, Burney, and many others—led her to aspire to literature with greater depth. Perhaps as she grew older and became, through various kinds of losses, more aware of the tragic side of life, her characters gained in dimension. In Austen's adolescent fiction we meet a brash young artist experimenting with and destroying all kinds of one-dimensional stock characters, overused plots, and hackneyed expressions, as if needing to establish what literature should *not* be before adopting a style and form of her own.

It is impossible to know exactly when Jane Austen began thinking of herself as a writer—a real writer, rather than just a teenager trying to make her parents, siblings, and cousins laugh at her audacity and verbal cleverness. Even as a youngster Jane Austen seems to have enjoyed calling herself an author and imagining her works reaching a wider audience. Here are three typical dedications:

> Memoirs of Mr Clifford To Charles John Austen Esqre Sir, Your generous patronage of the unfinished tale, I have already taken the Liberty of dedicating to you, encourages me to dedicate to you a second, as unfinished as the first. I am Sir with every expression of regard for you & yr noble Family, your most obe^{dt} &c.&c. . . . THE AUTHOR (*MW,* 42)

> Amelia Webster an interesting & well written Tale is dedicated by Permission to Mrs Austen by Her humble Servant THE AUTHOR (*MW,* 47)

> The Mystery: An Unfinished Comedy Dedication to the Revd George Austen Sir, I humbly solicit your Patronage to the following Comedy, which tho' an unfinished one, is I flatter myself as *complete a Mystery* as any of its kind. I am Sir your most Hum^{le} Servant THE AUTHOR (*MW,* 55)

Two decades before she would *actually* publish a novel, Jane Austen joked with Cassandra that her works had "obtained a place in every library in the Kingdom":

> Catharine, or The Bower To Miss Austen MADAM Encouraged by your warm patronage of The beautiful Cassandra, and The History of England, which through your generous support, have obtained a place in every library in the Kingdom, and run through threescore Editions, I take the liberty of begging the same Exertions in favour of the following Novel, which I humbly flatter myself, possesses Merit beyond any already published, or any that will ever in future appear, except such as may proceed from the pen of Your Most Grateful Humble Ser^{vt}
>
> THE AUTHOR(*MW,* 192)

The capitalization used here comes not from me but from THE AUTHOR!

Even though at this point (at about age sixteen) Jane Austen is only bantering with her sister, she clearly has on her mind artistic merit, publishing success, multiple editions, and fame. Why else would she write about it? She even is contemplating the notion of earning money through her writing, as either she or her brother Henry added a postscript to the dedication to "Lesley Castle" asking a fictitious bank called "Demand & Co." to "please pay Jane Austen Spinster, the sum of one hundred guineas" (*MW*, 110).

Like a young girl trying on costumes, Jane Austen seems in her adolescent works to be playing with roles, including that of successful author. She displays boastful high spirits, or "an excess of *cockylorum*," a word she italicized but then later deleted from one of her early sketches.[30] Austen's delight in these exuberant, youthful experiments in writing must have encouraged her to pursue a vocation as a novelist—to really *be* "THE AUTHOR" determined to create bold works possessing "Merit beyond any already published."

3

Only Genius, Wit, and Taste
Northanger Abbey

Great God! What a genius I had when I wrote that book.
        –Jonathan Swift about *The Tale of the Tub*

I have nothing to declare but my genius.
        –Oscar Wilde to a customs officer

Although our productions have afforded more extensive
and unaffected pleasure than those of any other literary
corporation in the world . . . there seems almost a general
wish of decrying the capacity and undervaluing the labour
of the novelist, and of slighting the performances which
have only genius, wit, and taste to recommend them.
        –Jane Austen, *Northanger Abbey*

Readers in search of Jane Austen may find more of her in *Northanger Abbey* than in any other novel she would write. Like Oscar Wilde telling a New York customs officer, "I have nothing to declare but my genius," Jane Austen in *Northanger Abbey* seems more interested in displaying her own artistic powers than in telling a particular story.[1] She brilliantly demonstrates that while she could have written in a variety of popular styles of the day, she instead has grander goals for her own novels. Despite the fact it was published posthumously, *Northanger Abbey* appears to have undergone fewer revisions than *Sense and Sensibility* or *Pride and Prejudice* and thus sounds more like the young Jane Austen. Like "Henry and Eliza," "Love and Freindship," and other early burlesques, *Northanger Abbey* remains in some ways a bold, rebellious exercise in literary demolition.

Perhaps because Austen spends so much time in *Northanger Abbey* pillorying the improbable sentimental and gothic best-sellers of her day, it has seemed in some ways more topical and dated than her other novels. Even Austen observed in her advertisement for *Northanger*

Abbey that it included "parts . . . which thirteen years have made comparatively obsolete" (12). Few Austen readers and critics over the last two centuries have chosen *Northanger Abbey* as their favorite Austen novel or as her greatest masterpiece. A. Walton Litz observes that the novel "lacks the narrative sophistication of the later works" because Austen was "experimenting . . . with several narrative methods she had not fully mastered," and biographer Park Honan calls the narrator "a lithe and slithery eel of great energy which is less than fully controlled."[2] Paradoxically, the weakness of *Northanger Abbey* becomes its strength. Trying to pin the narrative tale on that "slithery eel" becomes a game well worth playing. Who is this protean storyteller who moves in and out of the novel, sometimes praising, sometimes mocking her characters and her readers?

Northanger Abbey opens with an ironic narrator informing us indirectly that the characters, plots, and diction of other books bear little resemblance to real life and that conduct books for girls stifle a young woman's intellect and spirit:

> No one who had ever seen Catherine Morland in her infancy, would have supposed her born to be an *heroine*. Her situation in life, the character of her father and mother, her own person and disposition, were all equally against her. . . . She had a thin awkward figure, a sallow skin without colour, dark lank hair, and strong features;–so much for her person;–and not less unpropitious for *heroism* seemed her mind. She was fond of all boys' plays, and greatly preferred cricket not only to dolls, but to the more *heroic* enjoyments of infancy, nursing a dormouse, feeding a canary-bird, or watering a rose-bush. . . . she was moreover noisy and wild, hated confinement and cleanliness, and loved nothing so well in the world as rolling down the green slope at the back of the house. . . . Catherine . . . had by nature nothing *heroic* about her . . . [and] prefer[red] cricket, base ball, riding on horseback, and running about the country. . . . she fell miserably short of the true *heroic* height. (13–16; my italics)

This stands as a revolutionary opening. Catherine may not have ridiculously greasy tresses and a swelling back like Rebecca in "Frederic and Elfrida," Austen's first adolescent sketch, but she is sallow with lank hair. She may not get drunk, raise armies, and commit murder, as did the delinquent women of the youthful burlesques, but she rejects domesticity, confinement, and personal cleanliness.

Yet Austen's mock-assault actually forces readers to see Catherine's superiority to other heroines. She played this same trick on readers in the earlier "Love and Freindship" when she disguised praise as censure in her description of a young woman named Bridget. Like Catherine, Bridget is seventeen, "one of the best of ages," but lacks beauty: "Alas! she was very plain and her name was Bridget. Nothing therefore could be expected from her—she could not be supposed to possess either exalted Ideas, Delicate Feelings, or refined Sensibilities—She was nothing more than a mere good-tempered, civil, and obliging Young Woman; as such, she was only an Object of Contempt" (*MW*, 100–101). Here, too, Austen uses negation—nothing, not supposed, nothing more—to disparage Bridget, yet her words celebrate Bridget's redeeming virtues. Similarly, Austen makes sure her readers know in the opening chapter of *Northanger Abbey* that the supposedly unheroic Catherine Morland "had neither a bad heart nor a bad temper" (14).

Despite being more naive than her counterparts, Catherine Morland is the only Austen protagonist to be called the heroine. The term appears over twenty times in *Northanger Abbey*, not at all in *Pride and Prejudice, Sense and Sensibility, Mansfield Park,* or *Persuasion*, and only once in *Emma* (and, in that instance, *not* linked to the heroine, Emma). In all, Austen uses *heroine, hero, heroism, heroic, heroines* more times in *Northanger Abbey* than double that of the five other novels combined.

Why might Austen seem to have this—to coin a phrase—heroine addiction? Why does she tell us over and over that Catherine is her heroine but feel no compulsion to use that term in relationship to Marianne and Elinor of *Sense and Sensibility,* Elizabeth Bennet of *Pride and Prejudice,* Fanny Price of *Mansfield Park,* Emma of *Emma,* or Anne Elliot of *Persuasion?* Why call our attention to whether or not Henry Tilney is a hero or whether the characters are behaving heroically?

Could it be that neither Catherine Morland nor Henry Tilney is the true star? Rather, Jane Austen is the heroine and hero of *Northanger Abbey,* deliberately outshining both her fictional creations. *Northanger Abbey* is more about storytelling than it is a story, more about the author's craft than about her characters' lives. In *Northanger Abbey* not only does Austen use words like *heroine* more often than the other works, but it is also the only novel in which she uses the word *novelist* and repeats the term *novel.* Only in *Northanger Abbey* does Austen mention *reviewers, the press, abridgers,* and *publishers,* refer to her work as a *fable* or a *volume* with *chapters,* call herself the *author* and *contriver* wielding a *pen* and following *rules of composition,* and announce with linguistic flourish that "the eight *parts of speech* shone out most expressively" from her heroine's eyes (120). This novel also employs the word *adventure* more ("my heroine was involved in one of her most alarming adventures"), even though Austen's other novels present young women who nearly die, are knocked unconscious, go to sea on a man-of-war, or get accosted by a band of gypsies. It is not that *Northanger Abbey has* more adventures; it just *talks* about them more.

In addition, *Northanger Abbey* is the only Austen novel to refer to a readership. Why choose phrases such as "for the reader's more certain information," "that the reader may be able to judge," "passed in review before the reader," "I leave it to my reader's sagacity," and "the bosom of my readers" except to make readers aware of the author's power over them (18, 19, 97, 247, 250)? *Northanger Abbey* is by far the most self-conscious novel Jane Austen would ever write.

So the better opening sentence of *Northanger Abbey* might read, "No one but Jane Austen, the discerning author, who had ever seen Catherine Morland in her infancy, would have supposed her born to be an heroine." The entire opening chapter of *Northanger Abbey* is less about Catherine than about her creator. Austen regrets to inform us that she will not give us the standard melodramatic features of popular fiction: no father "addicted to locking up his daughters"; no mother dying pathetically during childbirth; no dazzlingly beautiful heroine who seems to be born already possessing every possible accomplishment and feminine grace; no mysterious lords or foundling children. This is Jane Austen mocking all the literary conventions she knows how to use but will not.

The pervasive narrative references to heroines, heroes, novels, and readers in *Northanger Abbey* link this work to the juvenilia. In her adolescent "Jack and Alice: A Novel," Jane Austen adopts a breezy omniscient tone and uses the "I" voice to call readers' attention to her novelistic choices: "Before I proceed to give an account of the Evening, it will be proper to describe to my reader, the persons and Characters of the party introduced to his acquaintance"; "It may now be proper to return to the Hero of this Novel . . . of whom I believe I have scarcely ever had occasion to speak" (*MW,* 12, 24–25). In the youthful "Catharine, or the Bower," Austen interrupts the story (as she does in *Northanger Abbey*) to compare her character to other fictional creations: "Catharine had the misfortune, *as many heroines have had before her*, of losing her Parents when she was very young" (*MW,* 192; my italics).

Only in *Northanger Abbey* does Austen continue this adolescent practice of commenting repeatedly about her novelistic role and about her characters' heroism or lack thereof. As Catherine leaves her native Fullerton for Bath in the company of the gouty Mr. Allen and his vapid wife, Austen tells us all the sensational events that do not occur. Catherine's busy, no-nonsense mother does not have "a thousand alarming presentiments of evil . . . from this terrific separation," sorrow does not "oppress her heart with sadness," nor does she drown her beloved daughter in tears or in warnings against "the violence of such noblemen and baronets as delight in forcing young ladies away to some remote farm-house." Instead, Mrs. Morland tells Catherine to stay warm and keep track of expenses. "Every thing indeed relative to this important journey was done, on the part of the Morlands, with a degree of moderation and composure, which seemed rather consistent with the common feelings of common life, than with the refined susceptibilities, the tender emotions which the first separation of a heroine from her family ought always to excite" (18–19). Austen obviously delights in juxtaposing melodramatic language (anxiety, severe, alarming, terrific) with mundane reality.

In *Northanger Abbey* Austen uses language of authorial disappointment ("unpromising") to describe Catherine's humdrum trip: "Under these unpromising auspices, the parting took place, and the journey began. It was performed with suitable quietness and uneventful safety. Neither robbers nor tempests befriended them, nor one lucky overturn to introduce them to the hero. Nothing more alarming occurred than a fear on Mrs. Allen's side, of having once left her clogs behind her at an inn, and that fortunately proved to be groundless" (19). Misfortunes are lucky befrienders of any author in search of a potboiler plot. Sorry, readers, Austen seems to be saying. All I will give you is a man with gout, a woman with clog fears, and a nonheroine with an unremarkable mind who is leaving her common, moderate, composed family.

What, then, makes *Northanger Abbey different* from the adolescent burlesques? Do we care about Catherine Morland more than we do about Laura, Isabel, Augusta, Sophia, or other women of "Love and Freindship"?

Yes, I would argue, and it happens by the second chapter of the novel. Catherine does not speak in the opening chapter (we are simply told all the ways she is unheroic or in training to be a heroine), but she does voice an opinion once she and Mrs. Allen enter the crowded Upper Rooms of Bath for the first time: "How uncomfortable it is," whispered Catherine, "not to have a single acquaintance here! . . . What shall we do? . . . Had not we better go away as it is?"

Anyone who has hung around awkwardly at a high school dance hoping to be approached by a would-be partner, and anyone who has tried to break into small conversational groups of strangers at a cocktail party can immediately identify with Catherine Morland. As Austen writes, "she longed to dance, but she had not an acquaintance in the room" and "felt yet more the awkwardness of having no party to join, no acquaintance to claim, no gentleman to assist them." Although knowing that "now was the time for a heroine, who had not yet played a very distinguished part in the events of the evening, to be noticed and admired," Catherine inspires no "rapturous wonder" in the heart of any young man in attendance, "nor was she once called a divinity by any body" (22–23).

Although Austen still intrudes her narrative voice to tell us whether or not Catherine is leading a heroine's life, she simultaneously has created a character that inspires empathy in her own right. At a second dance, Catherine silently sits with the wallflowers: "Catherine . . . was sharing with the scores of other young ladies still sitting down all the discredit of wanting a partner. To be disgraced in the eye of the world, to wear the appearance of infamy while her heart is all purity, her actions all innocence, and the misconduct of another the true source of her debasement, is one of those circumstances which peculiarly belong to the heroine's life, and her fortitude under it what particularly dignifies her character" (53). Readers are invited to laugh at the juxtaposition of overwrought language with prosaic reality (lacking a dance partner is hardly "infamy"), and we think of Austen's bathetic tales of young women pretending to make a dramatic "first entreé into Life"—a "mighty affair" that fills them with fear, expectation, and raptures—when they are only going next door to have tea at the neighbors ("A Collection of Letters," *MW,* 150). Yet we are also forced to feel Catherine's actual discomfort as she waits for a partner.

This is not the slapstick, unrealistic environment of the early sketches, with people falling out of windows, getting poisoned, or dying of grief. Austen is quick to tell us all the forms of melodramatic behavior Catherine does *not* engage in: "instead of turning of a deathlike paleness, and falling in a fit on Mrs. Allen's bosom, Catherine sat erect, in the perfect use of her senses, and with her cheeks only a little redder than usual" (53). We no longer need to beware of swoons, as Laura told Sophia in "Love and Freindship": in *Northanger Abbey* Austen gives her "simple and probable" heroine no fits. At times *Northanger Abbey* begins to sound like a realistic novel of a rather ordinary, naive young woman coming of age and experiencing typical frustrations and humiliations. Austen invites the universal empathy of her female readers by announcing, "Every young lady may feel for my heroine . . . for every young lady has at some time or other known the same agitation" (74). Throughout *Northanger Abbey*, Austen links Catherine to *every young lady* and *all* of us rather than to every young *heroine*. No matter how hard Catherine tries to play her literary part, "feelings rather natural than heroic" possess her (93).

Like Pinocchio evolving from wooden puppet in Gepetto's hands to a real boy, so Catherine Morland takes on a life of her own. At the same time, Austen never lets her readers forget who created Catherine Morland—and who is laughing at and sympathizing with her youthful inexperience and ignorance.

In her adolescent sketches Austen describes young women who seem to have been born talented and gifted, offering "infantine tho' sprightly answers" and boasting "wonderfull Acquirements" (*MW*, 33, 78). In contrast, the opening chapter of *Northanger Abbey* shows Catherine Morland having trouble on her road to accomplishment: "She never could learn or understand any thing before she was taught; and sometimes not even then, for she was often inattentive, and occasionally stupid. . . . She learnt [the piano] a year, and could not bear it; . . . The day which dismissed the music-master was one of the happiest of Catherine's life. Her taste for drawing was not superior. . . . At fifteen, appearances were mending; she began to curl her hair and long for balls; her complexion improved" (14–15). The narrator implies that other novelists are wrong to create precocious female paragons and that society mistakenly thinks that a layering of cosmetics will convert a girl into a woman. Why not continue to roll down green slopes and play "base ball" (a name the *Oxford English Dictionary* claims Austen coined) rather than tiptoe around the house in delicate inanity?

When Catherine prepares for heroinehood, she tends to her stylish appearance and learns to extract quotations from the books she reads so that she can trot them out for special occasions, like donning a piece of clothing or jewelry. Austen tells us, "from fifteen to seventeen she was in training for a heroine; she read all such works as heroines must read to supply their memories with those quotations which are so serviceable and so soothing in the vicissitudes of their eventful lives" (15). Perhaps Catherine feels a heroine's life will be eventful and full of vicissitudes, but we have seen no evidence of this yet. She trains for such events by memorizing lines that are soothing, like a pacifier given to calm a child, and serviceable, like a useful pair of shoes.

In a seemingly aimless fashion, Jane Austen gives samples of Catherine's quotations. Just as she loved playing charades and writing riddles for her family, so it seems she wants to play games with the readers of *Northanger Abbey*. I will give you just a few words and you figure out why, she seems to be saying, as she begins rattling off a series of partial quotations from poets Alexander Pope, William Gray, and James Thomson (spelled "Thompson" by Austen):

> From Pope, she learned to censure those who
>   "bear about the mockery of woe."
> From Gray, that
>   "Many a flower is born to blush unseen
>   And waste its fragrance on the desert air."
> From Thompson, that
>   —"It is a delightful task
>   "To teach the young idea how to shoot." (15)

As the narrator moves on without comment, readers are left to ponder.

We first wonder why Catherine has learned in Heroine Training 101 to censure those who "bear about the mockery of woe," half a line from Alexander Pope's eighty-two-line "Elegy to the Memory of an Unfortunate Lady." The entire poem describes a woman who would rather kill herself than endure hopeless love; she dies unmourned. The poem warns that in the end, "beauty, titles, wealth, and fame" matter not at all because death turns all of us into "a heap of dust." This unfortunate woman will not even have friends around her to *pretend* to mourn her loss:

> What though no friends in sable weeds appear,
> Grieve for an hour, perhaps, then mourn a year,
> And bear about the mockery of woe
> To midnight dances, and the public show?[3]

Catherine obviously has not absorbed the meaning of the line she memorized because she cannot distinguish between people with genuine versus counterfeit emotion. Although Catherine fails to see that her "friend" Isabella is one who will "bear about" into public the mockery of feeling, Austen signals readers in this opening chapter to keep this theme in mind. Austen also invites readers who know Pope's poem to sense the irony of Catherine's learning a "soothing" or "serviceable" quotation from an elegy to a suicidal lovesick woman.

Catherine's rote memorization of a few words of someone else's wisdom does not constitute "training" for anything.

The quotations from Gray and Thomson likewise go right over the curls on Catherine's head but offer much to the reader-sleuth. In "Elegy Written in a Country Churchyard," Gray warns against Ambition, Grandeur, "the pomp of power," and all that beauty and wealth can offer, suggesting that such pursuits lead nowhere but to the grave.[4] Perhaps Austen wants readers to keep this in mind when she introduces them a few chapters later to the fashion-obsessed Mrs. Allen, wealth-seeking Thorpes, and pompous, power-hungry General Tilney.

Pomp, beauty, and wealth are also rejected in Thomson's "Spring" from *The Seasons*. Austen quotes only the lines celebrating the joy of instructing an innocent youth ("Delightful task! to rear the tender thought, / To teach the young idea how to shoot"), ironic verse in view of the fact that Catherine hardly seems to have received a solid education. Again the context of these lines is revealing: Thomson describes an ideal couple rejecting both a mercenary marriage in which a man "from sordid parents buys the loathing virgin" and a sexually demeaning marriage in which tyrannical men rule "bosom-slaves, meanly possessed of a mere lifeless, violated form." Instead, Thomson's ideal husband and wife ignore worldly greed and superficial appearances, searching instead for something dearer than beauty. Loving soul mates, they form an emotional and intellectual partnership. Instead of beauty, they think of the "mind-illumined face" and value "Truth, goodness, honour, harmony, and love, / The richest bounty of indulgent Heaven!"[5] Some of the married couples we meet in *Northanger Abbey* hardly live up to Thomson's ideal vision, whether it is the intellectually impoverished marriage of Mr. and Mrs. Allen or the loveless union between General Tilney and his late wife. But Henry Tilney, like Thomson, can imagine a different sort of marriage than that of his parents, telling his sister to expect a sister-in-law who is "open, candid, artless, guileless, with affections strong but simple, forming no pretensions, and knowing no disguise" (206). Innocence, or spring, will triumph in *Northanger Abbey*, but not without encountering the blasts of worldly winter.

When Austen then turns in her parade of quotations from Thomson to Shakespeare, the allusions continue to be rich in irony and implication:

> from Shakespeare she gained a great store of information—
> amongst the rest, that

>   —"Trifles light as air,
>   "Are, to the jealous, confirmation strong,
>   "As proofs of Holy Writ."
>
> That
>
>   "The poor beetle, which we tread upon,
>   "In corporal sufferance feels a pang as great
>   "As when a giant dies."
>
> And that a young woman in love always looks
>   —"like Patience on a monument
>   "Smiling at Grief."
>
> So far her improvement was sufficient. (16)

Although Austen insists that her sufficiently improved heroine now has a "great store of information," readers are silently invited to look for more. Why these three quotations, we ask.

The wicked Iago in *Othello* speaks the first quotation as he plots to use a handkerchief to frame Desdemona, inciting Othello's jealous, murderous rage. Catherine may have learned a few of Iago's words, but what would she do if she actually met an Iago? By the twenty-sixth chapter of *Northanger Abbey*, Catherine still wonders naively of the duplicitous General Tilney, "Why he should say one thing so positively and mean another all the while, was most unaccountable! How were people, at that rate, to be understood?" (211). By quoting Iago in the opening chapter, Austen may be signaling her readers to watch for what Catherine finds "unaccountable": the many varieties of human evil, hypocrisy, dishonesty, and double-dealing.

The second quotation ("the poor beetle") belongs to Isabella in *Measure for Measure* as she pleads with her brother Claudius to accept his own death rather than ask that she sacrifice her honor by having sex with Angelo, the acting Duke. Isabella struggles with life and death, love and honor, holiness and evil. How ironic that a few pages later in *Northanger Abbey* we will meet Isabella Thorpe (is Austen's choice of the name "Isabella" only coincidence?), a vain coquette using trickery to snare a husband with money and class and encouraging her brother to do the same. Shakespeare's saintly Isabella speaks of heavenly "prayers from preserved souls" and "fasting maids whose minds are dedicate / To nothing temporal." Austen's worldly Isabella prattles of fashions, beaux, and best-selling potboilers. Though Austen's Isabella and Catherine speak in hyperbole about agonies, one's whole life, and all the world, they have no inkling about real suffering and genuine moral dilemmas.

What might Austen be telegraphing to her readers by choosing for Catherine's final Shakespearean quotation an excerpt from *Twelfth Night* comparing women in love to Patience on a monument? Viola speaks these lines while disguised as a man. When Duke Orsino disparages women as incapable of strong passions or constancy ("they lack retention"), Viola describes to him a woman who loves faithfully in silence:

> She never told her love,
> But let concealment, like a worm i' the bud,
> Feed on her damask cheek. She pined in thought;
> And, with a green and yellow melancholy,
> She sat like Patience on a monument,
> Smiling at grief. Was not this love indeed?
> We men may say more, swear more; but indeed
> Our shows are more than will; for still we prove
> Much in our vows but little in our love.
> (*Twelfth Night*, 2.4.110–18)

Besides allowing Austen to highlight the dramatic irony of a highly articulate woman putting down men while pretending to be a man, this passage also foreshadows what will come in *Northanger Abbey*. Like Viola, Catherine will fall in love first. Rather than conducting herself with feminine modesty, Catherine blurts out, "Let us go to-morrow" when offered an opportunity to walk with Henry and his sister (80). This is not as exaggerated as the behavior of the aggressive heroines of the juvenilia ("She flew to Frederic, and in a manner truly heroick, spluttered out to him her intention of being married the next day"), but it is nevertheless highly unusual (*MW,* 11). Austen seems to alert readers to how different her healthy, active, outspoken heroine is from the fading, suffering, patient woman on a pedestal.

One wonders why Austen lists these six quotations in her opening chapter. Perhaps she wishes to attack women's education as superficial: they learn sweet literary phrases and a little tinkling music as decoration, not as a means toward a higher or deeper end. Perhaps they should have sought a different sort of *soothing*, as in the older meaning of truth telling. Shakespeare and other authors can indeed be soothsayers. Furthermore, Austen invites her readers to become conspirators, to play a game of hide-and-seek. Here are a few words of text, but you go find the context, Austen seems to insist. It is as if we are given a glimpse of a piece of a red jacket but must look behind the bush to see who is hiding there.

Austen's playful irony in some ways compliments the readers, as if she is saying, "I believe you, too, will laugh at my characters, find the hidden meanings, and get my point." In a letter to her sister Austen insisted (through a clever rewrite of Sir Walter Scott) that she wrote for readers with intelligence: "I do not write for such dull Elves / As have not a great deal of Ingenuity themselves" (29 January 1813). Within the same letter, she goes on to mention her delight in trying to solve her sister's verbal puzzles: "We admire your Charades excessively, but as yet have guessed only the 1st. The others seem very difficult." She describes the pleasure both in the language Cassandra uses for her charades and in "the finding them out."

Even after the opening chapter of *Northanger Abbey,* Jane Austen continues to intrude: "In addition to what has been already said of Catherine Morland's personal and mental endowments, when about to be launched into all the difficulties and dangers of a six weeks' residence in Bath, it may be stated, for the reader's more certain information, lest the following pages should otherwise fail of giving any idea of what her character is meant to be; that her heart was affectionate, her disposition cheerful and open, without conceit or affectation of any kind—her manners just removed from the awkwardness and shyness of a girl; her person pleasing, and, when in good looks, pretty—and her mind about as ignorant and uninformed as the female mind at seventeen usually is" (18). More than half the words in that lengthy sentence are about *Austen*—what she will state, how this will aid the reader, and so forth. She could simply have written, "Catherine had an affectionate heart, cheerful and open disposition, and pleasing person." Instead, she calls our attention to the *act* of describing a character ("lest the following pages should otherwise fail of giving any idea of what her character is meant to be"), and she shows her own wit and realism through nonhyperbolic comments like "when in good looks, pretty." Though she tells readers that female minds are usually ignorant and uninformed, she has already by this early point in the novel convinced her readers that her own mind possesses wisdom and information.

Northanger Abbey can delight most if read as a double-track novel: the story of Catherine the naive character ("Catherine Morland is a goose," writes one critic) and the story of Jane Austen the savvy author.[6] Jane Austen displays her superiority not only to her artless young heroine and Oxford-educated hero, but also to all the other men and women in the vicinity.

If Catherine's mind is unremarkable, what adjectives should describe the mind of her supposed chaperone, the fashion-obsessed

Mrs. Allen? She would win any contest for female ignorance: with a complete "vacancy of mind and incapacity for thinking," she spends her days in "busy idleness," a marvelous Austen oxymoron capturing the waste of a woman with "no real intelligence to give" (60, 67, 69). Before letting Mrs. Allen speak (or rather, natter), Austen once again delays her story to focus on her own *creation* of a character for her "work": "It is now expedient to give some description of Mrs. Allen, that the reader may be able to judge, in what manner her actions will hereafter tend to promote the general distress of the work, and how she will, probably, contribute to reduce poor Catherine to all the desperate wretchedness of which a last volume is capable" (19–20). Just as tempests and carriage spills are lucky befrienders of an author, so "distress" and "desperate wretchedness" are expedient contributors to a work's promotion.

When Austen turns in the next paragraph to a supposed description of Mrs. Allen, she demonstrates her own wit by leveling an attack on rampant female ignorance: "Mrs. Allen was one of that numerous class of females, whose society can raise no other emotion than surprise at there being any men in the world who could like them well enough to marry them. . . . The air of a gentlewoman, a great deal of quiet, inactive good temper, and a trifling turn of mind, were all that could account for her being the choice of a sensible, intelligent man, like Mr. Allen" (20). Austen goes on to suggest that men prefer trifling women so they can feel superior. She ironically pretends to embrace ignorance in another generalization beginning with "people" but ending with "a woman especially": "Where people wish to attach, they should always be ignorant. To come with a well-informed mind, is to come with an inability of administering to the vanity of others, which a sensible person would always wish to avoid. A woman especially, if she have the misfortune of knowing any thing, should conceal it as well as she can" (110–11). Here Austen paraphrases Dr. Gregory's advice to his daughters, "If you have any learning, keep it a profound secret, especially from the men."[7] Yet Austen undermines the words by displaying her own fortune of knowing many things, including how to write books. Not surprisingly, Austen follows that mock praise of female ignorance with a direct reference in the very next sentence to "a sister author," reminding readers that not *all* women are ignorant. In addition, she may want readers to remember Frances Burney's description in *Camilla* of the ways men dote on the empty-headed, fair-haired Indiana but are repelled by the learned Eugenia.

If, as Austen tells us, some men want imbecilic women and the rest want ignorant ones, where does a woman like our author fit in? Perhaps she fits in best with Henry Tilney, sharing his delight in the absurd. Thinking about Catherine stuck all day in Mrs. Allen's company, Henry exclaims, "What a picture of intellectual poverty!" (79). How to survive such impoverishment? Turn it to humor, Henry Tilney demonstrates, as he joins in a mock conversation with Mrs. Allen on the merits of muslin. Like Austen, Henry Tilney "indulged himself a little too much with the foibles of others" (79).

Henry Tilney seems to be one of the few Austen heroes invested with his creator's dry humor, flair for words, and ability to mock society. When he first meets Catherine, he engages in deliberately fake small talk with "affected astonishment" and jokingly tells her that she should write in her journal that she danced with "a very agreeable young man [who] seems a most extraordinary genius" (27). The ultimate straight woman, Catherine keeps responding literally to Henry's wit, as when he launches into a mock-panegyric on the wonders of female letter writing:

> "As far as I have had opportunity of judging, it appears to me that the usual style of letter-writing among women is faultless, except in three particulars."
> "And what are they?"
> "A general deficiency of subject, a total inattention to stops, and a very frequent ignorance of grammar." (27)

How Henry relishes Catherine's inability to see the punch line coming!

Henry's earlier question to Catherine, "Shall I tell you what you ought to say?" hints at the danger of being a female without a voice—in contrast to being a female author controlling the voices of others. If Catherine knows nothing, she will allow this Oxford-educated man to speak for her and think for her. "It was no effort to Catherine to believe that Henry Tilney could never be wrong . . . and what she did not understand, she was almost as ready to admire, as what she did" (114). Like Petruchio telling Katherine in *The Taming of the Shrew* that the sun is the moon, Henry Tilney plays with Catherine's perceptions of reality and her ability to speak about it. By the time Henry has "talked of fore-grounds, distances, and second distances—side-screens and perspectives—lights and shades" to his "hopeful scholar" Catherine, has he truly "improved" her ability to appreciate nature (111)? She ends up afraid to take a walk alone because "she should not know what was picturesque when she saw it" (177). Perhaps Catherine could have avoided this insecurity and helped Henry appreciate fore-grounds if she had gotten him to quit pontificating long enough to roll down a green slope with her.

Henry enjoys feeling superior to both Catherine and his own sister, Eleanor. When Eleanor insists that he must dispel the impression that he has left with Catherine that he is "a great brute in [his] opinion of women in general," Henry responds with another wise-crack: "Miss Morland, no one can think more highly of the under-standing of women than I do. In my opinion, nature has given them so much, that they never find it necessary to use more than half" (113–14). He condescendingly tells Catherine that "teachableness of disposition in a young lady is a great blessing" (174).

Behind the patronizing Henry Tilney stands a self-confident woman author with an unshakable belief in herself. Jane Austen bra-zenly dangles the strings of her Henry Tilney puppet to remind us that *she* has created *him* and is telling him what to say, sometimes laughing at his vanity or pedantry. Oxford may not have been open to women during Austen's lifetime, but this does not seem to have hindered her ability to give voice to a witty and well-spoken Oxford-educated male character. As Henry makes fun of women's lack of understanding, readers remain aware of his "mother" author, Jane Austen. Henry's putdowns of women's ignorance become ironic in light of Austen's earlier narrative jibes about men preferring empty-headed women who flatter their vanity.

Wisdom for Austen did not mean condescension or academic pretentiousness. In *Northanger Abbey* she makes Henry acknowledge that Catherine has unknowingly accomplished "a brilliant satire on modern language" when she confesses to him, "I cannot speak well enough to be unintelligible" (133). Austen undoubtedly would have a good laugh at the way even that passage about unintelligibility con-tinues to generate turgid prose two centuries later:

> An uncanny effacement of the binary, or an uncanny re-turn of the repressed, does indeed render unstable the op-tions between the primitive and the civilized that is every-where operable in Henry's ethnocentric ideology of the *heimlich*. . . . *Northanger Abbey* is everywhere given to a gen-der specific version of the modality of power that Foucault, who will also figure prominently in what follows, terms "apanoptic" or "disciplinary." . . . *Northanger Abbey*, I shall argue, reinscribes the gothic carceral as the carceral posi-

tioning of the reading subject, a fully gendered subject, in relation to the literature of the carceral. "I cannot speak well enough to be unintelligible," Catherine tells Henry, and therein lies the principle of her claustration: in the panoptic hold of a gender-specific intelligibility or legibility from which there is no escape.[8]

What a relief it is to turn to Catherine Morland and her candid remarks such as "I am come in a great hurry" and "I never mind dirt" (102, 82)!

Although Catherine initially accepts Henry Tilney as the end-all of knowledge, Austen shows us that sometimes the pupil knows more than the teacher; the fool sees more than the king. Nearly two hundred years before the popularization of "herstory," Catherine articulates the problem of male-dominated history: "history, real solemn history, I cannot be interested in. . . . I read it a little as a duty, but it tells me nothing that does not either vex or weary me. The quarrels of popes and kings, with wars or pestilences, in every page; the men all so good for nothing, and hardly any women at all—it is very tiresome." Catherine's remarks echo Mary Astell's observation in the early eighteenth century: "The Men being the historians, they seldom condescend to record the great and good Actions of Women."[9] Catherine's irreverent view of history reminds us of Austen's dismissal of king after good-for-nothing king in her adolescent "History of England." Catherine's remarks about history also point out another truth besides the omission of women: although history may be presented as fact, it often is little more than the biased fictional creation of its author. As Catherine observes of history books full of the tales of heroes, "a great deal of it must be invention" (108).

Throughout *Northanger Abbey*, Catherine's remarks are refreshingly blunt. She has not acquired adult dishonesty, indirection, or guile. As Henry quips, "your mind is warped by an innate principle of general integrity" (219).

Whether describing her heroine, her hero, or any of the supporting cast, Jane Austen rarely lets readers forget that they are her own fictional creations. Bold, self-confident, keenly intelligent, and undeniably inventive, Jane Austen emerges as the true hero of *Northanger Abbey*.

In particular, Austen shows off her heroic powers of invention in *Northanger Abbey* by demonstrating that she could have written best-selling gothic romances. In Austen's hands, imitation becomes pillory, not flattery. With great one-upwomanship, Austen spoofs her era's taste for exotic, sensational adventures bearing no resemblance to real life.

Horace Walpole had ushered in the fad for the gothic with his *Castle of Otranto* (1765), starring a trembling princess named Isabella pursued by supernatural horrors and lively room furnishings:

> "Heaven nor hell shall impede my designs," said Manfred, advancing again to seize the Princess. At that instant the portrait of his grandfather, which hung over the bench where they had been sitting, uttered a deep sigh, and heaved its breast . . . He saw it quit its panel, and descend on the floor with a grave and melancholy air. "Do I dream?" cried Manfred . . . "or are the devils themselves in league against me? speak, infernal spectre! . . . Isabella shall not escape me!"
>
> That lady, whose resolution had given way to terror . . . recollected a subterraneous passage. . . . She seized a lamp that burned at the foot of the staircase, and hurried towards the secret passage. [10]

All the standard ingredients are here: a haunted castle, noble villains, nubile heroines-in-distress, secret passageways, and a plenteous heaping of exclamation marks to go all around. Although no gothic action figures were marketed as part of the trend, Walpole did redesign his house with gothic trappings, as did many of his countrymen. At the time Austen began writing *Northanger Abbey* in the 1790s, she knew that overwrought gothic novels were her era's best-sellers.

Gothic novels become the favorite topic of conversation for Isabella and Catherine in *Northanger Abbey*. They display their "delicacy, discretion, originality of thought, and literary taste" through breathless gushings over a pile of romances. When Catherine exclaims, "Oh! I am delighted with the book! I should like to spend my whole life in reading it," Isabella responds, "Dear creature! . . . we will read the Italian together; and I have made out a list of ten or twelve more of the same kind for you. . . . Castle of Wolfenbach, Clermont, Mysterious Warnings, Necromancer of the Black Forest, Midnight Bell, Orphan of the Rhine, and Horrid Mysteries. Those will last us some time" (40). The titles Isabella lists come from actual Gothic novels of the time by Mrs. Parsons, Regina Roche, Peter Teuthold, Francis Lathom, Eleanor Sleath, and Peter Will. One suspects that Austen somehow knew even *before* she became a famous author that these lightweight gothic writers of the day would never become household words; that they lacked her own gift of universality. Can one imagine thousands of Mrs. Parsons Society members with bumper stickers on their cars proclaiming, "I'd rather be reading Mrs. Parsons"?

Another gothic thriller mentioned in *Northanger Abbey* is Lewis's *The Monk*, which Isabella's boorish brother calls a "tolerably decent" novel (48). Perhaps John Thorpe has learned to pursue women aggressively by encountering not particularly "decent" passages like this one in *The Monk:* "'For your sake, fatal beauty,' murmured the monk, while gazing on his devoted prey, 'for your sake have I committed this murder and sold myself to eternal tortures. Now you are in my power; the produce of my guilt will at least be mine.' . . . He lifted her, still motionless, from the tomb. . . . Scarcely could he command his passion sufficiently to restrain himself from enjoying her while yet insensible. . . . Naturally addicted to the gratification of the senses, in the full vigour of manhood and heat of blood, he had suffered his temperament to acquire such ascendancy that his lust was become madness." [11] *The Monk* tells of Antonia, Ambrosio, and other passion-ridden Italians duking it out in various graveyards.

Similarly, Ann Radcliffe's *The Italian* features characters named Paulo, the Marchesa, Schedoni, Spalatro, Marco, Signora Bianchi, Vincento di Vivaldi, and Father Ansaldo. A typical sentence of *The Italian* reads, "The door closed, with a thundering clap that echoed through all the vaults; and Vivaldi and Paulo stood for a moment aghast!" Austen's banal John Thorpe is no Giovanni Thorponi, no exotic fiend; he can only bore his "prey," lie to her, and plot to get her money. He lacks demonic dash, appearing only as "a stout young man of middling height . . . with a plain face and ungraceful form" (45).

The gothic novel Austen mentions the most in *Northanger Abbey* is Radcliffe's *The Mysteries of Udolpho* (1794) with its skeletons, veils, and secret murders. Isabella refers to its characters and events, Catherine pronounces it "the nicest book in the world," and Henry Tilney jokes that he spent two days reading *Udolpho*, his "hair standing on end the whole time" (107, 106). Gothic novels such as *The Mysteries of Udolpho* generally featured the victimization of a highly angelic heroine. The exquisitely perfect Emily St. Aubert speaks foreign languages and converses with her father in high-falutin' diction. Rather than being unable to pen sonnets or tolerate the piano, like Catherine Morland, Emily writes poetry and delicately plays the lute. Emily quivers her way through *Mysteries of Udolpho* as she encounters tumultuous storms, ruined castles, mysterious bloodstains, and ubiquitous ghosts.

Jane Austen shows in *Northanger Abbey* that she *could* have written a Radcliffian best-seller every bit as bloodcurdling as *Mysteries of Udolpho*. When Catherine is invited to visit Northanger Abbey, ancestral home of the Tilneys, she imagines a setting like the ones she has read about in gothic fiction. Knowing this, Henry Tilney teases her on the way to the abbey with a mock narrative of what she will find: "Will not your mind misgive you when you find yourself in this gloomy chamber—too lofty and extensive for you, with only the feeble rays of a single lamp to take in its size—its walls hung with tapestry exhibiting figures as large as life, and the bed, of dark green stuff or purple velvet, presenting even a funereal appearance? " (158). Catherine obligingly utters phrases like "Oh! Mr. Tilney, how frightful!" to flatter his authorial vanity, so he goes on at length to narrate his tale of unconquerable horrors, unquiet slumber, frightful gusts of wind, vaulted rooms, ominous furniture, and blood-stained daggers (160).

Just a few paragraphs later, Austen will pick up the mock-gothic pen where Henry left off. Catherine arrives at the disappointingly unalarming abbey without even the cooperation of the weather: "The breeze had not seemed to waft the signs of the murdered to her; it had wafted nothing worse than a thick mizzling rain." Poking fun of words like "waft" and "presentiment," Austen leads Catherine and readers through pseudo-gothic moments at the abbey (161). Her language out-horrifies and out-agitates even Henry's as she describes Catherine's nocturnal discoveries: "Catherine's . . . quick eyes directly fell on a roll of paper pushed back into the further part of the cavity, apparently for concealment, and her feelings at that moment were indescribable. Her heart fluttered, her knees trembled, and her cheeks grew pale. She seized, with an unsteady hand . . . the precious manuscript. But alas, her candle was extinguished. Darkness impenetrable and immovable filled the room. A violent gust of wind, rising with sudden fury, added fresh horror to the moment. Catherine trembled from head to foot" (169–70). By having first Henry and then her narrator demonstrate the art of blood-curdling, hair-raising, storm-pounding, light-extinguishing moments, Austen shows that she could have made *Northanger Abbey* as gothic as any best-seller.

Why go through the mock-gothic narrative twice? Both Henry and Austen-as-narrator describe trembling, fainting, alarmed, and eager young women impelled by their curiosity to seize precious treasures while violent storms, receding footsteps, and expiring lamps create incomprehensible, indescribable horrors. One effect of replaying the mock-gothic narrative is in order to double the effect of Catherine's precipitous fall from heroism into a mundane heap of not-very-spooky laundry: "Could it be possible, or did not her senses play her false?–An inventory of linen, in coarse and modern characters, seemed all that was before her! If the evidence of sight might be trusted, she held a washing-bill in her hand" (172). Catherine already had been disappointed to find the abbey rather modern looking and the cabinet filled with nothing but linen; now she holds a laundry bill. Yet even this anticlimactic moment fails to deter Catherine from her quest for evidence that General Tilney has killed his wife. Catherine *wants* to be scared–to find a crime, to encounter a ghost–because her own life lacks excitement.

When Catherine sneaks into the bedroom of General Tilney's deceased wife, she thus ignores the sunny windows and ordinary appearance of the room in order to nurse her own desire to be afraid. One turning point in the novel comes when Henry catches her there, realizes she has suspected his father of murdering his mother, and scolds her for being irrational: "If I understand you rightly, you had formed a surmise of such horror as I have hardly words to–Dear Miss Morland, consider the dreadful nature of the suspicions you have entertained. What have you been judging from?" (197). Of course, Catherine has been judging from the gothic novels she has pored over rather than from common sense or her own observations of the abbey, with its contemporary furnishings and renovated rooms. So far, we are "with" Henry as he chastises Catherine. He has helped remove her blinders: "The visions of romance were over. Catherine was completely awakened" (199).

Some have assumed that Henry is a mouthpiece for Austen and that her double gothic descriptions are meant to show her oneness with her hero. Instead, could it not be a deliberate set up? As Henry continues his spiel to the mortified Catherine, he launches into a parochial defense of English life that no longer sounds like Jane Austen: "Remember the country and the age in which we live. Remember that we are English, that we are Christians. Consult your own understanding, your own sense of the probable, your own observation of what is passing around you–Does our education prepare us for such atrocities? Do our laws connive at them? Could they be perpetrated without being known, in a country like this, where social and literary intercourse is on such a footing . . . ? Dearest Miss Morland, what ideas have you been admitting?" (197–98). Murder, according to Henry, cannot occur in such a pious, law-abiding, cultured, literate society as England. Yet we know from Austen's "History of England" that she saw the progression of monarchs as a series of bloody murders and dastardly intrigues. English prisons were filled with criminals. Although Henry boasts about the superior literary discourse in England, readers of *Northanger Abbey* remember that the Oxford-educated John Thorpe boasts "I never read novels; I have something else to do" and that English anthologies often contain no more than "a dozen lines of Milton" (48, 37). Austen seems now to have moved beyond her hero, separating herself from his voice and vision. Henry Tilney may be as blind in his own way as the girl he has just "awakened."

Catherine, however, views Henry as the oracle of Delphi and converts to a British patriot after hearing Henry's speech. In the following chapter, she concludes that fiendish characters only live across the English Channel: "Charming as were all Mrs. Radcliffe's works . . . it was not in them perhaps that human nature, at least in the midland counties of England, was to be looked for. . . . Among the Alps and Pyrenees, perhaps, there were no mixed characters. There, such as were not as spotless as an angel, might have the dispositions of a fiend. But in England it was not so; among the English, she believed, in their hearts and habits, there was a general though unequal mixture of good and bad" (200). Catherine congratulates herself that she has finally, under Henry's instruction, acquired "the greatest good sense," but readers detect her narrow parochialism.

Although Catherine thinks Radcliffe's works give a "faithful delineation" of Europe, Austen seems unconvinced by gothic settings unrecognizable to geographers. Just what sort of representation can authors offer of countries they have never actually visited? Catherine has acquired this habit from Radcliffe, as when she tells Henry that Beechen Cliff reminds her of the south of France.

> "You have been abroad then?" said Henry, a little surprised.
>
> "Oh! no, I only mean what I have read about. It always puts me in mind of the country that Emily and her father travelled through, in the 'Mysteries of Udolpho.'" (106)

This passage carries double irony as Austen mocks Catherine for being reminded of French scenery when she only has read about it in a book by an English author who never went to France![12]

Austen seems determined to outsmart each of her characters and each of her fellow authors. Through the double gothic episodes, Austen has wrested the narrative away from Henry by the middle of the novel. Although Henry has been the one to inform and instruct Catherine, now we discover that Henry has much to learn. He needs to admit that he has been raised in no home sweet home—or abbey. His father *is* guilty: not of murdering his wife but of making her life hard to endure; not of torturing his children but of oppressing them daily.

Catherine has not been as stupid as Henry thinks. Violating every rule of hospitality and chivalry, General Tilney summarily ejects Catherine Morland from his home solely because he has discovered that she is not rich. Now her mind is occupied not with storms and haunted chambers but with "the contemplation of actual and natural evil" (227). Though Austen pillories gothic melodrama in *Northanger Abbey*, she simultaneously shows that the world really does offer horrible moments, despicable men and women, and hidden evils. I like both Claudia Johnson's suggestion that Austen "relocates the gothic in ordinary domestic life in England" and Paul Morrison's conclusion that "Horror, like charity, begins at home."[13] Villainy does exist—even in central England behind the elegant façades of renovated mansions.

Villainy need not wear dark mustaches and a bloodstained Italian cloak; in fact, it may wear a courteous face and the best English trousers. Henry's reprobate brother, Captain Tilney, may not abduct the heroine with the help of "three villains in horsemen's great coats," but he lacks principle and purpose. Henry's father, General Tilney, is well mannered yet unscrupulous; well spoken but bad intentioned. His letter to Mr. Morland is "very courteously worded in a page full of empty professions," just as his social politeness masks his moral bankruptcy (252). Catherine's seemingly silly encounter with the cabinet in her bedroom at the abbey takes on new meaning. Like the ornate cabinet empty of all but a bill for laundry, so the well-dressed, articulate General Tilney is hollow at the core, motivated only by a crass desire for material goods.

Some readers may share Catherine's disappointment in finding real problems rather than exciting gothic Adventures. Most amusing is the way a 1965 American publisher marketed *Northanger Abbey* as a "paperback literary gothic." Want a cheap thrill? The front cover observes under the title, "The terror of Northanger Abbey had no name, no shape—yet it menaced Catherine Morland in the dead of night!" A lurid illustration shows a distraught Catherine, her hand clutching her low-necked gown, fleeing a mansion and a dark, forbidding man whose hands come together as if pointing at his genitals. A blurb teases readers with the thrilling horrors that await them should they choose to buy this novel: "A HOLIDAY ENDS AS TERROR BEGINS—STALKING CATHERINE MORLAND FROM EVERY

SHADOWY CORNER OF NORTHANGER ABBEY! FAR FROM HOME AND CLOSE TO DANGER, CATHERINE HAS NO-WHERE TO TURN!"[14] Readers who bought this edition must have minded the anticlimactic abbey as much as Catherine. In the twenty-first century, a Teacher's Video Company catalog describes a *Northanger Abbey* film as if marketing Radcliffe: "This gothic Austin [*sic*] story takes place in a sinister castle in 18th-century Bath. Will evil or good win out?" Scan the titillating titles *(Scream)* and plots ("a psycho killer targets a past victim's daughter") of recent movies or the back covers of grocery store best-sellers ("A shrieking, freezing horror . . . turns a beautiful woman into a shriveled husk before she has time to scream"). Perhaps *Northanger Abbey* is timelier than we like to think.

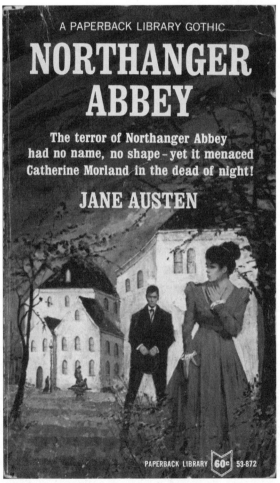

Gothic cover illustration for 1965 *Northanger Abbey*

In addition, any dismissal of Catherine as a dense and silly goose perhaps should compare her to contemporary adolescents. Instead of poring over gothic novels and imitating literary heroines, Isabella and Catherine today might be movie junkies aping the fashions of the stars. Why, Austen suggests, must an adolescent girl be portrayed in books as anything other than a work in progress, a mixture of self-doubt and confusing cultural pressures, a combination of good instincts and bad judgment? As Austen seems to suggest early on in *Northanger Abbey*, Catherine's mind is "about as ignorant and uninformed as the female mind at seventeen usually is" (18).

Catherine has begun to change by the end, but Austen makes character development less central in *Northanger Abbey* than in her other novels. We become so involved in the story of Elizabeth Bennet's changed feelings about Mr. Darcy *(Pride and Prejudice)*, Marianne Dashwood's new personality after her illness *(Sense and Sensibility)*, or Sir Thomas Bertram's painful recognition of his parental negligence *(Mansfield Park)* that we often forget to think about Jane Austen "THE AUTHOR." In *Northanger Abbey*, however, Jane Austen always remains in the face of her readers, reminding us that these are *her* characters; this is *her* work.

Indeed, the most famous and oft quoted passage from *Northanger Abbey* is not a dialogue between hero and heroine or a climactic moment in the abbey but rather a narrative passage about novels. Early on in the novel, Austen uses the reading habits of the instantly intimate Isabella and Catherine as an excuse to launch into a rare and eloquent essay on her own craft: "They . . . shut themselves up, to read novels together. Yes, novels;—for I will not adopt that ungenerous and impolitic custom so common with novel writers, of degrading by their contemptuous censure the very performances, to the number of which they are themselves adding . . . scarcely ever permitting them to be read by their own heroine. . . . Alas! if the heroine of one novel be not patronized by the heroine of another, from whom can she expect protection and regard? I cannot approve of it." Throughout Austen's nearly five-hundred-word argument, she uses the pronoun "I" and "we" to link herself to the guild of novelists: "Let us not desert one another; we are an injured body" (37).

And who is this "we"? It is not just *all* novelists, nor is it all writers. Austen compliments "our productions" and attacks "our foes," including in the opposition "the press," "the Reviewers," and the "thousand pens" who praise the works of *male* prose writers and editors:

> Although our productions have afforded more extensive and
> unaffected pleasure than those of any other literary corpo-
> ration in the world, no species of composition has been so
> much decried. From pride, ignorance, or fashion, our foes
> are almost as many as our readers. And while the abilities
> of the nine-hundredth abridger of the History of England,
> or of the man who collects and publishes in a volume some
> dozen lines of Milton, Pope, and Prior, with a paper from
> the Spectator, and a chapter from Sterne, are eulogized by a
> thousand pens,–there seems almost a general wish of de-
> crying the capacity and undervaluing the labour of the nov-
> elist, and of slighting the performances which have only
> genius, wit, and taste to recommend them. (37–38)

The "eulogized" male writers abridge and collect rather than create,
and the reviewers who praise them write in "threadbare strains," min-
ing even the *phrases* of others. The men who do the collecting and
publishing of anthologies choose only other male writers: Milton, Pope,
Prior, Addison, and Steele. The anthologies obviously lack depth;
after all, how much justice to *Paradise Lost* does one do by selecting
"some dozen lines of Milton"?

By referring to the *Spectator* (an eighteenth-century journal with
essays by Addison and Steele), Austen may also be reminding readers
of its misogynist tone, as the periodical took frequent jibes at women
for being thoughtless and frivolous. Austen uses words like "decrying" and "slighting" to capture the patronizing tone of those who belittle women's novels–and women in general. Steele, for instance, who
had sprinkled his essays in the *Spectator* and the *Tatler* with comments
"for the better improvement of the fair sex" or "for the benefit of my
female readers," claimed that if women's minds were laid open, their
thoughts would be shown to be only of tippets, muffs, fans, and other
"gewgaws and trifles," and advised his fellow superior men that "if
you speak to women in a style and manner proper to approach them,
they never fail to improve by your counsels." [15]

But Austen wants to give, not receive counsel; to inform, not be
improved. In her famous essay imbedded in *Northanger Abbey*, she speaks
in the voice of a female novelist more directly and extensively than in
any other place in her writing. She quips that novels display "only
genius, wit, and taste." In particular, she praises novels by women:
"'And what are you reading, Miss–?' 'Oh! it is only a novel!' replies
the young lady; while she lays down her book with affected indifference, or momentary shame.–'It is only Cecilia, or Camilla, or Belinda;'

or, in short, only some work in which the greatest powers of the mind are displayed, in which the most thorough knowledge of human nature, the happiest delineation of its varieties, the liveliest effusions of wit and humour are conveyed to the world in the best chosen language" (38). *Cecilia* (1782) and *Camilla* (1796) are by Fanny Burney; *Belinda* (1801) is by Maria Edgeworth. Austen ironically uses the phrase "in short" to introduce five superlatives describing these novels by women ("greatest . . . most thorough . . . happiest . . . liveliest . . . best chosen") and to present the large scale of the novel's content and readership ("powers of the mind . . . knowledge of human nature . . . conveyed to the world").

Why these three novels in particular? In all three cases, the titles center on a young woman (as *Emma* will do); in all three cases, the novels focus on social customs and flaws and on young women lacking in formal education or appropriate guidance. Burney and Edgeworth also had an ear for realistic dialogue and paved the way for Austen's own coming-of-age novels of manners and morals. Later in *Northanger Abbey*, Austen mocks those men who disparage the lives and works of female novelists by making the boorish John Thorpe into a Burney detractor. When Catherine acknowledges that she has never read *Camilla*, John explains that she has missed nothing worthwhile: "Novels are all so full of nonsense and stuff. . . . They are the stupidest things in creation. . . . [*Camilla* is a] stupid book written by that woman they make such a fuss about, she who married the French emigrant. . . . I guessed what sort of stuff it must be before I saw it: as soon as I heard she had married an emigrant, I was sure I should never be able to get through it. . . . You had no loss I assure you; it is the horridest nonsense you can imagine" (48–49). If John just added "like" and "you know" to his use of the word "stuff" in this probing literary analysis, he would fit in with many modern groups of teens. He seems to have spent more time at Oxford drinking than thinking. By putting anti-women, anti-French invective in the mouth of the crude John Thorpe, Austen challenges both forms of his chauvinism.

Austen closes her impassioned defense of novels in *Northanger Abbey* with a parting shot at the *Spectator*, already mentioned in the same paragraph as one of the choices of male anthologists: "Now, had the same young lady been engaged with a volume of the Spectator, instead of such a work, how proudly would she have produced the book, and told its name; though the chances must be against her being occupied by any part of that voluminous publication, of which either the matter or manner would not disgust a young person of taste;

the substance of its papers so often consisting in the statement of improbable circumstances, unnatural characters, and topics of conversation, which no longer concern any one living; and their language, too, frequently so coarse as to give no very favourable idea of the age that could endure it" (38). In this voluminous sentence, Austen argues that realistic, lively novels filled with natural characters are superior to stilted works by past masters of prose. She flings back at the writers of the *Spectator* precisely those abuses (improbable circumstances and unnatural characters) that they had hurled against popular novelists.

Perhaps Jane Austen also viewed this passage in *Northanger Abbey* as part of her ongoing exchange of ideas with her witty brothers. In the *Loiterer*, published at Oxford from 1789–90, James and Henry Austen had made grandiose claims for their prose and had included an attack on novels as a "species of production" so growing in number "as to render the necessity, or even the propriety of adding to their number rather doubtful, and which might perhaps be considerably lessened without any great diminution of our knowledge, wit or taste." [16] Those comments appear in the *Loiterer* directly after a request for fiction from "Sophia Sentiment," thought to be Austen herself. Perhaps Austen's attack on periodicals and praise of novels in *Northanger Abbey* stands in answer to her brothers' earlier disparagement of the genre.

Austen shows how many kinds of writers she could have been if the spirit so moved her. Readers are made to see that *Northanger Abbey* could have been a hair-raising gothic potboiler, a sentimental epistolary novel ("My dearest Catherine"), a saga complete with the story of many generations ("This brief account of the family is intended to supersede the necessity of a long and minute detail from Mrs. Thorpe herself, of her past adventures and sufferings, which might otherwise be expected to occupy the three or four following chapters"), a moral fable for the edification of wayward young girls, a literary essay on the novel genre, a bildungsroman tracing a character's growth from childhood to adulthood, or a blistering satire exposing England's political, economic, and social wrongs (34).

Austen, not her hero or heroine, has the last word and the last laugh in *Northanger Abbey*. From start to finish of this novel, she seems less interested in telling a good tale than in making her readers conscious of the tale teller. Not only does she reintroduce the phrase "my heroine" as she brings Catherine back home but she once again calls our attention to her own role as disappointed author of a work without a grand plot:

A heroine returning, at the close of her career, to her native village, in all the triumph of recovered reputation, and all the dignity of a countess, with a long train of noble relations in their several phaetons, and three waiting-maids in a travelling chaise-and-four, behind her, is an event on which the pen of the contriver may well delight to dwell; it gives credit to every conclusion, and the author must share in the glory she so liberally bestows.—But my affair is widely different; I bring back my heroine to her home in solitude and disgrace; and no sweet elation of spirits can lead me into minuteness. A heroine in a hack post-chaise, is such a blow upon sentiment, as no attempt at grandeur or pathos can withstand. (232)

Austen reminds us of her role as pen-wielding contriver seeking credit and glory, and she emphasizes that the author is a woman: "the author . . . she." But just as similar passages in the opening chapters sent the clear message that she is a more realistic author than most other authors, so here Austen's mock-apology becomes self-affirmation. Countesses in phaetons need not apply.

In a book about writing, it is not surprising that Austen comes in near the end to remind us of her power over the storyline. Just watch me give you a happy ending, Austen warns us: "The anxiety, which in this state of their attachment must be the portion of Henry and Catherine, and of all who loved either, as to its final event, can hardly extend, I fear, to the bosom of my readers, who will see in the tell-tale compression of the pages before them, that we are all hastening together to perfect felicity" (250). Spreading literary artifice all around, Austen tells us that Eleanor Tilney will also find her happy ending through marriage to a wealthy nobleman. Look at me playing with the plot, Austen says to her readers, and note that I will not violate "the rules of composition" by introducing "a character not connected with my fable" (251).

Although she calls the novel a fable, Austen mocks simplistic homilies by asking in her final sentence, "I leave it to be settled by whomsoever it may concern, whether the tendency of this work be altogether to recommend parental tyranny, or reward filial disobedience" (252). What ultimately is the lesson of *Northanger Abbey?* Why does Henry marry Catherine, and what does this happy ending suggest? Austen reminds us that Henry's motives are primarily gratitude because Catherine has been far more open and precipitous in declaring her feelings for him: "though Henry was now sincerely attached to her, though he felt and delighted in all the excellencies of her character and truly loved her society, I must confess that his affection originated in nothing better than gratitude, or, in other words, that a persuasion of her partiality for him had been the only cause of giving her a serious thought. It is a new circumstance in romance, I acknowledge, and dreadfully derogatory of an heroine's dignity; but if it be as new in common life, the credit of a wild imagination will at least be all my own" (243). The derogatory circumstances are just a subtler version of the bathetic end of "Frederic and Elfrida," Austen's first sketch. Faced with Elfrida's "heroick" declaration that she wants to marry him the next day, Frederic ultimately gives in: "he flew to her & finding her better than he had been taught to expect, was united to her Forever—" (*MW*, 12).

As *Northanger Abbey* ends, readers under the control of a satirical narrator also may wonder if Henry marries Catherine because, like Mr. Allen and most men, he wants an ignorant woman who will flatter his vanity and set up his jokes. Has he chosen her because of her charming comment, "Henry Tilney must know best," and because he treasures "all the civility and deference of the youthful female mind, fearful of hazarding an opinion of its own in opposition to that of a self-assured man"? (153, 48) Yet the marriage between Catherine and Henry is not merely a joke. Through Henry and Catherine, Austen makes fun of both intellectual pretentiousness and intellectual poverty, suggesting the importance of thinking and talking clearly. She derides men for wanting inferior women and chastises women for accepting ignorance.

Most striking in *Northanger Abbey* is Austen's brilliant mind—her creative power, wit, empathy, insight, and chutzpah. Through the narrative voice, Austen demonstrates mature womanhood. She conveys her affection for Catherine's warm heart and genuineness but laughs at her foolishness. She embraces Henry's wit but rejects his pedantry. How ironic Henry Tilney's misogynist discourse becomes when we realize a discerning woman has given him his voice: "I will be noble. I will prove myself a man, no less by the generosity of my soul than the clearness of my head. I have no patience with such of my sex as disdain to let themselves sometimes down to the comprehension of yours. Perhaps the abilities of women are neither sound nor acute—neither vigorous nor keen. Perhaps they may want observation, discernment, judgment, fire, genius, and wit" (112). Our heroine the author definitely possesses all the qualities Henry complains women may lack—observation, discernment, judgment, fire, genius, and wit—and she knows it.

No other Austen novel contains so much narrative intrusion, so much of that "I" voice asking readers to look at the book to see its superiority to the creations of other writers. No other Austen novel will end with a sentence using the words "I" and "myself" or a reference to "this work." More than in any other novel, *Northanger Abbey* explores what it means to be a woman author and how reality differs from romance.

Once we have discovered Austen's triumphant celebration of her creative powers in *Northanger Abbey*, we sense the unfairness of critical comments reducing the novel to the lamentations of a sex-starved, disappointed spinster. Here is an extreme example: "*Northanger Abbey* . . . shows her disillusionment and disappointment with life. . . . *Northanger Abbey* [is] the work of a caustic, disappointed woman. . . . *Northanger Abbey* shows her asking the old question: Where is the man for me?"[17] Instead, I hear Jane Austen asking, where is the discerning reader for me?

At one point Henry Tilney observes, "The person, be it gentleman or lady, who has not pleasure in a good novel, must be intolerably stupid" (106). In *Northanger Abbey* Austen invites readers, be they gentlemen or ladies, to take pleasure in novels like her own that use humor, the best chosen language, and the greatest powers of the mind to present a thorough knowledge of human nature. *Northanger Abbey* announces the arrival of a female novelist whose works are better than sentimental fiction, gothic novels, dry history books, nonfiction works by men, and moralistic conduct books. While showing us a heroine who lacks discernment and wit, Austen displays her own brilliance; while introducing us to a sophisticated, Oxford-educated hero with a gift for language, Austen demonstrates her own superiority of insight and expression. *Northanger Abbey* can best be enjoyed as an exuberant *tour de force;* a daring display of genius, wit, and taste.

4

An Excellent Heart
Sense and Sensibility

For there is no friend like a sister
In calm or stormy weather;
To cheer one on the tedious way,
To fetch one if one goes astray,
To lift one if one totters down,
To strengthen whilst one stands.
  —Christina Rossetti, *Goblin Market*

　　　　　　　　　. . . my troubles are two.
But oh, my two troubles they reave me of rest,
The brains in my head and the heart in my breast.
  —A. E. Housman, *Additional Poems: XVII*

She had an excellent heart;—her disposition was affectionate, and her feelings were strong; but she knew how to govern them: it was a knowledge which her mother had yet to learn, and which one of her sisters had resolved never to be taught.
  —Jane Austen, *Sense and Sensibility*

As Jane Austen worked to transform "Elinor and Marianne" into what would become *Sense and Sensibility*, she must have wondered whether any manuscript of hers would ever reach a readership or generate an income. Austen knew she could write novels with "genius, wit, and taste to recommend them," as she noted in the unpublished *Northanger Abbey*, but would any publisher agree (*NA*, 37)? Was there a public discriminating enough to prefer them to the improbable, sensational bestsellers of the day?

The changed title suggests that Austen perhaps added philosophical depth to what began primarily as a sketch of two characters. The new title, however, has in some ways hindered readings of *Sense and*

Sensibility. Yes, Austen links Elinor to sense ("Her own good sense so well supported her") and Marianne to sensibility ("too great importance placed by her on the delicacies of a strong sensibility"), but she continually muddies the semantic waters, using not just the title words but terms like sensitive, sensible, and sensation (141, 201). Marianne is "sensible and clever," Elinor is "most feelingly sensible," and Marianne ironically becomes "*insensible* of her sister's presence" when she focuses on the sensations of her own romance (6, 134, 175). Austen carefully crafts her fiction so that readers cannot, in all fairness, reduce these two sisters to mind and emotion. As Carol Shields observes, "we have real sisters here, not convenient contrarieties."[1] Furthermore, Austen presents a large cast of characters, both male and female, possessing varying degrees of sense and sensibility. By so doing, she joins Mary Wollstonecraft in inviting readers to reconsider the standard assumption that men have sense, women have feeling.

Though her narrative voice is less pronounced in *Sense and Sensibility* than in *Northanger Abbey*, Jane Austen still remains ever present between the lines of her novel. If you think this female character in *Sense and Sensibility* is an unbelievably greedy, selfish, mercenary schemer, be advised that she is better than half her sex, Austen asserts with acerbic irony. If you find this marriage loveless, this man's will and testament unfair, this woman insipid, this card party dull, this man idle, or this group's conversation boring, remember that they are typical, Austen insists. Phrases such as *no traits at all unusual, like every other place, like half the rest of the world, as usual,* and *often* dot the pages of this biting novel. The Jane Austen we discover in *Sense and Sensibility* indicts her era's anti-intellectualism, commercialism, and selfishness. Through her narrative voice, she reminds readers that scoundrels, wastrels, philistines, and bores are the norm, not the exception, in real life—a dark, cold, almost-tragic real life offset only by instances of individual growth and genuine affection.

As Eva Brann notes in an article about *Sense and Sensibility* entitled "Whose Sense? Whose Sensibility? Jane Austen's Subtlest Novel," Austen asks "the frequent question, unique to this book: Who is its heroine?"[2] Some critics find the easy answer to be Elinor: "*Sense and Sensibility* is the story of Elinor Dashwood. The action of the novel is hers; it is not Marianne's."[3] Yet two women move across center stage in this novel. What exactly are we meant to conclude about the differences between "Elinor and Marianne," the novel's original title? If Elinor is the heroine, do we automatically assume that her husband is more heroic than Marianne's? What does John Hardy lose by excluding

Marianne from his collection of Austen heroines?[4] In our search for Jane Austen, do we find her more on one heroine's side than the other?

Some have argued that Marianne is in fact "the life and center of the novel."[5] Biographers alert us to the fact that there may be greater similarities between Jane Austen and Marianne, Cassandra Austen and Elinor. According to a relative, Jane Austen reported that, faced with the death of her fiancé, Cassandra behaved "with a degree of resolution and Propriety which no common mind could evince in so trying a situation."[6] Could the book have started out as a tribute to Cassandra Austen's propriety and ended as a celebration of Jane Austen's vitality? As early as 1866 a reviewer noted, "Elinor is too good; one feels inclined to pat her on the back and say, 'Good girl!' but all our sympathy is with the unfortunate Marianne."[7] Other critics claim that Jane Austen meant for Elinor to be the heroine but that Marianne took on a life and power of her own: "Marianne . . . has our sympathy: she, and our response to her, are outside Jane Austen's control"; "The true heroine of *Sense and Sensibility* is Marianne. . . . The result is that a perfect comedy of manners was spoilt, and a great flawed novel written."[8]

I believe that Jane Austen deliberately constructs a tale of two heroines—or rather, two young women. The narrator shifts readers back and forth between the two sisters and everything they represent. To exclude Marianne from *Jane Austen's Heroines* shortchanges Austen's dual accomplishment in *Sense and Sensibility*—in particular, her ambivalent feelings toward revolutionary ideals, romantic notions, and youthful illusions.

If *Northanger Abbey* demonstrated that, had she chosen, Jane Austen could have written a gothic potboiler, then *Sense and Sensibility* proves that she could have created a romantic tragedy. The word *heart* appears in this novel far more than in any other she would write, often accompanied by adjectives such as *anguished, broken, sinking, wrung, wounded, sick,* and *heavy.* Austen censured and laughed at humiliated, desperate young women in her adolescent sketches (like Emma, who "continued in tears the remainder of her Life" after Edgar departs [*MW,* 33]), but in *Sense and Sensibility* she tempers her criticism with empathy. Marianne Dashwood may be silly at times ("I must feel—I must be wretched") but her heartache is raw—and real (190). As Victorian novelist George Moore notes, in *Sense and Sensibility* Austen "gives us all the agony of passion the human heart can feel" because "it is here that we find the burning human heart in English prose for the first, and alas, for the last time."[9]

Why might Austen delve more deeply into emotional states in this novel? As she worked on revising "Elinor and Marianne" into *Sense and Sensibility*, Austen encountered suffering too real to be ignored: her sister's loss of a fiancé to yellow fever in 1797, the death of a cousin in a road accident in 1798, her family's decision to leave their home in 1801, her father's death in 1805 and the corresponding need for Mrs. Austen, Jane, and Cassandra to find smaller living quarters (much like Mrs. Dashwood and her daughters moving to a smaller cottage), and Jane Austen's possible disappointments in love, whatever they may have been, before reaching the decision to don the garb of an old maid. Perhaps seeing grieving fiancées and devastated widows so close to home left Austen unwilling to write yet another light-hearted spoof of the sentimental heroine.

Nanine Vallain's *Liberty*, one of many representations of
Marianne (France)

Austen's portrayal of Marianne's romanticism differs in tone from her derision of Catherine Morland's fascination with the gothic. After all, Austen liked the same writers as Marianne: Austen praises Cowper and Scott in her letters, as well as Gilpin's writings on the picturesque.[10] Like Marianne, Austen enjoyed music and felt less restrained and proper than her elder sister, who preferred painting. In one letter Jane Austen jokes that Cassandra has more "starched Notions" than her own (4 February 1813). An acquaintance of the family praised Jane Austen's sparkling eyes and energy but observed, "her sister Cassandra was very lady-like but *very prim*."[11] By using adjectives such as *striking, brilliant, eager*, and *animated* to describe Marianne but never Elinor, Austen suggests that Marianne's romanticism gives her a fire lacking in her tamer sister. True, by staying inside during inclement weather rather than running wildly down a steep slope Elinor avoids spraining her ankle and getting thoroughly drenched, but one suspects she could have used the fresh air and the liberty.

Liberty seems central to Marianne's character—and perhaps to her name. At the time Austen began "Elinor and Marianne" in the mid-1790s, she would have been well aware that Marianne stood for France—in particular, revolutionary France—and was being captured in the iconography of the time as a half-clothed, vibrant young woman whose youth and spirit conveyed the dawning of a new era. In *Marianne into Battle*, Maurice Agulhon traces the official link between the female symbol of liberty and the French republic to 1792, just a few years before Austen began "Elinor and Marianne." Statues of Louis XV gave way to statues of Marianne; paintings depicted her as "young, active, with a short dress (that leaves her legs bare at least below the knee, and sometimes also a breast bared); rather a tomboy in short."[12] As Lynn Hunt observes, by the end of the 1790s, "Liberty was indelibly associated with the memory of the Republic she had represented. In collective memory, *La Republique* was 'Marianne.'"[13] Characters named Marianne figure prominently in French literature, often as young women of common origins who stand up to their so-called aristocratic betters.

Could Austen have chosen the name Marianne because she wanted readers to consider both the good and the bad side of French revolutionary ideals? Austen copied out the Marseillaise, dotted her letters and novels with French phrases and allusions, and was acutely aware through her brothers of military conflicts between France and England.[14] I disagree with George Moore, who patronizingly creates an apolitical, demure, sheltered voice for Jane Austen: "I know nothing . . . of politics. . . . I am a maiden lady, interested in the few people with whom my life is cast. If you care to know how So-and-so marries So-and-so, I will tell you." [15] Austen tells her readers far more than that. We recognize Marianne's idealism and scorn of outmoded conventions, but also her impracticality and zeal. Consider the words of Marat-Mauger, a French revolutionary, who wrote in 1793, "A revolution is never made by halves; it must either be total or it will abort." [16] This sounds much like Austen's comment about Marianne, "She could never love by halves" (379). Marat-Mauger also offers a definition— "Revolutionary means outside of all forms and all rules"—that seems to fit Marianne's proud disregard of propriety. Marianne's fervor is refreshing yet disturbing, admirable yet off-putting.

There also is a French connection the only other time that Austen chooses the name Marianne: Austen dedicates her juvenile sketch "Love and Freindship," composed as a series of letters to Marianne, to her flamboyant cousin Eliza de Feuillide, then married to a French count. When Austen wrote "Love and Freindship" in 1792, Count de Feuillide had not yet lost his head to the guillotine, so perhaps Austen felt freer to send her cousin this light-hearted burlesque. In "Love and Freindship," Laura tells Marianne that she and Sophia successfully persuaded a young woman to reject a sensible man because of his lack of romantic appreciation: "They said he was Sensible, well-informed, and Agreable; we did not pretend to Judge of such trifles, but as we were convinced he had no soul, that he had never read the Sorrows of Werter, & that his Hair bore not the slightest resemblance to Auburn, we were certain that Janetta could feel no affection for him, or at least that she ought to feel none. The very circumstance of his being her father's choice too, was so much in his disfavour, that had he been deserving of her, in every other respect yet *that* of itself ought to have been a sufficient reason in the Eyes of Janetta for rejecting him. . . . It was her Duty to disobey her Father" (*MW*, 91–92). Austen's readers would have known that Goethe's *Sorrows of Werther* (1774) epitomized romanticism and had already caused a rash of suicides. Tormented by passions and lost in dreams, Goethe's artistic hero eventually shoots himself in the head. As Marianne recognizes near the end of *Sense and Sensibility*, she comes perilously close to following after Werther: She exclaims, "Had I died—it would have been self destruction" (345). Austen must have sensed that one danger of European romanticism—whether French, English, or German—was its morbidity.

The passage from "Love and Freindship" describing Janetta's rejection of a man because he is Goethe-less and because he is her father's choice seems an exaggerated version of scenes Austen would later include in *Sense and Sensibility*. Marianne believes Elinor should reject Edward because he reads Cowper so lamely, and she and Willoughby scorn the fatherly Colonel Brandon because others respect him. People in love must be afflicted, Marianne suggests, and she assumes that Elinor cannot possibly love Edward because she acts so sensibly: "When is she dejected or melancholy?" (39). Although Marianne is not a mere caricature as are Laura and Sophia of "Love and Freindship," she displays some of the same affectations.

In passages in *Sense and Sensibility* giving voice to Marianne, Austen summons the affected diction, punctuation, and martyred tone of romantic poetry. Marianne's lyrical address to Norland expresses her regret that her childhood home cannot feel her pain and that the trees will not visibly register grief over the departure of owners with such good taste: "Oh! happy house, could you know what I suffer in now viewing you from this spot, from whence perhaps I may view you no more!—And you, ye well-known trees!—but you will continue the same.—No leaf will decay because we are removed, nor any branch become motionless although we can observe you no longer!—. . . No, you will continue the same; unconscious of the pleasure or the regret you occasion, and insensible of any change in those who walk under your shade!—But who will remain to enjoy you?" (27). Austen may be smiling here at Marianne's overblown use of language, but she also lets readers know that Marianne's feelings are real. Marianne does appreciate nature more than the new inhabitants do. The answer to her question of who will remain to enjoy nature is no one: later in the novel we discover that John and Fanny Dashwood, the new owners of Norland, have chopped down the old walnut trees to make room for a greenhouse.

Elinor twits her younger sister for delighting in romantic agony— her love of things desolate, dying, and dead. If Edward were at death's door, maybe Marianne would be attracted, Elinor jokes: "Had he been only in a violent fever, you would not have despised him half so much. Confess, Marianne, is not there something interesting to you in the flushed cheek, hollow eye, and quick pulse of a fever?" (38). Marianne, one suspects, could have written a moving "Ode to Autumn" à la Keats, "Ode to Dejection" à la Coleridge, or "Ode to the West Wind" à la Shelley ("the leaves dead / Are driven, like ghosts from the enchanter fleeing"):

"And how does dear, dear Norland look?" cried Marianne.

"Dear, dear Norland," said Elinor, "probably looks much as it always does at this time of year. The woods and walks thickly covered with dead leaves."

"Oh!" cried Marianne, "with what transporting sensations have I formerly seen them fall! How have I delighted, as I walked, to see them driven in showers about me by the wind! What feelings have they, the season, the air altogether inspired! Now there is no one to regard them. They are seen only as a nuisance, swept hastily off, and driven as much as possible from the sight."

"It is not every one," said Elinor, "who has your passion for dead leaves."

"No; my feelings are not often shared, not often understood." (87–88)

Marianne *cries;* Elinor *says.* Autumn brings Marianne "transporting sensations" and exclamations, while Elinor sees piles of dead leaves. In conversations like this one, Austen places readers in the middle with her, irritated that Marianne is carrying on excessively yet conscious that she genuinely delights in nature and spends more time outdoors than Elinor does.

Part of Marianne's appeal is her frankness, her lack of guile and concealment. In a society of fawning hypocrites and greedy schemers, Marianne is refreshingly open. Marianne has "neither shyness nor reserve" when talking to Willoughby and scorns her sister's suggestion that she has been too unrestrained: "'Elinor,' cried Marianne, 'is this fair? is this just? are my ideas so scanty? But I see what you mean. I have been too much at my ease, too happy, too frank. I have erred against every common-place notion of decorum; I have been open and sincere where I ought to have been reserved, spiritless, dull, and deceitful:—had I talked only of the weather and the roads, and had I spoken only once in ten minutes, this reproach would have been spared'" (47–48). Marianne believes that she can do no wrong because she can feel no wrong. Perhaps Austen felt that one limitation of romantic literature was its amorality. When Marianne asserts of a man, "Whatever be his pursuits, his eagerness in them should know no moderation," she little realizes that Willoughby has indeed followed just such a credo, seducing young women and pursuing women of fortune with plenty of eagerness and immoderation (45). Marianne has to learn that one can be eager, handsome, spirited, lively, passionate, musical, and well spoken—but despicable.

Austen clearly saw that too great an emphasis on feeling leaves one self-absorbed, uncontrolled, and vulnerable. Too great a faith in imagined worlds guarantees disillusionment. Those who embrace liberty may become libertines; instincts are not always divine. Colonel Brandon's melodramatic Tale of Two Elizas (is it coincidence Austen chose the name of her cousin?) stands as a warning to Marianne. Like Marianne, Eliza had a "warmth of heart" and "eagerness of fancy and spirits" that caused Colonel Brandon to fall in love with her (205). Scorning the values of their society, the romantic colonel and Eliza tried unsuccessfully to elope in order for Eliza to escape forced marriage to the colonel's older, more prosperous brother. Faced with disappointment, Eliza responds by becoming a fallen woman subject to her passions. As Colonel Brandon reports, "I could not trace her beyond her first seducer, and there was every reason to fear that she had removed from him only to sink deeper in a life of sin. . . . So altered—so faded—worn down by acute suffering of every kind!" (207). After Colonel Brandon rescues her from prostitution and imprisonment for debt, Eliza dies of consumption. There is real death, disease, poverty, and sex in *Sense and Sensibility*. Eliza's pursuit of sensuality leads to a real child, "a little girl, the offspring of her first guilty connection" (208). This second Eliza, also subject to "the violence of her passions," falls victim to Willoughby's seduction (322).

Although Marianne scorns Elinor for suggesting that it is improper for her to be wandering alone with Willoughby through the rooms of his relative's house and scoffs at the need for a formal engagement, the Tale of Two Elizas suggests that Marianne is foolish to discard rules designed not for her oppression but for her protection. Austen censures those like Lady Middleton who are too priggish to hear talk of pregnancy or illegitimacy, but she also warns against promiscuity, anarchy, and the unbridled pursuit of sensation.

Austen demonstrates that Marianne, despite her romantic taste and personal beauty, evinces antisocial behavior at times, making no effort to flatter others: "'What a sweet woman Lady Middleton is!' said Lucy Steele. Marianne was silent; it was impossible for her to say what she did not feel, however trivial the occasion; and upon Elinor therefore the whole task of telling lies when politeness required it, always fell" (122). Is Marianne's refusal to lie a refreshing sign of her integrity, winning our admiration? Or is it a sign that she has not learned to be an adult member of a community? Perhaps both: Austen simultaneously praises and censures the romantic emphasis on spontaneous, uninhibited emotion.

If Marianne illustrates the unbridled zeal of French revolutionaries, perhaps Elinor embodies the enduring British tradition of remaining composed under pressure, of keeping a stiff upper lip. Passages describing Elinor are dotted with words like *judgment, reason, duty, principle, observation, thought, restraint, command, civility, decorum,* and *knowledge.* Stay calm, she tells herself: "For a few moments, she was almost overcome—her heart sunk within her, and she could hardly stand; but exertion was indispensably necessary, and she struggled so resolutely against the oppression of her feelings, that her success was speedy, and for the time complete. . . . Elinor [spoke] with a composure of voice, under which was concealed an emotion and distress beyond any thing she had ever felt before" (134–35). Like the British explorer Stanley, Elinor might have observed calmly, "Dr. Livingstone, I presume?" when encountering a countryman in the heart of an African jungle.

Elinor uses her calm, steady, reasoned judgment to keep her family functional throughout the novel. With a mother acting like little more than a teenager, two younger sisters whose eyes are glazed over with romance, and a father so cheerfully sanguine that he dies without obtaining written documentation providing adequately for his widow and daughters, Elinor must become wise beyond her nineteen years. She seems the calm, rational head of the household. Calmness does not win as many admirers as passion, though: as one critic laments, "Elinor, not to mince words, is what some have forthrightly called a stick."[17] Mark Twain crowned Elinor the queen of waxwork, unable to warm up and feel a passion.[18]

Elinor is no prudent stick without emotion, however. Austen first introduces Elinor as a woman of feeling—a loving daughter and sister with an "excellent heart" and "affectionate but genuine feeling" (6). Elinor falls in love with Edward before Marianne ever meets Willoughby. What draws us to Elinor is her genuine concern for her family, her ability to suffer without wallowing in misery, her pride when she faces rejection or disappointment, her discernment, her skill at handling awkward social situations, her empathy for others, and her masterful efforts at self-control.

Yet Austen shows that Elinor is not as objective as she thinks. Because she is attracted to Edward Ferrars with a "blind impartiality," she invests him with artistic potential: "Had he ever been in the way of learning, I think he would have drawn very well" (19). Austen will later give this silly thought to Lady Catherine de Bourgh in *Pride and Prejudice*, who insists that she and her daughter are naturally musical, though neither can play (*PP*, 173). Elinor's keen eyes seem to play tricks on her at times. When Elinor sees Edward wearing a ring with hair in it and hears him falsely assert that the hair is his sister's, Elinor jumps to a conclusion without evidence: "That the hair was her own, she instantly felt" (98). Like Marianne, Elinor indulges in instant feelings and, like Marianne, her judgment can thus be wrong. The hair is not hers, nor is Edward free to propose marriage.

Austen gives readers no answer as to what an intelligent, sensitive woman with sense and sensibility ought to do when forced to spend evenings with tasteless, insensitive neighbors and relatives. Marianne withdraws; Elinor adapts. While Marianne solipsistically pours out her emotions into the piano, Elinor "joyfully profit[s]" from the subterfuge of using "the powerful protection of a very magnificent concerto" to hide her secret conversation with a rival, "and thus by a little of that address, which Marianne could never condescend to practise, gained her own end" (149, 145). Are we to admire Elinor for using a hypocritical means to a social end, or applaud Marianne for refusing to play the game?

Marianne needs to be more like Elinor in order to find a welcome place in society, yet along with Colonel Brandon we applaud Marianne's audacity, ardor, and candor. We all, in a sense, would like to tell the Mrs. Jennings, Mr. Palmers, Lady Middletons, and Mrs. Ferrars of the world that they are nosy, rude, boring, and mean, rather than continuing to exchange Christmas cards and pleasantries with them. Of course Marianne should not be as rude as Mr. Palmer, who perhaps stands as a warning of social "honesty." Mr. Palmer calls his mother-in-law "ill bred," labels Willoughby's house "as vile a spot as I ever saw in my life," and constantly opposes his wife, who informs him, "My love, you contradict every body. . . . Do you know that you are quite rude?" (111–12). Marianne's bluntness and contrariness place her in danger of becoming as outspoken and opinionated as Mr. Palmer.

Both sisters have affectionate hearts, but Elinor masks hers and strains for social correctness, even if it means dissembling. When Marianne makes blunt remarks, Elinor assumes "the whole task of telling lies when politeness required it" (122). Elinor stands somewhere in the middle between the open, direct Marianne and the manipulative Lucy Steele, an artful woman who skillfully and insincerely uses the art of flattery to worm her way into favor. Austen invites readers to compare differing social responses by having Elinor, Marianne, Lucy and Nancy Steele (as eldest, called Miss Steele) all present when Lady Middleton and Fanny Dashwood argue over the earthshaking matter of their sons' comparative heights:

One subject only engaged the ladies till coffee came in, which was the comparative heights of Harry Dashwood, and Lady Middleton's second son William, who were nearly of the same age. . . .

Lucy, who was hardly less anxious to please one parent than the other, thought the boys were both remarkably tall for their age, and could not conceive that there could be the smallest difference in the world between them; and Miss Steele, with yet greater address gave it, as fast as she could, in favour of each.

Elinor, having once delivered her opinion on William's side, by which she offended Mrs. Ferrars and Fanny still more, did not see the necessity of enforcing it by any farther assertion; and Marianne, when called on for her's, offended them all, by declaring that she had no opinion to give, as she had never thought about it. (233–34)

A key question here is *what does Austen think?* Which approach does she recommend? The Steele sisters are social hypocrites, but it is precisely Lucy's cunning use of flattery that will land her a wealthy husband by the novel's end. Did Elinor need to give an opinion about the boys' heights at all? Was Marianne's approach—to abstain entirely and display obvious indifference—the only one with integrity?

I see no "triumph of politeness over sincerity" here, to use Susan Morgan's phrase; no clear victor or clear heroine.[19] In a later scene at the Palmer house as the other women do carpet-work and chat of children and social engagements, Austen again shows two sisters responding differently to vapid conversation: Elinor "however little concerned in it, joined in their discourse," while Marianne makes a bee line for the library (304). Who made the right decision? Where is our heroine? Elinor maintains a civility sorely absent in Marianne, yet she lacks Marianne's refreshing openness.

Since pain triggers growth, Marianne emerges the most altered of the two sisters by novel's end. As if to underscore the idea of character development, Austen leaves Marianne at the same age (nineteen) as Elinor was at the novel's beginning. How much can happen in just two years if people are open to learning from their erroneous judgment and behavior, Austen implies.

Elinor's stance at the end of the novel differs dramatically from her earlier complacency. In an early chapter, she had smugly observed of Marianne, "A few years will settle her opinions on the reasonable basis of common sense and observation. . . . A better acquaintance with the world is what I look forward to as her greatest possible advantage" (56). By the novel's end Elinor has dropped this irritatingly parental tone because she knows that her own maturing process was far from over. Perhaps she might now admit the truth of Blaise Pascal's remark, "Le coeur a ses raisons que la raison ne connait point" (The heart has its reasons which reason knows nothing of).[20] Readers, too, may feel differently now about that earlier moment in the novel when Marianne and Elinor parted from their mother before heading for London for a few weeks. At the time, the narrator implied that Elinor was the only reasonable one: "Elinor was the only one of the three, who seemed to consider the separation as anything short of eternal" (158). But by showing readers that this almost *was* a final farewell, Austen invites reconsideration of Elinor's perceptions.

In a novel with two heroines rather than one, it is interesting that the only time the term "heroism" appears is when *both* sisters are present—and both progressing. When Marianne stifles the spasm in her throat and does *not* burst out passionately, Elinor hails this evolution in her sister: "Such advances towards heroism in her sister, made Elinor feel equal to any thing herself" (265). Austen celebrates the growth (or "advances") of both heroines. To leave out either Elinor or Marianne from a discussion of Austen's heroines does an injustice to Austen's dual focus. *Sense and Sensibility* invites readers to compare and contrast Elinor and Marianne, not choose between them.

Similarly, *Sense and Sensibility* emerges as the only Austen novel to present two men running for election as the hero. Some vote for Colonel Brandon; others for Edward Ferrars. If real life has more than one central character, why not a novel, Austen seems to suggest. To reinforce the realism of her art, Austen contrasts both men with John Willoughby, a man resembling "the hero of a favourite story" (43). Contemporary moviemakers miss the point of Austen's characterization when they give white horses, soul-searching glances, or a taste for poetry to Colonel Brandon or Edward, as if distrusting audiences ever to accept an unheroic hero.[21] Austen asks more of her readers.

Austen ironically demonstrates that although John Willoughby has "manly beauty" and reads Cowper "with all the sensibility and spirit" Edward lacked, he apparently has ignored the poet's message (42, 48). Did Austen hope readers would think of the following Cowper lines, which contain the title words of her novel?

> I would not enter on my list of friends
> (Though graced with polish'd manners and fine sense,

Yet wanting sensibility) the man
Who needlessly sets foot upon a worm.[22]

Willoughby definitely is "graced with polish'd manners and fine sense," yet even he admits that he has trampled on Marianne's feelings: "It is astonishing . . . that my heart should have been so insensible!" (320).

During Marianne's illness, Colonel Brandon both feels and thinks, cares and acts. With quick helpfulness, he brings Mrs. Dashwood to her daughter's bedside: "*He,* meanwhile, whatever he might feel, acted with all the firmness of a collected mind, made every necessary arrangement with the utmost dispatch, and calculated with exactness the time in which [Elinor] might look for his return. Not a moment was lost in delay of any kind" (312). I disagree with those who find Colonel Brandon a disappointing match for Marianne. Poor Colonel Brandon has been called a "wooden and undeveloped character . . . unexciting and remote," a "vacuum," and a "stolid sad sack."[23] Colonel Brandon's primary fault resembles that of British colonialists in general, even those claiming to be enlightened: he has a paternalistic tendency to enjoy rescuing the weak and less fortunate. But Colonel Brandon's character is hardly "undeveloped." True, he is an awkward narrator, but he admits this about himself. His inarticulateness hints at depth not dearth of feeling: "it would be impossible to describe what I felt," he tells Elinor (199). As Austen notes of this man who uses both his head and his heart, "Colonel Brandon . . . was in every occasion *mindful* of the *feelings* of others" (62; my italics).

In fact, one begins to wonder along with Mrs. Jennings why Austen did not pair this chivalrous man of action with Elinor. The two spend far more time talking to each other than to their prospective mates. So what does Edward Ferrars add to the novel, and why might Elinor prefer him? We have our dastardly villain (Willoughby) and our manly hero (Colonel Brandon) paired literally in a duel: "we met by appointment, he to defend, I to punish his conduct" (211). Willoughby marries for money while Colonel Brandon marries for love. Willoughby looks the part of the perfect gentleman; Colonel Brandon acts like one. Why might Austen have added Edward Ferrars to her gallery of gentlemen?

Although Edward may seem weak, inexperienced, or idle compared to the older, well-traveled Colonel Brandon, he possesses at least one trait Austen knows is lacking in both the Colonel and in Marianne: wit. Edward has self-deprecating humor and can banter with the ever-serious Marianne in a way slightly reminiscent of Henry Tilney's exchanges with Catherine Morland and Eleanor Tilney in

Northanger Abbey. Instead of praising the picturesque as Henry does, Edward dryly mocks the affectations of its sentimental proponents: "I have no knowledge in the picturesque . . . I shall call hills steep, which ought to be bold, surfaces strange and uncouth, which ought to be irregular and rugged, and distant objects out of sight, which ought only to be indistinct through the soft medium of a hazy atmosphere" (96–97). Marianne takes Edward seriously and wonders why he boasts of his ignorance, but Elinor recognizes his pose. When Edward continues to assert, "I do not like crooked, twisted, blasted trees . . . ruined, tattered cottages . . . nettles, or thistles, or heath blossoms" and boasts that he would prefer "a troop of tidy, happy villagers" to "the finest banditti in the world," Marianne looks at him with amazement while Elinor laughs (98). Throughout the novel only Elinor and Edward—and of course the narrator—display the ability to see life ironically.

If we free ourselves from the image of Edward as a dull, mother-dominated milquetoast and look carefully at his conversation, we see that he displays a flair for discerning character. In a conversation with Marianne, he drolly imagines what she would do if she inherited a fortune: "And books!–Thomson, Cowper, Scott–she would buy them all over and over again; she would buy up every copy, I believe, to prevent their falling into unworthy hands; and she would have every book that tells her how to admire an old twisted tree. Should not you, Marianne? Forgive me, if I am very saucy. But I was willing to shew you that I had not forgot our old disputes" (92). Marianne replies in utter seriousness, failing to catch Edward's friendly jibes. Although Edward tells Elinor that "gaiety never was a part of *my* character," one senses that the esprit he displays here while unhappily engaged to Lucy has the potential to turn to genuine mirth once he is blessed with a happy marriage (93).

Our final view of Edward shows him with greater integrity than his more pragmatic wife-to-be. Edward refuses to cave in to his mother: "I can make no submission–I am grown neither humble nor penitent," he insists, but Elinor argues that "a little humility may be convenient." Although finally he agrees to visit his mother, he "still resisted the idea of a letter of proper submission" (372). Throughout, Edward displays democratic notions, observing that he feels more at home among the lower classes than with the gentility. Edward remains steady in his principles, secure in his exceptional decision to forfeit the right of eldest son, and happily engaged in his parish duties. Austen turns her milquetoast into a mensch.

As narrator, Austen reserves some of her censure for her minor characters, particularly for those who do not grow. Edward Ferrars's younger brother has become a pretentious dandy who regards his decorated toothpick case as a necessity of life:

> The correctness of his eye, and the delicacy of his taste, proved to be beyond his politeness. He was giving orders for a toothpick-case for himself; and till its size, shape, and ornaments were determined, all of which, after examining and debating for a quarter of an hour over every toothpick-case in the shop, were finally arranged by his own inventive fancy, he had no leisure to bestow any other attention on the two ladies, than what was comprised in three or four very broad stares. . . . At last the affair was decided. The ivory, the gold, and the pearls, all received their appointment, and the gentleman having named the last day on which his existence could be continued without the possession of the toothpick-case, drew on his gloves with leisurely care, and bestowing another glance . . . as seemed rather to demand than express admiration, walked off with an happy air of real conceit and affected indifference. (220–21)

This passage perhaps hints at the devastating effects of "empire" on those who decadently reap its rewards without possessing any awareness of the labor and injustice supporting their own luxurious lifestyle. We see Robert Ferrars giving orders and making demands. The repetition of words like "leisure" and "bestow" captures his idleness and imperiousness. Austen's readers would have recognized that ivory, gold, and pearls were among the fruits of colonialism. Although this passage contains the only reference to ivory in Austen's novels, there are other brief allusions to the slave trade and to the West and East Indies. Earlier in *Sense and Sensibility* Willoughby's references to "nabobs, gold mohrs, and palanquins" would similarly have reminded readers that British extravagance came only through the harsh labor of others (51).[24]

Robert Ferrars thinks only of himself, not those exploited for the sake of his country's wealth. He loves ornaments and is "adorned in the first style of fashion." Little else occupies his time. He reminds one of Mary Wollstonecraft's depictions of women more interested in what they will wear on a trip than in where they will go. In a chapter called "The State of Degradation to Which Woman is Reduced,"

Wollstonecraft asks, "Can dignity of mind exist with such trivial cares?" She concludes that rich men have become honorary women: "Women, in general, *as well as the rich of both sexes*, have acquired all the follies and vices of civilization, and missed the useful fruit."[25] An idle, wealthy gentleman like Robert Ferrars is ladylike in the worst sense of the epithet. Robert Ferrars's act of drawing on his gloves "with leisurely care" shows his uselessness. Austen's oxymoronic description of Robert Ferrars's "sterling insignificance" captures the link between British imperialism ("sterling" suggests the British unit of value) and the pettiness of its leisured, pampered upper class (221).

Austen includes many other sterling examples of insignificant men and women in this novel. Mr. Palmer "idled away the mornings at billiards, which ought to have been devoted to business" and displays "Epicurism . . . selfishness . . . conceit" (305). Sir John Middleton has no resources for solitude, displays a "total want of talent and taste," and feels no purpose in life beyond hunting, shooting, and throwing pleasure parties (32). Nancy Steele uses bad grammar and thinks of nothing but herself, her pink ribbons, and her conquest of beaux, while the vulgar Lucy Steele schemes her way up the social ladder. A dense woman, the "everlasting talker" Mrs. Jennings fails to see that her raillery causes pain or that her comments lack depth ("Mrs. Taylor did say this morning that one day Miss Walker hinted to her, that she believed Mr. and Mrs. Ellison would not be sorry to have Miss Grey married") (54, 194). Both her daughters are vapid, uneducated, frivolous women who display a few trivial "accomplishments" for the sake of catching a husband, then promptly drop the effort: Lady Middleton celebrates her marriage by giving up music and now passes the time elegantly "saying little and doing less"; Charlotte Palmer hangs above her mantlepiece "a landscape in coloured silks of her performance, in proof of her having spent seven years at a great school in town to some effect" and now spends her time lounging, dawdling, laughing, and whiling away the time while her servants do the work (175, 160).

Why are Lady Middleton, Charlotte Palmer, Fanny Dashwood, the Steele sisters, and women of their ilk so insipid and illiberal? Again, Austen suggests that idleness and lack of education are much to blame, just as in the case of the many dissipated and indolent men in this novel. Wollstonecraft had warned of self-indulgent fine ladies "brimful of sensibility, and teeming with capricious fancies" as well as "mere notable women" with "a shrewd kind of good sense, joined with worldly prudence" who possess "neither greatness of mind nor taste."[26]

Without ever writing a line of a political treatise as Wollstonecraft had done, Austen offers an equally revolutionary argument for educating both men and women to be whole human beings. Only then can they live in harmony and fulfillment.

Like Wollstonecraft, Austen rejects the notion that "man was made to reason, woman to feel." [27] Perhaps Austen was tired of reading passages in conduct books suggesting that young women were innately sensitive, quivering, emotional messes, such as the Reverend John Bennett's *Letters to a Young Lady, on a Variety of Useful and Interesting Subjects, Calculated to Improve the Heart, to Form the Manners, and Enlighten the Understanding:* "The timidity, arising from the natural weakness and delicacy of your frame; the numerous diseases to which you are liable; that exquisite sensibility, which, in many of you, vibrates to the slightest touch of joy or sorrow, . . . the sedentariness of your life, naturally followed with low spirits or *ennui;* whilst we are seeking health and pleasure . . . will expose you to a number of *peculiar* sorrows." [28] Austen also might have objected to Tennyson's later lines, "Man with the head and woman with the heart: . . . All else confusion." [29] In *Sense and Sensibility* Austen insists that all will be confusion unless *both* men and women possess *both* sense and sensibility.

John Halperin writes, "Somewhere between *Sense and Sensibility* lies what is just plain *sensible,* and it is here that Jane Austen wishes us to stand." [30] Austen argues this not only in *Sense and Sensibility* but in all her other novels: as Joan Ray notes, "the phrase *sense and sensibility* is key to reading Austen, whichever of her novels we pick up." [31] Sensibility need not be delicate weakness or self-indulgence, but rather a genuine ability to feel for others. Sense need not be cunning or narrow pragmatism but rather an enlightened use of one's mind. In Austen's world, any *human* needs both. As Joseph Wiesenfarth observes, "to be a whole person, one must have sensibility enlightened by sense." [32]

Austen suggests that it may be particularly difficult to achieve such wholeness, such humanity, in an economically exploitative society. For many men and women, sense becomes little more than a calculated self-interest in obtaining cents and percents for oneself. In *Sense and Sensibility* more than in any other novel, Austen links the pursuit of money to the destruction of finer feelings.

This novel is permeated with remarks about fortunes, annuities, moieties, inheritances, salaries, and livings, as if each character comes with a price tag attached. From start to finish, money determines behavior. Money, not love, seems to make most of the world of *Sense and*

Sensibility go round. Perhaps W. H. Auden had *Sense and Sensibility* in mind when he wrote these lines about Jane Austen:

> You could not shock her more than she shocks me;
>   Beside her Joyce seems innocent as grass.
> It makes me most uncomfortable to see
>   An English spinster of the middle class
>   Describe the amorous effects of "brass",
> Reveal so frankly and with such sobriety
> The economic basis of society.[33]

We certainly see the amorous effects of brass in the loveless marriages of Lucy Steele, Colonel Brandon's brother, and John Willoughby. As Willoughby admits, "My affection for Marianne . . . was all insufficient to outweigh that dread of poverty, or get the better of those false ideas of the necessity of riches, which I was naturally inclined to feel, and expensive society had increased" (323) Willoughby has managed to hit the jackpot, snaring Miss Grey and her fifty thousand pounds. As he notes in a rare moment of integrity, "In honest words, her money was necessary to me" (328). Edward Ferrars could have been the equivalent of a millionaire as well, for if he had married Miss Morton he "would settle on him the Norfolk estate, which, clear of land-tax, brings in a good thousand a-year," land her thirty thousand pound fortune, gain a wife with a title, and be assured of receiving his inheritance from his pleased mother (266). Mrs. Jenning's "ample jointure" (a financial settlement providing for a widow) allows her to see both her daughters "respectably married" with expensive and extensive estates (36). If money can't buy you love, it certainly can buy you marriage.

In *Sense and Sensibility* we meet a society so based on economics that it uses income to measure the worth not only of prospective marriage partners but also of people in general. John Dashwood would probably approve of having people wear name tags saying "Hello, my name is ___ and I make ___ pounds a year." He compliments Mrs. Ferrars because she has "such very large fortune" and indeed "never wished to offend anybody, especially anybody of good fortune" (222, 267). When Colonel Brandon arrives, John Dashwood "only wanted to know him to be rich, to be equally civil to him" (223). As the grieving Marianne declines in health, John Dashwood ticks off her declining market value: "I question whether Marianne *now*, will marry a man worth more than five or six hundred a-year, at the utmost" (227). The only purpose of John Dashwood's life seems to be to acquire money, spend it on himself and his immediate family, and keep it away from others, including the relatives he had promised to help. His concept of the ultimate spiritual horror is the loss of property: "Can anything be more galling to the spirit of a man than to see his younger brother in possession of an estate which might have been his own?" (269).

Is John Dashwood's first name of significance? In a novel where "Marianne" may symbolize revolutionary France, does Austen invoke the spirit of John Bull—the prosaic, mercenary, soulless symbol of England—by naming three of her English gentlemen "John"? John Dashwood is a selfish materialist, Sir John Middleton an aristocrat without taste or inner resources, and John Willoughby an idle, dissipated, extravagant "gentleman" who marries for money and seduces for pleasure, leaving broken hearts and lives in his wake. Young John Middleton, a boy of six, monopolizes the conversation, harasses his female cousins, searches their bags, steals their belongings, and displays his "spirits" by "monkey tricks" such as throwing Lucy's handkerchief out the window—hardly a good omen of little John Bulls to come (121). If we add to Austen's collection the crass, philistinistic, fortune-hunting John Thorpe of *Northanger Abbey*, the dissolute "Honorable" John Yates of *Mansfield Park*, the rather dour, reserved attorney John Knightley of *Emma*, and the "civil, cautious" lawyer John Shepherd in *Persuasion*, John Bull definitely comes out in need of amendment.

Austen heightens the contrast between those with and without feeling by presenting two Mrs. Dashwoods. As Isobel Armstrong observes, "The novel imagines a world with too much sensibility in Mrs. Dashwood, and too little in the other Mrs. Dashwood, Fanny."[34] The first Mrs. Dashwood's warm-blooded personality and possession of "a sense of honour so keen, a generosity so romantic" make her a far cry from the coldly objective and selfishly calculating Mrs. John Dashwood (6). Austen shows how Fanny perverts the language of maternal feelings ("our poor little boy") to talk her easily convinced husband out of any sense of charity, duty, or justice (9). The original plan to give three thousand pounds to needy relatives is reduced in just a few minutes to nothing more than an occasional present of fish and game, when in season. Fanny succeeds as a mother in looking out for the interests (literally) of her child, but at what social and moral cost?

Using words like *observe, certainly, undoubtedly, to say the truth,* and *I am convinced,* John and Fanny Dashwood conclude that the late Mr. Dashwood was not "in his right senses" when he asked his son to share his fortune (9). By sprinkling the word *sense* throughout this novel, Austen demands that we question its meaning. When Colonel Brandon decides to give Edward a living as rector that he could have sold for profit, John Dashwood responds with utter amazement: "This living of Colonel Brandon's—can it be true?—has he really given it to Edward? . . . this is very astonishing! . . . and now that livings fetch such a price! . . . a man of Colonel Brandon's *sense*! . . . It is truly astonishing! . . . what could be the Colonel's motive?" (294–95). John Dashwood's definition means it makes *sense* for Willoughby to marry the heiress Miss Grey. It makes *sense* for Mrs. Ferrars to want Edward to marry the wealthy, titled Miss Morton. As Miss Steele observes, "Miss Godby told Miss Sparks, that nobody in their *senses* could expect Mr. Ferrars to give up a woman like Miss Morton, with £30,000 to her fortune, for Lucy Steele that had nothing at all" (273; my italics).

As narrator, Austen pretends to admire the fact that Lucy's sense pays off: "The whole of Lucy's behaviour . . . the prosperity which crowned it . . . may be held forth as a most encouraging instance of what an earnest, an unceasing attention to self-interest . . . will do in securing every advantage of fortune, with no other sacrifice than that of time and conscience" (376). Why might Austen call this behavior "encouraging" or refer to John Dashwood as "respectable"? Austen pretends as narrator to adopt her era's prevailing opinions—to assume the majority voice of her era. Yet by ironically praising characters with obviously flawed values, Austen invites her readers to go against the norm. She demonstrates that those with a "sensitive conscience" like Marianne, a respect for principles like Edward and Elinor, or a generosity of spirit like the brotherly Colonel Brandon must look senseless to the Steeles and John and Fanny Dashwoods of the world (350).

While Austen attacks the money-mindedness of society, she also exposes the vulnerability of those too romantic to cope with financial reality. Mrs. Dashwood's inability to save money in the past makes her ill equipped to handle her newfound adversity. Marianne's naivete about money matters makes her too blind to Willoughby's expensive lifestyle and the lengths he will go to preserve it. At least Elinor and Edward face real life: "They were neither of them quite enough in love to think that three hundred and fifty pounds a-year would supply them with the comforts of life" (369). The happiest characters in Austen's fictional world are those who understand money but are not destroyed by its corrupting power. Colonel Brandon's act of giving a living to Edward Ferrars may not make "sense" to John Dashwood, but it is consistent with the ideals of brotherhood celebrated in this novel.

Austen does not come in as narrator to tell us her ideals or even to indicate whether we are to prefer Elinor to Marianne, Edward to Colonel Brandon. Instead of intruding as she did in *Northanger Abbey* to tell us about the hero and heroine of her "tale," she inserts her presence in *Sense and Sensibility* for a different purpose: to remind readers that her seemingly exaggerated characters and events are *not unusual.* All of society stands indicted here through Austen's frequent references to the characters' resemblance to others of their sex, class, or era.

Throughout this novel, Austen reminds us that selfish, unfair people will be deemed respectable if they have money. Rather than presenting the unfair disinheritance of Mrs. Dashwood and her daughters as unusual, Austen informs us in the opening chapter that such occurrences are the norm: "The old Gentleman died; his will was read, and *like almost every other will,* gave as much disappointment as pleasure" (4; my italics here and in the next quotation). Rather than expressing surprise at Fanny and John Dashwood's selfish disregard for the claims of their relatives, Austen matter-of-factly states, "It was *very well known* that no affection was *ever* supposed to exist between the children of *any man* by different marriages" (8). Throughout *Sense and Sensibility,* Austen sprinkles in clauses such as *still more common, in many cases of a similar kind, like many others, too common, in common use, the common opinion, in the common phrase, as any other man, as ladies always [do], by no means unusual, in the usual style, like other parties, like the half the rest of the world, like every other place.* Austen makes her opinion clear that mean-spirited, crass, tasteless people, loveless marriages, and boring events are the norm, not the exception.

What are we to think of the state of women if the illiterate Lucy Steele (described as "capable of the utmost meanness of wanton ill-nature") is pronounced to be "superior in person and understanding to half her sex"? (366). What are we to think of men if our narrator tells us that the rude, hedonistic Mr. Palmer possesses "no traits at all unusual in his sex and time of life"? (304).

The dreadful marriage of the Palmers—one of insults and abuse on the one hand and escapist oblivion on the other—is described as too usual, too common, to make Elinor wonder about it. Indeed, Elinor considers "the strange unsuitableness which *often* existed between husband and wife" (118; my italics). She mistakenly assumes that since Mr. Palmer's mistaken reasons for marriage are *common,* it must not do any harm: Mr. Palmer's "temper might perhaps be a little soured by finding, *like many others of his sex,* that through some unaccountable bias in favour of beauty, he was the husband of a very silly woman,—but she [Elinor] knew that this kind of blunder was *too common* for any sensible man to be lastingly hurt by it.—It was rather a wish of distinction she believed, which produced his contemptuous treatment of everybody, and his general abuse of every thing before him. It was the desire of appearing superior to other people. The motive was *too common* to be wondered at" (112; my italics). This is a fascinating passage. Mr. Palmer, like Mr. Allen in *Northanger Abbey* and like Mr. Bennet in *Pride and Prejudice*, has joined "many others of his sex" in valuing beauty at the expense of sense, a far "too common" blunder. Austen implies that many men marry inferior women, and that this action reflects a more universal desire of looking superior to others. Austen seems to separate herself from Elinor Dashwood in this paragraph. Elinor stops wondering about Mr. Palmer because his circumstances seem so common. But readers are left to conclude that a man of sensibility may indeed be lastingly and devastatingly hurt by a bad marriage and by inflated egotism.

Perhaps more than in any book she would write, Austen aims her satiric gaze at the ignorance, dullness, and tastelessness of *the public*—of everyone. If the empty-headed Robert Ferrars is "as well fitted to mix in the world as any other man," God help the world (251). The ostentatious residence of the Palmers is "like every other place of the same degree of importance" (302). When Austen describes a "musical" party consisting of people who talk through performances and have no real taste or appreciation for the music, she points out that such events are "not very remarkable" because they are "like other musical parties" in general where the majority of listeners have no taste and the "performers themselves were, as usual" arrogant in assuming themselves the best performers in England (250). John Middleton's vapid pleasure parties are conducted in "the usual style." Lady Middleton utters "the most common-place inquiry or remark," and Mrs. Jennings offers "common-place raillery." The "common cant" usually distorts the truth, Austen notes. Austen indicts all people as empty talkers with her comment about Mrs. Ferrars's concise use of words: "She was not a woman of many words: for, *unlike people in general*, she proportioned them to the number of her ideas" (232; my italics). Rather than singling out the selfish Fanny Dashwood as unusual, Austen relates her cruelty to her relatives to the behavior of people in general.

Throughout *Sense and Sensibility* Austen categorically suggests that something profound is *wanting* in society. Mrs. Ferrars evinces a "want of liberality," Mrs. Palmer a "want of recollection and elegance" (90, 304). Lucy Steele evinces a "want of real elegance and artlessness" and "want of information in the most common particulars," as well as a "thorough want of delicacy, of rectitude, and integrity of mind" and "want of liberality" stemming from her "want of instruction" and "want of education" (124, 127, 367). Sir John and Lady Middleton resemble each other only "in that total want of talent and taste," and the audiences at their musical parties show a "shameless want of taste" (32, 35). The cumulative effect of all these references to wants is to leave readers deeply aware that something is lacking in human society.

Austen's narrative intrusions point out that her society lacks not only culture but also morality. Although critics have sometimes faulted Austen for creating a stage villain in Willoughby, she seems to me to have gone to great lengths to make Willoughby quite unsurprising to those around him.[35] She reduces him at the end not to shameful ignominy or penitent remorse, but just to ordinariness. True, once he finds out that Mrs. Smith might have left him her fortune even if he had married Marianne, he regrets choosing a woman for money rather than love. Yet he expresses no concern about his seduction of Eliza, and he goes on to lead an unremarkable life: "But that he was for ever inconsolable, that he fled from society, or contracted an habitual gloom of temper, or died of a broken heart, must not be depended on—for he did neither. He lived to exert, and frequently to enjoy himself. His wife was not always out of humour, nor his home always uncomfortable; and in his breed of horses and dogs, and in sporting of every kind, he found no inconsiderable degree of domestic felicity" (379). Willoughby will fit in fine. Maybe Sir John Middleton will stop labeling him "as good a kind of fellow as ever lived," but he still will take him out hunting (43). Lady Middleton decides to visit rather than snub Mrs. Willoughby because she is rich enough to be elegant. Like spraying air freshener on the source of a bad odor rather than removing it, society masks over any stink, any scandal (if the perpetrator be male), any injustice, and proceeds with elegance. The well-bred Lady Middleton may rush out of the room to avoid hearing talk of a love-child or a pregnancy, but the true horror lies in her own indifference, ignorance, and false elegance.

Although Marianne stands out as exceptional, striking, and refreshingly unconventional compared to the Lady Middletons of her milieu, even she becomes less extraordinary in the hands of our ironic narrator. When Marianne misjudges others, falls for the superficially graceful, polished Willoughby, or displays selfishness, she merely resembles many others in the world: "Elinor [was] . . . assured of the injustice to which her sister was often led in her opinion of others, by the irritable refinement of her own mind, and the too great importance placed by her on the delicacies of a strong sensibility, and the graces of a polished manner. *Like half the rest of the world, if more than half there be that are clever and good,* Marianne, with excellent abilities and an excellent disposition, was *neither reasonable nor candid.* She expected from other people the same opinions and feelings as her own, and she judged of their motives by the immediate effect of their actions on herself" (201; my italics). Does Austen insert this perplexing passage to inform readers that most of us, Marianne included, are neither reasonable nor candid in its earlier sense of being unprejudiced and, as Dr. Johnson puts it in his famous dictionary, "free from malice; not desirous to find fault"? Even those who are clever and good with excellent dispositions and abilities may fall victim to irrationality and partiality, she suggests. Through an inserted "if" clause, Austen makes us question whether the majority of people are clever and good. By this point in the novel, Austen has demonstrated that more than half the characters are silly and selfish. The whole world seems implicated here, since even a character with cleverness and feelings judges others according to "the immediate effect of their actions on herself."

Such narrative potshots at the world perhaps explain why many critics are quick to call *Sense and Sensibility* a bleak book written in a foul mood by an embittered spinster.[36] Perhaps Austen's anger stemmed not from her inability to find a mate but to find a readership. How did she feel as lightweight pulp fiction brought fame and fortune to lesser writers while her manuscripts of *First Impressions* and *Susan* remained unpublished? Did her experience of watching across the Channel as the French Revolution dissolved into the Reign of Terror leave her convinced of the selfishness of all concerned? As her family moved from Steventon to Bath, did she find herself condemned to a hollow life of unbearably petty activities in the company of stupid people? Did Austen's acquaintance with real emotional pain (as in the case of Cassandra's loss of a fiancé) darken her vision?

Although Marianne in *Sense and Sensibility* comes closer to death than any other Austen heroine does, it is interesting that even in this novel Austen refuses to write unadulterated tragedy. The word "almost" occurs at climactic moments. Feeling "almost choked by grief," Marianne "almost screamed with agony" when confronting Willoughby's rejection (182). In turn Willoughby "almost ran out of the room" when departing forever from Marianne and Elinor, "almost ran out of the room" when responding to the news of Edward's liberty (332, 360). Through qualifiers like these, Austen keeps her narrative reins in check, giving us something that is almost tragedy, almost melodrama. The same Jane Austen who burlesqued fainting heroines in "Love and Freindship" perhaps still distrusts tear-jerking sentimental fiction but knows that life really does contain tragic losses and dark despair. As Eudora Welty put it, Jane Austen's novels are "profound in emotion" for "in her writing there deeply lies, as deeply as anything in her powers, a true tenderness of feeling."[37] *Sense and Sensibility* leaves us no doubt that Austen could have written a poignant deathbed scene, with Mrs. Dashwood and Elinor consumed with grief at the side of a lifeless Marianne, with a power that would have rivaled the ability of Charles Dickens to describe Little Nell's final moments or Louisa May Alcott to describe the loss of Beth March.

In our search for Jane Austen, we often found her in *Northanger Abbey* using the personal pronoun "I," whether telling us of "my heroine" or delivering her ironic opinions. For the most part, that "I" voice is gone from *Sense and Sensibility*. The only direct use of the narrative "I" in this novel appears at the beginning of a passage describing Fanny Dashwood's frustration at having to send a carriage for Marianne and Elinor. I quote this passage at length because it illustrates several features of the narrator:

> I come now to the relation of a misfortune, which about this time befell Mrs. John Dashwood. It so happened that while her two sisters with Mrs. Jennings were first calling on her in Harley-street, another of her acquaintance had dropt in—a circumstance in itself not apparently likely to produce evil to her. But while the imaginations of other people will carry them away to form wrong judgments of our conduct, and to decide on it by slight appearances, one's happiness must in some measure be always at the mercy of chance. In the present instance, this last-arrived lady allowed her fancy so far to outrun truth and probability, that on merely hearing the name of the Miss Dashwoods, and understanding them to be Mr. Dashwood's sisters, she immediately concluded them to be staying in Harley-street; and this misconstruction produced within a day or two afterwards, cards of invitation for them as well as for their brother and sister, to a small musical party at her house. The consequence of which was, that Mrs. John Dashwood was obliged to submit not only to the exceedingly great inconvenience of sending her carriage for the Miss Dashwoods; but, what was still worse, must be subject to

all the unpleasantness of appearing to treat them with attention. . . . The power of disappointing them, it was true, must always be her's. But that was not enough; for when people are determined on a mode of conduct which they know to be wrong, they feel injured by the expectation of any thing better from them. (248–49)

This "I" ironically adopts Fanny's point of view by pretending that the obviously trivial incident of sending a carriage is a "misfortune," an "evil," and an "exceedingly great inconvenience." This same narrator refuses to let readers put Fanny's selfish, snobbish behavior at arm's length from their own. She interrupts this account to talk about "*our* conduct" and ends with a general comment on "*people.*"

The final chapters of *Sense and Sensibility* provide further glimpses of Jane Austen, simply from the emphasis she chooses to give at the end. To the irritation of many critics, Austen chooses to withdraw as narrator rather than give us tender romantic scenes between her two pairs of lovers. When Edward finally has the freedom to propose to Elinor, Austen states matter-of-factly, "How soon he had walked himself into the proper resolution, however, how soon an opportunity of exercising it occurred, in what manner he expressed himself, and how he was received, need not be particularly told" (361). Why need it not particularly be told? Why do we also hear no spoken words between Marianne and Colonel Brandon in the final chapter?

Some have speculated that Austen distances herself from such romantic moments because, as an unmarried woman, she had no familiarity with such scenes and a prudish reluctance to dwell on them. Yet since she displayed no such inhibition in giving us Marianne's passionate outburst to Willoughby or Colonel Brandon's narrative of his attachment to Eliza, one suspects a different reason. Could it be that in a novel exploring the relationship between solitude and society, between intimacy and public life, Austen demonstrates through her respectful silence that there are some emotions and moments understood only in private? She need never back off from dialogue between Sir John and Lady Middleton, for Sir John's idea of intimacy is a noisy crowd. We know that John and Fanny Dashwood will never talk of anything unrelated to money and property. Perhaps Austen leaves readers outside the homes of Edward and Elinor, Colonel Brandon and Marianne, to signal that indoors these two couples have found their own very private domestic happiness—the exchange of ideas and reciprocity of affection possible only to men and women with both sense and sensibility. Her stance as author—respectful of her lovers' privacy—places her in diametric opposition to Nancy Steele, hovering outside the door to eavesdrop on her sister's conversation with Edward. "La! . . . do you think people make love when any body else is by? . . . all I heard was only by listening at the door. . . . And I am sure Lucy would have done just the same by me" (274). Nancy and Lucy Steele will listen through the door; Austen will not.

In the final paragraph of *Sense and Sensibility*, Austen delivers an injunction to her readers: "Between Barton and Delaford, there was that constant communication which strong family affection would naturally dictate;—and among the merits and the happiness of Elinor and Marianne, let it not be ranked as the least considerable, that though sisters, and living almost within sight of each other, they could live without disagreement between themselves, or producing coolness between their husbands" (380). The narrator ranks as considerably important the fact that the sisters remain close to their mother and to each other; their two husbands have warmth between them. The final image is of a world of rational discourse ("constant communication") *and* natural emotion (the "happiness" resulting from the natural dictates of "strong family affection"). Austen ends her novel about the prevalence of cold, selfish, dull people bickering over money and status with the image of a close-knit family.

Even though that final sentence suggests that the main characters lived happily ever after in perfect harmony, Austen does not lapse into saccharine Walt Disney–like writing here. She could have written, "because they were sisters, they lived within sight of each other in harmony and their husbands enjoyed a warm relationship." Instead, she writes "*though* sisters, and living *almost* within sight of each other, they could live *without disagreement* between themselves, or producing *coolness* between their husbands." Just as when we are told "whatever you do, do not think of an elephant" we must think of the elephant, so here by being reminded of disagreement and coolness, we keep those problems with us as we close the pages of the novel. Austen continues to the end to insert into *Sense and Sensibility* her biting perception that the majority of human beings—and their countries—lack the true sense and sensibility needed to live in harmony.

Perhaps in *Sense and Sensibility* more than in any other novel she would write, Austen opines that most men and women are selfish, competitive, dull, greedy, petty, vain, and insufferably insipid. Create your own oasis of family warmth, intellectual stimulation, personal growth, and social altruism, Austen suggests in the conclusion to *Sense and Sensibility*, for little hope exists of reforming or even escaping "the rest of the world."

5

The Liveliness of Your Mind
Pride and Prejudice

Wit is more necessary than beauty; and I think no young woman ugly who has it, and no handsome woman agreeable without it.

   —William Wycherley, *The Country Wife* (1673)

A chief event of life is the day in which we have encountered a mind that startled us.

   —Ralph Waldo Emerson, *Character* (1844)

"My beauty you had early withstood. . . . Now be sincere; did you admire me for my impertinence?"
  "For the liveliness of your mind, I did."

   —Elizabeth and Darcy in *Pride and Prejudice*

With *Pride and Prejudice* finally completed, Jane Austen wrote her sister a mock-apology for its lack of depth. "I had had some fits of disgust. . . . The work is rather too light & bright & sparkling;— it wants shade;—it wants to be stretched out here & there with a long Chapter—of sense, if it could be had, if not of solemn specious nonsense—about something unconnected with the story; an Essay on Writing, a critique on Walter Scott, or the history of Buonaparte—or anything that would form a contrast & bring the reader with increased delight to the playfulness & Epigrammatism of the general stile.—I doubt your quite agreeing with me here—I know your starched Notions" (4 February 1813). Some critics have responded to this as evidence of Jane Austen's insecurity, concluding, "Jane Austen did not appear to have liked *Pride and Prejudice* nearly as much as we have. To her its 'playfulness and epigrammatism' appeared excessive and unrelieved."[1] Instead, I view this letter as yet another instance of Austen's ability to write a tongue-in-cheek disparagement of her work while actually celebrating its power. Austen knew full well that she needed no history of Napoleon or any "solemn specious nonsense" grafted onto her carefully crafted comic novel.

In fact, Austen demonstrates in *Pride and Prejudice* that one can have substance and sense without sacrificing playfulness or pleasure. After all, Jane Austen boasted to Cassandra in that same letter, "I am quite vain enough and well satisfied enough" with that "darling child," *Pride and Prejudice*. Generations of readers have agreed, hailing *Pride and Prejudice* as perhaps Jane Austen's all-time greatest creation. In this supposedly "too light, and bright, and sparkling" novel, Jane Austen introduces a dramatically different kind of young woman. Austen herself claimed that there had never been a heroine like Elizabeth Bennet, calling her "as delightful a creature as ever appeared in print" (29 January 1813). Austen creates a lively, intelligent young woman who thinks, reasons, argues, sparkles, and laughs her way through a series of absurd and unfair social circumstances. Many readers have found the witty Elizabeth to be much like Austen herself, yet such a link may obscure an equally important connection between Austen and the more problematic Mr. Bennet. Austen structures the novel so that we as readers initially share Mr. Bennet's point of view, yet she ultimately severs us—and perhaps herself—from his dangerously attractive cynicism. In *Pride and Prejudice* Austen calls into question the very nature of truth, rejects the notion of love at first sight, challenges notions of class, and explores the proper function of humor. Readers in search of Jane Austen can find in *Pride and Prejudice* her most probing analysis of the power and danger of her own comic art.

Before Austen introduces readers of *Pride and Prejudice* to her highly unconventional heroine, she forces them to question convention itself. The famous ironic opening of *Pride and Prejudice* ("It is a truth universally acknowledged, that a single man in possession of a good fortune, must be in want of a wife") invites us to rewrite the very first sentence of her novel. If we deduce that single women want husbands with fortunes, we simultaneously must conclude that ironic authors want readers with perception. From the start, Austen asks us to approach her whole novel in the spirit of intelligent and subversive questioning.

Too often the first sentence is quoted in isolation rather than in the important context of the paragraph that follows:

> It is a truth universally acknowledged, that a single man
> in possession of a good fortune, must be in want of a wife.
> However little known the feelings or views of such a man

may be on his first entering a neighbourhood, this truth is so well fixed in the minds of the surrounding families, that he is considered as the rightful property of some one or other of their daughters. (3)

Before Austen ever introduces us to Elizabeth Bennet and other key characters in the novel, she calls our attention to the more general process of arriving at "truth."

Self-interested, materialistic inhabitants of this neighborhood, as yet unnamed, instantly seize on a "little known" man of good fortune as "property" for their daughters the minute he arrives in town ("on his first entering the neighbourhood"). Their assumption that the man will belong to "some one or other of their daughters" indicates a society where partners in marriages of convenience seem interchangeable pawns. To hide this reality, these neighbors construct false "universal truths" for all to implant in their minds with "well fixed" glue. *Pride and Prejudice* explores the conformity and blindness of communities, particularly small country villages unaware of their own provincialism. The "neighbourhood" (a term repeated far more frequently in *Pride and Prejudice* than any other Austen novel) transforms rumor and opinion into fact, unthinkingly perpetuating antiquated customs and rigid notions of class.

The neighborhood emerges as remarkably intrusive and unreliable. At varying points in *Pride and Prejudice*, Austen interrupts the story to remind us that private news, whether bad or good, accurate or false, rapidly permeates a neighborhood. A typical sentence reads, "The good news quickly spread through the house; and with proportionate speed through the neighbourhood" (309). Tell one neighbor and the whole town will know: "Mrs. Bennet was privileged to whisper it to Mrs. Philips, and *she* ventured, without any permission, to do the same by all her neighbours in Meryton" (350). This reminds us of Austen's quip in an early letter that Mr. Harvey's marriage "is a great secret, & only known to half the Neighbourhood" (5 September 1796).

In *Pride and Prejudice* Austen delays the tale of her principal characters in order to show how falsehoods start and multiply:

Mr. Bingley was obliged to be in town the following day. . . . [Mrs. Bennet] began to fear that he might be always flying about from one to another, and never settled at Netherfield as he ought to be. Lady Lucas quieted her fears a little by starting the idea of his being gone to London only to get a large party for the ball; and a report soon followed that Mr. Bingley was to bring twelve ladies and seven gentlemen with him to the assembly. The girls grieved over such a number of ladies; but were comforted the day before the ball by hearing, that instead of twelve, he had brought only six with him from London, his five sisters and a cousin. And when the party entered the assembly room, it consisted of only five altogether; Mr. Bingley, his two sisters, the husband of the eldest, and another young man. (10)

A paragraph like this leads some of my undergraduates to observe in dismay, "I've read three chapters of *Pride and Prejudice*, and *nothing's* happening!" The paragraph does indeed describe much ado about nothing. Why, instead of just telling us that Mr. Bingley arrived with two sisters, a brother-in-law, and a friend, does Austen delay the plot to tell us of the town's erroneous expectation of a large party, nineteen people, and other possibilities? As with the opening paragraphs of the novel, Austen calls to our attention the inaccurate and therefore wasteful nature of neighborhood discourse.

The population of Meryton tends to judge others too quickly and categorically, forming opinions collectively rather than individually. At first the crowd admires Mr. Darcy, but "the tide of his popularity" turns (10). "Every body" feels the same. "His character was decided. He was the proudest, most disagreeable man in the world, and every body hoped that he would never come there again," "every body [was] disgusted with his pride," "every body was pleased to think how much they had always disliked Mr. Darcy . . . by every body else Mr. Darcy was condemned as the worst of men," "the general prejudice [was] against Darcy" (11, 78, 138, 226). In contrast, the "universally liked" Wickham quickly earns "the general approbation of the neighbourhood" (90, 206). The verdict on Wickham is unanimous: "the good opinion which *all* the neighbourhood had of him" (285). All Meryton functions as a unit, swayed too easily to label people as bad or good, villainous or angelic. Consider the town's response when Wickham changes from paragon to blackguard: "All Meryton seemed striving to blacken the man, who, but three months before, had been almost an angel of light. . . . Every body declared that he was the wickedest young man in the world; and every body began to find out, that they had always distrusted the appearance of his goodness" (86). Through the ridiculously illogical phrase "began to find out, that they had always," Austen exposes the way we rewrite our pasts to conceal our own mistakes.

Only Jane Bennet stands apart from the crowd, speculating that there must be additional circumstances "of which we can form no idea" and that conclusions might be drawn because "people have perhaps misrepresented" the facts. Rather than making up her mind, Jane determines that it is "impossible for us to conjecture the causes or circumstances": "It is difficult indeed—it is distressing.—One does not know what to think," Jane says. "I beg your pardon;—one knows exactly what to think," replies Elizabeth (86). One would expect that Austen would make her unconventional heroine, Elizabeth, the one to stand apart from the crowd, but she does not. She makes Elizabeth quick to censure and Jane quick to praise. The truth seems to lie somewhere between these two sisters.

Yet our focus never shifts between them, as it does in *Sense and Sensibility*. We rarely hear Jane's voice in this novel *except* in conversation with Elizabeth. The narrator clearly stays with Elizabeth, not Jane. When we do encounter Jane, she is often lying in bed apologizing for her illness, sitting and looking lovely, blushing deeply, consoling others, or trying to resign herself to permanent separation from Mr. Bingley. We never hear Jane talk to Mr. Bingley or Mr. Darcy in the course of *Pride and Prejudice*, an astonishing authorial choice on Austen's part. In contrast, Austen shows us the conversational sparks flying between Elizabeth and virtually every other character in the novel. Rather than easing into a marriage with an easy-mannered man, as Jane does, Elizabeth fights and argues her way from dislike to love in some of the most electrifying romantic scenes in literature. Both Jane and Elizabeth earn happy endings, but as Elizabeth quips, "I am the happiest creature in the world. I am happier even than Jane; she only smiles, I laugh" (383). From the opening chapter of this novel to its final paragraphs, Jane Austen celebrates her witty, energetic, and changing heroine, Elizabeth.

Austen introduces her heroine indirectly in the opening chapter by having the witty Mr. Bennet speak of her with affection ("my little Lizzy") and distinction ("something more . . . than her sisters"), while the scatterbrained Mrs. Bennet puts her down ("not half so handsome as Jane, nor as good-humoured as Lydia"). Much as in *Northanger Abbey* Austen invites our sympathy for Catherine Morland by showing her waiting for a dance partner in Bath, so in *Pride and Prejudice* she elicits our response to Elizabeth by having her slighted by Mr. Darcy ("She is tolerable; but not handsome enough to tempt *me*"). Austen keeps the camera eye not on Jane happily dancing with Mr. Bingley but on Elizabeth sitting on the sidelines and overhearing humiliating conversations.

No wallower, Elizabeth transforms rejection into amusement: "Mr. Darcy walked off; and Elizabeth remained with no very cordial feelings towards him. She told the story however with great spirit among her friends; for she had a lively, playful disposition, which delighted in any thing ridiculous" (12). Elizabeth Bennet is the first Austen heroine to share her creator's love of narration ("She told the story") and wit. Elizabeth's response to this moment at the dance resembles Austen's own breezy tone in her letters when describing a dance: "I do not think I was very much in request–. People were rather apt not to ask me till they could not help it; . . . There was one Gentleman . . . who I was told wanted very much to be introduced to me;–but as he did not want it quite enough to take much trouble in effecting it, We never could bring it about" (9 January 1799). Elsewhere in her letters to her sister, Austen seems grateful to disagreeable neighbors for serving as comic fodder to her imagination: "Whenever I fall into misfortune, how many jokes it ought to furnish to my acquaintance in general, or I shall die dreadfully in their debt for entertainment" (22 January 1799). A niece's description of her aunt Jane Austen's "playful talk" and "playfulness of spirits" could apply equally well to Elizabeth Bennet, as could a nephew's comment that his aunt Jane's "unusually quick sense of the ridiculous led her to play with all the commonplaces of everyday life, whether as regarded places or things."[2] Humor can animate: two nieces recall that Jane Austen "would suddenly burst out laughing, jump up and run across the room" or "rub her hands, laugh to herself and run up to her room" to write.[3] Like her creator, Elizabeth Bennet delights in studying characters and can be moved by her observations to run and laugh. There is something sharp and impertinent about Elizabeth that makes us think she could, like Austen, write in a private letter that a neighbor's wife was "discovered to be everything that the Neighbourhood could wish her, silly & cross as well as extravagant"(18 December 1798).

How interesting that the sneering Miss Bingley condemns Elizabeth Bennet's lively expression with the same tone that some biographers even to this day have used to censure Jane Austen's appearance as presented in Cassandra's portrait: "I must confess that I never could see any beauty in her. Her face is too thin; her complexion has no brilliancy; and her features are not at all handsome. Her nose wants character . . . and as for her eyes, which have sometimes been called so fine, I never could perceive any thing extraordinary in them. They have a sharp, shrewish look, which I do not like at all; and in her air altogether, there is a self-sufficiency without fashion,

which is intolerable" (271). Now consider a recent critic's description of Jane Austen's portrait: "Cassandra's drawing [of Jane Austen]
shows a woman more sharp-featured than appealing: the eyes are
large and beautiful, glancing keenly . . . and the mouth itself looks
small and mean. She looks like a peevish hamster. . . . Her nose was
narrow and possibly rather long."[4] Just as Miss Bingley criticizes
Elizabeth for possessing "self-sufficiency," "abominable . . . conceited
independence," and "impertinence," so biographers at times have found
Austen's prepossessing appearance disconcerting (271, 35–36).

Liveliness defines Elizabeth Bennet's character throughout *Pride
and Prejudice*, from the first description of her "lively, playful disposition" to our final picture of her lively imagination, spirits, talents,
and speech (12). Elizabeth uses a "lively, sportive" way of talking to
Mr. Darcy, who "wants liveliness" and admits himself attracted to her
precisely because of her "liveliness of mind" (387–88, 325, 380). This
sets Elizabeth Bennet apart from other Austen heroines. In *Northanger
Abbey* Catherine Morland is eager but too dense to share the lively
Henry Tilney's intellectual repartee, and in *Sense and Sensibility* Elinor
Dashwood cautions Edward Ferrars against mistaking Marianne's
sparkling eyes for liveliness: "Gaiety never was a part of *my* character," says Edward. "Nor do I think it a part of Marianne's. . . . I should
hardly call her a lively girl," replies Elinor. (*SS*, 93). Marianne is too
melancholy, Elinor too reserved to be called lively, and the men they
marry are both in search of animation. Only in *Pride and Prejudice* does
Austen let her heroine speak with unrepressed wit. No wonder she
had trouble imagining any reader disliking her Elizabeth: "how I shall
be able to tolerate those who do not like *her* at least, I do not know"
(29 January 1813).

Liveliness allows Elizabeth Bennet to survive social circumstances
full of as much ennui and pettiness as any dinner party in *Sense and
Sensibility*. Sir John and Lady Middleton and John and Fanny Dashwood
would feel at home in the neighborhood of Meryton, where the shallow Miss Bingley ironically complains of "the insipidity and yet the
noise; the nothingness and yet the self-importance of all these people!"
(27). On a twenty-four-mile carriage ride with the tedious Sir William
Lucas and a daughter "as empty-headed as himself," Elizabeth has to
listen to the conversation of two people with "nothing to say that
could be worth hearing" offering "about as much delight as the rattle
of the chaise" (152).

Unlike Marianne Dashwood, Elizabeth does not succumb to
despair at this sort of inanity. Elizabeth survives such conversation

by rallying her spirits, willing herself into better humor, and finding delight in absurdities. Even in the middle of Mr. Collins's longwinded marriage proposal to her, Elizabeth is "near laughing" at the ludicrous idea of his being run away with by his feelings (105). Throughout *Pride and Prejudice* Austen shows us "Elizabeth's spirits soon rising to playfulness again" (380). Personal disappointment also can be overcome through humor, as when she discovers Wickham's absence after she had dressed with special care for a ball: "She . . . turned away with a degree of ill humour, which she could not wholly surmount. . . . But Elizabeth was not formed for ill-humour; and though every prospect of her own was destroyed for the evening, it could not dwell long on her spirits. . . . she was soon able to make a voluntary transition to the oddities of her cousin" (90). The delightful absurdity of her cousin Mr. Collins again helps distract her from disappointment about Wickham's absence.

Elizabeth's cheerful disposition helps her cope with change. Because "it was her business to be satisfied—and certainly her temper to be happy," she can adjust to news that her much-anticipated trip to the Lakes has been canceled (239). When the haughty Miss Bingley and Mrs. Hurst snub her, Elizabeth counters their rudeness with laughter, repartee, and an energetic exit:

> Then taking the disengaged arm of Mr. Darcy, [Miss Bingley] left Elizabeth to walk by herself. The path just admitted three. Mr. Darcy felt their rudeness and immediately said.—
>
> "This walk is not wide enough for our party. We had better go into the avenue."
>
> But Elizabeth, who had not the least inclination to remain with them, laughingly answered,
>
> "No, no; stay where you are.—You are charmingly group'd, and appear to uncommon advantage. The picturesque would be spoilt by admitting a fourth. Good bye."
>
> She then ran gaily off, rejoicing as she rambled about, in the hope of being at home again in a day or two. (53)

Throughout *Pride and Prejudice* Elizabeth jumps, springs, rejoices, smiles, and laughs, causing conventional young women to gasp in horror. Miss Bingley and Mrs. Hurst find her shockingly unladylike. Mrs. Bennet admits that even though Elizabeth is twenty, she has maintained her girlhood right to scamper, ramble, and "run on in a wild manner" (42). Austen's portrayal of Elizabeth with muddy petticoats and a face glowing with exertion defies the vision of a young woman portrayed in conduct books of the time. Elizabeth Bennet seems not to have read Hannah More's *Essays on Various Subjects, Principally Designed for Young Ladies* (1777): "That bold, independent, enterprising spirit, which is so much admired in boys, should not, when it happens to discover itself in the other sex, be encouraged, but suppressed."[5]

Elizabeth Bennet also ignores Hannah More's advice that "Girls should be taught to give up opinions betimes, and not pertinaciously carry on a dispute, even if they should know themselves in the right. . . . They should acquire a submissive temper and a forbearing spirit."[6] Rather than submitting, Elizabeth faces adversity with pertinacity and courage. When she arrives at Lady Catherine's formidable mansion, "Elizabeth's courage did not fail her" and she enters "without trepidation" (161). As Elizabeth puts it, "There is a stubbornness about me that never can bear to be frightened at the will of others. My courage always rises with every attempt to intimidate me" (174).

This courage also allows her to face her own mistakes and her own sorrows. When Elizabeth confronts real pain—her sister Lydia's disgrace, her sister Jane's heartache, her own feelings of mortification and self-reproach—she can no longer laugh her problems away, but her dauntless spirits do help her ward off depression. She refuses to let nostalgia or regret paralyze her, announcing that her philosophy is, "Think only of the past as the remembrance gives you pleasure" (369). Unlike Marianne Dashwood, who courted misery and nourished grief, Elizabeth refuses "to increase her vexations, by dwelling on them . . . to fret over unavoidable evils, or augment them by anxiety" (232). Optimism, laughter, and courage seem the best medicines for keeping Elizabeth Bennet resilient, ready to go forward and encounter more of the world's folly and injustice.

Yet bold liveliness has its limits—and dangers. We can foretell Elizabeth Bennet's vulnerability if we remember that the charming scoundrel Willoughby in *Sense and Sensibility* is described as "very lively," with a lively imagination, lively spirits, and lively manner, and that the sensual Eliza Brandon is "so lively" before she falls into prostitution (*SS,* 50, 206). Austen will return to this theme in both *Mansfield Park* and *Emma* by presenting seductively attractive characters (Mary and Henry Crawford, Frank Churchill) possessing a store of liveliness to mask a shortage of steady principle. Just as Henry Tilney's lively wit in *Northanger Abbey* makes him better able to banter than to see life clearly, so Elizabeth Bennet's playful disposition can at times keep her from confronting the truth. Liveliness can be energy, brilliance, and animation, a zest for life; it also can connote a lightness and ease not altogether commendable. When confronting a terminal illness, would one want a lively nurse? Phrases that appear elsewhere in Austen such as "lively and . . . thoughtless," "lively impudence," "talents for the light and lively," or "lively, and . . . unthinking" suggest that Austen thought it possible to have a "too lively mind" (*NA*, 152; *E,* 369; *MP,* 350, 69).

Often in her novels Jane Austen uses minor characters as exaggerated versions of her protagonists' flaws, as if allowing them to view themselves in a distorted amusement park mirror. Just as the fallen Eliza stands as a warning to Marianne in *Sense and Sensibility,* so in *Pride and Prejudice* the "naturally lively" Lydia Bennet illustrates to Elizabeth that lively spirits, a sense of youthful playfulness, and the courage to defy authority are not enough unless governed by an educated mind, a loving, generous heart, and a moral conscience (284).

Austen goes to great lengths to draw parallels between Elizabeth and Lydia Bennet. The youngest of the five Bennet sisters, Lydia has "youth, health, and good humour," qualities she shares with Elizabeth (283). If Elizabeth is "almost wild," Lydia is off the charts (35). Like some of the hoydens in Austen's adolescent sketches, Lydia displays a "wild giddiness," "wild volatility," "exuberant spirits," and "all too natural . . . high animal spirits" (213, 231, 45). She delights in unladylike behavior: "Dear me! We had such a good piece of fun the other day at Colonel Foster's. . . . What do you think we did? We dressed up Chamberlayne in woman's clothes, on purpose to pass for a lady,—only think what fun! . . . Lord, how I laughed! . . . And then when we came away it was such fun! . . . And then we were so merry all the way home! We talked and laughed so loud" (221–22). Energy in young women may be refreshing, as in Catherine Morland's noisy and wild escapades on the green slopes, Marianne's outdoor rambles, and Elizabeth's brisk walks. But Lydia is little more than a silly, self-indulgent, obstreperous girl: "Lydia was Lydia still; untamed, unabashed, wild, noisy, and fearless" (315).

What are we to think of Lydia's fearlessness? Like Elizabeth, Lydia is undaunted by authority or convention. Lydia has a "sort of natural self-consequence" and is "self-willed" with a "disdain of all restraint" and an "ungovernable" temper (45, 231, 385). She is "absolutely resolved" to stay with Wickham, married or unmarried, because it pleases her to do so (322). Both Elizabeth and Lydia give their opinions decidedly for such young women and display a rebelliousness, irreverence, and audacity. We may admire Elizabeth for asserting herself against the dictatorial Lady Catherine, but what do we think when Lydia cavalierly disregards duty, honor, and gratitude in order to seek her own instant happiness?

Austen reinforces the parallels between Elizabeth and Lydia by showing them both attracted to the same seemingly charming man: Captain Wickham. "Whatever he said, was said well," Elizabeth thinks of Wickham, "and whatever he did, done gracefully" (84). Similarly, Lydia insists that Wickham "did every thing best in the world" (318). When Elizabeth first meets Wickham, she quickly shares with this handsome stranger her verdict on Mr. Darcy ("I think him very disagreeable") and Lady Catherine ("she is an arrogant, conceited woman"), thus joining her youngest sister in acting with a "total want of propriety" (77, 84, 198). When Wickham seems surprised by her vehemence and bluntness, Elizabeth boasts that she would deliver those opinions in almost any house in the neighborhood. Elizabeth comes to realize the danger of such frankness when she hears her own thoughts presented in Lydia's voice:

> Lydia laughed and said . . . "There is no danger of Wickham's marrying Mary King. . . . I will answer for it he never cared three straws about her. Who could about such a nasty little freckled thing?"
> Elizabeth was shocked to think that, however incapable of such coarseness of *expression* herself, the coarseness of the *sentiment* was little other than her own breast had formerly harboured and fancied liberal. (220)

Elizabeth's shock here and elsewhere comes from recognizing a likeness in thinking between herself and her profligate younger sister. Like Lydia, Elizabeth has an unladylike tendency to be playful and teasing. Elizabeth speaks "laughingly" and makes glib comments in the early chapters of *Pride and Prejudice* that sound Lydia-like: "Did not you think, Mr. Darcy, that I expressed myself uncommonly well just now, when I was teasing Colonel Forster to give us a ball at Meryton?" (53, 24). *Both* Elizabeth and Lydia dearly love a laugh.

Austen distinguishes between the two by using the word "fun" only in association with Lydia, not Elizabeth. Lydia titters, "we had such fun," "it was such fun," "such a good piece of fun," and "very good fun" even when describing her own disgraceful behavior. A relatively new noun in Austen's day, *fun* connoted cheating and clowning and earned Dr. Samuel Johnson's condemnation as a "low cant word" to describe "high merriment" and "frolicksome delight."[7]

Lydia also laughs with as much readiness as a hyena. "You will laugh when you know where I am gone," she writes her friend after taking off with Wickham, "and I cannot help laughing myself at your surprise . . . I can hardly write for laughing" (221–22). In her own letters Austen had mocked the hyperbolic expression, "'I could die of laughter at it,' as they used to say at school" (1 September 1796), and she gives this clichéd utterance to the giddy Lydia: "Lord! how I laughed! . . . I thought I should have died . . . I was ready to die of laughter" (221–22). Just as Elizabeth is constantly urged by her more sober older sister and by her aunt to respond to their questions seriously, so Lydia seems to take life as little more than a joke. Lydia carries this to an incredible extreme, taking not even her own future or the feelings of her family seriously: "What a good joke it will be! . . . Good gracious! when I went away, I am sure I had no more idea of being married till I came back again! though I thought it would be very good fun if I was" (291, 316). Unlike Elizabeth, who feels genuine sorrow, Lydia seems impervious to any emotions other than impatience and "fun." Austen's readers would have recollected a passage in Ecclesiastes: "Sorrow is better than laughter; for by the sadness of the countenance the heart is made better. The heart of the wise is in the house of mourning, but the heart of fools is in the house of mirth" (7:3–4). Elizabeth had previously defended laughter against the grave Mr. Darcy's attack on people "whose first object in life is a joke," but here in the figure of her own sister stands just such a heartless creature (57). Laughter has its place: and that place is not first.

Elizabeth recognizes the cause of her youngest sister's folly: "She has never been taught to think on serious subjects. . . . She has been given up to nothing but amusement and vanity. She has been allowed to dispose of her time in the most idle and frivolous manner" (283). Those strong words of Austen's Elizabeth Bennet about her sister sound surprisingly like Mary Wollstonecraft lamenting the state of degradation to which women are reduced: "The grand source of female folly and vice has ever appeared to me to arise from narrowness of mind. . . . Pleasure is the business of woman's life, according to the present modification of society, and while it continues to be so, little can be expected from such weak beings."[8] Austen's narrow-minded, uneducated Lydia Bennet has become idle and frivolous because she has been indulged by her mother, neglected by her father, and undervalued by society. Lydia is careless, ignorant, and vain, acting with impudence and imprudence.

In fact, this "silliest" girl in the county has such an "ignorance and emptiness of her mind" that she is literally "thoughtless, thoughtless Lydia" (29, 231, 292). It is easy to imagine Lydia Bennet today, skipping school in order to flirt shamelessly at a shopping mall in between credit card purchases and snacks paid for by others: "We mean to treat you all . . . but you must lend us the money, for we have just spent ours at the shop. . . . Look here, I have bought this bonnet. I do not think it is very pretty, but I thought I might as well buy it as not. . . . Have you seen any pleasant men? Have you had any flirting?" (219, 221). Time moves slowly for a young woman with no inner resources: "Nothing less than a dance on Tuesday, could have made such a Friday, Saturday, Sunday, and Monday endurable" (88).

Not only her head but also her heart seems vacant. Not choosy about her dance partner, she seems ready to have any man who will flatter her vanity. Like many a bride-to-be today preoccupied with expensive wedding arrangements rather than the impending marriage, so Lydia on her wedding day worries only about whether Wickham will wear his blue coat (319). When she returns home as Mrs. Wickham, she ignores the disgraceful circumstances of her marriage and the pain she has caused others. She gloats about preceding her "old maid" sisters into the dining room: "Ah! Jane, I take your place now, and you must go lower, because I am a married woman" (317). Rather than facing the fact that she has married a profligate man who stays with her only because he is paid to do so, Lydia milks her moment of wedded importance: "Oh! mamma, do the people here abouts know I am married to-day? I was afraid they might not; . . . so I . . . took off my glove, and let my hand just rest upon the window frame [to show] the ring, and then I bowed and smiled like any thing" (316). In direct contrast to the loyal, affectionate Elizabeth, Lydia displays selfish indifference to her family and inattentiveness to her sisters' feelings.

Although Austen does not discuss religion in *Pride and Prejudice* as directly as she will in the later *Mansfield Park*, she seems to use Lydia Bennet to reveal the danger of a young woman having no moral principles, no conscience, and no belief in a higher power. Lydia's love of gambling—she is "extremely fond of lottery-tickets," "talk[s] incessantly of the lottery," and loves making bets—and Wickham's extensive gaming debts suggest they are fortune's fools, moving about restlessly without a higher purpose (76, 84). Lydia blithely uses the Lord's name in vain: "Lord how tired I am!" "Lord, how ashamed I should be of not being married before three and twenty! . . . Lord! how I should like to be married before any of you . . . Lord! how I laughed!" "Oh, Lord! yes" (103, 221, 317).

Why might Austen give us two Bennet sisters described as wild, bold, and laughing, one to admire and the other to censure? Perhaps, as Claudia Johnson suggests, Lydia serves for the reader as "a decoy who attracts the disapproval to which Elizabeth herself could otherwise be subject."[9] Austen's readers can accept Elizabeth's remarkable unconventionality, impertinence, impropriety, and violation of conduct-book standards because *compared to Lydia* she seems quite restrained, feminine, and virtuous. We see that Elizabeth, despite her muddy petticoats, self-confidence, and love of laughter, has both sense and sensibility, qualities woefully lacking in the unintelligent, unfeeling, and "absolutely uncontrouled" Lydia (231).

Yet how can we blame Lydia for her behavior when she has succeeded so marvelously in becoming like her mother? Much as she devoted many pages of *Sense and Sensibility* to showing the similarities between Marianne Dashwood and her equally romantic and imprudent mother, so Jane Austen makes it abundantly clear in *Pride and Prejudice* that "dear Lydia" is her mother's favorite daughter. Repetitions of words link daughter to mother. For example, the only times in *Pride and Prejudice* in which Austen uses *distracted* and *merry* are in conjunction with these two unthinkingly happy-go-lucky women:

"I should have gone quite distracted." (Lydia, 319)

"I shall go distracted." (Mrs. Bennet, 378)

"We were so merry all the way home!" (Lydia, 222)

"How merry we shall be together!" (Mrs. Bennet, 306)

Like her mother, Lydia has been raised to be a creature of appetite and pleasure without virtue or reason, and Austen leads us to suspect that the cycle will continue if the uneducated, unreformed, and unrepentant Lydia ever has daughters of her own.

Much as Lydia shows off her ring to passersby, so Mrs. Bennet focuses on the wedding clothes ("a privilege without which her marriage would scarcely seem valid"), boasts of Lydia's marriage to the whole neighborhood, and laments that the newspaper write-up is so brief (310). Her comments echo Jane Austen's joking remark in a letter, "One may as well be single if the Wedding is not to be in print" (late February 1815). Just as Lady Middleton and Fanny Dashwood argued over the heights of their sons in *Sense and Sensibility*, so Mrs. Bennet and her peers compete over their ability to land propertied husbands for their daughters.

But Austen sees to it that her readers understand rather than merely scorn Lydia and her mother. Denied education and power by society, Mrs. Bennet and Mrs. Wickham are left at the financial mercy of irresponsible husbands. Mrs. Bennet articulates the economic powerlessness of women when she notes of her husband's passive acceptance of the entail, "I am sure if I had been you, I should have tried long ago to do something or other about it" (62). In the last letter she writes in *Pride and Prejudice,* Lydia shrewdly uses her connections to try *to do something or other about* getting her feckless husband an income:

> "MY DEAR LIZZY,
>
> "I wish you joy. . . . It is a great comfort to have you so rich, and when you have nothing else to do, I hope you will think of us. I am sure Wickham would like a place at court very much, and I do not think we shall have quite money enough to live upon without some help. Any place would do, of about three or four hundred a year." (386)

Austen shows that despite their shallowness, Mrs. Bennet and Lydia at least take action and try to survive in economic circumstances stacked against them.

Just as "Lydia was Lydia still" at the end of the novel, unreformed and unimproved, so Mrs. Bennet remains exactly the same woman of "mean understanding, little information, and uncertain temper" whom we met at the beginning (315, 5). In one of the few narrative intrusions in *Pride and Prejudice,* Austen inserts her "I" voice to lament Mrs. Bennet's inability to grow: "I wish I could say [that she became] a sensible, amiable, well-informed woman for the rest of her life," but in fact Mrs. Bennet remains still "nervous and invariably silly" (385).

Like Mrs. Bennet and Lydia, Mary Bennet never grows or changes in the course of this novel. Yet her faults are profoundly different from theirs. "In consequence of being the only plain one" in the family, Mary spends her time practicing the piano, "always impatient for display" of her talent (25). She reads prose works so she can extract sayings of "thread-bare morality" for the edification of others (60). If Lydia is too flighty, Mary is too heavy: "Mary piqued herself upon the solidity of her reflections" (20). If we accept Blake's notion that to generalize is to be an idiot, then Mary's abstractions are another form of idiocy in a book filled with fools. Why talk generically of "virtue in a female" when scandal affects your youngest sister (289)? Mary only gives the illusion of having sense and sensibility; in fact, she has neither. Her musical performances display her lack of taste and genius, and her pompous reactions to her sisters demonstrate her dearth of compassion and empathy. Reading brings no wisdom, as Mary refers to pride and vanity without recognizing her own. Her remarks in fact plagiarize Hester Chapone's *Letters on the Improvement of the Mind* (1773), one of the many conduct books Austen debunked throughout her juvenilia.[10] In addition, Mary's comment about a woman's reputation being "no less brittle than it is beautiful" steals from Mr. Villars's insistence in a Fanny Burney novel that "the reputation of a woman . . . is, at once, the most beautiful and most brittle of all human things."[11]

Perhaps Austen includes the prose-reading, pontificating Mary Bennet to prevent any reader from reaching easy conclusions about how to keep young women from following in Lydia's wild footsteps. Mary stands as a reminder to readers that the best way to raise daughters is not to feed them a diet of essays, conduct books, and sermons, forbid them from reading fanciful novels and lyrical poems, admonish them to avoid wit and laughter, and teach them to acquire fine arts for display rather than for their souls.

Again, Austen tempers her portrait of a female fool. She places Mary as the middle daughter out of five, thus excluded from both the close affection between Elizabeth and Jane and the camaraderie between the giddy Lydia and Kitty; she is the favorite of neither parent. Is it her fault that even though she "worked hard" at her music she has no innate talent (25)? Is it her fault that she is plain? What bad *luck* (a word repeated throughout this novel) that she was not first or second in line in the Bennet family to be married and that Elizabeth's mortifying rejection of Mr. Collins caused him to switch his "affections" to Charlotte Lucas. Mary actually *liked* Mr. Collins (she prizes his letters) and probably would have made an excellent wife for him. Perhaps Austen tells us of Mary's favorable response to Mr. Collins ("Mary might have been prevailed on to accept him") to remind us that coincidences, accidents, and sheer luck often influence just which women will capture those single men with large fortunes looking for wives (124).

Austen's final paragraph about this middle Bennet sister shows Mary continuing to moralize about others rather than developing herself. Her punishment is to be stuck permanently as the only daughter at home, forced therefore to keep Mrs. Bennet company. Mary's only comfort is that "she was no longer mortified by comparisons between her sisters' beauty and her own," a parting reminder from Austen that in a culture valuing appearance, Mary's destiny might have been different had she been blessed with a pretty face (386).

The fretful Kitty, who seems to have inherited her mother's frenzied nerves and Lydia's folly, has at least a chance of improvement, we are told, because she spends time with Elizabeth and Jane: "Kitty, to her very material advantage, spent the chief of her time with her two elder sisters. In society so superior to what she had generally known, her improvement was great. . . . she became, by proper attention and management, less irritable, less ignorant, and less insipid" (385). Give a young woman guidance ("management") and education and she can make great improvement, Austen suggests.

Austen frequently sets the "two elder sisters" apart from the rest of Meryton. When the regiment of officers leaves town, only Elizabeth and Jane respond sensibly: "All the young ladies in the neighbourhood were drooping apace. The dejection was almost universal. The elder Miss Bennets alone were still able to eat, drink, and sleep" (229). They are without question Mrs. Bennet's "two most deserving daughters," both possessing intelligence, compassion, virtue, and fortitude (385). Unlike the contrast Austen developed between Elinor and Marianne in *Sense and Sensibility*, Jane and Elizabeth join forces to conceal their sufferings and to keep their disordered family from further harm. Trying unsuccessfully but valiantly to act as surrogate parents, "Elizabeth had frequently united with Jane in an endeavour to check the imprudence of Catherine and Lydia" (213). In many ways, they function as husband and wife–like soul mates. Their close relationship perhaps reflects Jane Austen's own lifelong partnership with Cassandra. As a relative observed, "No one was equal to Jane in Cassandra's eyes. And Jane looked up to Cassandra as one far wiser and better than herself. They were as their mother said 'wedded to each other.'"[12] Austen's focus in *Pride and Prejudice* on two sisters' candid, animated, and supportive conversation may reflect her own joy in sharing with Cassandra "the pleasures of Friendship, of unreserved Conversation, of similarity of Taste & Opinions" (1 July 1808).[13] Of the 150 surviving Jane Austen letters, over 90 are addressed to Cassandra. Jane Austen clearly considers her sister a sympathetic, intelligent listener and acknowledges her superiority in a way reminiscent of Elizabeth Bennet's praise of Jane: "my only fear is of your being so agreeable, so much to [Mrs. Knight's] taste, as to make her wish to keep you with her for ever" (7 January 1807).

Like a married couple silently catching each other's eyes in public in order to find strength and comfort, "Jane and Elizabeth looked at each other" when stuck in a public place with the noisy, imprudent Lydia (221). At another point, a "glance from Jane invited Elizabeth to follow her upstairs" (116). Elizabeth admits that during hard times, she wants nothing better than to be with her sister: "I was very uncomfortable, I may say unhappy. And with no one to speak to, of what I felt, no Jane to comfort me and say that I had not been so very weak and vain and nonsensical as I knew I had! Oh! how I wanted you!" (226). At several points in this novel, Jane and Elizabeth rationally and feelingly discuss what action to take, using each other as a sounding board. When Elizabeth is away from home and news breaks of Lydia's disgrace, Jane deeply feels the loss of a partner to share the sorrow and plan the future: "I am truly glad, dearest Lizzy, that you have been spared something of these distressing scenes; but now as the first shock is over, shall I own that I long for your return?" (275). Elizabeth responds by feeling "wild to be at home—to hear, to see, to be upon the spot, *to share with Jane* in the cares that must now fall wholly upon her, in a family so deranged" (280; my italics). Austen makes sure readers not only hear extensive dialogue between the sisters but also are told that their reunion means "half the night spent in conversation" (374).

Too often labeled just a "courtship novel," *Pride and Prejudice* contains many passages demonstrating that Jane and Elizabeth care deeply about each other. Austen fills this novel with phrases such as "her thoughts naturally flew to her sister" or "the happiness of a most beloved sister" (262, 190). Jane's illness prompts Elizabeth's four-mile walk through the mud, and Elizabeth rejects Darcy in part because of his efforts to separate Jane from the man she loves. Throughout, Elizabeth maintains Jane's superiority, viewing her as "all loveliness and goodness" with "her understanding excellent, her mind improved, and her manners captivating" (186). In turn, Jane is quick to see why the wealthy Mr. Darcy would want to marry Elizabeth because of "the strong sisterly partiality which made admiration of Elizabeth appear perfectly natural" (224). Rather than competing, they love each other wholeheartedly: for example, instead of stewing about the fact that Jane had more dance partners and received more compliments than she did, Elizabeth "instantly read her feelings . . . and every thing else gave way before the hope of Jane's being in the fairest way for happiness" (95). At another point, Elizabeth "felt Jane's pleasure" (12). Austen emphasizes the sisters' reciprocity of affection: "Each felt for the other" (334). Much as she ended *Sense and Sensibility* with a description of the closeness between two sisters, so Austen tells us in the closing chapter of *Pride and Prejudice* that "Jane and Elizabeth, in addition to every other source of happiness, were within thirty miles of each other" (385).

Why, then, if we have two intelligent, compassionate women who love each other do we not have two equal heroines? The first conversation Austen includes between Jane and Elizabeth answers that question:

> "I was very much flattered by his asking me to dance a second time. I did not expect such a compliment."
>
> "Did not you? *I* did for you. But that is one great difference between us. . . . He could not help seeing that you were about five times as pretty as every other woman in the room. . . . Well, he certainly is very agreeable, and I give you leave to like him. You have liked many a stupider person."
>
> "Dear Lizzy!"
>
> "Oh! you are a great deal too apt you know, to like people in general. You never see a fault in any body. All the world are good and agreeable in your eyes. I never heard you speak ill of a human being in my life." (14)

We cannot help but find Elizabeth more compelling, and we already know that the witty Mr. Bennet prefers her. Elizabeth is droll, self-deprecating, perceptive, and loving. And, as Austen expressed it in a letter, Elizabeth is more delightful than previous heroines, different from anything that "ever appeared in print." We may have encountered sweet, angelic, beautiful, modest Jane Bennets before in literature, but no one like Elizabeth. It is not surprising that Elizabeth troubled some in Austen's era, who felt Jane was the novel's true heroine. Author Mary Mussell Mitford, for instance, deplored Elizabeth Bennet for possessing an "entire want of taste" and for being "so pert, so worldly a heroine."[14]

Jane Bennet is too good to be true in two senses of the phrase—both in the conventional sense that she does not ring true to imperfect readers and also in the sense that her goodness keeps her from seeing the truth. Elizabeth views her older sister as perfect in an imperfect world: "My dear Jane! You are too good. Your sweetness and disinterestedness are really angelic. . . . *You* wish to think all the world respectable, and are hurt if I speak ill of anybody. *I* only want to think *you* perfect" (134). Like the naive Catherine Morland who is so "warped by an innate principle of general integrity" that she fails for hundreds of pages to detect Isabella's dissembling manners and mercenary ulterior motives, the "honestly blind" but well-intentioned Jane Bennet persists for an unbelievably long time in finding the odious Miss Bingley and Mrs. Hurst charming, pleasing, friendly women (*NA,* 219; *PP,* 14). "Caroline is incapable of willfully deceiving anyone," Jane insists of the blatantly duplicitous Miss Bingley (119). Elizabeth quickly sees through this sneering, backstabbing woman because Elizabeth has "more quickness of observation and less pliancy of temper than her sister" (15).

Elizabeth has more "quickness" not only in terms of keenness of perception but also in terms of speed. It takes her one moment, not scores of chapters, to reject Miss Bingley and Mrs. Hurst. She does not share the sweet, steady Jane's cautious approach: "I would wish not to be hasty in censuring any one," Jane calmly states (14). Elizabeth's prejudice stems primarily from her tendency to jump to conclusions as quickly as she jumps over stiles. In a race, one definitely would bet on Elizabeth: "Away ran the girls . . . Jane, who was not so light, nor so much in the habit of running as Elizabeth, soon lagged behind" (301). Elizabeth has to learn to form her own judgments more slowly and cautiously. "All I can promise you . . . is not to be in a hurry," she eventually tells her aunt (145).

Jane is calmer than Elizabeth and fights against strong emotions like anger. The phrase "pliancy of temper" suggests the narrator's ambivalence about Jane Bennet (15). Certainly one would not wish to have a rigid, unyielding, utterly stubborn temper, but Jane's pliancy allows her to be too easily bent, influenced, and manipulated by others. She is constantly described as "sweet" and "mild," adjectives suggesting goodness but also a kind of feminine weakness. We cannot imagine Jane standing up so boldly to Lady Catherine, as Elizabeth does. Instead of pertinaciously fighting her adversaries with wit, Jane pliantly withdraws, stays composed, blames herself, and suffers stoically in silence, for "whatever she felt she was desirous of concealing" (129).

Interestingly, Austen shows us that the truth lies somewhere between Jane's steady faith in universal human goodness and Elizabeth's quick rush to total condemnation. When Elizabeth hears of Charlotte Lucas's engagement to Mr. Collins, she blasts her friend:

> "Charlotte's marriage . . . is unaccountable! in every view it is unaccountable!"

"My dear Lizzy, do not give way to such feelings as these. They will ruin your happiness. You do not make allowance enough for difference of situation and temper. Consider Mr. Collins's respectability, and Charlotte's prudent, steady character. Remember that she is one of a large family; that as to fortune, it is a most eligible match; and be ready to believe for everybody's sake, that she may feel something like regard and esteem for our cousin."

". . . My dear Jane, Mr. Collins is a conceited, pompous, narrow-minded, silly man; you know he is, as well as I do; and you must feel, as well as I do, that the woman who marries him, cannot have a proper way of thinking. . . . You shall not, for the sake of one individual, change the meaning of principle and integrity, nor endeavour to persuade yourself or me, that selfishness is prudence, and insensibility of danger, security for happiness."

"I must think your language too strong in speaking of both," replied Jane, . . . "But enough of this." (135–36)

Elizabeth speaks categorically, accusing Charlotte of sacrificing "*every* better feeling to worldly advantage." In fact, readers see that the unromantic, plain-faced Charlotte Lucas has made a practical choice with her eyes open, seeing an establishment with Mr. Collins as her "pleasantest preservative from want" (122–23). She pursues this marriage, setting out "to meet him accidentally in the lane" and making an effort to flatter him at the right time (121). Once married, the "sensible, intelligent . . . prudent, steady" Charlotte develops her own coping strategy—encouraging Mr. Collins to garden so he will be out of the house and taking the worst room of the house so he will not bother her there (135). Jane may be wrong to think any regard or esteem can exist between this couple, but Elizabeth is too vehement in her scorn. Jane is in danger of blind optimism; Elizabeth of disillusionment.

Austen uses the husbands of Mrs. Bennet's "two most deserving daughters" to explore notions of gentlemanly behavior, a recurring theme in all six of her novels. Like the contrast Austen sets up between Elizabeth and Jane—Elizabeth quick to censure everyone whereas Jane finds only goodness—Mr. Darcy and his friend Mr. Bingley respond in radically different ways to the same social scene: "Between [Bingley] and Darcy there was a very steady friendship, in spite of a great opposition of character. . . . The manner in which they spoke of the Meryton assembly was sufficiently characteristic. Bingley had never met with pleasanter people or prettier girls in his life; every body had been most kind and attentive to him, there had been no formality, no stiffness, he had soon felt acquainted with all the room; and as to Miss Bennet, he could not conceive an angel more beautiful. Darcy, on the contrary, had seen a collection of people in whom there was little beauty and no fashion, for none of whom he had felt the smallest interest, and from none received either attention or pleasure" (16). Both are blind: Bingley sees no evil because of his easy, open temper; Darcy sees no good because of his overweening pride.

Like Mary Bennet ironically uttering reflections about vanity and pride without recognizing her own, Mr. Darcy speaks in humorless abstractions: "Nothing is more deceitful . . . than the appearance of humility. It is often only carelessness of opinion, and sometimes an indirect boast" (48). "Yes, vanity is a weakness indeed. But pride— where there is a real superiority of mind, pride will be always under good regulation" (57). True, Lydia and Kitty Bennet spend far too much time thinking about the next merry dance, but does Darcy have to condemn it ("Every savage can dance") as primitive (25)? He moves in social circles with cold silence, "grave propriety," and formal bows that signal his disdain (26). He cannot take a joke ("Mr. Darcy is not to be laughed at!" Elizabeth notes) and seems full of self-love: "Mr. Darcy may hug himself," as Miss Bingley puts it (57).

Austen presents Darcy as a thinking, feeling man with a blunt core of integrity ("disguise of every sort is my abhorrence," he insists) who must learn in the course of the novel to behave with gentler manners and "perfect civility" to everyone, including those society deems beneath him (192, 251). Though no glib reciter of poetry or singer of duets, he has enough appreciation of the arts to enjoy Elizabeth's performances, to suggest dancing a reel to "a lively Scotch air," and to maintain the grounds of his Pemberley estate without ostentation in a style "neither formal, nor falsely adorned" (52, 245). Darcy's ability to nurture the natural beauty of his extensive grounds separates him from his aunt, a tasteless, showy woman, and from Mr. Collins, whose approach to houses and landscape is to count every item and calculate every price.

Darcy is, like Colonel Brandon, a gentleman in need of an animated woman. As Mrs. Gardiner concludes of Darcy, "His understanding and opinions all please me; he wants nothing but a little more liveliness, and *that* . . . his wife may teach him" (325). Elizabeth already had reached that same conclusion: "It was an union that must have been to the advantage of both; by her ease and liveliness, his mind might have been softened, his manners improved, and from his judgment, information, and knowledge of the world, she must have received benefit of greater importance" (312). Austen suggests that marriage succeeds only if both partners become more whole, more complete, through the union.

As if to underscore the need for complementarity rather than similarity in marriage partners, Austen gives some of Elizabeth's qualities—liveliness, ease, good-humored playfulness—to Mr. Bingley but does not present Bingley and Elizabeth as attracted to each other. Bingley has the very strengths Darcy lacks: he can laugh at himself, act graciously to others, take pleasure in any surroundings, and democratically accept as his equals those with less money. He is a newly made gentleman whose family fortune came from trade, not inherited titles and estates, but he has not acquired the nouveau riche hauteur of his sisters nor the aristocratic pride of his friend, Mr. Darcy. Bingley is a respectable "good-looking and gentlemanlike" man with "a pleasant countenance" and "perfect good breeding," a man others call "sensible, good humoured, lively" with "unaffected cordiality . . . a greater sweetness of address, and a stronger desire of generally pleasing than any other man" (10, 14, 16, 261).

Bingley is the only character Austen ever describes as possessing a "ductility" of temper, a word reminding us of Jane Bennet's pliancy and tractability (16). Unlike Darcy (to whom nothing comes easily), Bingley has "easy, unaffected manners," "so much ease," an "easiness of temper," "good-humoured ease," and "ease and cheerfulness" (10, 14, 15, 133, 261, 345). Like *lively*, the term *ease* is loaded with ambivalence. Bingley's ease suggests his relaxed informality and cheerful social poise, but it also indicates a too ready acceptance of whatever happens (such as Darcy sending him away from Jane) and an almost lazy resignation to his gentlemanly lot. "I am an idle fellow," he confesses (38). Elizabeth bemoans Bingley's "want of proper resolution which now made him the slave of his designing friends," and Darcy admits of his easygoing friend, "He had a stronger dependence on my judgment than on his own" (133, 199). Bingley speaks with wit (he jokes with his sisters and joshes Darcy), but he never takes *action* unless directed to do so by Darcy. Bingley and Jane may live happily, easily, and sweetly ever after, but they will remain passive and at the mercy of others. As Mr. Bennet puts it to Jane, "Your tempers are by no means unlike. You are each of you so complying, that nothing will ever be resolved on; so easy, that every servant will cheat you" (348).

As in *Sense and Sensibility*, Austen suggests in *Pride and Prejudice* that idleness and easy wealth threaten to make men effeminate. If Bingley is too pleasing and pliant, Wickham is downright soft, resembling what Austen knew to be the negative stereotype of a woman: "His appearance was greatly in his favour; he had all the best part of beauty, a fine countenance, a good figure, and very pleasing address," "a captivating softness . . . in manners," "every charm of air and address," "every charm of person and address," "He smiled, looked handsome, and said many pretty things" (72, 180, 206, 284, 330). Like Bingley, Wickham is "a young man of most gentlemanlike appearance" who seems all that is "amiable and pleasing," with an "easy assurance," "easy address," and "good-humoured ease" (72, 152, 315, 316). Austen's repetition of identical phrases for Bingley and Wickham seems designed to draw readers' attention to the similarities—and ultimately the key differences. To a *far* greater extent than Bingley, Wickham has acquired the exterior of a gentleman without ethics. Bingley is a rather weak but good man, whereas Wickham is a downright scoundrel, a man whose "vicious propensities—the want of principle" propel him into "a life of idleness and dissipation" (200, 201).

Austen expands her exploration of the gentleman in *Pride and Prejudice* by introducing a gallery of minor male characters with various degrees of gentlemanliness. Mr. Hurst, for instance, "merely looked the gentleman" but is "an indolent man, who lived only to eat, drink, and play at cards" (35). Colonel Fitzwilliam is "not handsome," but his well-informed mind and manner of conversing make him "most truly the gentleman" (170–71). The only titled gentleman in *Pride and Prejudice* is Sir William Lucas, a knight with "the complaisance of a courtier" who is little more than a timid, unintelligent man in awe of the nobility (126). Joining Sir William Lucas in his adulation of the rich and titled is William Collins, a ridiculous "mixture of pride and obsequiousness, self-importance and humility" who utters "pompous nothings" and allows himself to be slavishly ruled by the opinions and decrees of Lady Catherine de Bourgh (70). Mr. Collins is more than stupid: he is mean-spirited. As a way of punishing Elizabeth for refusing his offer, he takes pleasure in spreading the gossip about Lydia and in gloating in his letters to Mr. Bennet that he has not married into their pitiful family: "Let me advise you then, my dear Sir, to console yourself as much as possible, to throw off your unworthy child from your affection for ever, and leave her to reap the fruits of her own heinous offence" (297). Austen shows this clergyman using biblical language ("reap the fruits") to preach a lack of mercy and forgiveness. This is no gentleman, just as this is no man of God.

Although Mr. Bennet can see Mr. Collins's pomposity, he fails to overcome his *own* failings as a gentleman. Mr. Bennet casually ignores his daughters' plight due to the entail and seeks merely "leisure and tranquillity," not the proper discharge of his duties (71). Yes, he is literate ("with a book he was regardless of time"), but he approaches life's vicissitudes with "calm unconcern" (12, 111). His neglect of his giddy daughters and ridicule of his wife in part contribute to Lydia's disgrace. Mr. Bennet sums up his laissez-faire approach to the world when he quips, "I am quite at leisure" (377). By placing into Mr. Bennet's mouth a rhetorical question—"For what do we live, but to make sport for our neighbours and laugh at them in our turn?"—Austen indirectly steers us toward a different conclusion (364). Mr. Bennet has too little sense of duty or responsibility.

Mr. Bennet's brother-in-law, Mr. Gardiner, would answer that a gentleman lives to help his family and neighbors, not to laugh at them. Austen describes Mr. Gardiner as "a sensible, gentlemanlike man, greatly superior to his sister [Mrs. Bennet] as well by nature as education," a "well-bred and agreeable" man with "intelligence . . . taste and . . . good manners" who marries an equally well-bred, sensible, and loving woman, functions as a loving husband, father, brother, and uncle, and takes dignified action to help the Bennet family with their Lydia troubles (139, 255). Although, horror of horrors, he "lived by trade, and within view of his own warehouses," Mr. Gardiner is more gentlemanly in manner and deed than those considered his social betters (139). In passages throughout *Pride and Prejudice* describing "gentlemanlike" behavior, Austen warns readers not to view handsome, leisured men as gentlemen until their just principles, informed understanding, liberal generosity, and active discharge of duties prove them worthy of the name.

One form of prejudice Austen explores in *Pride and Prejudice* is our tendency to prejudge men and women by "First Impressions," as the novel was originally called—in particular, by first impressions based on appearance. Mary Bennet and Charlotte Lucas know full well that they have fewer options because of their plain faces, while Mrs. Bennet has been able to land herself a good husband solely because of her youth and beauty. Bingley instantly gravitates toward Jane because she is the most beautiful woman in the room, and Elizabeth finds Wickham charming and virtuous simply because he is handsome. When Elizabeth and Jane consider the true nature of Darcy and Wickham, they marvel at the difference between semblance and substance, the fact that "one has got all the goodness, and the other all

The rectory at Steventon where Jane Austen wrote her early version of *Pride and Prejudice* (Reproduced by permission of the Jane Austen Memorial Trust)

the appearance of it" (225). Elizabeth had labeled Wickham "the most agreeable man I ever *saw*," a phrase suggesting she has judged with her eyes rather than her mind (144).

In answer to Marvell and Shakespeare's question, "Who ever lov'd that lov'd not at first sight?" (Marvell's *Hero and Leander*, 1.176, quoted by Shakespeare's Phebe in *As You Like It*, 3.5.82), Austen could have answered, the hero and heroine of *Pride and Prejudice*. Austen rejects the notion of love at first sight—both the emphasis on appearance and the emphasis on speed—by showing the slow-developing relationship between Elizabeth and Darcy. Discussions of haste and hurry throughout the novel make readers conscious of the need for love to develop slowly and thoughtfully. Unlike Laura and Edward of the adolescent "Love and Freindship," who marry within two minutes of meeting each other, Elizabeth and Darcy take their time. As Elizabeth explains to Jane, "It has been coming on so gradually, that I hardly know when it began" (373).

Darcy shares this bewildered inability to pinpoint the moment when love began. He confesses to Elizabeth, "I cannot fix on the hour, or the spot, or the look, or the words, which laid the foundation. It is too long ago. I was in the middle before I knew that I *had* begun"

(380). I do not recall a passage like this in any previous literary work. It seems a deliberate rejection on Austen's part of the love-at-first-sight formula expected of courtship romances. Darcy moves from regarding Elizabeth as "not handsome enough to tempt" him, to finding Elizabeth's face "rendered uncommonly intelligent" by her sparkling eyes, to considering in general that a truly accomplished woman must possess "something more substantial, in the improvement of her mind by extensive reading," to discovering that he has indeed become "bewitched" by Elizabeth's lively mind and playful spirit (12, 23, 39, 52). Darcy clearly wants a woman with a mind, not just a pretty face or superficial skills. Despite his gravity, Darcy cannot help but smile at several points because of Elizabeth's pointed retorts. Like Henry Tilney in *Northanger Abbey*, Elizabeth Bennet mocks conventional small talk: "It is *your* turn to say something now, Mr. Darcy.—*I* talked about the dance, and *you* ought to make some kind of remark on the size of the room, or the number of couples" (91). Austen notes here and at many other moments after Elizabeth speaks, "Darcy smiled." Elizabeth thinks quickly and perceptively, as in her response to Darcy's justification for his antisocial behavior:

> "I certainly have not the talent which some people possess," said Darcy, "of conversing easily with those I have never seen before. I cannot catch their tone of conversation, or appear interested in their concerns, as I often see done."
>
> "My fingers," said Elizabeth, "do not move over this instrument in the masterly manner which I see so many women's do. They have not the same force or rapidity, and do not produce the same expression. But then I have always supposed it to be my own fault—because I would not take the trouble of practising. It is not that I do not believe *my* fingers as capable as any other woman's of superior execution."
>
> Darcy smiled and said, "You are perfectly right." (175–76)

Elizabeth insists on her inalienable right to banter: "it belongs to me to find occasions for teasing and quarreling with you as often as may be" (381). She makes Darcy think, challenges his complacency, and thus enlivens him. Darcy falls in love with Elizabeth because she is "a rational creature speaking the truth from her heart" with wit and perception (109).

In fact, if we try to find the precise moment when Darcy becomes "bewitched" by Elizabeth and is prompted through a very un-Darcy-like impulse to ask her to "seize . . . an opportunity of dancing a reel," we discover that the conversation right before this pits the two against each other like skilled lawyers in a courtroom (52). In a passage worth quoting at some length, Darcy argues the "case" with Elizabeth against Bingley's yielding personality until Bingley finally protests the dispute. Darcy says,

> "Your conduct would be quite as dependant on chance as that of any man I know; and if, as you were mounting your horse, a friend were to say, 'Bingley, you had better stay till next week,' you would probably do it, you would probably not go—and, at another word, might stay a month."
>
> "You have only proved by this," cried Elizabeth, "that Mr. Bingley did not do justice to his own disposition. You have shewn him off now much more than he did himself." . . .
>
> "You expect me to account for opinions which you chuse to call mine, which I have never acknowledged. Allowing the case, however, to stand according to your representation, you must remember, Miss Bennet, that the friend who is supposed to desire his return . . . has merely desired it, asked it without offering one argument in favour of its propriety."
>
> "To yield readily—easily—to the *persuasion* of a friend is no merit with you."
>
> "To yield without conviction is no compliment to the understanding of either."
>
> "You appear to me, Mr. Darcy, to allow nothing for the influence of friendship and affection. A regard for the requester would often make one readily yield to a request, without waiting for arguments to reason one into it. . . . "
>
> "Will it not be advisable, before we proceed on this subject, to arrange with rather more precision the degree of importance which is to appertain to this request, as well as the degree of intimacy subsisting between the parties?". . .
>
> "Arguments are too much like disputes [Bingley later interjects]. If you and Miss Bennet will defer yours till I am out of the room, I shall be very thankful." (49–51)

Indeed, Elizabeth and Darcy do enjoy arguing, much as professional chess players suffering through matches against amateurs would feel grateful to find formidable opponents to challenge their skills. Austen reinforces our perceptions of Elizabeth and Darcy as equals by giving them matching amounts of speaking time. In addition to the debate about Bingley's personality, there are over a dozen other major dialogues between Darcy and Elizabeth.[15] Readers hear Elizabeth and Darcy talk as intellectual equals far more than any other pair of lovers in Austen's novels. What a far cry the animated Elizabeth-Darcy exchanges are from the mismatched opening "conversation" between Mr. and Mrs. Bennet. One reason Mr. Bennet misses Elizabeth so much when she is away from home is that she functions as his substitute soul mate, the one person with whom he can engage in verbal sparring and a witty exchange of ideas.

By getting to know and respect Elizabeth's mind and heart, Darcy moves from coldly dismissing her appearance (Darcy is reported to have said, "*She* a beauty!—I should as soon call her mother a wit") to admiring her as "one of the handsomest women" he has met (271). This is love at fourth or fifth sight, perhaps—and not just by sight. Darcy attributes his attraction to the liveliness of Elizabeth's *mind*, not to the liveliness of her eyes or delicacy of her features. His attraction is not just cerebral, though, as he seems struck in part by Elizabeth's intense affection for Jane. Like Elizabeth, Darcy values the love of a sister. He has faithfully loved Georgiana, trying to protect her honor and nurturing her growing intimacy with Elizabeth.

Elizabeth takes many more chapters to fall in love and has to overcome active dislike of Darcy as "the last man in the world whom [she] could be prevailed on to marry" (193). In Elizabeth's list of attributes that eventually attract her to Darcy, his height and "noble mien" get nary a mention (10). For Elizabeth, Darcy's natural taste, educated mind, moral judgment, and honorable conduct reveal his gentlemanliness. Unlike her father, infatuated by beauty, Elizabeth will not form a hasty "unequal marriage" leaving her the "grief" of being "unable to respect [her] partner in life" (376).

Austen intrudes as narrator to tell us that a gradually developed love between a man and a woman, in this case Darcy and Elizabeth, may be less romantic to write about but more satisfying in its depth: "If gratitude and esteem are good foundations of affection, Elizabeth's change of sentiment [toward Darcy] will be neither improbable or faulty. But if otherwise, if the regard springing from such sources is unreasonable or unnatural, in comparison of what is so often described as arising on a first interview with its object, and even before two words have been exchanged, nothing can be said in her defence, except that she had given somewhat of a trial to the latter method, in her partiality for Wickham, and that its ill-success might perhaps authorise her to seek the other less interesting mode of attachment" (279). Much as in *Northanger Abbey* Austen pretended to apologize for the ways Catherine failed to resemble heroines in other books, so here she pretends that her description of mature love based on a solid foundation is "less interesting" than the love at first sight which "is so often described" in typical romances.

As if to emphasize that she is more interested in the *process* of falling in love than the romance itself, Austen again chooses to withdraw the camera lens (or at least turn off the sound equipment) right as Darcy proposes to Elizabeth: "he expressed himself on the occasion as sensibly and as warmly as a man violently in love can be supposed to do" (366). Here Austen uses the clichéd expression ("violently in love") she called into question earlier in the novel as "so hackneyed, so doubtful, so indefinite, that it gives . . . very little idea," a phrase "as often applied to feelings which arise from an half-hour's acquaintance, as to a real, strong attachment" (140–41). By the time we are told in the third volume that Darcy is "violently in love," we know it is the latter, more slowly grown and therefore genuine form of attachment; it is not based on beauty (Mr. Bennet), convenience (Mr. Collins), or sensuality and money (Wickham), but rather esteem.

It is easy (to use a Bingley term) to be so charmed by the growing love between Elizabeth and Darcy that we fail to recognize the radical social nature of their marriage—and of the novel as a whole. In *Sense and Sensibility* Marianne marries a man with an annual income of two thousand pounds, but she was the daughter of a gentleman from a long-established, respectable family with no vulgar relations in the closet. In contrast, Elizabeth Bennet secures a man worth ten thousand pounds per year and can offer him little besides an embarrassing assemblage of relatives. Not only that but Darcy has noble, titled ancestors while Elizabeth has the taint (also called "pollution" and "impurities") of relatives in trade and in the law (141, 388). As Austen economics expert Edward Copeland notes, this is "a Cinderella match of great wealth and comparative poverty, across significant social lines," a union of "dizzying" stakes between "potentially one of the most impoverished" heroines and the wealthiest Austen hero.[16]

There is no denying that Austen turns the class system upside down and inside out in this novel. Why else would she go to such lengths to show that the woman at the top of the social ladder—the aristocratic Lady Catherine de Bourgh—has less breeding than the lowly, totally untitled Mrs. Gardiner, the novel's true "lady"? Mrs. Gardiner is "an amiable, intelligent, elegant woman" who shares with her husband "affection and intelligence," or sensibility and sense (139, 240).

Aristocracy based on birth gives power to those who may not deserve it, Elizabeth Bennet recognizes, and she refuses to feel afraid of Lady Catherine simply because of her title: "Mere stateliness of money and rank, she thought she could witness without trepidation" (161). Elizabeth feels unafraid of Lady Catherine because she possesses no talents or virtues that justify her title and rank. Elizabeth probably shared the thoughts of Figaro in his daring monologue from *Marriage of Figaro:* "Because you're a great lord, you think you've a great mind as well! Nobility, fortune, rank, power, it makes a man proud. What have you done to deserve all that? You went to the trouble of being born, nothing more."[17] Although Lady Catherine enjoys condescending to her social inferiors and "likes to have the distinction of rank preserved," she occupies a superior position merely through accident of birth, not through any talent or merit of her own (161). Mr. Collins is sure that Elizabeth will temper her "wit and vivacity" when she comes face to face with the great Lady Catherine ("the silence and respect which her rank will inevitably excite"), but Elizabeth in fact responds by voicing her opinions and registering her lack of awe (106). She feels herself to be Lady Catherine's equal, despite Lady Catherine's noble line and insistence that Elizabeth is "a young woman of inferior birth, of no importance in the world" (355). In her interchanges with Lady Catherine, Elizabeth's firm insistence on equality marks a glorious instance of civil disobedience. An iconoclast, Elizabeth is "the first creature who had ever dared to trifle" with the formidable Lady Catherine (166). As if proving Mary Wollstonecraft's assertion that women can think and reason, Elizabeth uses calm logic in her pointed arguments with the enraged Lady Catherine.

In some ways, Austen presents Lady Catherine as an upper-class version of Mrs. Bennet. Darcy feels "ashamed of his aunt's ill breeding" much as Elizabeth feels mortified by her mother's vulgarity (173). Both women shamelessly put forward their daughters, lack taste and depth, and oppress others with their interference. Both make ridiculously absurd remarks that show they do not know themselves or their own limitations. When it rains and Jane must therefore stay with the Bingleys, Mrs. Bennet acts "as if the credit of making it rain were all her own" (31). Similarly, Lady Catherine is happy to gather a party around her so she can "determine what weather they were to have on the morrow" (166). Mrs. Bennet claims that nobody suffers the way she does, while Lady Catherine insists, "Nobody can feel the loss of friends more than I do" (210). Why might Austen create these parallels? Perhaps she wishes readers to sense that class and wealth are mere accidents of birth and no guarantees of refinement. Give Mrs. Bennet a title, a showy estate, and a sickly unmarried daughter and she could fill Lady Catherine's elegant shoes admirably.

Mrs. Bennet, however, only has the power to make her own family cringe. Lady Catherine inflicts herself on the entire multitude around her, a sort of heartless cross between Louis XIV and Marie Antoinette sallying forth to the poor in order to "silence their complaints, and to scold them into harmony and plenty" (169). Like contemporary bosses micromanaging every aspect of their employees' lives, Lady Catherine gives authoritative commands about everything from the arrangement of furniture to the proper size of joints of meat. She cannot bear Elizabeth's obstinacy, her refusal to kowtow to authority, her upstart ideas, and her nerve in thinking she could marry into such a noble family. In a telling exchange Lady Catherine says to Elizabeth,

> "My daughter and my nephew are formed for each other. They are descended on the maternal side, from the same noble line; and, on the father's, from respectable, honourable, and ancient, though untitled families. Their fortune on both sides is splendid. They are destined for each other by the voice of every member of their respective houses; and what is to divide them? The upstart pretensions of a young woman without family, connections, or fortune. Is this to be endured! But it must not, shall not be. If you were sensible of your own good, you would not wish to quit the sphere, in which you have been brought up." . . .
>
> "Whatever my connections may be," said Elizabeth, "if your nephew does not object to them, they can be nothing to *you*. . . . How far your nephew might approve of your interference in *his* affairs, I cannot tell; but you have certainly no right to concern yourself in mine." . . .
>
> "Are the shades of Pemberley to be thus polluted?" (356–57)

This is an extraordinarily revolutionary scene. As if to underscore the political overtones of this clash, Austen uses terms like *dictatorial, magistrate, power, rights, commands,* and *authoritative* to describe the conflict between the imperial Lady Catherine and her defiant subject,

Elizabeth. We hear echoes of Lady Catherine in Gilbert and Sullivan's absurdly haughty Pooh-Bah, The Lord High Everything Else in *The Mikado:* "I can trace my ancestry back to a protoplasmal primordial atomic globule. Consequently, my family pride is something inconceivable. I can't help it. I was born sneering."[18]

Austen does not simplify her presentation of class by implying that all people in lower classes are worthy. Yes, Elizabeth has the very well-bred Aunt and Uncle Gardiner, more deserving of praise than their upper-class "betters," but she also has Aunt and Uncle Phillips, characterized by their vulgarity and strong smell of port. Whether she turns her eyes on aristocrats or those of the middle class, Austen suggests each case must be judged (not prejudged) on its merits.

Rather than concluding *Pride and Prejudice* with a paragraph describing Darcy and Elizabeth's romantic love for each other, Austen chooses to end with an emphasis on the breakdown in walls between the classes. Formerly, Elizabeth had assumed that a marriage to Darcy would have meant separation from her relatives in trade ("my aunt and uncle would have been lost to me"); the Gardiners, she assumes, would be unable to visit Pemberley because of their lower social status (246). The final paragraphs of this novel assure readers that in fact such visits are welcomed:

> Lady Catherine was extremely indignant on the marriage of her nephew. . . . But at length . . . she condescended to wait on them at Pemberley, in spite of that pollution which its woods had received, not merely from the presence of such a mistress, but the visits of her uncle and aunt from the city.
>
> With the Gardiners, they were always on the most intimate terms. Darcy, as well as Elizabeth, really loved them; and they were both ever sensible of the warmest gratitude towards the persons who, by bringing her into Derbyshire, had been the means of uniting them. (388)

Darcy's ability to overcome his snobbish sense of superiority in order to accept Elizabeth as his equal and to measure her relatives (and his own) by worth rather than birth marks perhaps the greatest personal evolution any Austen hero undergoes.

Darcy has not finished evolving by the end of the novel, though: he has just *begun* to learn how to be laughed at. Laughter is a leveler, so Elizabeth's teasing will keep Darcy from ever becoming a Lady Catherine de Bourgh who condescends to scowl at those of "inferior" ranks. If a wife can laugh at her husband, she claims a kind of equality and security; a right to judge. She is no doormat or admiring doll that, like many a political candidate's wife, claps and smiles no matter how inane her husband's speech. She has a mind of her own and the courage to give voice to her thoughts, however subversive.

To be able to laugh at oneself is to admit weaknesses; to recognize therefore the possibility of change. Could Mrs. Bennet ever laugh at her whininess, Mary at her pedantry, or Mr. Collins at his pomposity, they would be on their way to improvement.

To laugh at others, however, can border on cruelty. For example, Miss Bingley and her sister "indulge their mirth" at Elizabeth's expense, utter "witticisms" designed to skewer her, and display a kind of liveliness: "They could describe an entertainment with accuracy, relate an anecdote with humour, and laugh at their acquaintance" (37, 46, 54). The phrase "laugh *at*" says it all. Elizabeth may laugh at follies and nonsense whenever she can, but she will not join Miss Bingley in laughing at other people in a mean, disloyal, or cutting way.

Like Caroline Bingley, Mr. Bennet likes "set downs" of others (13). He humiliates his daughter Mary by saying "you have delighted us long enough" when her musical performance wearies others, a sharp remark that makes Elizabeth feel sorry for her sister (101). He makes sarcastic jokes at Mrs. Bennet's expense, thus "exposing his wife to the contempt of her own children," and copes with his disastrous marriage through his "powers of entertainment": "To his wife he was very little otherwise indebted, than as her ignorance and folly had contributed to his amusement" (236). For Mr. Bennet, laughter serves as an escape vent, not a means for reform. Elizabeth realizes that her father's approach to his silly youngest daughters does much harm: "Her father, contented with laughing at them, would never exert himself to restrain the wild giddiness of his youngest daughters" (213). Instead of caring that Mr. Collins will evict the Bennet women from Longbourne, Mr. Bennet only seems glad to discover that he has a relative stupid enough to be amusing: "Mr. Bennet's expectations were fully answered. His cousin was as absurd as he had hoped, and he listened to him with the keenest enjoyment" (68).

As she considers her father's inappropriate use of humor, Elizabeth realizes she must check her own tendency to put down others. She knows that one reason she likes disliking Darcy is because it gives her a chance to display her wit: "I meant to be uncommonly clever in taking so decided a dislike to him, without any reason. It is such a spur to one's genius, such an opening for wit to have a dislike of that kind. One may be continually abusive without saying any thing just; but one cannot be always laughing at a man without now and then stumbling on something witty" (226). Like her father, Elizabeth also is so keenly aware of the world's folly that she veers toward cynicism. "Stupid men are the only ones worth knowing, after all," Elizabeth quips on her way to visit Mr. Collins, a man "who has not one agreeable quality, who has neither manner nor sense to recommend him" (154). Mrs. Gardiner warns her at that point, "Take care, Lizzy; that speech savours strongly of disappointment." Like Mr. Bennet taking refuge from his disappointing marriage in witty barbs, Elizabeth "delight[s] in any thing ridiculous" and "loves absurdities" (12, 152). "Follies, nonsense, whims and inconsistencies *do* divert me," she admits, "and I laugh at them whenever I can" (57).

But unlike her father, Elizabeth grows in her understanding that humor can be abused. Mr. Bennet's response to Jane's grief at Bingley's departure is to joke about how women like to be jilted ("I congratulate her. Next to being married, a girl likes to be crossed in love a little now and then"), a remark demonstrating no compassion or understanding of genuine emotion (137). Elizabeth cannot get her father to take seriously her remonstrances about how Lydia and Kitty are behaving in discreditable, harmful ways. Late in the novel, Mr. Bennet assumes Elizabeth will still be diverted by his comments about the foibles of Lady Catherine, Mr. Collins, and Mr. Darcy, not sensing that he has "most cruelly mortified her" by his remarks and has made her feel "It was necessary to laugh, when she would rather have cried" (369). She recognizes that her father's witty repartee indicates an "ill judged . . . direction of talents" (237).

In searching for Jane Austen in *Pride and Prejudice*, we find her not only in the witty, lively, good-humored voice of her heroine but also in the more destructive sarcasm of Mr. Bennet. Austen goes to great lengths in this novel to place her readers in the same position as Mr. Bennet. Like Mr. Bennet, we laugh at the absurdity of fools so blind that they seriously utter hilariously ironic remarks. Miss Bingley yawns directly after saying she never tires of a book and accuses Elizabeth of practicing "a paltry device, a very mean art" of putting down women in order to captivate men, the very act Miss Bingley is guilty of herself (40). Lady Catherine boasts of her musical superiority (and her daughter's) while revealing that neither can play a note.

And how can we not help sharing Mr. Bennet's delight in Mrs. Bennet's absurdity? She accuses the Lucases of being artful people "all for what they can get" without recognizing that she has competed for the same wealthy sons-in-law (140). When Mrs. Bennet says, "I should not mind any thing at all," "I am frightened out of my wits," or "I shall go distracted," we chuckle to ourselves that she has no mind at all and has gone witless and distracted long ago (130, 288, 378). We appreciate our narrator's wit in informing us that Lady Lucas is "not too clever to be a valuable neighbour to Mrs. Bennet" (18). Some of Mrs. Bennet's unconsciously funny comments are priceless:

> "She is a selfish, hypocritical woman, and I have no opinion of her." (6)

> "I told you . . . that I should never speak to you again, and you will find me as good as my word. . . . Not that I have much pleasure indeed in talking to any body. People who suffer as I do from nervous complaints can have no great inclination for talking. Nobody can tell what I suffer!—But it is always so. Those who do not complain are never pitied." (113)

> "I am determined never to speak of it again to anybody. I told my sister Philips so the other day." (227)

> "My comfort is, I am sure Jane will die of a broken heart, and then he will be sorry." (228)

We feel indebted to Mrs. Bennet for comic relief, just as Mr. Bennet credits his wife for contributing to his amusement.

Austen shows off her own Mr. Bennet-like ability to use words as weapons. She can produce brilliant oxymorons that capture the split between image and reality. Lady Catherine radiates "dignified impertinence" and is "all affability and condescension," Miss Bingley displays "sneering civility" and is "all that was affectionate and insincere," and Mrs. Bennet can do no better than to be "restored to her usual querulous serenity" (166, 157, 269, 383). It seems to me that Austen leads her readers into a trap. We share in Mr. Bennet's ironic vision and laugh along with him at the follies and inconsistencies of his relatives and neighbors, but suddenly we find ourselves uncomfortable with his irresponsible and insensitive behavior. Like Elizabeth, we as readers are forced to check our laughter—and think about it.

Pride and Prejudice, begun as "First Impressions" only a few years after the juvenilia, perhaps marks Austen's departure from the high-spirited, rollicking hilarity of her adolescent works, where murders are funny if described wittily enough. One acquaintance of Austen remembered her as being much like Mr. Bennet: "I remember her as a tall thin spare person, with very high cheek bones great colour—sparkling Eyes not large but joyous & intelligent . . . her keen sense of humour I quite remember, it oozed out very much in Mr. Bennett's [*sic*] Style."[19] One early critic describes Austen's biting humor in a way that could apply to Mr. Bennet: "Jane Austen was always to delight in her fools: without compunction she mocks their follies so as to get all the amusement out of them she can."[20] But by showing Elizabeth and her father taking different comic bends in the road, Austen asks readers and perhaps herself to question that amusement—to consider the proper and improper uses of humor. Be on guard, she seems to say, against humor that divides, pains, or destroys. Austen would have known the saying that laughter is the work of the devil.

Yet most of all, *Pride and Prejudice* celebrates not the damning but the redeeming power of comic fiction; its ability to educate and entertain its readers, to expand their definition of humanity and their knowledge of themselves. When Mr. Collins boasts that he "never read[s] novels," he echoes Reverend Fordyce's attack on novels as an "infernal brood of futility and lewdness" that should be avoided because "Instructions they convey none."[21] However, readers are left thinking that Mr. Collins would have been better off putting down Fordyce's *Sermons* and picking up an insightful novel like *Pride and Prejudice* (68). Austen adds additional humor by reminding readers of a scene in Richard Brinsley Sheridan's *The Rivals:* a hairdresser uses pages of Fordyce's *Sermons* as curling-papers, and a heroine named Lydia Languish reads novels instead of preachy essays.[22] Mrs. Bennet would probably agree with Sheridan's Mrs. Malaprop, "I would by no means wish a daughter of mine to be a progeny of learning. I don't think so much learning becomes a young woman." By echoing Sheridan, Fordyce, and other male authors, Austen demonstrates that learning becomes a woman writer, particularly one with the ability to give earlier works a witty twist. No wonder Sheridan called *Pride and Prejudice* "one of the cleverest things he ever read."[23]

Our narrator makes it clear that she is writing no mere travelogue ("It is not the object of this work to give a description of Derbyshire, nor of any of the remarkable places through which their route thither lay") and no love-at-first-sight romance (240). Instead *Pride and Prejudice* fits exactly the description Austen had given of novels in *Northanger Abbey*, bought but not published at this point: "'It is only *Cecilia*, or *Camilla*, or *Belinda*'; or, in short, only some work in which the greatest powers of the mind are displayed, in which the most thorough knowledge of human nature, the happiest delineation of its varieties, the liveliest effusions of wit and humour are conveyed to the world in the best chosen language" (*NA*, 38).

In that passage from *Northanger Abbey*, Austen refers to *Cecilia* by Fanny Burney, and it is interesting that she takes the title of *Pride and Prejudice* from that novel. "The whole of this unfortunate business," says Dr. Lyster in *Cecilia*, "has been the result of PRIDE and PREJUDICE. . . . Yet this, however, remember; if to PRIDE AND PREJUDICE you owe your miseries . . . to PRIDE AND PREJU-DICE you will also owe their termination." [24] In Burney's novel, however, only the hero was guilty of pride and prejudice while the heroine was faultless from the beginning, much like Jane Bennet. The narrative voice of *Cecilia* is hardly funny. In contrast, Austen writes a witty novel that claims for both men and women the right to be flawed and struggling, to experience evolutionary and revolutionary moments like Elizabeth's sense of mortification: "She grew absolutely ashamed of herself.–. . . she had been blind, partial, prejudiced, absurd. 'How despicably I have acted! . . . I, who have prided myself on my abilities! . . . How humiliating is this discovery!. . . Till this moment I never knew myself'" (208). Mr. Bennet only feels self-reproach for a few brief moments and then lapses back into cynicism, noting that he will see to it that Kitty spends at least ten minutes a day in a rational manner. Elizabeth has learned to balance her amused, detached stance with serious reflection and self-knowledge.

Austen may ask us to check our laughter, but definitely not stop it altogether. In fact, she closes *Pride and Prejudice* with the young, shy Georgiana Darcy learning from her new sister-in-law, Elizabeth, that a woman may adopt a lively, sportive manner with her husband and "take liberties" with him (388). The humor between Elizabeth and Darcy will enrich, not polarize, their union.

In *Pride and Prejudice* Austen celebrates a marriage of sorts in her own approach as author–what Twain would later call "seriously scribbling to excite the laughter of God's creatures." [25] Like Elizabeth and Darcy blending liveliness and judgment, Austen's own fiction offers sparkling amusement and serious instruction, barbed wit and gentle wisdom.

6

All the Heroism of Principle
Mansfield Park

Be strong and of good courage; be not afraid, neither be
thou dismayed; for the LORD thy God is with thee wherever thou goest.

–Joshua 1:9

No coward soul is mine,
No trembler in the world's storm-troubled sphere:
I see Heaven's glories shine,
And faith shines equal arming me from fear.

–Emily Brontë, *Last Lines*

Fanny . . . was nearly fainting: all her former habitual dread
of her uncle was returning. . . . Too soon did she find herself at the drawing-room door; and after pausing a moment
for what she knew would not come, for a courage which
the outside of no door had ever supplied to her, she turned
the lock in desperation. . . . She had all the heroism of principle, and was determined to do her duty.

–*Mansfield Park*

With the successful publication of *Sense and Sensibility* (1811) and
Pride and Prejudice (1813), both revisions of novels begun in the
1790s, Jane Austen could have chosen to publish as her third novel a
new tale of a lively, laughing heroine like Elizabeth Bennet or an eager, impassioned young woman like Marianne Dashwood. Instead,
she seems deliberately to have chosen something new and challeng-
ing to her powers, acknowledging in a letter that this novel about a
shy, pious heroine and clergyman-hero would be "not half so entertaining" as her previous work (6 July 1813). *Mansfield Park* (1815) is
the only Austen novel permeated with religious imagery and termi-
nology such as altars, crosses, clergy, morals, principles, ordination,

chapel, church, religion, sermon, prayer, piety, and pulpit. Perhaps the death of her father, a clergyman and tutor, in 1805 and the rising careers of two clergymen brothers gave her reason in this novel to pay homage to a religious life and to consider questions of piety, loyalty, and conscience. Morality forms the basis for heroism in *Mansfield Park*.

As narrator, Austen leaves little doubt that she approves of her moral heroine (Fanny Price) and serious hero (Edmund Bertram). At the same time, she refuses to join this grave couple in abandoning wit, humor, and clever game playing. From the very first paragraph of *Mansfield Park*, the narrator adopts a brightly ironic voice, as when she observes, "there certainly are not so many men of large fortune in the world as there are pretty women to deserve them" or refers to Mr. and Mrs. Norris's "career of conjugal felicity" while demonstrating the opposite (3). Wit and learning, Austen suggests in *Mansfield Park*, can be gateways to wisdom, not necessarily distractions from it. If the novel asks readers to value the humorless but virtuous Fanny Price more than the sparkling but tainted Mary Crawford, the narrative voice simultaneously reassures us that we can have *both* morality and wit. Through clever allusions and hints, Austen invites perceptive readers to play a game of detection with her. Searching for Jane Austen between the lines of *Mansfield Park* leads to a veritable pot of gold.

No other Austen creation has provoked more widely divergent responses than the one and only Fanny Price. In an essay called "What Became of Jane Austen?" novelist and critic Kingsley Amis wondered why the creator of Catherine Morland, Marianne and Elinor Dashwood, and Elizabeth Bennet invented such an unappealing weakling as the heroine of *Mansfield Park*. Kingsley Amis calls Fanny "a monster of complacency and pride" operating "under a cloak of cringing self-abasement."[1] Although some early readers praised Fanny's quiet, modest, moral nature, others were disappointed with her passivity. "Insipid Fanny Price," Jane Austen's own mother remarked, and Austen's lively niece Anna similarly "could not bear Fanny" ("Opinions of Mansfield Park and Emma," *MW,* 432). Many later readers have agreed with Mrs. Austen and have found the heroine insufferably self-righteous and unendurably timid: Fanny has been called a bore, "the most terrible incarnation we have of the female prig-pharisee," an "unyieldingly charmless heroine," and "the prig in your first-grade class who never, ever misbehaved and who told the teacher when anyone else did."[2] Lionel Trilling concludes that readers of *Mansfield Park* cannot help but be "repelled by its heroine."[3]

For the first and only time in Austen, we meet a "supine" heroine who cries frequently, tires easily, and acts "exceedingly timid and shy, and shrinking from notice" (395, 12). Austen uses phrase after phrase to portray Fanny as the *opposite* of courage, self-confidence, importance, and energy. She is described as *afraid of everybody, trembling, trembling about everything, trembling and fearing to be sent for, so low and wan and trembling, forlorn, fearful, disheartened, awed, overcome, mortified, abashed, so shy and reluctant, most shy and uncomfortable, nearly fainting, fearful of notice, too much frightened to have any enjoyment, dependent, helpless, friendless, neglected, forgotten, very timid, and exceedingly nervous, always so gentle and retiring, all agitation and flutter, almost stunned, delicate and nervous, on the point of fainting away, timid, anxious, doubting, finding something to fear in every person and place*. As Lydia Bennet might exclaim, Good Lord!

No athletic tomboy rolling down green slopes or jumping over fences, Fanny Price gets a headache after walking half a mile or being out in the sun to cut roses, for "every sort of exercise fatigues her so soon" (95). Unlike Jane Austen, who observed in a letter, "There were twenty Dances & I danced them all, & without any fatigue" (24 December 1798), Fanny Price gets "breathless," "knocked up," and "tired so soon" at a dance and feels "fatigued and fatigued again" throughout this novel (279, 387). We long to give her iron supplements.

Fanny also could use public speaking classes. If she utters anything at all, it is in a *faltering voice*, a *low voice*, a *shrinking accent*, a *self-denying tone*, or a *quiet way*. Excluded from most of the dialogue, Fanny relishes her wallflower role and shrinks from notice: "She was not often invited to join in the conversation of the others, nor did she desire it" (80). When Fanny does speak up at one point, this "creepmouse" is "shocked to find herself at that moment the only speaker in the room" (145–46). At another instance when she says *two sentences* in opposition to Henry Crawford's cavalier attitude about Sir Thomas, she trembles and blushes at the thought of having spoken "so much at once" (225).

We know from the juvenilia that Austen could create heroines who were outspoken and fearless. For example, Eliza in "Henry and Eliza" sails on a man-of-war, raises an army, climbs out of a dungeon, and walks thirty miles without stopping. Sukey in "Jack and Alice" heaves rivals out the window. Why might Austen choose in *Mansfield Park* to present such a physically weak, self-deprecatory, and cowering heroine?

In *Mansfield Park* Austen seems interested in examining the causes of timidity. Readers meet Fanny at a younger age than other Austen heroines: she is ten when she comes to Mansfield Park in a state of homesickness, mortification, and delicate puniness. Austen emphasizes Fanny's small size by having others refer to her as the *little girl*, the *little visitor*, *poor little thing*, and *the dear little cousin* with the *little heart* and *little soul*. The naturally sensitive daughter of an alcoholic father and a slatternly mother who neglects her, Fanny Price arrives at the formidable mansion of her relatives primed to feel insignificant. "I can never be important to any one," Fanny laments (26). Thinking "too lowly of her own claims" and "too lowly of her own situation," Fanny becomes "much too humble" (20, 35, 176). She accepts Aunt Norris's admonition, "Remember, wherever you are, you must be the lowest and last" and ends up "as usual, believing [her]self unequal to anything!" (221, 351).

Certainly Fanny seems unequal to humor. Readers may discover Fanny giving an occasional smile ("Fanny could not avoid a faint smile") or feeling "not unamused" by her observations of others, but even those faintly amused moments are rare (363, 131). In the nearly five hundred pages of Chapman's edition of *Mansfield Park*, Fanny only gets close to laughing one time. When Tom Bertram must rapidly shift subjects, Austen writes ambiguously, "Fanny, in spite of every thing, *could hardly help laughing*" (119; my italics). Readers have to guess as to whether Fanny actually emitted an audible laugh. Fanny has only two other close encounters with near-mirth: at one point we see Fanny "*almost* laugh," and in another scene we are told she "*tried* to laugh"—but cannot (64, 411). As she admits of herself, "I suppose I am graver than other people" (197).

Why did the brilliantly comic Austen choose as her heroine someone that even Mary Bennet and Mr. Collins might find too gravely serious? Why create such a distance between her own fiercely ironic narrative voice ("Mrs. Norris . . . consoled herself for the loss of her husband by considering that she could do very well without him") and the low-pitched, pious, unjoking, private utterances ("Heaven defend me from being ungrateful!") of the painfully shy Fanny Price (23, 323)?

Perhaps the audacious, self-confident Elizabeth Bennet of *Pride and Prejudice* made success seem too easy. Elizabeth, we suspect, *enjoys* standing up to Lady Catherine, arguing with Mr. Darcy, or opposing her mother. In contrast, Fanny Price recoils against such self-assertion. By choosing a bashful heroine unable to use humor as a defense, Austen presented herself with a fictional "problem case" in *Mansfield Park* unlike anything else she had written.

In previous novels Austen had touched only briefly on the topic of shyness (the awkward Edward Ferrars in *Sense and Sensibility* and bashful Georgiana Darcy in *Pride and Prejudice*), but in *Mansfield Park* shyness takes center stage. One senses in the vivid descriptions of Fanny's timidity and sense of isolation that Jane Austen knew shyness well. Perhaps she drew on memories of her emotions as a young girl sent off from home to attend school. Biographer Park Honan calls the young Jane Austen "a shy country girl" and draws from family accounts a portrait of a Fanny Price-like mouse: "[Jane] seemed an agreeable mouse. Then, and for years later, Jane was shy, mute and uncertain with her peers. . . . At nine and ten she was a timid, imitative observer hovering near a circle of slangy, half-sophisticated girls who talked over her head and laughed at everything. . . . Jane Austen, however mousy and inconsequential she seemed, did not play false to herself, and her shyness was in some ways an advantage."[4] Such a portrait cannot be documented, but it is true that even later in life Austen continued to shun the limelight. Biographical accounts of Austen give the impression that she could resemble *either* Elizabeth Bennet *or* Fanny Price, depending on how comfortable she felt with her visitors.[5]

Rather than viewing Fanny Price as an aberration and asking, "What became of Jane Austen?" Kingsley Amis might have noted the close link between Fanny Price's personality and some of Jane Austen's less well-known letters and prayers. Austen could at times be devout—like Fanny. Readers used to Austen's comic bite may wait in some serious letters for a joke that never comes. For example, Austen writes to condole an acquaintance, "The loss of so kind and affectionate a Parent, must be a very severe affliction to all his Children. . . . the Goodness which made him valuable on Earth, will make him Blessed in Heaven" (8 April 1798). To her brother Frank, Austen writes tenderly and reverently:

> My dearest Frank,
> I have melancholy news to relate, and sincerely feel for your feelings under the shock of it. . . . Our dear Father has closed his virtuous & happy life, in a death almost as free from suffering as his Children could have wished. . . . Heavy as is the blow, we can already feel that a thousand comforts remain to us to soften it . . . the consciousness of his worth and constant preparation for another world. (21 and 22 January 1805)

Though savagely funny at times, Austen could also write sober, heart-felt words confessing her sense of sin and doubt; her worries about her conscience; her awareness of the ephemeral nature of human concerns. Fanny Price could have uttered the same prayers that Austen wrote herself:

> Give us grace almighty father. . . . Teach us to understand the sinfulness of our own hearts, and bring to our knowledge every fault of temper and every evil habit in which we have indulged to the discomfort of our fellow-creatures, and the danger of our own souls. May we now, and on each return of night, consider how the past day has been spent by us, what have been our prevailing thoughts, words and actions during it, and how far we can acquit ourselves of evil. Have we thought irreverently of thee, have we disobeyed thy commandments, have we neglected any known duty, or willingly given pain to any human being? Incline us to ask our hearts these questions oh! God, and save us from deceiving ourselves by pride and vanity. (*MW*, 453–54)

Austen's three surviving prayers contain reminders to herself to be thankful for blessings, to avoid "discontent or indifference," to resist temptations, to make better use of each hour of the day, to rise each morning "with every serious and religious feeling," and to "endeavour after a truly christian spirit to seek to attain that temper of forbearance and patience." Undoubtedly thinking of her brothers in the navy, she offers special prayers for the safety of loved ones who travel by land or sea. I believe that this Austen voice—the one striving to conquer irreverence and rise above discontent in order to be a better soul—comes out most directly in Fanny Price. This is not to suggest that Austen *was* Fanny, nor that she wanted to be like her serious heroine, but only that she understood aspects of her character. Austen adds an autobiographical touch by having William Price give Fanny a cross, just as she and Cassandra had received topaz crosses from Charles Austen.

Austen seems deliberately to present Fanny Price as a blend of all the characteristics her era found desirable in women: modesty, delicacy, piety, and submissiveness. Fanny possesses "looks and voice so truly feminine," "unpretending gentleness," "ineffable sweetness and patience," "gentleness, modesty, and sweetness," and "that sweetness which makes so essential a part of every woman's work in the judgment of man" (169, 296, 294). She perfectly fits conduct-book

Topaz crosses Charles Austen gave his sisters
(Reproduced by permission of the Jane Austen Memorial Trust)

descriptions of women such as this one in *Wisdom in Miniature* (1795):
"The utmost of a woman's character is contained in domestic life;
first, her piety towards God; and next in the duties of a daughter, a
wife, a mother, and a sister."[6] Austen shows us Fanny's reverence for
the church and her loyal behavior as a surrogate daughter to Sir Thomas and Lady Bertram, her faithfulness toward Edmund, her moth-
erly kindness toward her younger sisters, and her ardent love for her
brother William. Fanny also satisfies the requirements of Chase Amos's
On Female Excellence (1792), which praised "mildness, moderation, and
kindness towards all" in women and opined that "delicacy of manners and purity of speech are so much expected from an amiable,
modest female."[7] The Reverend Fordyce would have approved of
Fanny Price, as he calls in his frequently reprinted *Sermons for Young
Women*, 1761, for "meekness and modesty . . . soft attraction and virtuous love," as well as the capacity to be "agreeable and useful."[8]

Austen read not only Fordyce (which made Lydia Bennet gape
in *Pride and Prejudice*) but also Dr. Gregory's *A Father's Legacy to His
Daughters*, which praises a girl's blushing as "the most powerful charm
of her beauty."[9] Indeed Fanny "colours" more than any other Austen
heroine. In direct contrast to the imperviously disgraceful Lydia Bennet
of *Pride and Prejudice*, who shows "no variation of colour" in her cheeks
when returning home from her Wickham escapades, the virginal Fanny
Price blushes her way through *Mansfield Park* (*PP,* 316). Henry extols
Fanny's "colour beautifully heightened" and her "soft skin . . . so
frequently tinged with a blush" (296, 229; my italics). Austen makes
sure we know that Fanny offers not just any old tinge but "so deep a

blush" and "the deepest blushes" growing "deeper and deeper" on a "face . . . like scarlet" (362, 259, 313, 316).

Sir Thomas Bertram emphasizes the value of Fanny Price's deeply blushing feminine modesty and gentle submissiveness when he orders Fanny off to bed in front of her would-be husband, Henry Crawford, as a way of demonstrating her obedience: "It might occur to him, that Mr. Crawford had been sitting by her long enough, or he might mean to recommend her as a wife by shewing her persuadableness" (281). Henry indeed seems attracted to Fanny as a sort of angelically gentle, docile woman. He pictures her as a kind of worshipping doll-slave: "I will not do her any harm, dear little soul! only want her to look kindly on me, to give me smiles as well as blushes, to keep a chair for me by herself wherever we are, and be all animation when I take it and talk to her; to think as I think, be interested in all my possessions and pleasures, try to keep me longer at Mansfield, and feel when I go away that she shall be never happy again" (231). As his sister concludes when Henry declares his intention of making the "innocent and quiet" Fanny marry him, "You will have a sweet little wife; all gratitude and devotion" (292).

Fanny may be sweet and little, but her gratitude and devotion are offered only to those *she* chooses. For an angel in the house, Fanny has surprisingly independent thoughts, solid integrity, and hidden power: "Her manner was incurably gentle, and she was not aware how much it concealed the sternness of her purpose" (327). Austen presents Fanny as a paradoxical combination of steely determination and feminine manners, "a woman, who firm as a rock in her principles, has a gentleness of character so well adapted to recommend them" (351).

Although our first impression of Fanny may be of a conduct-book weakling who does nothing but tremble in a corner or yield supinely to others, she in some ways has the most strength of any Austen heroine. She stays loyal to Sir Thomas in his absence, repulses Henry Crawford's advances, refuses either to reveal or to abandon her unrequited love for Edmund, and remains unswayed by the persuasions of her social superiors. Despite her obliging temperament, she resolutely asserts her right to her own feelings. When Sir Thomas Bertram displays his wrath at her refusal of the wealthy Henry Crawford, Fanny feels miserable but does not back down. She speaks politely (using "Sir" in every sentence) but firmly: "I–I cannot like him, Sir, well enough to marry him" (315). Fanny's voice may waver, but not her will. Although Sir Thomas calls Fanny "wilful and perverse" and insists that "independence of spirit . . . in young women is offensive and disgusting beyond all common offense," we treasure Fanny's resoluteness, particularly because we have waited so long for it and because we recognize that it is harder for the innately timid Fanny Price to stand up to Sir Thomas than for the feistier Elizabeth Bennet to hold her ground against her mother or Lady Catherine (318).

Austen demonstrates in *Mansfield Park* that even a shy, traditionally feminine, economically dependent, and yielding young woman can summon from within herself the necessary strength to refuse to compromise her beliefs. When Fanny waits at the door trying to muster up enough courage to speak to Sir Thomas, we are told that this is a familiar situation: "pausing for a moment for what she knew would not come, for a courage which the outside of no door had ever supplied her" (177). The "courage which she knew would not come" finally *does* come. Even shrinking violets and wallflowers can blossom. To make even small changes in one's self can require tremendous inner courage, Austen suggests. For Fanny to act and speak in her own person—*in propria persona*, as Austen notes near the end of the novel—requires far greater growth than for a heroine already endowed with self-assurance.

Despite her heartache, Fanny Price has enough inner resources to take pleasure in topics other than Edmund. Excluded from conversation, "Her own thoughts and reflections were habitually her best companions" (80). As Mary Crawford observes, "Why, Fanny, you are absolutely in a reverie!" (360). Frequently deep in thought or musing, engaged in soliloquies, or finding solace in meditation, Fanny contemplates nature, humanity, religion, politics, literature, architecture, and friendship. Austen makes sure that we acknowledge Fanny's fullness of mind by telling us that when Fanny thinks about male and female styles of letter writing, she had "such thoughts as these *among ten hundred others*" (376). Fanny is "clever," with "a quick apprehension as well as good sense, and a fondness for reading" (22). Unlike the chattering majority of men and women who make idle small talk, Fanny speaks infrequently but deliberately. She seems to be the only person in this novel who wants to know where British wealth comes from: "The evenings do not appear long to me. I love to hear my uncle talk of the West Indies. . . . Did not you hear me ask him about the slave trade last night? . . . there was such a dead silence!" (197–98). The shy Fanny asks a politically charged question. Her cousins do not join in the discussion, nor does her uncle give her an answer. Lady Bertram expresses interest in the East or West Indies only as the source of luxury items: "I wish that he may go the East Indies, that I may have my shawl," she says of her son, seemingly indifferent to the danger of such a voyage or the slave labor required for the production (305). The wealthy plantation-owning Bertrams (and, by implication, British society) maintain "dead silence" about the slave trade.

Austen adds irony to scenes like this one by showing that Sir Thomas and Edmund Bertram respond inappropriately to Fanny's seriousness. Right after Fanny talks of the West Indies, Edmund changes the subject and reduces her to a beauty pageant contestant: "Your uncle thinks you very pretty, dear Fanny—and that is the long and the short of the matter. Anybody but myself would have made something more of it, and any body but you would resent that you had not been thought very pretty before; but the truth is, that your uncle never did admire you until now—and now he does. Your complexion is so improved!—. . . and your figure—Nay, Fanny, do not turn away about it—. . . You must really begin to harden yourself to the idea of being worth looking at.—You must try not to mind growing up into a pretty woman" (198). As a plain girl Fanny was ignored; as a pretty woman Fanny is noticed only for her appearance. She blushes and squirms with vexation, not pleasure. As Edmund notes, "Ask your uncle what he thinks, and you will hear compliments enough; and though they may be chiefly on your person, you must put up with it, and trust to his seeing as much beauty of mind in time" (197).

Austen makes Fanny's "beauty of mind" clear any time she contemplates the wonder and miracle of creation. Her quietly spoken words are uttered like a philosopher, as in these remarks about memory: "If any one faculty of our nature may be called MORE wonderful than the rest, I do think it is memory. There seems something more speakingly incomprehensible in the powers, the failures, the inequalities of memory, than in any other of our intelligences. The memory is sometimes so retentive, so serviceable, so obedient— at others, so bewildered and so weak—and at others again, so tyrannic, so beyond controul!—We are to be sure a miracle every way—but our powers of recollecting and of forgetting, do seem peculiarly past finding out" (208-9). Such mature discourse is lost on her only listener, the "untouched and inattentive" Mary Crawford. Readers, however, may be startled by Fanny's level of insight and the fact that she is thinking this way at all. Rather than talking of new hair ribbons or smartly dressed officers, like Lydia Bennet, or wallowing in her lovesickness, like Marianne Dashwood, Fanny vividly describes the mysterious, uncontrolled workings of the human brain. Indeed, Fanny articulates the baffling way our minds torment us with memories we do not want yet deny us access to information we need to retrieve.

Often in *Mansfield Park* Austen reminds readers that Fanny is following a "train of thought" or that the "tender ejaculation" she utters results from reflection and meditation (151, 208). The sight of evergreens, for instance, leads her to consider ecological diversity and differences among countries: "I am so glad to see the evergreens thrive! . . . The evergreen!–How beautiful, how welcome, how wonderful the evergreen!–When one thinks of it, how astonishing a variety of nature!–In some countries we know the tree that sheds its leaf is the variety, but that does not make it less amazing, that the same soil and the same sun should nurture plants differing in the first rule and law of their existence" (209). Though equally filled with exclamation marks, this is a very different kind of response than Marianne's melancholy and solipsistic ode to dead leaves in *Sense and Sensibility*. Fanny's thoughts take her out of herself and lead to heightened pleasure and reverence. As she explains to Mary, "You will think me rhapsodizing; but when I am out of doors. . . . I am very apt to get into this sort of wondering strain" (209). This is the only time in her novels Austen uses the idea of rhapsody. Contemplating the stars enables Fanny to appreciate the sublimity of Nature: "When I look out on such a night as this, I feel as if there could be neither wickedness nor sorrow in the world; and there certainly would be less of both if the sublimity of Nature were more attended to, and people were carried more out of themselves by contemplating such a scene" (113). Although Fanny assumes that everyone could respond this way to the sky or to evergreens ("One cannot fix one's eyes on the commonest natural production without finding food for a rambling fancy"), she seems to be the only "one" in this novel to do so. While Fanny rhapsodizes about trees and stars, Mary Crawford thinks of herself and Edmund thinks of Mary Crawford.

Fanny's remarks seem to echo Wordsworth's notion of Nature as a nurse and gateway to the divine, the "guide, the guardian of my heart, and soul / Of all my moral being."[10] As if Austen wants to call attention to this poem, transparencies of Tintern Abbey decorate Fanny's room. Throughout *Mansfield Park* Fanny applies her poetic fancy to the natural scenes she encounters: "the trees, though not fully clothed, were in that delightful state, when farther beauty is known to be at hand, and when, while much is actually given to the sight, more yet remains for the imagination" (446–47). To destroy an

avenue or grove of trees is to eliminate a source of imaginative pleasure and spiritual health. "Cut down an avenue! What a pity! Does
not it make you think of Cowper? 'Ye fallen avenues, once more I
mourn your fate unmerited'" (56). Like Marianne Dashwood, Fanny
cites romantic nature writers Austen liked such as William Cowper
and Sir Walter Scott.

Fanny's romanticism also shows in her warmth of heart and acute
feelings. Fanny helps to smooth over disputes between her younger
sisters, writes to her sailor-brother, worries about leaving her incom-
petent Aunt Bertram alone, cares about Sir Thomas's feelings, helps
the clueless Mr. Rushworth study his dramatic part, listens kindly to
Edmund and Mary, and soothes the spirits of her vexed cousins, Maria
and Julia. Fanny's frequent tears throughout the novel result both
from her loving, empathetic nature and from her timidity and sensitivity.

Unlike Marianne Dashwood of *Sense and Sensibility* feeding her
sorrow and openly exhibiting her grief, Fanny Price can hide her feelings. She suffers real pain (Austen repeats the word "stab") but immediately strives to conquer her emotions by praying for strength and
consulting her reason: "It was a stab. . . . He would marry Miss
Crawford. It was a stab. . . . Till she had shed many tears . . . Fanny
could not subdue her agitation; and the dejection which followed could
only be relieved by the influence of fervent prayers for his happiness.
It was her intention, as she felt it to be her duty, to try to overcome all
that was excessive, all that bordered on selfishness in her affection for
Edmund. . . . She would endeavour to be rational. . . . She had all the
heroism of principle, and was determined to do her duty" (264–65).
Fanny has Marianne Dashwood's excessive feelings but is determined
to govern them. Yet Fanny refuses to go as far as the self-controlled
Elinor does in dissembling and lying for the sake of social acceptability.
Artless Fanny cannot ever play a role: "I could not act any thing. . . .
No, indeed, I cannot act. . . . I really cannot act," she insists truthfully—
and redundantly (145–46).

Fanny can stand up to her peers and to her elders if she feels a
request will violate her principles. Even the tainted Henry Crawford
knows that Fanny is the one truly spiritual person he has met: "Henry
Crawford had too much sense not to feel the worth of good principles
in a wife. . . when he talked of her having such a steadiness and
regularity of conduct, such a high notion of honour, and such an
observance of decorum as might warrant any man in the fullest dependence on her faith and integrity, he expressed what was inspired

by the knowledge of her being well principled and religious" (294). Like Edmund acknowledging Fanny's goodness and "mental superiority," Henry grants her "touches of the angel" and admits to her, "You are infinitely my superior in merit. . . . You have qualities which I had not before supposed to exist in such a degree in any human creature" (471, 344, 343).

Did an author who claimed in a letter not to like literary pictures of perfection decide in *Mansfield Park* to create a flawless, angelic heroine? As Edmund tells his father, "Fanny is the only one who has judged rightly throughout" (187). Fanny seems a mixture of thinking and feeling, sense and sensibility, displaying both a literate mind and an affectionate heart. So does Austen present Fanny as the model of womanhood? Is anything *wrong* with Fanny Price?

Austen implies that Fanny's chief fault is a tendency to be too overwhelmed by circumstances. Fanny not only must learn to find her voice—to speak up no matter how shy and intimidated she feels inside—but also to "buck up" rather than give up. Fanny's sensitivity is so great that she feels guilty when she does not mourn her stern uncle's absence: Fanny "really grieved because she could not grieve" (33). She flagellates herself for her own emotions, as when for her rival she experiences "feelings so near akin to envy, as made her hate herself for having them" (413). Austen notes that Fanny feels so embarrassed by her unrequited love of Edmund that "she would rather die than own the truth" and feels melodramatically convinced that "she was miserable for ever" (317, 321).

Austen gently mocks Fanny for being too devastated even by the misbehavior of others. Like Jane Bennet, loath to admit humanity's capacity for evil, Fanny seems too thunderstruck by all-too-common moral frailty. For example, when Fanny learns of her married cousin's disgraceful adultery, she indulges in "shudderings of horror" because this "horrible evil" is "too horrible a confusion of guilt, too gross a complication of evil, for human nature, not in a state of utter barbarism, to be capable of!" (440–41). How healthy and helpful is it when Fanny contemplates a sort of mass suicide for the whole Bertram-Rushworth-Crawford family? Fanny thinks "it scarcely possible for them to support life and reason under such disgrace; and it appeared to her, that as far as this world alone was concerned, the greatest blessing to every one of kindred with Mrs. Rushworth would be instant annihilation" (442). Through this hyperbolic language, Austen demonstrates that Fanny needs a thicker skin to withstand the world, whether her parents' noisy, squalid home or the teeming, corrupted metropolis of London. Otherwise she will display a virtue so cloistered that it represents an escape from life rather than an embrace of its true reality.

Much as she gently mocked seventeen-year-old Marianne Dashwood's arrogance of youth in *Sense and Sensibility* ("At my time of life opinions are tolerably fixed," [*SS,* 93]), so Austen smiles at Fanny's realization that maybe at age eighteen she has not yet experienced all life might offer: "She began to feel that she had not yet gone through all the changes of opinion and sentiment, which the progress of time and variation of circumstances occasion in this world of changes. The vicissitudes of the human mind had not yet been exhausted by her" (374). Fanny may be sweet and angelic, but she is a *young,* inexperienced woman who still has a long way to go, Austen suggests. She needs to see more of the world without being "instantly annihilated" by the experience or, like Mary Crawford, corrupted by the encounter.

Although Austen presents Fanny Price as the indisputable heroine of this novel, she goes to great lengths to make Mary Crawford seem a more appealing character in many ways—and one whose voice at times sounds remarkably like Austen's. A mixture of attractive features and unfortunate deficiencies, the witty, energetic, self-assured Mary can draw readers' attention away from Fanny Price as easily as she does Edmund Bertram's. After reading *Mansfield Park,* one of Austen's own nephews was "interested by nobody but Mary Crawford" (*MW,* 431).

While Fanny trembles to hear even *talk* of horses, Mary proves herself a bold horsewoman: "Miss Crawford's enjoyment of riding was such, that she did not know how to leave off. Active and fearless, and, though rather small, strongly made, she seemed formed for a horsewoman" (66). Boasting "I am very strong," Mary has "the conviction of very much surpassing her sex in general by her early progress" in horsemanship (68, 67). By making Mary small, like Fanny, Austen removes the chance that size can be used as any excuse for Fanny's timidity and fragility. Described as "gifted by nature with strength and courage," Mary claims to be a "woman of spirit" who was "not born to sit still and do nothing" (69, 243). Mary would excel in a marathon while Fanny would quit with a headache after a quarter of a mile.

Mary shines indoors as well as outdoors. Instead of wanting to let others beat her at cards, Mary boasts, "I will stake my last" and promptly wins the game (243). She enlivens any drawing room because she possesses genuine artistic accomplishments (like Marianne Dashwood) and a flair for witty conversation (like Elizabeth Bennet). Like Elizabeth Bennet believing that Wickham is virtuous because he appears to be so charming, Edmund feels for Mary "an ecstasy of admiration of all her many virtues, from her obliging manners down to her light and graceful tread" (112).

Like Austen, Mary is well read and loves word play. Joking about the poor morals of the rear admirals and vice admirals she has met, Mary quips, "Of Rears and Vices, I saw enough. Now, do not be suspecting me of a pun, I entreat" (60). She is the only Austen character to *announce* that she is constructing a parody of a parody:

> "Sir Thomas is to achieve mighty things when he comes home," said Mary, after a pause. "Do you remember Hawkins Browne's 'Address to Tobacco,' in imitation of Pope?–
> > 'Blest leaf! whose aromatic gales dispense
> > To Templars modesty, to Parsons sense.'
> I will parody them:
> > 'Blest Knight! whose dictatorial looks dispense
> > To Children affluence, to Rushworth sense.'
> Will not that do . . .?" (161–62)

Mary's choice of Isaac Hawkins Browne's parody of Alexander Pope is significant: Browne was a minor poet known for wit, repartee, frivolity, and a squandered talent; a man who admitted that wealth, "the downy couch of ease," and associations with "the vulgar herd" had kept him from contemplation and loftier thoughts.[11] In a novel mentioning the slave trade and Sir Thomas's sugar plantations, perhaps Austen also includes the reference to tobacco as a reminder of another crop in which extensive slave labor in the East Indies and in America was used to provide a luxury for England. Like Browne, Mary Crawford seems to waste her wit on idle, irreverent doggerel.

Austen gives Mary Crawford the breezy tone and sharp bite of her own letters. In private letters, Austen shows her fondness for puns and alliteration, quipping that Alexander Pope is the "one infallible Pope" (26 October 1813) and describing a life of "Candour & Comfort & Coffee & Cribbage" (9 February 1813). Which of the following is an Austen letter and which is a remark by Mary Crawford?

> "What a difference a vowel makes! If his rents were but equal to his rants!"

> "It is a Vile World, we are all for Self & I expected no better from any of us. But though *Better* is not to be expected, *Butter* may, at least from Mrs Clement's Cow."

Both Mary and Austen laugh at themselves. Again, which is which?

> "Expect a most agreeable letter; for not being overburdened with subject—(having nothing at all to say)—I shall have no check to my Genius from beginning to end."

> "It is impossible to put an hundredth part of my great mind on paper."

(Answer: first and fourth are Mary [394, 415]; second and third are Austen's letters of 23 January 1817 and 21 January 1801.) Some of Mary Crawford's remarks also sound like those attributed to Austen's flamboyant, Frenchified cousin, Eliza de Feuillide, who used private theatricals to flirt with Austen's brothers and remarked, "I always find that the most effectual mode of getting rid of temptation is to give way to it."[12]

Austen has Mary Crawford drop into conversation phrases such as *menus plaisir*, *esprit de corps*, *adieu*, *bon vivant*, and *lines passionées*. In contrast, the plain-speaking, very English Edmund insists that he cannot produce a *bon mot*, rejecting the sparkling but empty repartee of Parisian wits. Yet Austen herself dots her fiction and her letters with French phrases, as when she notes with greater spirit than accuracy, "What a Contretems!—in the Language of France" (9 February 1807). At the same time, Austen links the witty Mary Crawford to the decadence and selfishness of French culture by having Mary compare herself to the narcissistic Doge in the court of Louis XIV. In addition, Mary's insistence that her brother's adulterous relationship with Maria is just a moment's *étourderie* suggests a thoughtlessness consistent with this character who is "careless as a woman and a friend" (437, 260). Mary's casual, affected language shows that she deems her brother's real act of wrongdoing a trifling matter.

Even when playing the harp Mary seems more bent on uttering clever remarks than on responding genuinely to the music. Like the apocryphal story of Marie Antoinette suggesting that the poor eat cake, Mary Crawford has no compunction against demanding a cart for transporting her harp even if farmers need it for the harvest. She is surprised to find that her selfish arrogance "offended all the farmers, all the labourers, all the hay in the parish" (58). As she tells Fanny at another point, "Selfishness must always be forgiven you know, because there is no hope for a cure" (68). Austen links Mary to the corruption of the city by having her cite "the true London maxim, that every thing is to be got with money" (58).

Mary's cynicism extends to all aspects of society, including the church. Just as Mrs. Ferrars and Fanny Dashwood in *Sense and Sensibility* reject the church as not "smart" enough a profession for Edward Ferrars, Mary Crawford totally opposes Edmund's choice of entering the clergy and advises him to go into the law. Mary also has little faith in those who attend church. In the same chapel where Fanny expects awe and magnificence and praises the value of families assembled together for prayer, Mary thinks of the many parishioners who would prefer to sleep late or whose minds are somewhere else entirely.

Austen certainly shared Mary Crawford's irreverence toward those merely pretending to be godly and had already included in her novels young women in church thinking about their clothes rather than the message. In *Mansfield Park* she validates Mary's views by portraying Dr. Grant as a clergyman more interested in his dinners than his duties. Like Mary, Austen saw through many instances of "seeming piety" (87). But Mary shows no sign of allegiance to any higher purpose, sense of duty or conscience, or inner spiritual guide. As Edmund concludes, Mary's faults are "faults of principle—blunted delicacy and a corrupted, vitiated mind" (456).

Mary Crawford is nonetheless one of the most discerning and self-aware characters in Austen's fictional universe. She does not sleep through the novel, like the childish Lady Bertram; sponge off others while boasting of generosity, like the mean-spirited Aunt Norris; or join Maria and Julia Bertram in thinking that rattling off the names of kings, cruel emperors, and heathen gods constitutes an education. Mary looks both in the mirror and out the window and knows something is profoundly wanting. An orphan raised by a debauched admiral and his embittered wife in a metropolis teeming with corrupted people, Mary has been robbed of faith. "A tinge of wrong" mars her behavior and taints her mind (269). Frequently restless and discontented, Mary sometimes forces laughter, but her gaiety seems empty: Austen describes her as "trying to appear gay and unconcerned" or trying "to speak carelessly; but she was not so careless as she wanted to appear" (288, 458). A lively, charming, accomplished young woman, Mary Crawford *could* have been truly admirable had she been given a moral education to counter the inescapable corruption of the world around her.

The narrator of *Mansfield Park* combines Mary's wit with Fanny's conscience. Like Mary, Austen delights in irreverence and parodies classical syntax. "Much was said, and much was ate, and all went well," the narrator observes, much as Austen in a letter had noted, "They came & they sat & they went" (6 November 1813). But like Fanny, the narrator demonstrates genuine appreciation of nature and an uncompromising moral integrity. By the end of *Mansfield Park*, neither Mary Crawford nor Fanny Price has changed much in essentials. Instead, the narrative voice offers readers an alternative combining the best of both women.

In this novel Austen reserves the language of character transformation and moral journey for three male characters: Sir Thomas Bertram and his two sons, Tom and Edmund. This is the only novel to portray a blind father who sees the light, a dissolute elder son who finds goodness, and a serious younger son who has to *learn* to love the heroine.

No other Austen father grows as much as Sir Thomas Bertram does. Mr. Morland stays in the background of *Northanger Abbey*, Mr. Dashwood dies in the opening chapter of *Sense and Sensibility*, Mr. Bennet lapses back into cynicism by the end of *Pride and Prejudice*, Mr. Woodhouse remains a childhood hypochondriac throughout *Emma,* and Sir Walter Elliot continues his vanity and snobbery from start to finish of *Persuasion*. It is far more difficult to label Sir Thomas of *Mansfield Park*. A complex figure, Sir Thomas illustrates the danger of imperialism and patriarchy but also the redeeming power of humility, morality, charity, and love.

From the start, Sir Thomas has good intentions. Austen's phrase "well-meant condescensions" captures her ambivalent view of this slave-holding aristocrat and imperious father (13). Sir Thomas scares Fanny with his harsh, severe demeanor, but his charity in welcoming his sister-in-law's puny daughter into his household suggests his sense of honor and generosity. Proud to be "master at Mansfield Park," he is a serious, dignified, undemonstrative man characterized by "steady sobriety and orderly silence" and a strict sense of decorum (370, 240). His offspring not surprisingly respond by craving laughter and a release from restraint.

A political and social product of his time, Sir Thomas does his duty in Parliament and strives to make his plantations in Antigua profitable. Sir Thomas seems a no-nonsense, unimaginative man who believes "there should be moderation in everything" (313). At home, he composedly accepts a wife as a sleepy ornament, prides himself on having given his children everything they need, and views Fanny Price as socially inferior in rank and rights. In "leaving his daughters to the direction of others at their present most interesting time of life" when he travels to Antigua, he errs in thinking his sister-in-law, Mrs. Norris, would make a good director (32). He also errs in agreeing to a marriage between his eldest daughter and the stupid but wealthy Mr. Rushworth. Devoid of "romantic delicacy," Sir Thomas egotistically views the alliance as beneficial: He is "happy to secure a marriage which would bring *him* such an addition of respectability and influence" (331, 201; my italics). Sir Thomas sees nothing wrong with his children's education, nor does he detect Aunt Norris's lack of judgment, morals, and compassion until everything falls apart. He becomes wrathful when thwarted, as when he subjects a disobedient Fanny to an abusive harangue or dismisses her to her squalid home as a "medicinal project" designed to teach her a lesson (369).

Yet Sir Thomas absolutely should not be viewed as a Simon Legree. Even in the early sections of *Mansfield Park* Sir Thomas has a keener sense of honor than many around him. Certainly he shines next to Fanny's drunken, callous, vulgar father, Lieutenant Price, who ignores his daughters and indulges his rowdy sons. A moral man, Sir Thomas encourages Edmund to be the sort of clergyman who lives in his parish and takes his duties seriously. Sir Thomas sadly recognizes that his eldest son lacks Edmund's integrity and sense of responsibility. "I blush for you, Tom," Sir Thomas says as he learns that the future Sir Thomas's extravagant, hedonistic ways have caused debts that will hurt Edmund's opportunities (23). Sir Thomas may be angry with Fanny for refusing to marry Henry Crawford, but he also is appalled to discover that Aunt Norris has never allowed a fire in Fanny's room. As master of the house, he immediately orders a fire to be lit even when he is angry with her.

Most remarkable is Sir Thomas's capacity to admit his errors, feel the sting of self-reproach, and change his ways. Although Austen wraps up *Mansfield Park* with a breezy tone ("Let other pens dwell on guilt and misery") promising readers their expected happy ending for hero and heroine, she makes sure that we know that Sir Thomas has suffered longest: "Sir Thomas, poor Sir Thomas, a parent, and conscious of errors in his own conduct as a parent, was the longest to suffer. He felt that he ought not to have allowed the marriage, that his daughter's sentiments had been sufficiently known to him to render him culpable in authorising it, that in so doing he had sacrificed the right to the expedient, and been governed by motives of selfishness and worldly wisdom" (461). Austen spends several pages dwelling on Sir Thomas's guilt and misery, reminding us that although his sense of loss deadens and he finds new sources of comfort, the pain always remains: "the anguish arising from the conviction of his own errors in the education of his daughters was never to be entirely done away with" (463). Had Mr. Bennet or Mr. Price felt their own errors so deeply, they would be on the road to becoming not only far better fathers but also far better men.

Sir Thomas knows that his repression of his children has led them to rebel (could this be a swipe at King George III's approach to that "strange business . . . in America" mentioned earlier in the novel?), and he admits that delegating authority to Aunt Norris has been "grievous mismanagement" (119, 463). Most importantly, Sir Thomas recognizes that his concept of education has been sorely deficient: "Something must have been wanting *within.* . . . He feared that principle, active principle, had been wanting, that they had never been properly taught to govern their inclinations and tempers, by that sense of duty which can alone suffice. They had been instructed theoretically in their religion, but never required to bring it into daily practice. To be distinguished for elegance and accomplishments . . . could have had . . . no moral effect on the mind" (463). Sir Thomas bitterly, wretchedly confesses that he has meant well but done ill, spent much but accomplished little. His reference to fancy balls in Antigua suggests that, like many British colonialists, he has himself led a life of luxury too far removed from hard work and self-denial. Tom, Maria, and Julia are idly rich yet morally impoverished. Knowing now that he has spoiled his children, Sir Thomas can "acknowledge the advantages of early hardship and discipline, and the consciousness of being born to struggle and endure," recognize the selfish, bossy Aunt Norris as an evil "part of himself," and feel "sick of ambitious and mercenary connections" (465–66, 471). Austen uses strong, repetitive language in the final page of *Mansfield Park* ("Sir Thomas saw repeated, and for ever repeated, reason to rejoice in what he had done for them all") to show that Sir Thomas reaps rewards for his early charity in bringing Fanny into his house (473).

Again Austen keeps the spotlight on the distance Sir Thomas has traveled, literally and figuratively. He has faced disorder in Antigua, thousands of miles away, as well as disaster at home. In the concluding chapter of *Mansfield Park*, Austen spends far more time on Sir Thomas than on her supposed hero and heroine. She reminds us that Sir Thomas now finds felicity in a union he had originally shuddered to contemplate: "The high sense of having realised a great acquisition in the promise of Fanny for a daughter, formed just such a contrast with his early opinion on the subject when the poor little girl's coming had been first agitated, as time is for ever producing between the plans and decisions of mortals, for their own instruction, and their neighbours' entertainment" (472). Growth occurs not just in youthful, romantic heroes and heroines but also in fathers. Not all drama happens on the way to the altar. Austen's sentence widens its focus from Sir Thomas to "mortals" in general, suggesting that all of us possess the potential over time to become wiser and better human beings. By referring to the "instruction" and "entertainment" produced by contemplating such character changes, Austen reminds readers of her own dual mission as a moral but comic novelist.

Austen suggests that a gentleman is made, not born—and made only through a painful process of self-reflection and discovery. Along with their father, Tom and Edmund Bertram also are significantly transformed by the novel's end, Tom in his behavior and Edmund in his perception.

As eldest son and the future Sir Thomas, Tom Bertram has been raised to do little but pursue his own pleasures, spend money, and view life as an extended holiday. Unlike his grave younger brother, Tom is full of liveliness, "cheerful selfishness," and the gift of gab, with "easy manners, excellent spirits . . . and a great deal to say" (24, 47). He has bad friends, a penchant for drink, and an aversion to work. Because he has never had to strive, Tom seems restless, "having so much leisure as to make almost any novelty a certain good" (123). For Tom, as for Marianne Dashwood in *Sense and Sensibility*, illness brings change. As his brother nurses him back to health, Tom begins recovering from both a physical and moral sickness, shedding his "thoughtlessness and selfishness" and becoming "what he ought to be, useful to his father, steady and quiet, and not living merely for himself. (462)

Edmund does not need to reproach himself for gambling and drinking as does his brother, but he knows that his infatuation with the dazzling Mary Crawford has blinded him and led him to compromise his own standards. As Fanny notes when Edmund agrees to act in love scenes with Mary in theatricals that he knows his absent father would oppose, "the scruples of his integrity, seemed all done away" (367). Like Marianne finding the handsome Willoughby perfect, Edmund gives Mary Crawford "merits which she had not" and labels her "sweet and faultless" (264, 269). A serious man with "not the least wit" in his nature, Edmund avoids gallant flattery and vapid small talk, but he nevertheless seems drawn to the witty Mary Crawford like a moth to a flame (94).

Edmund possesses all the necessary ingredients for a gentleman ("strong good sense and uprightness of mind," "his sincerity, his steadiness, his integrity") but lacks backbone and discernment (21, 65). He seems to have absorbed some of his father's paternalism, commenting in patronizing tones about how he has shaped, formed, and directed Fanny's mind. Just as Sir Thomas fails to understand Fanny's feelings but likes to advise her, so Edmund trivializes Fanny's emotions when he assumes that it can make no difference to her whether or not she stays at Mansfield Park, or when he speaks of a possible marriage to Henry Crawford as a coup for her. A superior listener and perceiver, Fanny knows Edmund far better than Edmund knows Fanny—or himself.

Like Catherine Morland's awakening, Marianne Dashwood's transformation, and Elizabeth Bennet's enlightenment, Edmund Bertram undergoes a metamorphosis. By the novel's end, he confesses of his infatuation for Mary Crawford, "My eyes are opened. . . . How have I been deceived!" (456, 459). Edmund now can return to the role suggested by the meaning of his name: Edmund signifies "a gentleman who prospers by helping others." Just as he acted as a true gentleman by serving as kind guardian of the young Fanny from the time she arrives at Mansfield Park, so he now can flourish by nursing his brother Tom, loving the worthy Fanny, helping his afflicted parents, and comforting and guiding his parishioners.

Cassandra Austen faulted her sister for marrying Fanny to the staid Edmund Bertram rather than to the more charming Henry Crawford. As niece Louisa Knight observed, "Cassandra tried to persuade Miss Austen to alter *Mansfield Park* and let Mr. Crawford marry Fanny Price . . . but Miss Austen stood firm and would not allow a change."[13] Fanny stands firm as well, proclaiming her right to say no: "I should have thought . . . that every woman must have felt the possibility of a man's not being approved, not being loved by some one of her sex, at least, let him be ever so generally agreeable. Let him have all the perfections in the world, I think it ought not to be set down as certain, that a man must be acceptable to every woman he may happen to like himself" (353). Elinor Dashwood in *Sense and Sensibility* said wryly of planned marriages, "The lady, I suppose, has no choice in the affair" (*SS,* 296). Never wry, Fanny Price straightforwardly defends a woman's right to select her own partner in life.

Just as it takes the shy Fanny greater courage to speak up to Sir Thomas than for Elizabeth to bandy words with Lady Catherine, so Fanny faces a greater challenge in rejecting Henry Crawford than any other Austen heroine will face from a suitor. Marianne and Elinor Dashwood receive no extra marriage proposals, and it is easy for Catherine Morland to reject the boorish John Thorpe or for Elizabeth Bennet to disappoint the pompous Mr. Collins. In *Mansfield Park*, however, the devil-as-suitor is more cleverly disguised; the temptation to accept him thus is greater. Fanny's powers of discernment allow her to acknowledge that Henry surpasses other men in some respects ("he had more confidence than Edmund, more judgment than Thomas, more talent and taste than Mr. Yates"), but she remains convinced that this "best actor of all" is wrong for her—and tinged with wrong himself (165).

Henry Crawford's flirtation with other women and his adultery with Maria stem from his vanity, selfishness, restlessness, and immorality. Deeming it his "right" to gain Fanny, Henry arrogantly assumes he can *make* Fanny like him and relishes the glory of forcing her to love him. Henry changes for the better in the process of pursuing Fanny, but even when he speaks of his kindly intentions, his ego cannot be suppressed: "My Fanny . . . my happiness . . . I am the doer . . . I am the person to give the consequence. . . . What can Sir Thomas and Edmund together do . . . to what I *shall* do?" Henry exclaims, delighting like a competitor in the fact that he can do more for her than others (297). Ego also drives Henry's adulterous relationship with Maria Bertram. Mortified by her rejection of their former intimacy, Henry's vanity is pricked and "he began the attack," determined "to subdue" Maria and make her "wholly at his command" (468).

What makes Henry a harder figure to relegate to the villain heap is that he, like his sister, has an excuse. Orphaned, they have been raised by guardians who have exposed them to corruption and cynicism. Austen seems determined in this novel to call readers' attention to the importance of upbringing. "The admiral's lessons have quite spoiled him," Mary admits of her brother (43). Also like Mary, Henry sees himself in the mirror and finds himself wanting. Nowhere is that more evident than in his envy for Fanny's sailor-brother, the "frank, unstudied, but feeling and respectful" William Price (233).

Unlike Henry, William has faced hardship, whether struggles to transcend a disordered home or adversity at sea for seven years. An open, unsophisticated, loving young man with both skills and scruples,

William inspires Henry Crawford's envy: "Henry Crawford . . . longed to have been at sea, and seen and done and suffered as much. His heart was warmed, his fancy fired, and he felt the highest respect for a lad who, before he was twenty, had gone through such bodily hardships, and given such proofs of mind. The glory of heroism, of usefulness, of exertion, of endurance, made his own habits of selfish indulgence appear in shameful contrast; and he wished he had been a William Price, distinguishing himself and working his way to fortune and consequence with so much self-respect and happy ardour, instead of what he was!" (236). Like many a New Year's resolution, however, Henry's desire for self-improvement lasts but a moment: "The wish was rather eager than lasting. He was roused from the reverie of retrospection and regret produced by it, by some inquiry . . . as to his plans for the next day's hunting; and he found it was as well to be a man of fortune at once with horses and grooms at his command" (236–37). Henry Crawford remains a man of fortune at the end of *Mansfield Park,* punished only by whatever momentary regrets he may feel. Like Willoughby in *Sense and Sensibility,* Henry will continue to shine in society's drawing rooms by using charm and elocution to mask inner discord. As a woman, Maria will be left disgraced and in exile; as a man, Henry (like Willoughby) can go on with his life. In a bitingly feminist narrative voice, Austen observes, "That punishment, the public punishment of disgrace, should in a just measure attend *his* share of the offence, is, we know, not one of the barriers, which society gives to virtue" (468).

Austen adds an unusual sentence after her description of the unpunished Henry Crawford: "*In this world,* the penalty is less equal than could be wished; but without presuming to look forward to *a juster appointment hereafter,* we may fairly consider a man of sense like Henry Crawford, to be providing for himself no small portion of vexation and regret" (468; my italics). This is the only passage I have found in which Jane Austen invites readers (albeit indirectly, "without presuming") to consider the eternal punishment waiting for scoundrels who blithely walk away scot-free from the wreckage they cause. Of all Austen's novels, *Mansfield Park* reminds us most that even if we obtain checkered "happiness à la mortal" or a marriage "as secure as earthly happiness can be," this does not begin to address immortality or the soul.

Another way Austen shows an interest in immortality in *Mansfield Park* is by spending far more time exploring the value of a clerical life. In *Pride and Prejudice* readers can hardly take the Reverend Mr. Collins seriously when he boasts, "I consider the clerical office as equal in point of dignity with the highest rank in the kingdom" (*PP,* 97). In Collins's case, this is hardly true, as he is a man of limited intellect, little heart, and less spirituality who cringes before anyone of rank. In *Mansfield Park*, however, Jane Austen shows the truth of Mr. Collins's statement. As a clergyman, Edmund Bertram *does* rank as high—or higher—in moral principle as any other man in the novel. Mary Crawford is wrong to label the profession nothing and to assume that it would be stooping for her to ally herself with Edmund if he adopts such a career. As Edmund responds, a clergyman who honors his work can be of "first importance to mankind" because he serves as the guardian "of religion and morals" and affects individuals and groups of people "both temporally and eternally" (92).

If Edmund is correct that "as the clergy are, or are not what they ought to be, so are the rest of the nation," then the nation is a mixture (93). Austen gives us both Dr. Grant, a selfish, claret-drinking clergyman who dies of "three great institutionary dinners in one week," and the upright, conscientious Edmund. As if to underscore the religious focus of this novel, Austen ends *Mansfield Park* not with a conversation between the happily married Fanny and Edmund but with a reference to the parsonage. Edmund's replacement of the Reverend Mr. Norris and the Reverend Dr. Grant offers evidence that "the Nation" may be moving in the right direction—at least in the isolated rural world "within the view" of Mansfield Park (473).

Mansfield Park emphasizes not only spiritual life but also "a more fraternal"—brotherly love—rather than the romantic love invariably described in popular fiction. When William Price and Henry Crawford depart from Mansfield Park, Sir Thomas mistakenly assumes that Fanny's heart will be saddened as much by the absence of her handsome suitor as by her sailor brother. The narrator tells us otherwise: "She sat and cried *con amore* as her uncle intended, but it was con amore fraternal and no other" (282). Much as *Sense and Sensibility* concludes with the image of close sisters and brothers living in harmony and equality, so *Mansfield Park* celebrates fraternity as the soundest basis for human relationships.

Those lacking in fraternal love are morally bankrupt. Lady Bertram and Aunt Norris have cast off their less fortunate sister, Mrs. Price, and the "absolute breach between the sisters" points to their shortage of sensibility and humanity (4). When Tom Bertram becomes dangerously ill, Mrs. Price feels as little for his mother as Lady Bertram would feel for her in a similar predicament: "So long divided, and so differently situated, the ties of blood were little more than nothing. . . . Mrs. Price did quite as much for Lady Bertram, as Lady Bertram would have done for Mrs. Price. Three or four Prices might have been swept away, any or all, except Fanny or William, and Lady Bertram would have thought little about it; or perhaps might have caught from Mrs. Norris's lips the cant of its being a very happy thing, and a great blessing to their poor dear sister Price to have them so well provided for" (428). Like Jonathan Swift but without his irony, Aunt Norris could have written a modest proposal suggesting that killing some of the Price children would help solve her sister's economic distress.

These three sisters' uncaring relationship contrasts sharply with the warm love between William and Fanny Price. Some have found the scenes between William and Fanny nearly incestuous, including William's plan near the end of the novel for a little cottage "in which he and Fanny were to pass all their middle and latter life together" (375).[14] I disagree. Just as Jane and Cassandra Austen lived together happily, forming a warm family life and living primarily off income provided by generous brothers, so William and Fanny Price imagine an alternative domestic oasis, should neither one find a suitable mate. Knowing that life together with William is a possibility, Fanny need not marry for the wrong reasons: she does not have to escape her parents (like Maria and Julia), gain an income (like Mary's ambitious, mercenary friend Mrs. Fraser), or find a moral mentor (like Henry and Mary Crawford). Perhaps their youthful picture of adult life together in a cottage is a bit naive and puerile, overly virginal, but it does offer an alternative form of love should romance be denied them.

Watching Fanny with her brother leads not to prurient discomfort but to admiration in "all who had hearts to value any thing good" (235). Some of Fanny's purest and happiest moments occur when she is with her brother. In a novel laced with political overtones, it is interesting that Austen describes Fanny's felicitous relationship with her brother as lacking in restraint, hierarchy, and repression: it is "unchecked, equal, fearless" (234).

Austen interrupts the tale of her fictional siblings reminiscing about their shared childhood to insert a general paragraph about the superiority of fraternal to conjugal ties: "An advantage this, a strengthener of love, in which even the conjugal tie is beneath the fraternal. Children of the same family, the same blood, with the same first associations and habits, have some means of enjoyment in their power, which no subsequent connections can supply; and it must be by a long and unnatural estrangement, by a divorce which no subsequent connection can justify, if such precious remains of the earliest attachments are ever entirely outlived. Too often, alas! it is so.–Fraternal love, sometimes almost every thing, is at others worse than nothing" (234–35). Just as *Pride and Prejudice* overturned romantic notions of love at first sight and celebrated gradually developed esteem, so this description of the long-lasting ties of fraternal love posits a new model for any love: love based on shared memories, mutual enjoyment, and unbroken connections.

To reinforce that idea, Austen shows the relationship between Edmund and Fanny as fraternal affection transformed into conjugal love. Is this another instance of incest? Aunt Norris certainly thinks so, as when she declares to Sir Thomas that it is "morally impossible" for those raised as brother and sister to fall in love (6). Edmund initially looks to Fanny with "the kind smile of an affectionate brother" and refers to her even near the end as "my Fanny–my only sister" (222, 444). Yet ultimately Edmund comes to realize (as Fanny has for hundreds of pages) that "her warm and sisterly regard for him would be foundation enough for wedded love" (470). Implied in that comment is the radical concept of "unchecked, equal, fearless" intercourse between husband and wife.

As narrator, Austen clearly approves of Fanny and Edmund's morality and their felicitous, slow growing "wedded love." At the same time, she ends the novel with vagueness about the details of their courtship ("I purposely abstain from dates"), part of a general pattern in this novel of avoiding the sound of full omnipotence (470). After all, Austen's very first word in *Mansfield Park* is a guess ("*About* thirty years ago, Miss Maria Ward") places her at a distance from her material. She speculates ("I have no inclination to believe") rather than announces that Fanny would not be as unconquerable as the "young ladies of seventeen one reads about" (231). She remains vague on how long Fanny expects Henry's affections to last ("It would not be fair to enquire") as well as on how long it takes for Edmund to switch his affections from Mary to Fanny (331). When Mrs. Norris is bundled off with the disgraced Maria to a remote, private establishment in another country, Austen does not follow them there but merely concludes, "it may be reasonably supposed that their tempers became their mutual punishment" (465).

Why this narrative vagueness? Why never give us a conversation between Fanny and Edmund once they have moved beyond fraternal to conjugal affections? John Halperin assumes another "botched ending" resulting from Jane Austen's inability to render romantic scenes.[15] This, however, would fail to explain why she also backs away from the specific fates of her villainous characters ("Let other pens dwell on guilt and misery") and acts as if she does not fully know any of her characters. In a novel about inner lives—the thoughts, reflections, and contemplations of people in solitude—Austen perhaps wishes to remind readers that none of us can really enter into the private recesses of another human mind.

At the same time, she invites us to become mental travelers following her clues. The mind seems a major topic in this novel, whether it is Fanny's struggle to have her "beauty of mind" recognized rather than her pretty figure or the narrator's demonstration of her own wise and witty thoughts. Take, for instance, Fanny's reference to little more than a line of William Cowper's "The Task": "Ye fallen avenues! once more I mourn / Your fate unmerited." This is all we are given on the surface. But what happens if we track down the allusion? The line comes from "The Sofa," book 1 of Cowper's six-book poem. Like Austen describing Lady Bertram lounging on the sofa rather than tending to more important duties, Cowper warns in "The Sofa" that society's move from no furniture to simple stools to elegant sofas may be a loss, not a gain; our increasingly refined, idle rich have obtained an unhappy leisure rather than an active usefulness. Cowper's phrasing ("languid eye," "vapid soul," "tedious card parties") parallels Austen's, as does his attack on cities filled with vice, schools without discipline, and pulpits without honor.[16]

I speculate that Austen hoped her readers would take her quotation of one line from "The Task" as an invitation to dig more deeply into Cowper's poem. It simply seems too coincidental that the poem also includes a ringing indictment of clerical abuses, an attack on the immorality of slavery, and a celebration of the divine power of nature.

In strong poetic language, Cowper calls on his fellow clergymen not to seek applause, perform theatrics, follow fashion, or cultivate empty figures of speech. "Avaunt all attitude and stare, / And start theatric, practised at the glass," Cowper insists. Good preachers can reform their listeners by plainly speaking the truth from their hearts: "I seek divine simplicity in him / Who handles things divine." Austen's creation of Edmund Bertram gives fictional life to the very sort of clergyman Cowper imagines. Edmund's avoidance of bon mots and oratorical flourishes makes him a better conduit for religious truths. Cowper makes it clear that clergymen should reject "lightness of speech," beware the seduction of "popular applause" and avoid jests, grins, "foppish airs and histrionic mummery" that "let down / The pulpit to the level of the stage." If religion relaxes its hold on "the roving and untutored heart," the result is that "the laity run wild."

Those who fault Austen for not going further in her attack on colonialism might revise their thinking if they follow her Cowper allusions. Austen's readers would have known Cowper in a way few of us do today. An ardent abolitionist, Cowper launches an eloquent tirade against "the wrong and outrage" of slavery in the very next book of "The Task," denouncing it as an offense against human brotherhood. Those with "a skin not coloured" the same become "lawful prey" of cruel masters, who chain them, work them to exhaustion, and lash their bodies "with stripes that Mercy, with a bleeding heart, / Weeps when she sees inflicted on a beast." Cowper's words are strong:

> Then what is man? And what man seeing this,
> And having human feelings, does not blush
> And hang his head, to think himself a man?
> I would not have a slave to till my ground,
> To carry me, to fan me while I sleep,
> And tremble when I wake, for all the wealth
> That sinews bought and sold have ever earned.

Cowper concludes, "We have no slaves at home.—Then why abroad?" a question which goes as unanswered in the poem as it does when Fanny raises the topic at Mansfield Park. Perhaps had Maria and Julia Bertram read this lengthy poem they might have joined their reflective cousin in questioning the source of their wealth.

As if she were writing in invisible ink, I believe Jane Austen uses the allusion to Cowper's "The Task" to bring his stirring words into readers' minds. She can thus attack the inhumanity of slavery without turning *Mansfield Park* into an abolitionist tract. Her brother Frank had already spoken out against the "harshness and despotism" of "land-holders or their managers in the West India Islands," observing, "Slavery however it is modified is still slavery."[17] Jane Austen knew that her father served as trustee of a profitable slave-tended estate in Antigua. I find it no accident that Austen gives Fanny Price quotations from an abolitionist poet. Had Virginia Woolf caught such indirect references, perhaps she would not have called Austen "too little of the rebel," a woman who "accepted life too calmly as she found it."[18]

Austen's father read Cowper aloud to the family, and Austen even asked her gardener to plant certain flowers in response to floral references in Cowper's verse (see letters of 18 December 1798 and 8 February 1807). By having Fanny and Edmund cite or echo Cowper, Austen links her heroine and hero to her own poetic tastes, spiritual values, and love of rural beauty.

Austen uses another Cowper allusion to describe Fanny's desire to return to Mansfield Park: "Her eagerness, her impatience, her longings to be with them, were such as to bring a line or two of Cowper's Tirocinium for ever before her. 'With what intense desire she wants her home,' was continually on her tongue, as the truest description of a yearning which she could not suppose any school-boy's bosom to feel more keenly" (431). No longer content just to quote Cowper verbatim, Fanny now has enlarged Cowper's vision to include women. Cowper's "Tirocinium; or a Review of Schools" refers exclusively to a school*boy's* homesickness, his experiences at school, and his bond to his father. Austen has Fanny substitute "she" and "her" in Cowper's original line, "With what intense desire *he* wants *his* home," and she claims her right to yearn as keenly as any schoolboy. Although Cowper's poem encourages fathers to lead their sons to some "philosophic height" for their "wondering eyes," in *Mansfield Park* the only philosophizing, wondering being is Fanny. The only time Cowper mentions women in "Tirocinium" is for the sake of a disparaging analogy:

> Boys, once on fire with that contentious zeal,
> Feel all the rage that female rivals feel:
> The prize of beauty in a woman's eyes
> Not brighter than in theirs the scholar's prize.[19]

Refuting this suggestion that boys strive for learning while girls value looks, Austen offers in Fanny a thinking, reading, meditating woman eager to gain "information for information's sake," not a female preening herself (418).

As in "The Task," Cowper's "Tirocinium" indicts clergymen who are "Christian in name, and infidel in heart," so interested in playing a fashionable part that they are "mere church furniture at best." The poem attacks poorly disciplined schools that do not prepare boys to become men of conscience and integrity. But why, Austen must have wondered, should a poem stressing the need "to cultivate and keep the morals clean" be aimed exclusively at fathers and sons? Why are only school*boys* thought to feel deeply and crave learning? *Mansfield Park* answers and extends "Tirocinium" by demonstrating that (to use Charlotte Brontë's later words), "Women feel just as men do, and they need exercise for their faculties as much as their brothers." [20]

Given the depth of Cowper's poetry, it is not surprising that Fanny has transcended the petty men and women around her, gained empathy, and learned to draw pleasure from her environs. Knowing that lyrics can elevate, Fanny wants to buy books of poetry to share with her younger sister. Austen describes Fanny playing the very role with Susan that Cowper envisioned fathers playing with their sons: that of warm mentor encouraging "clean morals" and "philosophic heights."

Austen also asks her readers to consider why Fanny quotes Sir Walter Scott's "Lay of the Last Minstrel": Fanny laments that the chapel at Sotherton has no banners blown by "the night wind of Heaven" and no signs that a "Scottish monarch sleeps below" (85–86). Fanny has obviously read canto 2 of Scott's long poem, as she takes her first quotation from book 10 and the second from book 12 of this second canto. Between the two lines she chooses, Scott describes a hero who "trampled the Apostate's pride" (book 11). Scott's poem celebrates pastoral values and suggests that some are so busy pursuing worldly gains that they have no time for prayer. Scott's description of human beings enamored with "titles, power, and pelf" and "concentred all in self" applies to many of the worldly, selfish men and women of Mansfield Park.[21]

Although Fanny quotes only Cowper and Scott, she has other books in her room, including Crabbe's *Tales*. As Park Honan notes, "Readers might grasp or miss the joke of Fanny Price's having the poet Crabbe's Tales among her books since the joke depends on our knowing that Fanny Price is the name of Crabbe's own 'meekly firm' heroine in The Parish Register."[22] The name appears at the end of part 2 (called "Marriages") in Crabbe's long poem in verse called "Parish Register":

> Last on my List appears a Match of Love,
> And one of Virtue;–happy may it prove!–
>
> . . . .
>
> For *Fanny Price* was lovely and was chaste.

An "amorous Knight" tries to seduce Fanny by offering to lift her into a life of luxury, wealth, and fashion. Soft carpets and tall mirrors will fill her room, and she will be an admired and adored object "by the Hands of Wealth and Fashion drest / By Slaves attended and by Friends carest."[23] Just as Henry Crawford's flattery and bribery cannot move Fanny Price to accept his marriage proposals, so Crabbe's "meekly firm" Fanny Price fixes her mind on heavenly comforts, the power of virtue, and her own faithfulness. Like Cowper, Crabbe was both an ordained minister and a writer, perhaps suggesting to Austen the abil-ity to be both literary and religious. Austen joked that she would like to become Mrs. Crabbe.[24] Did Austen take Fanny Price's name from Crabbe's principled heroine just to play a joke or to link her own themes to those Crabbe explored in his extensive theological writings?

Austen also adds extra layers to *Mansfield Park* by including ref-erences to a prose work: Dr. Johnson's *Rasselas*. Again, although the actual allusion goes by quickly and unobtrusively, the quotation in its broader context yields rich dividends. The reference comes as Fanny compares the disagreeableness of her Portsmouth home to the elegance of Mansfield Park: "In a review of the two houses . . . Fanny was tempted to apply to them Dr. Johnson's celebrated judgment as to matrimony and celibacy, and say, that though Mansfield Park might have some pains, Portsmouth could have no pleasures" (392). When Dr. Johnson's Rasselas says it is better not to marry because discord exists within so many marriages and families, his sister responds that unmarried people become peevish and malevolent "outlaws of hu-man nature."[25] Right before the sentence Austen quotes from *Rasselas,* we find a perfect description of someone like Aunt Norris: "To live without feeling or exciting sympathy, to be fortunate without adding to the felicity of others, or afflicted without tasting the balm of pity, is a state more gloomy than solitude; it is not retreat but exclusion from mankind. Marriage has many pains, but celibacy has no pleasures." Exiled to a remote country at the end of *Mansfield Park*, the callous, greedy, resentful Aunt Norris cannot elicit even Fanny's pity: "Mrs. Norris's removal from Mansfield Park was the great supplementary comfort of Sir Thomas's life. . . . To be relieved from her . . . was so great a felicity. . . . She was regretted by no one at Mansfield. She had never been able to attach even those she loved best. . . . Not even Fanny had tears for aunt Norris—not even when she was gone for ever" (465–66). Aunt Norris never truly marries, as she feels nothing when her husband dies, and she appears in the exact state Dr. Johnson's princess describes: a hell worse than solitude in which one is inca-pable of feeling or stimulating love.

Mansfield Park has been called Austen's least humorous novel, but sometimes as I follow the allusions I can sense her smiling as she writes. I would argue that one such moment might be the discussion in *Mansfield Park* of how important Shakespeare is to *men*. Shakespeare is "a part of an Englishman's constitution," Edmund Bertram and Henry Crawford agree, and they also lament the neglect of reading aloud in *boys'* schools (338). But Austen demonstrates in this novel (as well as in her other novels) that Shakespeare is also part of *her* constitution. Austen helps to characterize Henry Crawford by having him read the part of Cardinal Wolsey, a vain, ambitious, "fair-spoken, and persuading" churchman who proves "ever double both in his words and meaning" (*Henry VIII*, 4.2.52, 38–39). Henry's claim that he could play any character from Richard III to Shylock links him to two greedy, power-hungry, merciless men. Henry can quote *Paradise Lost* and read Shakespeare, much as Richard III can cloak his hollow interior with pleasing words:

> And thus I clothe my naked villainy
> With odd old ends stol'n forth of holy writ,
> And seem a saint when most I play the devil.
> (*Richard III,* 1.3.335–37)

Austen also includes echoes of King Lear: Sir Thomas's inability to see Fanny's superiority to her two spiteful "sisters," Maria and Julia, resembles Lear's dismissal of the virtuous Cordelia, only to find himself unloved by the selfish Regan and Goneril.

Like Shakespeare providing illuminating plays within the plays in *Hamlet* and *Midsummer Night's Dream*, so Austen weaves the play *Lover's Vows* into *Mansfield Park*. Although many chapters are filled with discussions of the play and descriptions of rehearsals, readers only hear one quoted line from Mrs. Inchbald's 1798 play. Austen evidently trusted readers to know or seek out the play (based on an earlier German drama called *The Love Child*), particularly its warning that the English were confusing wealth with virtue. When Amelia calls the clergyman Anhalt "a very good man," the dissolute Count Cassel defines the term by nationality:

> *Count.* "A good man." In Italy, that means a religious man; in France, it means a cheerful man; in Spain, it means a wise man; and it England, it means a rich man.–Which good man of all these is Mr. Anhalt?
> *Amelia.* A good man in every country, except England.
> (Appendix, *MP,* 498)

The *only* line from the play that Austen includes in *Mansfield Park* is "When two sympathetic hearts meet in the marriage state, matrimony may be called a happy life," a line that Mary as the heiress Amelia rehearses with Edmund as the clergyman Anhalt (358). Readers who go in search of more can find that as that line continues in *Lover's Vows,* Anhalt offers a brilliant description of the joyful and horrifying possibilities of marriage:

When two sympathetic hearts meet in the marriage state, matrimony may be called a happy life. When such a wedded pair find thorns in their path, each will be eager, for the sake of the other, to tear them from the root. . . . Patience and love will accompany them in their journey, while melancholy and discord they leave far behind.—Hand in hand they pass on from morning till evening, through their summer's day, till the night of age draws on, and the sleep of death overtakes the one. . . . This picture is pleasing; but I must beg you not to forget that there is another on the same subject.—When convenience, and fair appearance joined to folly and ill-humour, forge the fetters of matrimony, they gall with their weight the married pair. Discontented with each other—at variance in opinions—their mutual aversion increases with the years they live together. (Appendix, *MP,* 504–5)

Just one of many scenes from *Lover's Vows* relevant to *Mansfield Park,* this speech presents marriage as the best of times or the worst of times, a happy life or enslavement.

Anhalt's reference to a wedded couple journeying "hand in hand" suggests Adam and Eve—and Milton's portrayal of them ("They hand in hand . . . took their solitary way"). When Austen has Henry Crawford twist part of a line from *Paradise Lost,* readers recall the fuller passage. Henry defends his right to remain single and a horrible flirt by adding emphasis to a line from book 5 of *Paradise Lost:* "I am of a cautious temper, and unwilling to risk my happiness in a hurry. Nobody can think more highly of the matrimonial state than myself. I consider the blessing of a wife as most justly described in those discreet lines of the poet, 'Heaven's *last* best gift'" (43). As his sister notes, a smiling Henry dwells only on the word "last." In Milton, the line is spoken by an innocent, unfallen Adam as he sees his beautiful wife Eve sleeping beside him:

> "Awake
> My fairest, my espous'd, my latest found,
> Heaven's last best gift, my ever new delight."
> (*Paradise Lost,* book 5, 17–19)

Adam wakes Eve to rejoice with him in nature's beauty, but Eve is troubled by her dream of giving into temptation. Henry's jocular, distorted use of just four words from this passage suggests his inability to value the genuine "ever new delight" of marriage. His quip may seem witty at the time, but when he later throws away any chance of earthly paradise with Fanny by indulging in a moment's temptation with the forbidden Maria Rushworth, his carelessly spoken words seem empty. Henry seems to have taken as his text Andrew Marvell's "To his Coy Mistress": Austen shows Henry helping Maria escape with him through an iron gate, much as the seducer in Marvell's poem pushes through "the iron gates of life" to enjoy momentary pleasures with his mistress.[26] Austen uses patently moralistic terms (temptation, sacrifice, right) when she writes of Henry's seize-the-day approach to passion: "The temptation of immediate pleasure was too strong for a mind unused to make any sacrifice to right" (467).

Whether digging for Austen's references to Marvell, Milton, Shakespeare, Johnson, Crabbe, Scott, or Cowper, one never comes up empty. The same seems true of names. As Park Honan notes, Mansfield was "a name famous for high, honorable courage. As Lord Chief Justice the first Earl of Mansfield had struck at the roots of the African slave trade."[27] Joseph Wiesenfarth adds that the name Mansfield may link this novel to Richardson's *Sir Charles Grandison*, which includes references to a Mansfield House and an estate-owning Sir Thomas Mansfield.[28] Readers of Richardson's lengthy novel (one of Austen's favorites) might remember that the angelic heroine resists numerous suitors and argues for her right to marry only for affection: "Fortune without merit will never do with me, were the man a prince. . . . I must love the man to whom I would give my hand, well enough to be able . . . to *wish* to be his wife."[29] Austen's choice of the name "Norris" may echo the name of "the most villainous figure" in a book by Clarkson on African slavery.[30] Scratch the seemingly opaque surface of Austen's prose and one finds intricate designs hiding underneath. How *Mansfield Park* must have confounded the early reviewer who had called *Pride and Prejudice* "too clever to have been written by a woman"![31]

As I mentioned in chapter 3, Austen insisted in a letter to her sister that she designed her own novels for insightful readers: "I do not write for such dull Elves / As have not a great deal of Ingenuity themselves" (29 January 1813). Perhaps she should have added that her ingenious Elves also need access to an entire reference library. Virginia Woolf noted, "Austen is mistress of far deeper emotion than appears on the surface."[32] In *Mansfield Park* Austen brilliantly demonstrates that women can be mistresses of far deeper emotion *and thought* than centuries of men have believed them capable of possessing.

7

An Imaginist Like Herself
Emma

Even the whole world is not sufficient for the depth and
rapidity of the human imagination, which often sallies forth
beyond the limits of all that surrounds us.
                        —Longinus, "On the Sublime"

. . . so imagination bodies forth
The forms of things unknown, the poet's pen
Turns them to shapes, and gives to airy nothing
A local habitation and a name.
Such tricks hath strong imagination.
                        —Shakespeare, *A Midsummer Night's Dream*

Could a linguist, could a grammarian, could even a mathematician have seen what she did . . . without feeling
that circumstances had been at work to make them peculiarly interesting to each other?—How much more must
an imaginist, like herself, be on fire with speculation and
foresight!
                        —*Emma*

Jane Austen wrote disparagingly in a letter about her new novel,
Emma, "I am very strongly haunted with the idea that to those readers who have preferred P&P. [*Pride and Prejudice*] it will appear inferior in wit, and to those who have preferred MP. [*Mansfield Park*] very
inferior in good sense" (11 December 1815). Posterity has disagreed,
however, and has at times pronounced *Emma* "her greatest novel," the
"Book of Books . . . the very climax of Jane Austen's work," "the most
vivacious of the later novels," "the most perfect example in English
fiction in which character shapes events," "clearly Jane Austen's masterpiece," and even "the climax of Jane Austen's genius and the
Parthenon of fiction."[1] Noting "I used to think that men did everything better, but that was before I read Jane Austen," detective novelist Rex Stout considered *Emma* her masterpiece and reread it just a
few days before his death.[2]

In particular, Austen had predicted that readers would reject Emma as a heroine. Rather than calling her central figure "as delightful a creature as ever appeared in print," as she did Elizabeth Bennet of *Pride and Prejudice*, Austen told her family that in *Emma* she had created "a heroine whom no one but myself will much like." [3] She was right that some readers, including members of her own extended family, would dislike Emma Woodhouse—for example, niece Fanny Knight "could not bear" her, but others have pronounced Emma "part of our national heritage . . . the best-loved of English heroines."[4] The only one of Austen's novels to take a heroine's name as its title, *Emma* centers on a woman who centers on herself.

It is no wonder that *Emma* has been called "a novelist's novel" with a heroine who "is clearly an avatar of Austen the artist."[5] Despite the fact that Emma cannot stick to a course of steady reading, finish her paintings, or practice piano more than sporadically, she perhaps comes the closest of any Austen heroine to exhibiting artistic powers. What other young woman in Austen is described as an *imaginist*, a word Austen coins? Like Catherine Morland and Marianne Dashwood, Emma seems to have an active mind and colorful fancy. We learn that Emma is "such a fanciful, troublesome creature" and that her fancy is "that very dear part" of her (10, 14). As in the Cowper poem alluded to in this novel, Emma possesses a "fancy, ludicrous and wild" that allows her to imagine a more suspenseful, adventuresome world than the one she inhabits.[6] Emma creates analogies, as when she observes, "My playing is no more like her's, than a lamp is like sunshine" (231). When she hears that Jane Fairfax has received an anonymous gift of a piano, her mind creates a plot thick with sexual intrigue. Mischievous ideas run through her mind and offer an "ingenious and animating suspicion," giving sparkle to Emma's days (160). Making "plans and proceedings" for other people's lives becomes an "inspiriting notion" (69, 28). Like an author fired up by her task of creating characters and plots, Emma goes to work ("contriving things so well") on the people around her, finding an escape from boredom in "this state of schemes, and hopes, and connivance" (22, 343). Emma possesses "a mind delighted with its own ideas" (24).

Matchmaking becomes Emma's artistic specialty. She describes the marriage between Miss Taylor and Mr. Weston as an exhilarating personal victory: "One matter of joy to me . . . and a very considerable one [is] that I made the match myself. . . . [T]o have it take place, and be proved in the right . . . may comfort me for any thing" (11–12). Success brings triumph: "Emma felt the glory of having schemed successfully" (90). Emma tries to move people around and invent lives for them much like creating a cast of fictional characters and a romance plot. Calling it an interesting undertaking, she makes her evenings fly by as she invents a family background for Harriet Smith, a pretty orphan of doubtful birth residing at a nearby boarding school for girls. Emma labors to change Harriet's own "narrative" featuring her affection for the sensible farmer Robert Martin to a more exalted script starring Mr. Elton: "Emma could not feel a doubt of having given Harriet's fancy a proper direction" (42). Each day then offers an opportunity for Emma to further her plot, to propel Harriet and Mr. Elton toward the marital conclusion she has imagined for them. When pressed by Mr. Knightley to justify her actions, Emma invents a gentleman of fortune to be Harriet's missing father. She plants thoughts in Harriet's rather empty head and contrives excuses to bring Mr. Elton and Harriet together. Emma feels tremendous anger when it turns out that Mr. Elton has a plot of his own: to acquire Emma, her fortune, and her estate. Whenever her matchmaking fails, however, Emma quickly moves on to other fanciful schemes. As one Pulitzer Prize–winning author observes of Emma, "She is, in short, a novelist."[7] Emma's proposal "to arrange every body's destiny" resembles an omniscient author's manipulation of characters, and her endeavors bring her a feeling of "success . . . pleasure and triumph" (413, 12–13).

By the time Frank Churchill arrives in Highbury, Emma already has decided on his character and arranged his future to suit one she has imagined for herself. "He seemed . . . quite to belong to her" (119). Everyone will notice them together and know Frank is in love with her: "Emma divined what every body present must be thinking. She was his object, and every body must perceive it" (220). He will propose, and she will refuse him. The story offers material for her active, busy mind: "Emma . . . was still busy and cheerful . . . and farther, though thinking of him so much, and, as she sat drawing or working, forming a thousand amusing schemes for the progress and close of their attachment, fancying interesting dialogues, and inventing elegant letters; the conclusion of every imaginary declaration on his side was that *she refused him*. . . . Every thing tender and charming was to mark their parting; but still they were to part" (264). Emma thinks, forms, invents, fancies, and schemes her way out of boredom, imagining all sorts of "clever replies" and "delicate negatives" that she might give Frank, and rapidly planning that he will fall in love with the luckless Harriet Smith.

Once Emma has seized a notion (Harriet will marry Frank), she makes everything around her fit her plan: "She had taken up the idea . . . and made every thing bend to it" (134). When Frank rescues Harriet from some rowdy gypsies, Emma's mind immediately goes to work on the material with professional enthusiasm:

> Such an adventure as this,—a fine young man and a lovely young woman thrown together in such a way, could hardly fail of suggesting certain ideas to the coldest heart and the steadiest brain. So Emma thought, at least. Could a linguist, could a grammarian, could even a mathematician have seen what she did, have witnessed their appearance together, and heard their history of it, without feeling that circumstances had been at work to make them peculiarly interesting to each other?—How much more must an imaginist, like herself, be on fire with speculation and foresight!—especially with such a ground-work of anticipation as her mind had already made. (334–35)

Austen emphasizes Emma's brain, mind, thoughts, and ideas and creates a term for Emma's role ("imaginist") equivalent to specific careers (linguist, grammarian, and mathematician). Emma would excel as a romance or screenplay writer.

Or she could become a storyteller giving performances for children. When her nephews visit, Emma can transform the raw material of Harriet's encounter with the gypsies into a permanent source of entertainment: "The gipsies . . . took off in a hurry. . . . and the whole history dwindled soon into a matter of little importance but to Emma and her nephews:—in her imagination it maintained its ground, and Henry and John were still asking every day for the story of Harriet and the gipsies" (336). Again, Austen emphasizes Emma's imagination and her ability to change facts into a compelling narrative. Emma's ability to entertain children sounds like the description Caroline Austen gives of her aunt Jane's entertaining tales: "Everything she could make amusing to a child . . . she would tell us the most delightful stories chiefly of Fairyland, and her Fairies had all characters of their own—The tale was invented, I am sure, at the moment, and was sometimes continued for two or three days, if occasion served."[8] Like Emma, Austen evidently was an imaginist.

"A writer wastes nothing," William Faulkner observed.[9] Austen gives Emma the perspective and creativity of a resourceful writer by showing her standing still in a doorway of a shop, her mind active on the scene before her:

Emma went to the door for amusement.—Much could not be hoped from the traffic of even the busiest part of Highbury;—Mr. Perry walking hastily by, Mr. William Cox letting himself in at the office door, Mr. Cole's carriage horses returning from exercise, or a stray letter-boy on an obstinate mule, were the liveliest objects she could presume to expect; and when her eyes fell only on the butcher with his tray, a tidy old woman travelling homewards from shop with her full basket, two curs quarreling over a dirty bone, and a string of dawdling children round the baker's little box-window eyeing the gingerbread, she knew she had no reason to complain, and was amused enough; quite enough still to stand at the door. A mind lively and at ease, can do with seeing nothing, and can see nothing that does not answer. (233)

Both Austen and Emma seem more interested in observing people than in rhapsodizing, like Fanny Price, about the sky. Austen's passage about seeing "nothing that does not answer" anticipates Graham Greene's comment that "Everything is useful to a writer, you see—every scrap, even the most boring luncheon parties."[10]

Like Jane Austen, Emma uses her lively mind to transform what seems like nothing into something. In a letter, Austen perhaps is only partially ironic when she asks Cassandra, "Which of all my important nothings shall I tell you first? . . . You know how interesting the purchase of a sponge cake is to me" (15–17 June 1808). In other letters Austen transforms dull neighbors and trivial conversations into lively narratives for her sister and nieces. Not everyone thought such ordinary domestic scenes counted as *something:* even Jane Austen's publisher complained that *Emma* lacked incident and romance.[11] Unlike that publisher, Austen and her artistic heroine Emma see *nothing that does not answer.*

In fact, one senses a strong resemblance between Austen and her matchmaking, imaginative heroine. "I have got a Husband for each of the Miss Maitlands," Austen boasts in Emma-like fashion to Cassandra (1 October 1808). Like the clever Emma feeling bored by her neighbors, Austen laments, "There is nobody Brilliant nowadays" (23 September 1813) and complains, "It was stupidish . . . there was a lack of Talk altogether" (14 October 1813). In another letter, she confesses, "we are doing nothing ourselves to write about, & I am therefore quite dependant upon . . . my own Wit" (10 January 1809). Austen undoubtedly understood why Emma needed to transform the dullness of her environs into witty discourse, as she does much the same in her letters to Cassandra:

> We are therefore confined to each other's society from morning till night, with very little variety of Books and Gowns. (30 November 1800)

> My Adventures . . . have not been very numerous. . . . it was rather a dull affair. . . . I then got Mr Evelyn to talk to, & Miss Twistleton to look at; and I am proud to say that I have a very good eye at an Adulteress, for tho' repeatedly assured that another in the same party was the *She*, I fixed upon the right one from the first. . . . Another stupid party last night. . . . three old *Toughs* came in. . . . I cannot anyhow continue to find people agreable. . . . My Aunt has a very bad cough . . . and I think she is deafer than ever. My Mother's cold disordered her for some days. . . . Our Party last night supplied me with no new ideas for my letter. (12–13 May 1801; 21–22 May 1801)

> Lady Fagg will come. The Shades of Evening are descending and I resume my interesting Narrative. . . . Lady Elizabeth Hatton and Annamaria called here this morn^g;– (7 November 1813)

Austen admits to her sister that she exaggerates anecdotes for the sake of effect: "I made the most of the Story because it came in to advantage" (27 May 1801).

Like Emma, Austen feels pride in her own imagination and boasts that she can picture other lives: "I see your mournful party in my mind's eye under every varying circumstance of the day," she writes an absent Cassandra (25 October 1808). Perhaps Austen sheds light on why Emma is rude to Miss Bates when she writes of herself after making a sharp remark about a Widower, "I am forced to be abusive for want of a subject, having really nothing to say" (22 February 1807).

Austen gives Emma the outlook and even the language of an author. Emma calls Mr. Elton's charades as "a sort of prologue to a play, or motto to the chapter . . . soon followed by matter-of-fact prose" (74). Emma views others around her as characters, as when she looks across the room at Jane Fairfax and ponders "the fair heroine's countenance" (220). In Emma's ongoing narrative of her neighborhood, Jane stars in a scandalous relationship, and Frank becomes Harriet's husband. Both stories are fictions. Rather than acknowledging that she knows nothing of Frank's emotions, Emma is "contented with her view of his feelings" (265). But, like Mr. Elton, Frank has feelings and a plot of his own (his secret engagement to Jane Fairfax) completely surprising to Emma. Jane Fairfax has inner depths and is *not* a storybook character of Emma's creation. Because Emma prides herself in her own omniscience (she *divines* what others think and "courts the pre-arrangement of other people . . . shape[d] into the proper form"), she cannot understand that all the men and women around her also feel like central characters in novels of their own composition—novels that they write themselves (75).

Like Mary Crawford in *Mansfield Park*, Emma makes one think of Shakespeare's sister in Virginia Woolf's *A Room of One's Own:* a gifted woman trapped in a stifling society. We learn from Mr. Knightley

Cassandra Austen's sketch of a niece drawing
(Reproduced by permission of the Jane Austen Memorial Trust)

that the motherless Emma had precocious gifts: "At ten years old, she had the misfortune of being able to answer questions which puzzled her sister at seventeen" (37). Through Mr. Knightley's use of the word "misfortune," Austen reminds readers that Emma's cleverness may indeed be unlucky in an era advising women to avoid displaying wit and offering them little outlet for their intelligence.

To enliven her days, Emma has developed a talent for dialogue and can mimic the conversation of her sister ("Very true, my love") and Mr. Elton ("Exactly so") (113, 49). She can make even the straight-laced Mrs. Weston laugh at her skillful imitation of Miss Bates:

> "How would he bear to have Miss Bates belonging to him?—To have her haunting the Abbey, and thanking him all day long for his great kindness in marrying Jane?—'So very kind and obliging!—But he always had been such a very kind neighbour!' And then fly off, through half a sentence, to her mother's old petticoat. 'Not that it was such a very old petticoat either—for still it would last a great while—and, indeed, she must thankfully say that their petticoats were all very strong.'"
>
> "For shame, Emma! Do not mimic her. You divert me against my conscience." (225)

Emma could have succeeded as an actress, a comedian, or a writer. By showing Emma in the very process of amusing a listener by creating speech for Miss Bates, Austen makes us conscious of her own role as comic author. The danger, as with Mary Crawford's parodies and puns, is that amusement can come at the expense of conscience.

Emma's linguistic talents shine in comparison to those around her. Most neighbors offer only "long evenings of quiet prosings" (22). That "great talker upon little matters" Miss Bates cannot shape or edit the petty details of her life (21). Instead, she merely produces an oral dumping ground: "For, would you believe it, Miss Woodhouse, there he is, in the most obliging manner in the world, fastening in the rivet of my mother's spectacles.—The rivet came out, you know, this morning.—So very obliging!—for my mother had no use of her spectacles—could not put them on. And, by the bye, every body ought to have two pair of spectacles; they should indeed. Jane said so. I meant to take them over to John Saunders the first thing I did, but something or other hindered me all the morning; first one thing, then another, there is no saying what, you know" (236). There can be no paragraphs and few full stops in Miss Bates's remarks. Long before the unpunctuated, unparagraphed Molly Bloom chapter of James Joyce's *Ulysses*, Austen asks readers to consider the artistic limitations of stream-of-consciousness. Like automatic writing, Miss Bates's speech is spontaneous and therefore *realistic* (as Miss Bates puts it, "What is before me, I see"), but who would want to read pages and pages of it without the intervention of a controlling narrator (176)? All of us have sat next to Miss Bates at a dinner or on the airplane. At times, all of us perhaps have longed to *be* Miss Bates and force someone to listen to an excruciatingly detailed account of our day ("First I had to wait in a really long line at the post office, and then my bank statement said I was out of funds, and then . . ."). Austen must have recognized that even the author of *Sense and Sensibility* and *Pride and Prejudice* could generate Miss Bates-like prose in uninhibited letters to her sister: "I wonder whether the Ink bottle has been filled.—Does Butcher's meat keep up at the same price?—is not Bread lower than 2/6.—Mary's blue gown!—My Mother must be in agonies" (15 October 1813). Austen might write trivia-laden, unshaped prose in letters to a beloved sister, but she knew full well how much work—how much lopping and cropping, as she called it—it took to transform life into art.

Although Miss Bates seems modest, unassuming, and "obliging," there is a kind of egotism and tyranny in her monopoly of the airwaves to tell *her* story: "We have apple dumplings, however, very often. Patty makes an excellent apple-dumpling. . . . Thank ye, the gloves do very well—only a little too large about the wrist." (237). Such a monologue shuts out conversation: "Everybody's words, were soon lost under the incessant flow of Miss Bates" (322). Austen calls attention to the formlessness of Miss Bates's type of "art" (with no controlling shape or theme) by telling us that Miss Bates's long-suffering listeners follow her "without having any regular narration to attend to" (239). By talking about this *lack* of narration, Austen reminds us of her own. When a chattering Miss Bates pauses for a moment and asks, "What was I talking of?" Emma "wondered on what, of all the medley, she would fix" (237). Medley is a good description of Miss Bates's jumbled hodgepodge.

As if anticipating the impressionist movement, Austen also experiments with discourse that offers transient sensory reactions, as in Mrs. Elton's collage-like approach to strawberries: "The best fruit in England—every body's favourite—always wholesome.—These are the finest beds and finest sorts.—Delightful to gather for one's self—the only way of really enjoying them.—. . . Maple Grove—cultivation—beds when to be renewed—gardeners thinking exactly different—no general rule–" (359). Austen tells us that "such, for half an hour, was the conversation," but readers sense that if conversation is an *exchange* of thoughts and feelings, Mrs. Elton's speech does not qualify. The phrase Mrs. Elton uses for strawberry growing–"no general rule"– seems to apply to her principle of composition.

Throughout the novel Mrs. Elton dots her speech with foreign phrases *(carte blanche, al fresco, chaperon, rencontre, caro sposo* and *barouche landau)* but cannot see beyond her own provincial perspective. Like Mrs. Bennet thinking no neighborhood could be larger than Longbourne or Sir William Lucas stuck on his one moment of being presented at St. James Court, Mrs. Elton turns every utterance into an opportunity to mention, in broken record style, the unparalleled riches of Maple Grove, her brother-in-law's wealthy estate. Mrs. Elton's efforts to seem cosmopolitan and elegant ("I could immediately se- cure you some of the best society") fail when her bad grammar ("Nei- ther Mr. Suckling nor me . . .") stamps her as ill bred (275, 321).

Others in this novel also seem linguistically challenged or re- stricted. Like Mr. Collins, Mr. Elton speaks in affected compliments, and his riddles are sentimental twaddle. Harriet Smith provides only gushing exclamations and broken sentences ("Oh! dear no, never. . . . No, I do not; that is, I do not mean–What shall I do?"). When Harriet tries to tell a story, Emma detects the lack of method and "the feeble- ness and tautology of the narration" (409). Again, why would Austen include such a specialized phrase *(tautology of the narration)* except to call our attention to Emma's superior command of words and plot? Frank Churchill creates flowery purple prose, while on the other ex- treme the Knightley brothers speak and write with the imaginative flair of IRS accountants. Mr. Woodhouse merely whines ("My dear, how am I to get so far? . . . I could not walk half so far. . . . I am a very slow walker") and repeats himself (8, 58). In Highbury, only Emma views the world as the raw material for art.

In *Emma* Jane Austen suggests that a woman with artistic capa- bility but no sense of higher purpose or appropriate field for her pow- ers may waste her talent on useless pastimes and busywork. She may confuse matters of import with trivia. Emma refers to matchmaking as "the greatest amusement in the world" and elevates minor events in her life (for example, whether or not there will be a dance) to ma- jor events (12). The narrator ironically adopts this distorted view- point. A dance without a supper is hyperbolically pronounced "an infamous fraud upon the rights of men and women" (254). The idea of canceling a dance becomes an act of danger and grief: "It may be possible to do without dancing entirely. Instances have been known of young people passing many, many months successively, without being at any ball of any description, and no material injury accrue either to body or mind;—but when a beginning is made . . . it must be a very heavy set that does not ask for more. . . . The preparations must take their time . . . and for a few days they must be planning, proceeding and hoping in uncertainty—at the risk—in her opinion, the great risk, of its being all in vain. . . . Two days of joyful security were immediately followed by the overthrow of every thing. . . . The loss of the ball! . . . It was too wretched!" (247, 257). Like Robert Ferrars in *Sense and Sensibility* believing his ornate toothpick case to be required for "his existence [to] be continued" or Eliza in "Henry and Eliza" considering a gold watch one of the "usefull . . . necessaries" of life, the residents of Highbury seem to view leisure time activities as essential human "rights" rather than luxuries for the idle few (*SS,* 221; *MW,* 37). What are the begging gypsies and "poor sick family" doing while Emma wonders if life can go on without her taking the lead at a dance (83)?

Emma seems to be looking for ways to fill her time, as when she answers Harriet's question about her future ("But what shall you do?") by saying she will engage in the usual feminine tasks: "If I know myself, Harriet, mine is an active, busy mind, with a great many independent resources; and I do not perceive why I should be more in want of employment at forty or fifty than one-and-twenty. Woman's usual occupations of eye and hand and mind will be as open to me then, as they are now; or with no important variation. If I draw less, I shall read more; if I give up music, I shall take to carpet-work" (85). Like *Mansfield Park*'s Lady Bertram doing "some long piece of needle-work, of little use and no beauty" or Mrs. Grant feeling "in want of some variety" because she has "run through the usual resources of ladies," Emma seems to have few options for how to use her time in a genuinely creative or important way (*MP,* 19, 41). Emma envisions two decades of dilettantism without "important variation" from the feminine norm. Her intelligence and talent seem to have been squandered on a smattering of incomplete activities, like her unfinished drawings or neat lists of unread books.

Even at the age of twenty-one as she takes on the task of educating Harriet Smith, Emma continues to skim the surface: "it was much easier to chat than to study" (69). Unlike Fanny Price ordering books of history, biography, and poetry for her sister Susan and discussing their moral lessons, Emma and Harriet engage in no real reading.

Emma apparently encourages Harriet to scorn Robert Martin for reading *The Vicar of Wakefield* and *Elegant Extracts* rather than Ann Radcliffe's *The Romance of the Forest* and Regina Roche's *Children of the Abbey*, suggesting a feminine taste as silly and shallow as that of Isabella Thorpe and Catherine Morland in *Northanger Abbey*. Radcliffe's gothic thriller, for instance, contains passages like the following: "Adeline shuddered . . . an unaccountable dread came over her. 'Some horrid deed has been done here,' said she; . . . 'Murder has been committed.' The idea filled her with horror. . . . She threw herself on the turf, almost fainting with fear and languor. She knew if the Marquis detected her in an attempt to escape, he would, probably, burst the bounds which he had hitherto prescribed to himself, and that she had the most dreadful evils to expect. The palpitations of terror were so strong, that she could with difficulty breathe."[12] Why Robert Martin should be criticized for not reading this bosom heaver is unclear.

Though the thought never occurs to her, Emma might have profited from borrowing Goldsmith's *Vicar of Wakefield* from Robert Martin so that she, too, could refresh her memory about a kindly vicar's otherworldliness and his wife's foolish aspirations to gentility. Maybe Emma might have softened her snobbery had she remembered Goldsmith's comment that England's strength and pride was "its bold peasantry."[13] The narrator allies herself with Robert Martin by quoting Goldsmith later ("Goldsmith tells us, that when lovely woman stoops to folly . . .") rather than Radcliffe or Roche (387).

Emma also could have profited from Robert Martin's other choice: *Elegant Extracts*. Including excerpts from Shakespeare, Milton, and others, this popular anthology of verse and prose offered readers "a Copious Selection of Instructive, Moral, and Entertaining Passages from the Most Eminent British Poets." Sections entitled "False greatness," "Selfishness reproved," "The emptiness of riches," and "Various effects of pride" ("Let high birth triumph! what can be more great? / Nothing—but merit in a low estate") might have been quite edifying to Emma.[14]

The reference in *Emma* to the same sensational writers spoofed in *Northanger Abbey* suggests a link between the two novels. Austen does not mention *Northanger Abbey* in her letter to James Stanier Clarke about her "4th work" (really fifth), *Emma*, though she had tried unsuccessfully (and using a name with the initials M. A. D.) to reclaim the right to publish her early manuscript (11 December 1815; 5 April 1809). One wonders whether Austen deliberately wove into *Emma* some of the same ideas about the process of writing novels that she had made the main focus of the still unpublished *Northanger Abbey*. Whereas Austen chose to interrupt the storyline of *Northanger Abbey* to comment directly about novels, novelists, heroines, publishers, reviewers, and readers, in *Emma* she does so indirectly and subtly. By exploring books, storytelling, and types of language, Austen provides a fascinating Portrait of the Artist as a Young Woman.

The ironic narrator of *Emma* exposes Emma's literary affectation. Rather than helping Harriet with any serious reading, Emma encourages her to collect riddles in a decorated booklet: "the only literary pursuit which engaged Harriet at present, the only mental provision she was making for the evening of life, was the collecting and transcribing all the riddles of every sort that she could meet with, into a thin quarto of hot-pressed paper, made up by her friend, and ornamented with cyphers and trophies. In this age of literature, such collections on a very grand scale are not uncommon" (69). The narrator's mockery here is unmistakable, not only toward her youthful characters but also toward the pretentiousness of her era.

Emma may think she displays superior cultural knowledge when she quotes Shakespeare to Harriet, but Austen's readers would sense the unsuitability of the line's context:

> "You and Mr. Elton are by situation called together. . . .
> Your marrying will be equal to the match at Randalls. There
> does seem to be a something in the air of Hartfield which
> gives love exactly the right direction, and sends it into the
> very channel where it ought to flow.
> The course of true love never did run smooth–
> A Hartfield edition of Shakespeare would have a long
> note on that passage." (75)

Emma quotes Lysander's admission to Hermia in the first scene of *Midsummer Night's Dream* that obstacles often block lovers, but she leaves out the subsequent lines concerning the officiousness of matchmaking friends when Lysander says, "Or else it stood upon the choice of friends–" and Hermia replies, "O hell! to choose love by another's eyes." Emma will indeed cause Harriet pain by choosing Mr. Elton for her rather than letting her continue loving Mr. Martin.[15]

Mr. Knightley observes that matchmaking is hardly a "worthy employment" for a young woman of Emma's intelligence, but he posits no creative alternative (12). In an ironic voice reminiscent of Wollstonecraft or Austen herself, Emma insists that she will continue to make ambitious matches for the unclever Harriet "till it appears that men are much more philosophic on the subject of beauty than they are generally supposed; till they do fall in love with well-informed minds instead of handsome faces" (63). What motivation exists for a young woman to "be labouring to enlarge her comprehension or exercise it on sober facts" or ever to go beyond "a few first chapters, and the intention of going on to-morrow"? (69). Austen suggests that had her heroine been born male and a younger son in need of earning a living, she might have succeeded as a skilled attorney, like her brother-in-law. Austen uses militant language when she observes that Emma "combated the point" with her former governess (226). Emma spars with Mr. Knightley, enjoying the chance for one-upmanship and intellectual exchange. She finds herself arguing *for* Frank Churchill only because Mr. Knightley is arguing against him: "She . . . to her great amusement, perceived that she was taking the other side of the question from her real opinion" (145).

Emma is a portrait of an intelligent, strong, artistic woman in a society offering women no encouragement to use gifts of this kind. Austen adds pathos to her tale by showing just how static, dull, and confining life can be for such a woman—or for anyone forced to conform to the mind-numbing habits of others.

This novel captures the way we fall into repeated patterns, whether it be what side of the bed to sleep on or which place at a family dinner table to occupy; which food to select at a restaurant or on what side to part our hair. The trait seems innate, as when Emma's nephews insist that her narrative be exactly the same: "Henry and John were still asking every day for the story of Harriet and the gipsies, and still tenaciously setting her right if she varied in the slightest particular from the original recital" (336). While routines and habits can comfort, they can also stifle, limiting our opportunity to explore the world or develop ourselves. As Gibbon writes, "All that is human must retrograde if it does not advance."[16]

In *Emma* Austen captures the human tendency toward stasis through her portrayal of Mr. Woodhouse. Two recurring words in this novel, particularly in association with Mr. Woodhouse, are *usual* and *always:* "her father composed himself to sleep after dinner, as usual"; "Mr. Woodhouse going to bed at . . . the usual time"; "Everything safe in the house, as usual" (6, 211). Wherever Mr. Woodhouse goes, he makes "the usual stipulation" that there be little to vex his nerves or endanger his health (291). Like a male Lady Bertram, he is "without activity of mind or body" (7). Those around him seek to shield him from novelty of any sort. When Mr. Woodhouse worries about company coming, Emma reassures him that the rooms will be "just as usual, you know—Why should there be any change?" (79). Mr. Woodhouse, "hating change of every kind," sees the world as full of "lurking horrors," such as inclement weather or disagreeable food (7, 356).

When Mr. Woodhouse speaks to dinner guests, he employs the language of a dangerous outing *(venture, afraid, hurt)* to describe eating: "Mrs. Bates, let me propose your venturing on one of these eggs. An egg boiled very soft is not unwholesome. Serle understands boiling an egg better than any body. I would not recommend an egg boiled by any body else—but you need not be afraid—they are very small, you see—one of our small eggs will not hurt you. Miss Bates, let Emma help you to a *little* bit of tart—a *very* little bit. Ours are all apple tarts. You need not be afraid of unwholesome preserves here. I do not advise the custard" (24–25). Imagine dining out with Mr. Woodhouse and suffering through his running commentary on every culinary hazard! To avoid having anything to vex, distress, or scare you, Mr. Woodhouse advises, stay at home and have the same bland bowl of gruel prepared by the same cook and eat it in the company of the same people you are "used to," another phrase repeated in this novel. This conservative, "quaint and old-fashioned" valetudinarian sums up his philosophy with the comment, "Better not move at all" (302, 106). Mr. Woodhouse is the ultimate party-pooper, noting, "The sooner every party breaks up, the better" (210).

This novel opens and closes with Mr. Woodhouse's distaste for marriage precisely because it necessitates alteration: "Matrimony, as the origin of change, was always disagreeable" (7). To require no change—not only in oneself but also in others—smacks of arrogance and tyranny. Mr. Woodhouse sees no reason for Emma ever to leave Hartfield because he likes having her with him. Because he is "fond of society in his own way," Mr. Woodhouse only invites those whom he can command "as he liked" (20). He is too self-absorbed to be capable of empathy: "he could never believe other people to be different from himself" (19). If cake disagrees with him, no one should eat it. If he hates drafts, no one should open a window. Because he fears anything different or in motion ("The sea is very rarely of use to any body . . . nobody is healthy in London"), he advises others against traveling (101–2).

We sense Emma's bottled-up desire for change when she blurts out in response, "I must beg you not to talk of the sea. It makes me envious and miserable; I who have never seen it!" (101). She knows that she lacks her more stereotypically feminine sister's ability to content herself with sameness and safeness. Isabella Woodhouse has married a man almost as conservative as her father, a rather grumpy lawyer who grumbles about traveling anywhere or attending any party: "The folly of not allowing people to be comfortable at home—and the folly of people's not staying comfortable at home when they can! Here are we setting forward to spend five dull hours in another man's house, with nothing to say or to hear that was not said or heard yesterday, and may not be said and heard again tomorrow" (113). We sympathize with John Knightley's view when we see that parties in Highbury indeed consist of "nothing worse than every day remarks, dull repetitions, old news, and heavy jokes" (219). But John Knightley does little to enliven the scene for himself or for others.

No wonder Emma, who has "lived so secluded a life," feels starved for gossip, intrigue, suspense, and adventure, even if only in her own mind (275). Emma encounters the "sensation of listlessness, weariness, stupidity" after Frank Churchill leaves because he represents a change from the cast of characters she has always known (262). Unlike her father and her brother-in-law, Frank Churchill has a "love of change" (205). Emma knows that in general she is stuck in the same place with the same people, as in the case of Harriet and Mr. Elton: "Their being fixed, so absolutely fixed, in the same place, was bad for each, for all three. Not one of them had the power of removal, or of effecting any material change of society. They must encounter each other, and make the best of it" (143). Though this sentence refers to a specific trio, it could apply to most of the immobile, stagnant inhabitants of Highbury who suffer through "the common course of Highbury days" (262). Emma envies men with the freedom to change vistas, as when she tells Frank of his time at Weymouth, "If I had been there, I think I should have made some discoveries" (218).

In such an environment, news of any sort is welcome, as suggested by Austen's oxymoronic reference to "the happiness of frightful news" to describe Harriet's ambush by the gypsies (336). Hearing that someone has something to tell her, Emma responds, "News! Oh! yes, I always like news" (172). She fills her mind with possibilities during her suspenseful walk to the Westons' home to hear "something really important" (392). People who marry or die, we are told, are much appreciated because both events involve *change:* "Human nature is so well disposed towards those who are in interesting situations, that a young person, who either marries or dies, is sure of being kindly spoken of" (181).

Emma's matchmaking heightens her existence by giving interest to her bland days. Admitting that it is "adventuring too far," Emma calls a halt to planning others' lives but then suffers what Austen calls a "relapse," a term making her sound like an addict (137). Similarly, Emma experiences gossip as "an amusing supply" (or fix) to her fancy, much as Austen admits in her letters that she felt indebted to her neighbors for amusement (214). Emma adds spice to her life through such gossip as well as through narratives, riddles, conversations, and schemes, much as she would want to add spice to her father's basin of gruel if forced to eat it every day herself.

Yet the motherless Emma, we know, would steadfastly protect her father's right to eat that same unspiced basin of gruel each day. What redeems Emma from being a haughty, manipulative snob who practices her "art" at the expense of other people's feelings is that she has grown into a genuinely loving and loyal young woman with a warm heart who can admit her errors and seek to change her ways.

Austen emphasizes her heroine's imperfection by having Mr. Weston call Emma perfect immediately after she commits a blatantly rude act. Mr. Weston's little witticism (that the way to spell 'perfection' with two letters would be "MA" or Emma) makes Emma squirm because she knows it does not fit either her inner thoughts or outer behavior.

However, Emma's imperfection becomes part of her charm. Austen sees to it that readers are glad Emma is *not* a more tradition-ally perfect or conventional heroine. Would we really prefer Harriet Smith? At seventeen, Harriet is a very pretty, humble, sweet, grateful young woman whose lowly opinion of herself matches Fanny Price's. Like Marianne mooning over the music she and Willoughby sang together or Fanny Price saving a two-sentence note from Edmund, Harriet sentimentally gathers as her *"most precious treasures"* a bit of paste and an end of a pencil from her time with Mr. Elton (338). Today she would dot her i's with hearts. Harriet is simple, modest, and persuadable, as artless as Catherine Morland and as blushing as Fanny Price. She even faints.

Austen could have made Harriet Smith into the heroine of her novel. A decade before *Emma, Lady's Magazine* published a piece fea-turing a "Mr. Knightley" and "a deserted orphan" that some think may have been one source for Austen's novel: "Mr. Knightley, a coun-try-gentleman of not very large fortune . . . had married from the purest affection . . . a deserted orphan [left] at a boarding-school. . . . As by this union he made no addition to his property, nor formed any advantageous connexion, he was by some blamed, and by others ridiculed. He however found himself amply compensated . . . by the amiable qualities and virtues of his wife."[17] Had Austen followed this 1802 storyline, she would have made Harriet the heroine of her novel, rewarding her for her amiability with marriage to Mr. Knightley. Instead, Austen makes readers share Emma's growing sense that Harriet (and, by implication, any traditional, sweet, deferential heroine) lacks depth and interest. When Emma briefly thinks that she should be more like Harriet instead of a woman of "genius or intelligence," she acknowledges that it is too late "to set about being simple-minded and ignorant" (142). Emma may exclaim, "Dear Harriet!—I would not change you for the clearest-headed, longest-sighted, best judging female breathing," but by the end of this novel Emma and most readers find the "not clever" Harriet "dead weight" (269, 26, 450).

Austen also makes readers prefer Emma to her sister, who seems an upper class, nervous version of the simple, docile Harriet. Isabella is "slow and diffident" rather than "quick and assured," like Emma (37). She seems a diminutive angel of the house, "a pretty, elegant little woman of gentle, quiet manners" with "a disposition remarkably amiable and affectionate" (92). Our narrator damns Isabella with praise: "Poor Isabella, passing her life with those she doated on, full of their merits, blind to their faults, and always innocently busy, might have been a model of right feminine happiness" (140). Just as she added *"seemed"* to the opening sentence about Emma's blessings, so Austen adds *"might have been"* to her description of "poor" Isabella. Some might consider the torpid, submissive Isabella "a model of right feminine happiness," but the narrator and Emma obviously disagree.

Emma feels her own imperfections most acutely not in comparison to Isabella or Harriet but to an intelligent young woman exactly her own age: Jane Fairfax. Perhaps the title of this novel may keep us from doing justice to Jane Fairfax, the one truly accomplished artist in Austen's fictional world. Emma, who rarely practices and only performs "the little things which are generally acceptable," never achieves more than dilettantism: "She played and sang—and drew in almost every style; but steadiness had always been wanting" (227, 44). In contrast, Jane Fairfax works hard at her music and offers each time an "infinitely superior" performance on piano or voice (227). Jane has escaped the provincialism of London and developed her mind and talents: "She had . . . been given an excellent education. Living constantly with right-minded and well-informed people, her heart and understanding had received every advantage of discipline and culture; and Colonel

Campbell's residence being in London, every lighter talent had been done full justice to, by the attendance of first-rate masters" (164). Does Austen wish to illustrate, as she well knew herself, that an artist needed discipline and training, not just potential and imagination?

A beautiful, accomplished young woman whose life is fraught with hardship and secrecy, Jane Fairfax has endured the romantic deaths of both her father ("dying in action abroad") and her mother ("sinking under consumption and grief soon afterwards"); she has acquired that "slight appearance of ill-health" so becoming in an afflicted heroine (163, 167). Why is this "human perfection of body and mind" and "remarkably elegant" woman not the heroine we root for (167)? Perhaps the answer comes in the description of a Jane Fairfax-like heroine in Austen's sarcastic "Plan of a Novel According to Hints from Various Quarters":

> Heroine a faultless Character herself—, perfectly good, with much tenderness & sentiment, & not the least Wit—very highly accomplished . . . but particularly excelling in Music. . . . The heroine's friendship to be sought after by a young Woman in the same Neighbourhood, of Talents & Shrewdness . . . but having a considerable degree of Wit, Heroine shall shrink from the acquaintance. . . . often reduced to support herself & her Father by her Talents & work for her Bread; . . . worn down to a Skeleton. . . . Throughout the whole work, Heroine to be in the most elegant Society & living in high style. The name of the work *not* to be *Emma*. (*MW,* 428–30)

Austen makes us sense that, like the angelic Jane Bennet in *Pride and Prejudice*, the faultless Jane Fairfax would make a less interesting or believable heroine than the shrewd, talented, witty, often mistaken Emma. Emma's admission that she dislikes Jane Fairfax because of "that wickedness on my side which was prone to take disgust towards a girl so idolized and so cried up as she always was" reminds us of Austen's own remark in a letter, "pictures of perfection . . . make me sick and wicked" (203; letter of 23 March 1817). Emma enjoys discovering that the "amiable, upright, perfect Jane Fairfax was apparently cherishing very reprehensible feelings," and the two young women can only begin to become friends when both admit to jealousy, vulnerability, and error (243).

Jane Fairfax cracks no joke, nor does she shine with health and energy, as Emma does. Unlike her aunt, she is not a "standing lesson in how to be happy" (255). Like Fanny Price responding to news of Maria Rushworth's adultery with the thought that the whole family should be annihilated, so Jane Fairfax refers to the "evil day" when she may begin serving as a governess as if it were hard labor on a chain gang: "With the fortitude of a devoted novitiate, she had resolved at twenty-one to complete the sacrifice, and retire from all the pleasures of life, or rational intercourse, equal society, peace and hope, to penance and mortification for ever" (165). Jane's equation of the feelings of a governess in a well-to-do home to the emotions of a kidnapped slave in chains ("the sale—not quite of human flesh—but of intellect . . . as to the greater misery of the victims, I do not know where it lies") suggests an unappealing degree of self-pity and martyrdom (300–301). Yes, some governesses were treated abominably and subjected to the advances of male employers, but the comfortable life Miss Taylor led as a governess at Hartfield suggests rosier possibilities.

Jane may be perfectly behaved and musically proficient, but even the critical Mr. Knightley prefers Emma's openness and warmth, her tender heart and generous spirit. Most importantly, Emma achieves heroism because she undergoes a painful process of tremendous growth. This evolution fascinates Mr. Knightley early on: "There is an anxiety, a curiosity in what one feels for Emma. I wonder what will become of her!" (40). Far from remaining the never-vexed, never-distressed heroine introduced in the novel's opening sentence, Emma becomes agitated, mortified, grieved, depressed, wretched, and conscience-stricken, knowing by novel's end that she has acted with blindness, insufferable vanity, and unpardonable arrogance.

Austen calls our attention to the link between suffering and growth by telling us that Emma's "mind had never been in such perturbation" until Mr. Knightley scolds her, and that she experienced "all the perturbation that such a development of self . . . must create" after realizing her errors (133, 409). Austen tames her shrew, but not by forcing her to admit that the sun is the moon just because a man incorrectly but authoritatively says so. Austen's shrew is tamed when she gradually comes to see that her own perceptions and actions can be wrong.

The man who serves as the catalyst for Emma's growth is no badgering Petruchio but the gentlemanly Mr. Knightley, the only character to point out Emma's mistakes. Mr. Knightley's recognition that his beloved Emma is "faultless in spite of all her faults" suggests his embrace of her total and evolving humanity (433).

Although all six of Austen's novels contrast men who behave genteelly on the surface with those who are solid gentlemen, *Emma* explores this theme most directly and extensively. Austen calls attention to the topic by giving her hero a name with unmistakable chivalric overtones and by informing us that Mr. Knightley comes from "a family of such true gentility, untainted in blood" (358). Mr. Knightley is not technically a knight, like Sir William Lucas of *Pride and Prejudice*, but his generosity, dignity, loyalty, and morality mark him as deserving of a title. Although, as Emma notes, "You might not see one in a hundred, with *gentleman* so plainly written as in Mr. Knightley," he avoids exhibiting the trappings of his position, preferring to walk rather than use his handsome carriage (33). Mr. Knightley takes an active role as a magistrate and enters into the duties of William Larkins and others on his estate. While Emma is glib, saucy, and flippant, Mr. Knightley is the voice of reason and morality: "Where is your merit?—What are you proud of? . . . Respect for right conduct is felt by every body" (13, 147). Unlike Edmund Bertram and Henry Crawford, Mr. Knightley needs no Fanny Price to steer him toward truth and righteousness.

Austen contrasts Mr. Knightley's character with that of all the other versions of "gentlemen" in the novel. As Emma concedes of Mr. Knightley, "He is not a gallant man, but he is a very humane one" (223). How can Mr. Knightley be "quite the gentleman . . . a very gentleman-like man" yet "not a gallant man" (278–79)? What is the difference between behaving in a genteel as opposed to a gentlemanly way? Austen exploits the French origins and varying connotations of these and other terms pertaining to masculine behavior. After reading so many conduct books for young women written by men, Austen must have enjoyed the irony of writing (with a dedication to the profligate Prince Regent) a conduct novel for young men! Far more discussion takes place in this novel of gentlemanly than of ladylike behavior. Yet the two are related: before she can become the great lady of Highbury, Emma must grow up enough to recognize a true English gentleman and to dismiss any merely genteel impostors.

From the French *galant,* originally meaning "to rejoice" (as in the word "gala"), *gallant* carries the connotation of a light and lively form of courtesy. To "play the gallant" is to act the part of a showy, flirtatious ladies' man. Mr. Knightley is "not gallant" because he will not act a part; there is "nothing of ceremony about him" (57). Emma's recognition that Mr. Knightley is *humane* rather than gallant suggests she recognizes the difference between sincere generosity and empty compliments.

The term *gentleman* also derives from the French: from *gentilhomme,* or nobly-born man, giving rise to English words of varying meaning, such as gentility, gentleness, and gentleman. Like gallant, *genteel* carries both a positive sense (well bred, polite, gracious) and a negative connotation (affected, overrefined). *Gentle* can imply both kindness and weakness. Much as she explored the varying meanings of sense, sensible, sensation, sensitive, and sensibility in an earlier novel, in *Emma* Austen uses all these gentlemanly words in great abundance and complexity.

At the same time, its word origins also suggest *les gens,* or the people. Can a farmer be a gentleman? Can a titled gentleman be a brute? As a class marker, *gentleman* to Austen's readers would designate a man higher than a yeoman, meaning that technically Harriet is not a gentleman's daughter, nor is Robert Martin a gentleman. Yet Robert Martin's well written marriage proposal "would not have disgraced a gentleman," and he uses a Knightleyan form of "plain . . . strong and unaffected" English (51). Emma's snobbery leads her to label Robert Martin an uncouth, ungentlemanly clown simply because of his lower birth and lack of effete, affected, "gentle" mannerisms:

> "Well, Miss Woodhouse, is he like what you expected? What do you think of him? Do you think him so very plain?"
>
> "He is very plain, undoubtedly—remarkably plain:—but that is nothing, compared with his entire want of gentility. . . . I had no idea that he could be so very clownish, so totally without air. I had imagined him, I confess, a degree or two nearer gentility."
>
> "To be sure," said Harriet, in a mortified voice, "he is not so genteel as real gentlemen." (32)

Emma mentions a true gentleman's way of carrying himself, of walking and speaking. Her terms of praise are highly feminine: the "particularly gentle" and soft Mr. Elton has "not his equal for beauty or agreeableness," and her father has gentle softness and the "tenderest spirit of gallantry" (34, 68, 77).

More liberal in his notions of class, Mr. Knightley considers the rational, hardworking, affectionate yeoman a "respectable intelligent gentleman-farmer": "Robert Martin's manners have sense, sincerity, and good-humour to recommend them; and his mind has more *true gentility* than Harriet Smith could understand" (65; my italics).

Austen expands on the contrast between French fops and British men through Emma and Mr. Knightley's heated discussion of Frank Churchill and the term *amiable:*

> "I wish you would try to understand what an amiable young man may be likely to feel. . . ."
>
> "Your amiable young man is a very weak young man. . . . No, Emma, your amiable young man can be amiable only in French, not in English. He may be very 'aimable,' have very good manners, and be very agreeable; but he can have no English delicacy towards the feelings of other people: nothing really amiable about him." (148–49)

Viewing Frank as a puppy and "chattering coxcomb" with "smooth, plausible manners," Mr. Knightley dismisses his "life of mere idle pleasure" and pronounces Frank Churchill "a disgrace to the name of man" (150, 149, 148, 426).

So is Mr. Knightley perfect? Get rid of Frank and his Frenchified ways; get him to be frank (open) rather than franc (French). Speak in "the tone of decision becoming a man"—be a knightly man (146). Long live the British.

Austen has too great a vision for such chauvinism. Yes, Mr. Knightley outshines the other men in this novel, but he has his own limitations. If Mrs. Elton stands as a distorted version of Emma's dilettantism and self-importance, then the cool, ill-humored Mr. John Knightley illustrates in extreme form his brother George's rationality and reserve. Both brothers are quintessentially English, good at keeping a stiff upper lip: Austen informs us that John and George Knightley greet each other "in the true English style, burying under a calmness that seemed all but indifference, the real attachment which would have led either of them, if requisite, to do everything for the good of the other" (99). This reminds us of E. M. Forster's observation, "It is not that the Englishman can't feel—it is that he is afraid to feel. He has been taught . . . that feeling is bad form. He must not express great joy or sorrow, or even open his mouth too wide when he talks—his pipe might fall out if he did."[18]

Both Knightley brothers are keen, hard-working, no-nonsense men. But the danger for both is that they may leave no room for imagination and a sense of play. Just as John Knightley sees no point in journeying forth for a party, George Knightley complains that "surprises are foolish things" and dismisses dancing as nothing more than a "few hours of noisy entertainment" (228, 257). Napoleon might have backed up his comment that the English were a nation of shop-keepers by quoting John Knightley's pragmatic comment that "Business . . . may bring money, but friendship hardly ever does" (293). When the Knightley brothers get together, the conversation is literally down to earth: "As a farmer [Mr. Knightley] had to tell what every field was to bear next year. . . . The plan of a drain, the change of a fence, the felling of a tree, and the destination of every acre of wheat, turnip or spring corn, was entered into with as much equality of interest by John, as his cooler manners rendered possible" (100). When Mr. Knightley later insists to Emma that he would rather read an account book than dance, he sounds too much like his ever practical brother.

Mr. Knightley carries his "peculiar sort of dry, blunt manner" to such an extreme that his language lacks almost all ornamentation (356). Austen has her British gentleman use bare, Anglo-Saxon-laden diction, as in his plain proposal to Emma: "I cannot make speeches. . . . If I loved you less I might be able to talk about it more. But you know what I am. . . . You hear nothing but truth from me." He adds that "no other woman in England" would have borne his blunt behavior (430). Mr. Knightley's speech is reminiscent of Winston Churchill: "We shall fight on the beaches; we shall fight on the landing grounds; we shall fight in the fields and in the streets, we shall fight in the hills; we shall never surrender." Only *surrender* is a foreign (French) word here.[19] Austen's entire characterization of Mr. Knightley (old English, *cniht*) would change if she had him play *charades*, boast of his *barouche landau*, or ask for *carte blanche*. Instead, Mr. Knightley wears heavy leather (Old English, *hefig, lether*), gives apples (Old English *aeppel*) to Miss Bates, and points out that his shoes are not dirty and have not a speck on them (Old English, *scoh, drit, specca*). Austen informs us that the Knightley brothers avoid flourishes of speech (Old French, *flourir*) and deal only in the great (Old English, *daelen, great*). Mr. Knightley bluntly pronounces things good or bad (Old English, *god, baeden*).

Not surprisingly, Mr. Knightley feels disgust ("Bad . . . very bad. . . . This is very bad") after reading the ornate prose ("You must all endeavour to comprehend") Frank uses throughout his lengthy letter to Emma (445–56, 437). In contrast to Mr. Elton's gallant praise of Emma's inaccurate drawing of Harriet ("The attractions you have added are infinitely superior to what she received from nature"), Mr. Knightley baldly states a fact in monosyllables: "You have made her too tall" (Old English *getael*) (42, 48). Mr. Knightley

224

dismisses Frank as one who engages in Frenchified "manoeuvering and finessing" rather than in doing any true *work* (146). The Anglo-Saxon phrase *hard at work (hard aet woerc)* appears several times in association with Mr. Knightley. Frank's dalliance with Emma, pursuit of pleasure, delight in riddles and other trifles, flattering speech, and charming surface manners lead Mr. Knightley to view him as a selfish puppy in the Robert Ferrars style rather than a true gentleman.

But, as always, Austen invites readers to read between the lines and view *all* her characters as blind. Mr. Knightley has as much to learn from Frank as Frank does from Mr. Knightley. Discussion of Frank's foppery in traveling sixteen miles to London for a haircut must be reevaluated after we discover that his trip actually took place so that he could order a piano to be sent anonymously to Jane Fairfax. His generous gift and his enjoyment of singing duets suggest a genuine appreciation of art—and of his fiancée's talents. As one scholar notes, Frank demonstrates discriminating taste in instruments: "The Broadwood piano was the best that money could buy at the time."[20] Frank's "perfect knowledge of music" contrasts with the nouveau riche inhabitants of Highbury who lack the skill to use their own instruments (Mrs. Cole owns a "new grand pianoforte" but confesses, "I do not know one note from another"), those who pretend to love music yet have no intention of playing (Mrs. Elton claims to be "doatingly fond of music" yet seems now that she has snagged a mate to be "so determined upon neglecting her music"), and those too provincial ("I hate Italian singing—There is no understanding a word of it," Harriet complains) to appreciate foreign composers (227, 215, 276, 278, 232). Austen was ahead of her time in using England's reputation as *das Land ohne Musik*—country without music—to great fictional advantage.[21]

Frank also takes pleasure in dancing, including romantic waltzing. Mr. Knightley needs to get back into the dance, as Emma realizes when she sees him looking grave on the sidelines. Combine the best qualities of the disciplined Mr. Knightley and the lively Frank Churchill, Austen suggests, and the result might be a sturdy, honorable British gentleman ready to join the dance. One wonders if Austen consciously gave fictional representation to ideas about French and English character her brothers had explored in the *Loiterer*, their short-lived attempt to publish a witty periodical while at Oxford. James Austen had noted that Frenchmen find Englishmen "deplorably ignorant of the agréments of society" while British find "the Mounseers [*sic*] are all . . . ruffles without shirts." The *Loiterer* calls for balance, hoping that "the English would be convinced, that a man may be at once merry and wise."[22] Little did James and Henry Austen know back in 1789 that their merry and wise sister would illustrate that very point over two decades later in a novel dedicated by request to the Prince Regent of England.

Emma asks readers not only to consider national character but also to open their minds to new ideas about what a marriage should be. The novel opens and ends with wedding days and presents various forms of union. Mr. Knightley calls Miss Taylor "very fit for a wife" for Mr. Weston because she has learned "the very material matrimonial point of submitting [her] own will, and doing as [she is] bid" (6, 38). Mrs. Weston seems not to mind that her husband opens her mail. Although Austen has her hero praise such traditional subjection, she presents him as one who in actuality prefers a strong-willed woman, a counterpart. When Emma quips that "such a girl as Harriet is what every man delights in" rather than women with "well informed minds," Mr. Knightley retorts, "Men of sense . . . do not want silly wives" (63–64). He wants equality with Emma ("Cannot you call me George?") and romance ("Brother and sister! no indeed"), not a continuation of the teacherly role he has played in the past (463, 331). Unlike his brother John, George Knightley does not seek a wife who will merely murmur "Very true, my love" with uncritical devotion.

As in *Pride and Prejudice*, Austen contrasts traditional notions of romantic courtship with a slowly developing relationship. Mr. Knightley and Emma take their time on the way to the altar. As in *Mansfield Park*, semifraternal ties evolve into a conjugal union. Early on in *Emma*, Mr. Knightley admits that Emma seems as much his sister as does his sister-in-law, Isabella. He teases Emma with the air of a fond, rather patronizing older brother. Emma never even thinks of Mr. Knightley as a prospective husband until near the end, though her distress at his lack of dancing suggests she does not wish him relegated to the fuddy-duddy corner. Emma says to Mr. Knightley of the feasibility of their dancing together, "You know we are not really so much brother and sister as to make it at all improper" (331).

In a sense, Mr. Knightley and Emma have been behaving like a husband and wife for quite some time. From the beginning of the novel, Austen makes a point of showing Mr. Knightley and Emma functioning at dinner parties like a married couple skillfully maneuvering conversation to keep from distressing their guests. They share in their love of nieces and nephews and already seem to have created a cozy feeling of "home." Each is acutely aware of the other one's comings and goings. They talk with openness and equality: "We always say what we like to one another" (10). With years of friendship "all right, all open, all equal," it is not surprising that their eventual marriage can possess "something so like perfect happiness" (468, 432).

As in the case of the animated Elizabeth Bennet and reserved Mr. Darcy in *Pride and Prejudice*, Austen presents her happiest marriages in *Emma* as those where the union benefits both partners, like a completion of self. Presumably Emma, Harriet Smith, and Frank Churchill will acquire discipline and rationality; in turn, Mr. Knightley, Robert Martin, and Jane Fairfax may gain imagination and playfulness. As Mr. Knightley observes of the marriage between Frank and Jane, "I am very ready to believe his character will improve, and acquire from her's the steadiness and delicacy of principle that it wants . . . with such a woman he has a chance" (448). Frank and Emma realize in their final conversations that they would have been far too alike—both of them too fanciful, manipulative, and willful—to complement each other well as husband and wife. As Austen wrote in a letter, "Marriage is a great Improver" (20 November 1808).

But marriage can also be a great De-prover if partners bring out the worst in each other. The rejected Mr. Elton acquires a Mrs. Elton with "delightful rapidity" and soon becomes nearly as "hardened as his wife . . . growing like her" (181, 328). The only "finery" in their marriage is on the outside of their bodies. Every thing about this marriage is artificial, including Mrs. Elton's affected use of *caro sposo* to refer to her husband and her pretense that he is her "lord and master" when in fact she has the upper hand. Mrs. Elton gets the final spoken words in *Emma*—a condemnation of Emma and Mr. Knightley's wedding as a pitiful and shabby business because it lacks lace. One suspects that far too many modern-day Mrs. Eltons focus on display rather than substance, valuing the wedding day more than the perfect happiness of the union.

Austen adds a feminist twist to the ending of *Emma* by implying that her bossy, competitive heroine may still be scheming to stay more in control of her life than most married women. In a letter, Austen had discussed "pitying a young woman . . . because she cannot live in two places at the same time, & at once enjoy the comforts of being married & single" (8 February 1807). Emma comes the closest of any Austen heroine to proving a young woman *can* do just that. Emma will marry yet stay at home, remaining "always first and always right" to her father (84). Emma still thinks in competitive, egotistical terms, counting "on being *first* with Mr. Knightley" (415).

Like all other Austen heroines, Emma marries and supposedly lives happily ever after. Yet readers never forget the astonishing conversation Austen offers on celibacy between Emma and Harriet. Emma begins,

> "My being charming, Harriet, is not quite enough to induce me to marry; I must find other people charming—one other person at least. And I am not only, not going to be married, at present, but have very little intention of ever marrying at all. . . . I must see somebody very superior. . . . I cannot really change for the better. If I were to marry I must expect to repent it."
>
> "Dear me!—it is so odd to hear a woman talk so!"
>
> "I have none of the usual inducements of women to marry. . . . I believe few married women are half as much mistress of their husband's house, as I am of Hartfield; and never, never could I expect to be so truly beloved and important; so always first and always right in any man's eyes as I am in my father's." . . .
>
> "But still, you will be an old maid! and that's so dreadful!"
>
> "Never mind, Harriet, I shall not be a poor old maid; and it is poverty only which makes celibacy contemptible to a generous public! . . . [A] single woman, of good fortune, is always respectable, and may be as sensible and pleasant as anybody else." (84–85)

It is indeed, as Harriet Smith says, "so odd to hear a woman talk so." *Emma* contains some of the most direct discussions of women's hampered existences and threatened destinies in all of Austen. Emma speaks in the same bold voice Austen adopts herself in a letter to her niece: "Single Women have a dreadful propensity for being poor—which is one very strong argument in favour of Matrimony" (13 March 1817). Remove poverty as a factor and women acquire the freedom to say no.

Austen once again has her heroine argue that men are arrogant to assume that all women must and will marry. "It is always incomprehensible to a man that a woman should ever refuse an offer of marriage," Emma says, much as Elizabeth Bennet tried to explain to Mr. Collins, and Fanny Price insisted to Henry Crawford. In *The Watsons,* the novel Austen abandoned to write *Emma,* Elizabeth and Emma Watson debate the problem. Elizabeth says to her sister:

"You know we must marry. . . . It is very bad to grow old and be poor and laughed at. . . ."

"To be so bent on Marriage—to pursue a Man merely for the sake of situation—is a sort of thing that shocks me; I cannot understand it. Poverty is a great Evil, but to a woman of Education & feeling it ought not, it cannot be the greatest.—I would rather be a Teacher at a school (and I can think of nothing worse) than marry a Man I did not like."

"I would rather do any thing than be Teacher at a school" said her sister. (*MW,* 317–18)

In *Emma* Jane Fairfax sides with Emma Watson, deciding she would rather keep her dignity and accept loathsome work as a governess than marry a man she fears no longer loves her, despite the economic security and social acceptability she would gain from marriage.

Even the powerful, economically and socially secure Emma feels oppressed. Although she will be handsome, clever, and rich whether she marries or not, Emma laments women's lack of freedom and helplessness to shape their own economic futures: "She sat musing on the difference of woman's destiny" (384). Emma knows women do not have legal equality: "The world is not their's, nor the world's law," she says, applying a quotation about *poor* people from *Romeo and Juliet* to *women* in particular (400).

Emma is Austen's most unconventional heroine since the juvenilia—the one most "masculine" in the sense of intelligence, self-sufficiency, and bossiness. Camille Paglia goes so far as to call Emma a "Mercurius androgyne" with "latent masculinity."[23] Emma likes power and privilege. She utters paternalistic comments, as when she plans to elevate Harriet: "*She* would notice her; *she* would improve her; *she* would form her opinions and manners" (23). Austen's italics emphasize Emma's egotism. Emma acts like a father in control of his offspring's marital decisions, thinking, "Mr. Knightley must not marry! . . . I cannot at all consent to Mr. Knightley's marrying" (224). Emma could excel as a magistrate, lawyer, actor, or writer, though no such outlet exists for her talents. Perhaps Austen called Emma a heroine whom no one would like but herself because she knew her contemporaries were not ready for such an unusually opinionated woman—or woman author. She closes the novel with the usual wedding bells, but the surprisingly assertive voice of Emma Woodhouse ("I always deserve the best treatment, because I never put up with any other") lingers in readers' ears (474).

If *Mansfield Park* suggested that even a shy, quiet woman could find a voice, then *Emma* demonstrates that even a woman without "the power of removal" can change herself and, to some extent, her destiny. Emma never leaves Highbury, although Austen adds a nice touch by letting readers know that the wedding will be followed by a fortnight's "tour to the sea-side," perhaps helping to satisfy Emma's pent-up longing (483). Yet even before this trip, Emma undergoes a profound moral and emotional journey. Austen introduces frequent dates in this novel ("Sept. 28th," "26 June," "about ten days later," and so forth) to show readers that Emma's growth all occurs within little over a year: from September when she has lived "nearly twenty-one years in the world" to November of the following year, when she marries Mr. Knightley. The static ending of *Emma* is misleading. Yes, we find the same inert configuration of Emma, Mr. Knightley, and Mr. Woodhouse: "They sat down to tea—the same party round the same table—how often it had been collected!" (434). Yet despite this repeated tableau, Emma and Knightley are not the same—nor are readers. Both heroine and hero admit change: "At that time I was a fool," Emma says, and Mr. Knightley confesses, "I am changed also" (474). Their notion of an open, equal, and fair marriage radically redefines this institution. What other nineteenth-century novel besides *Emma* has an estate-owning hero move in with the heroine? One can imagine the Knightley-Woodhouses today not only taking on hyphenated names but also commuting great distances to accommodate two high-powered careers.

The very structure of *Emma* is ironic. The eponymous title reflects Emma's self-centered way of viewing the world, but Austen presents subplots and alternative readings. While Emma creates romantic storylines for others to follow, she herself becomes a chess piece in Austen's more realistic fiction. In addition, Austen perhaps delights in making her readers feel like Harriet Smith trying to solve riddles and piece together clues offered by someone of superior brilliance. Like Harriet, we do not know the answers to the charades and word puzzles until Emma tells us the answers, and we do not know the true relationship between Frank and Jane until Austen lets Emma and the rest of us in on the secret. What better way to demonstrate the power of the artist?

As Nobel Laureate Wislawa Szymborska notes in "The Joy of Writing," a poet can create woods, deer, and hunters and even stop the hunters' bullets in mid-flight. Writers have unrestricted, absolute power over their fictional worlds:

Not a thing will ever happen unless I say so.

. . . .

The joy of writing.
The power of preserving,
Revenge of a mortal hand.[24]

Had Mrs. Elton picked up a pen, she could indeed have had the *carte blanche* she wanted to arrange everything and everyone as she chose—though she might need to brush up on her grammar. An author need not give up that unfeminine evil, the godlike "power of having rather too much her own way" (6).

The intricate, ordered, balanced structure of this seriocomic detective novel with its "matchless symmetry . . . of design" and wizardry of technique reminds readers that while Emma Woodhouse may be a playful imaginist, she lacks the disciplined artistry of either a Jane Fairfax or a Jane Austen.[25] And unlike Jane Fairfax, Jane Austen not only knows how to create superior, elegant art but also how to radiate warmth and humor in the process. In this novel and in her work as a whole, Austen accomplishes what Emma can only imagine: "a mixture of the serious and the playful" and the power to shape her own narrative (129).

8

The Advantage of Maturity of Mind
Persuasion

That time is past,
And all its aching joys are now no more,
And all its dizzy raptures. Not for this
Faint I, nor mourn nor murmur; other gifts
Have followed; for such loss, I would believe,
Abundant recompense.
                    —William Wordsworth, "Tintern Abbey" (1798)

When all the fiercer passions cease
   (The glory and disgrace of youth);
When the deluded soul, in peace,
   Can listen to the voice of truth;
When we are taught in whom to trust,
   And how to spare, to spend, to give,
(Our prudence kind, our pity just.)
   'Tis then we rightly learn to live.
                    —George Crabbe, "Reflections" (1807)

There they returned again into the past, more exquisitely
happy, perhaps in their re-union, than when it had been
first projected; more tender, more tried, more fixed in a
knowledge of each other's character, truth, and attachment
. . . with the advantage of maturity of mind, consciousness
of right, and one independent fortune between them.
                    —*Persuasion*

In a letter written just a few months before her death, Austen informed a niece, "You may *perhaps* like the Heroine [of *Persuasion*],
as she is almost too good for me" (23 March 1817). In this final
completed novel, Austen does indeed present Anne Elliot as "a model
of female excellence . . . perfection itself, maintaining the loveliest

medium of fortitude and gentleness" (159, 241). The oldest heroine in Austen's novels, twenty-seven-year-old Anne demonstrates that those open to change over time can acquire maturity of mind and inner peace.

Many Austen readers find it impossible to read this final novel without being poignantly conscious of Austen's own declining health and the fact that she never lived to see *Persuasion* published. Passages describing the heroine's changed countenance ("her bloom had vanished early") and thin, faded appearance eerily remind us of letters from an ailing Austen to her relatives (6). In the same letter to a niece about the "too good" heroine of *Persuasion,* Austen writes that her own looks have become "bad enough, black and white" and "every wrong colour," symptoms now thought to be due to Addison's disease. "I must not depend upon being ever very blooming again," writes the forty-one-year-old Austen.

Yet throughout *Persuasion* Austen maintains her sense of humor and humanity, continuing to expose hypochondria, snobbery, idleness, materialism, and egotism. At the same time, she delineates happy alternatives available to those willing to wait and work. Although some critics have pointed to the melancholy, autumnal tone of this final novel, *Persuasion* in fact offers Austen's most optimistic celebration of possibilities for adults—whether male or female, single or married, rich or poor, aristocratic or "common," young or (as she puts it in *Sense and Sensibility* and *Emma*) on the "wrong side" of thirty-five. Readers in search of a mature Jane Austen may find glimpses of her in her late-blooming heroine with "seniority of mind," her unusually enterprising minor characters, and her still-biting narrative voice (101).

Self-assured, powerful Emma Woodhouse of *Emma* (1815) stands incongruously between two kinder, gentler, more traditionally feminine heroines: Fanny Price of *Mansfield Park* (1814) and Anne Elliot of *Persuasion* (completed in 1816 and published posthumously). Although Austen uses similar adjectives to describe Fanny and Anne, she makes her complex final heroine no simple remake. Anne Elliot is a decade older than Fanny Price, Catherine Morland, and Marianne Dashwood, so readers might expect Austen to display the triumph of reason over exuberance, propriety over passion. Instead, Austen tells us early in *Persuasion* that Anne Elliot "had been forced into prudence in her youth" but "learned romance as she grew older" (30). Romance, however, remains balanced with practicality: Austen presents the poetical, sensitive, warm-hearted Anne Elliot simultaneously as her most skilled, capable, and useful heroine.

Like Fanny Price, Anne Elliot lacks the liveliness of either Elizabeth Bennet or Emma Woodhouse. "Her spirits were not high," Austen writes of the delicate, mild-eyed, quiet, nervous, gently sighing Anne (15). Like Fanny, Anne tires on walks, blushes, suffers in silence when others label her an inferior nobody, and makes it her goal to stay out of everyone's way. A tender woman with gentle manners, Anne has both "elegances of mind and sweetness of character" (5). William Dean Howells's comment that "never was there a heroine so little self-assertive, so far from forth-putting" refers to Anne Elliot but could describe Fanny Price as well.[1] Also like Fanny, Anne reads poetry, appreciates nature, chides herself for emotions like envy and loneliness, listens to others attentively and patiently, tries to help those around her, and thinks deeply.

When Captain Wentworth first meets Anne, she is just shy of her twentieth year and seems to embody the feminine ideal: "an extremely pretty girl, with gentleness, modesty, taste, and feeling" (26). Nearly eight years later, as the novel opens, Anne knows that Captain Wentworth now regards her as possessing a "feebleness of character" and "weakness and timidity" for letting Lady Russell talk her into breaking off her youthful engagement to him (61). Nowhere else in Austen does a heroine have to suffer for many years because she has rejected the right man—one she loves and who loves her in return—simply because others advise her to do so. If *Northanger Abbey*'s Catherine Morland had been told to decline Henry Tilney's marriage proposal and had spent nearly a decade apart from him, watching as he flirted with other women, one suspects that she would have developed into an interesting woman rather than a "silly goose" with a penchant for scary novels. Austen thus leaves readers of *Persuasion* uncertain as to whether Anne's "prudent" youthful rejection of the unproven Wentworth was the right or wrong action. Although separation causes suffering for Anne and Wentworth, it also brings both the "advantage of maturity of mind" (248).

Jane Austen gives Anne some of her own experiences, tastes, opinions, and abilities. Like Austen, who supposedly fainted at the news her family had to move to Bath, Anne Elliot "disliked Bath . . . and Bath was to be her home" (14). Like Austen, Anne enjoys the piano not as an opportunity for display (like Mary Crawford playing the harp in *Mansfield Park*) but as a private recreation: "She knew that when she played she was giving pleasure only to herself. . . . In music she had been always used to feel alone in the world" (47). Anne defends the navy in a way that would have pleased Austen's

Jane Austen's writing table (Reproduced by permission of the
Jane Austen Memorial Trust)

two sailor brothers, and she values justice, honesty, and equity despite seeing little evidence of such qualities around her. Also like
Austen, Anne Elliot has a "more elegant and cultivated mind" than
the "thousands of other young ladies" around her who claim only
"the usual stock of accomplishments" (41, 40).

Anne also is the only Austen character described as having a
"collected mind" (242). Although Austen describes Anne as a reader
who likes to "clothe her imagination," she does not portray her as a
could-be novelist, as she did with the contriving, divining, "imaginist"
Emma Woodhouse (43). Instead, she makes Anne Elliot her most
useful, resourceful, skilled, *functional* heroine. Anne has "the hope of
being of real use" to those around her (100). As Captain Wentworth
concludes, there is "no one so proper, so capable as Anne" (114).
Anne serves as economic consultant when her spendthrift father and

sister land them in debt, unpaid but uncomplaining musician for the neighborhood's country dances ("how those little fingers of yours fly about!"), psychologist for her hypochondriacal sister, listener for every peeved relative in the vicinity, grief counselor to Captain Benwick, and nurse to those in distress (47). Austen's description of her sister Cassandra ("such an excellent Nurse, so assiduous and unwearying! . . . my dearest sister, my tender, watchful, indefatigable nurse") could also apply to the nurturing, hardworking, untiring Anne Elliot (letters of 25 March and 28 May 1817). Anne's usefulness brings her pleasure: she is "glad to be thought of some use, glad to have any thing marked out as a duty" and "extremely glad to be employed" (33, 71). Anne calls herself "extremely happy . . . to be of even the slightest use" to others (195). I like Natalie Tyler's witty description of Anne Elliot as "the indispensable Jane-of-all-trades."[2]

Austen underscores Anne's utility by contrasting it with other people's futility. Sir Walter finds the only "occupation for an idle hour" to be reading about himself in the baronetage, and Elizabeth Elliot has "no habits of utility"; neither of them thinks of helping others (3, 9). Henrietta and Louisa Musgrove may be amiable and affectionate, but they are hedonistically "living to be fashionable, happy, and merry" and to pursue delightful sensations (40). Charles Musgrove does "nothing with much zeal, but sport" and trifles the rest of his time away, while his ne'er-do-well younger brother, Dick, lacks purpose and discipline even when aboard a navy ship (43). Mary Musgrove responds to all events with useless hysteria and selfish hypochondria.

When Mary's son takes a bad fall, only Anne proceeds calmly, skillfully, and promptly: "Anne had every thing to do at once—the apothecary to send for—the father to have pursued and informed—the mother to support and keep from hysterics—the servants to control—the youngest child to banish, and the poor suffering one to attend and soothe;—besides sending, as soon as she recollected it, proper notice to the other house, which brought her an accession rather of frightened, enquiring companions, than of very useful assistants" (53). Austen emphasizes Anne's own competency by the sheer length and concreteness of this sentence's list of actions. When Charles Musgrove joins his whining wife in declaring his inability to help ("you see I can be of no use," Charles notes, while Mary insists, "I am of no more use at home than you are"), Anne sends both useless parents off to the party while she cares tenderly and properly for their son (55, 57). Anne's role leaves her isolated but brings her "many sensations of comfort" because she knows she is "of the first utility to the child"

(58). Even later she can look at this time and feel helped by her own helpfulness: "Her usefulness to little Charles would always give some sweetness to the memory of her two months visit there" (93).

In another unforgettable scene, Mary Musgrove's hysteria proves a literal hindrance. When Louisa Musgrove falls unconscious after a foolhardy jump, Mary and Henrietta Musgrove behave almost as helplessly as Laura and Sophia in "Love and Freindship," the neurotic young women who take turns fainting and running mad while their husbands lie bleeding to death in the road. Mary and Henrietta draw attention away from the seriously injured Louisa and prevent others from moving: "'She is dead! she is dead!' screamed Mary, catching hold of her husband, and contributing with his own horror to make him immoveable; and in another moment, Henrietta, sinking under the conviction, lost her senses too, and would have fallen on the steps, but for Captain Benwick and Anne, who caught and supported her between them" (109–10). In contrast, Anne once again instantly displays "strength and zeal and thought." While Captain Wentworth acts "as if his own strength were gone," groans for someone to help him, and staggers against a wall, Anne immediately functions as a paramedic. One Austen critic finds Anne's response so impressive that she dubs her "Dr. Anne Elliot."[3] Anne gives terse orders ("Rub her hands, rub her temples; here are salts"), dispatches Captain Benwick to fetch a surgeon, and instructs Charles to attend to Mary. She ignores the crowd that has gathered ostensibly "to be useful if wanted" but really "to enjoy the sight of a dead young lady, nay, two dead young ladies, for it proved twice as fine as the first report." Austen's narrative voice here takes a swipe at all of us more interested in gawking than helping. Anne has her hands full: she "tried to quiet Mary, to animate Charles, to assuage the feelings of Captain Wentworth"; the two men on the scene rather passively "seemed to look to her for directions." Anne must have felt a sense of relief when Captain Harville arrives, bringing with him "senses and nerves that could be instantly useful" (110–11).

Not surprisingly, Anne makes herself indispensable wherever she goes. Others frequently ask what they would do without her. Captain Wentworth wants Anne to be the one to stay at Lyme to nurse the ailing Louisa, but Mary Musgrove resents the slight to her own importance. "Why was not she to be as useful as Anne?" she fretfully asks (115). Why not indeed? Why has she become a hysterical self-absorbed woman incapable of helping anyone? She is not only useless to others but cannot even amuse or care for herself. Unlike Anne, Mary has "no resources for solitude" (37). Mary's uselessness leaves her discontented, whereas Anne "had the satisfaction of knowing herself extremely useful" (121).

Austen demonstrates that one key difference between Mary and Anne is that Anne has escaped the curse of "the Elliot self-importance" (37). Mary, Elizabeth, and Sir Walter all feel *ill used* rather than *of use* because they arrogantly expect one-way devotion and service from those around them. Ignoring the development of her inner self and her role as a contributing member of a community, Mary dwells only on the precedence due to her as a baronet's daughter. Why become an honorable, admirable person if your noble birth already entitles you to the best treatment?

In contrast, Anne has enough humility and perspective to know that her family does not deserve its rank. She admits that others—like the active Admiral and Sophy Croft, ingenious and hospitable Captain and Mrs. Harville, decent and well-meaning Musgrove parents, and courageous and enterprising Mrs. Smith—offer more to the world than her own poor excuse for a family. Her father may scorn those in the navy for their marred complexions and for their unorthodox way of ascending to titles, but Anne senses that Captain Wentworth, Captain Benwick, Captain Harville, and Admiral Croft outrank her father as true gentlemen. No snobs, the Harvilles and the old Musgroves know how to make a home warm and welcoming rather than cold and forbidding. Mrs. Smith may be a poor, disabled widow living in an unfashionable part of town, but Anne admires the way she works to support herself and do good to others. Through her portrayal of the ardent Captain Wentworth and the busy lives of a variety of unusual minor characters, Austen challenges traditional notions of class, gender, and success.

Austen readers may find Captain Frederick Wentworth a startling change from Austen's teacherly, rational heroes—sober men like Colonel Brandon, Mr. Darcy, and Mr. Knightley who balance the playful spirits of the heroines. When Anne first meets him, Captain Wentworth is a "fine dashing" man with "a great deal of intelligence, spirit and brilliancy" who displays a "bright eye, and curl of his handsome mouth," qualities more reminiscent of John Willoughby than Colonel Brandon. We are told that Captain Wentworth "looked and said everything in such exquisite grace," usually damning praise for an Austen man (26). Anne and Wentworth fall "rapidly and deeply in love," also a dangerous sign in Austen's fiction (52).

As "a stranger without alliance or fortune," the young captain appears to have a careless approach to his destiny and his budget:

Captain Wentworth had no fortune. He had been lucky in his profession, but spending freely, what had come freely, had realized nothing. But, he was confident that he should soon be rich;—full of life and ardour, he knew that he should soon have a ship, and soon be on a station that would lead to every thing he wanted. He had always been lucky; he knew he should be so still.—Such confidence, powerful in its own warmth, and bewitching in the wit which often expressed it, must have been enough for Anne; but Lady Russell saw it very differently.—His sanguine temper, and fearlessness of mind, operated very differently on her. She saw in it but an aggravation of the evil. It only added a dangerous character to himself. He was brilliant, he was headstrong. (27)

Austen's brilliant, headstrong, bewitchingly witty hero sounds more like Elizabeth Bennet and Emma Woodhouse than Mr. Darcy and Mr. Knightley. He seems the type of Austen man who often proves to be a rake—one seeking his own pleasure ("every thing he wanted") through luck and risk rather than through virtuous conduct and steady propriety.

Only Anne's rejection shakes Wentworth's faith in his lucky charm. In all other respects, his life validates his optimism: "All his sanguine expectations, all his confidence had been justified. His genius and ardour had seemed to foresee and to command his prosperous path. . . . He had distinguished himself [and had] made a handsome fortune" (29–30). Though hurt by Anne's rejection, he has not, like Anne, faded with time. Austen makes it clear that men age more gracefully than women by having her oldest heroine ruefully conclude of her former suitor, "the years which had destroyed her youth and bloom had only given him a more glowing, manly, open look, in no respect lessening his personal advantages" (61). Unlike Mr. Knightley remaining off to the sidelines at a dance, Captain Wentworth adds liveliness to any gathering and seems to "glow" his way through this novel.

Interestingly, Austen gives no simple answer as to whether Anne's action in rejecting the young Captain Wentworth was correct. As Anne puts it: "I have been thinking over the past, and trying impartially to judge of the right and wrong, I mean with regard to myself; and I must believe that I was right, much as I suffered from it, that I was perfectly right in being guided by [Lady Russell]. . . . To me, she was in the place of a parent. . . . I am not saying that she did not err in her advice.

239

It was, perhaps, one of those cases in which advice is good or bad only as the event decides" (246). In following Lady Russell's advice, was Anne caving in to class prejudice or displaying the obedience she owed an older advisor? Was Lady Russell wrong, seeming to distrust Providence, in feeling less sanguine than Captain Wentworth about his uncertain future? Does Austen describe Captain Wentworth's fearlessness and brash self-confidence in order to suggest that he was too young, too untested, and too unhumbled by adversity to be ready for marriage?

Some have called Anne's acquiescence to Lady Russell an error on her part. Marvin Mudrick, for instance, notes, "Her error was to let Lady Russell persuade her against his destiny, against the temper and fiery ambition that virtually guaranteed it."[4] Yet Austen seems to go to great lengths to overturn the common assumption (like that held by Marianne Dashwood in *Sense and Sensibility*) that the best romance is youthful romance. Had an adolescent Anne accepted Wentworth's first proposal, the conditions would hardly be inspirational: they fall in love then only because "he had nothing to do, and she had hardly any body to love" (26). Better wait for the real and tested thing, Austen implies with a sentence like that.

Captain Wentworth is the most *romantic* hero in Austen—like a dashing John Willoughby but with integrity. He disdains aristocratic condescension, is good with children, has acquired true manliness as a ship captain, shows empathy toward others, values spontaneity and energy, and displays fierce loyalty and generosity toward his friends. He has athletic grace (as when he clears a hedge at a leap) and is, like any self-respecting romantic, fond of music. Unlike Mr. Knightley, who speaks in blunt, no-nonsense terms and likes reading account books, Frederick Wentworth writes Anne a soulful letter about his heart and his feelings: "You pierce my soul. I am half agony, half hope. Tell me not that I am too late, that such precious feelings are gone for ever. I offer myself to you again with a heart even more your own, than when you almost broke it eight years and a half ago. . . . I can hardly write" (237). This sounds like something a tormented Charlotte Brontë character might write. Anne recognizes that she still loves Captain Wentworth in part because of his romantic temperament, for "warmth and enthusiasm did captivate her still" (161).

Austen links Captain Wentworth's animation and glowing spirits to his active pursuit of a vocation in the navy. Mrs. Dashwood of *Sense and Sensibility* would never need to say to Captain Wentworth, as she did to the idle, unanimated Edward Ferrars, "you would be a happier man if you had any profession to engage your time and give an interest to your plans and actions" (*SS*, 19). Captain Wentworth speaks of his ships and his voyages with obvious pride.

Captain Wentworth shares with Edward Ferrars an allegiance to a strict code of honor. Like Edward feeling duty bound to Lucy Steele, Captain Wentworth would have married Louisa Musgrove if she had misinterpreted his unguarded friendliness as commitment. "I was hers in honour if she wished it," he explains to Anne (242). Austen treats Captain Wentworth's insistence on an ancient notion of chivalry with ambivalence. On the one hand, his protectiveness toward women is admirably gallant: "There can be no want of gallantry . . . in rating the claims of women to every personal comfort *high*–and this is what I do. I hate to hear of women on board, or to see them on board; and no ship, under my command, shall ever convey a family of ladies any where, if I can help it" (69). On the other hand, Austen is quick to note that "This brought his sister upon him." The feisty Sophy Croft knows that such courtesy is antiquated and may in fact *harm* women by condemning them to a pampered and thus stifling existence: "Oh Frederick!–But I cannot believe it of you.–all idle refinement!–Women may be as comfortable on board, as in the best house in England. I believe I have lived as much on board as most women, and I know nothing superior to the accommodations of a man of war. . . . I hate to hear you talking so, like a fine gentleman, and as if women were all fine ladies, instead of rational creatures. We none of us expect to be in smooth water all our days" (69–70). Passages like that one make one suspect Austen had read Mary Wollstonecraft, who laments that, under the guise of chivalry and gallantry, "women are systematically degraded by receiving the trivial attentions which men think it manly to pay to the sex, when in fact, they are insultingly supporting their own superiority." [5] Like Wollstonecraft, Sophy Croft encourages her brother to drop his "superfine, extraordinary sort of gallantry" and grant women passage on board the ship–and life (69). Captain Wentworth and Anne Elliot have much to learn from Sophia Wentworth Croft and her unusual navy husband.

The Crofts contradict the anonymous old saying, "Marriage is a romance in which the hero dies in the first chapter." [6] Although Austen died a year before Byron began his satiric "Don Juan," she might have been amused by his observation that in most literary works, romance and marriage never seem to go together:

> Romances paint at full length people's wooing,
>   But only give a bust of marriages:
> For no one cares for matrimonial cooings,
>   There's nothing wrong in a connubial kiss:
> Think you, if Laura had been Petrarch's wife,
> He would have written sonnets all his life?[7]

Austen makes the Crofts remarkably unromantic (the Admiral has gout, and his wife has a blister "as large as a three-shilling piece"), yet she shows that this married couple remains deeply in love (170). Austen *does* care for "matrimonial cooings."

Unlike Charles and Mary Musgrove, who "might pass for a happy couple" but spend most of the time arguing and whining, or Mr. William Elliot and his first wife, who were "wretched together," Admiral and Mrs. Croft are both genuinely happy—and have been so for some time (43, 211). "Admiral and Mrs. Croft . . . seemed particularly attached and happy," Anne observes, and at another point notes, "They walked along in happy independence" (63, 168). Austen interrupts her narrative here and there to give readers a glimpse of the Crofts enjoying each other's company.

What makes this marriage so special? Austen clearly links the Crofts' happy fifteen-year marriage to their freedom from restrictive roles for men and women. Sophy Croft is an unusually self-assured, outspoken woman: "Mrs. Croft, though neither tall nor fat, had a squareness, uprightness, and vigour of form, which gave importance to her person. She had bright dark eyes, good teeth, and altogether an agreeable face; though her reddened and weather-beaten complexion, the consequence of her having been almost as much at sea as her husband, made her seem to have lived some years longer in the world than her real eight and thirty. Her manners were open, easy, and decided, like one who had no distrust of herself, and no doubts of what to do; without any approach to coarseness however, or any want of good humour" (48). Though a "genteel . . . lady," Sophy Croft asks questions about taxes and shows herself to be "more conversant with business" than her husband (22). She walks along "looking as intelligent and keen as any of the officers around her" (168). She rejects traditional notions of feminine refinement and argues eloquently for a woman's need for broader horizons: "I do assure you . . . that nothing can exceed the accommodations of a man-of-war; I speak, you know, of the higher rates. When you come to a frigate, of course, you are more confined—though any reasonable woman may be perfectly happy in one of them; and I can safely say, that the happiest part of my life has been spent on board a ship. While we were together, you know, there was nothing to be feared. Thank God! I have always been blessed with excellent health, and no climate disagrees with me" (70–71). Apparently Sophy Croft has not read the Reverend James Fordyce's sermon warning that "any young woman . . . that throws off all the lovely softness of her nature, and emulates the daring intrepid temper of a man—how terrible!" [8]

Rather than cultivating lovely softness, Sophy Croft shares adventures with her husband. She joins him whether they are on a ship crossing an ocean or on foot rambling about the countryside: "The Admiral and Mrs. Croft were generally out of doors together . . . dawdling about in a way not endurable to a third person, or driving out in a gig" (73). As Captain Wentworth notes, his sister is no timid, fainting lady when it comes to travel: "What glorious weather for the Admiral and my sister! They meant to take a long drive this morning; perhaps we may hail them from some of these hills. . . . I wonder whereabouts they will upset to-day. Oh! it does happen very often, I assure you—but my sister makes nothing of it—she would as lieve be tossed out as not" (84). Austen includes many references in *Persuasion* to the Crofts' unusual behavior as a metaphor for their unconventional marriage. For example, when Anne joins the Crofts in their carriage, she finds their driving style to be a metaphor for their partnership. Sophy Croft cries out, "My dear admiral, that post!—we shall certainly take that post" when they are about to have a collision: "But by coolly giving the reins a better direction herself, they happily passed the danger; and by once afterwards judiciously putting out her hand, they neither fell into a rut, nor ran foul of a dung-cart; and Anne, with some amusement at their style of driving, which she imagined no bad representation of the general guidance of their affairs, found herself safely deposited by them at the cottage" (92). Unlike many a contemporary husband resenting his wife for reading a map and implying that he might be lost, the Admiral happily shares the reins with his cool-headed wife and thus arrives safely at the right destination. In this, Admiral Croft differs from the arrogant Henry Crawford of *Mansfield Park,* who refuses to seek directions from anyone: "I lost my way . . . because I can never bear to ask" (*MP,* 241).

"Share" seems a key word with the Crofts, wherever they go. When Anne later encounters this unconventional couple in Bath, they remain each other's best friend: "They brought with them their country habits of being almost always together. He was ordered to walk, to keep off the gout, and Mrs. Croft seemed to go shares with him in every thing, and to walk for her life, to do him good" (168). Substitute "high cholesterol" for "gout" and one would find the Crofts today walking hand-in-hand around a track at a fitness club.

This unconventional marriage succeeds both because Mrs. Croft has spunk and because Admiral Croft has a solid, secure sense of identity. Austen emphasizes Admiral Croft's traditional manly qualities (he is hearty and hale and objects to the poetical Captain Benwick as "too piano" and to painters as "queer fellows") but then shows that this macho admiral has no need to dominate his wife (172, 169). A true man can share the power and form a genuine partnership with a woman without feeling his manhood threatened.

Both Crofts thrive not only because of their happy marriage but also because they have active lives and generous hearts. "Can I be of any use?" asks the admiral, a key question in this novel (169). Though Admiral Croft's manners seem coarse to the refined Lady Russell, Anne recognizes his irresistible and refreshing "goodness of heart and simplicity of character" (127). The Crofts squeeze together in the carriage to make room for a fatigued Anne, empathize with her feelings on quitting her birthplace, and set a fine example in the parish by giving "the best attention and relief" to the poor (125). As Anne concludes, Admiral and Mrs. Croft make "a most attractive picture of happiness" (168).

When Anne Elliot considers her youthful engagement to Captain Wentworth, she compares their love to the Crofts: "With the exception, perhaps, of Admiral and Mrs. Croft . . . there could have been no two hearts so open, no tastes so similar, no feelings so in union, no countenances so beloved" (63). Once married, the Wentworths may become as happy as the Crofts, but Austen implies that their marriage may involve more conversations and concerts than careening carriage rides. Captain Wentworth's lengthy analogy between a nut with a kernel and a human being with a strong character suggests that he has a more poetic outlook on life than the more down-to-earth admiral. It is hard to imagine Sophy Croft translating Italian songs at a concert, as Anne does. Austen shows readers that both Anne Elliot and Captain Wentworth are fond of children and good at caring for them, suggesting that they may not, like the Crofts, remain childless. The Wentworths can learn from the Crofts to form a joyous marriage but may choose different ways to spend their days together.

Austen's vision of a fulfilling, equitable marriage (that of the Crofts and of the Wentworths to come) seems way ahead of her time. Over a half-century later, John Stuart Mill can still only *imagine* such

an ideal: "What marriage may be in the case of two persons of cultivated faculties, identical in opinions and purposes, between whom
there exists that best kind of equality, similarity of powers and capaci-
ties with reciprocal superiority in them, so that each can enjoy the
luxury of looking up to the other, and can have alternatively the pleasure of leading and of being led in the path of development—I will not
attempt to describe."[9] Mill "will not attempt to describe" such a plea-
surable marriage (though perhaps he had in mind his union with the
unusual, highly intellectual Harriet Taylor), but Austen already had
done so in *Persuasion*.

Austen links a younger Sophy Croft to Anne Elliot by showing
both as brides married to captains. The choice for Anne is thus clear.
Stay at home alone with nothing to do and you may become as hypochondriacal as Mary Musgrove. Sophy Croft warns, "The only time
that I ever really suffered in body or mind, the only time that I ever
fancied myself unwell, or had any ideas of danger, was the winter that
I passed by myself" (71). Instead, Sophy Croft suggests, board that
metaphorical man-of-war and "go shares" with your partner in life.

By ending *Persuasion* with the idea of alarm off in the distance,
Austen presents the Anne Elliot–Frederick Wentworth marriage as a
voyage just beginning. Like Sophy Croft, Anne Elliot needs the skills
and the strength to endure whatever rough waters lie ahead. More
than in any other novel, Austen focuses in *Persuasion* on the need for
survival by presenting a variety of resilient characters—both married
and single—who have overcome adversity.

While Admiral and Mrs. Croft amble about the countryside
and overturn carriages, Captain and Mrs. Harville creatively turn
their tiny home into both a private haven and a warm oasis for
visitors. Especially when contrasted with the cold superciliousness
of Sir Walter and Elizabeth Elliot, the Harvilles seem to offer "a
bewitching charm in a degree of hospitality so uncommon, so unlike the usual style of give-and-take invitations, and dinners" (98).
This final Austen novel is full of characters and situations *so uncommon* and *so unlike the usual*.

Inside the Harville dwelling, visitors find "rooms so small as
none but those who invite from the heart could think capable of ac-
commodating so many" (98). Yet the Harvilles use their ingenuity to
transform little into much: "Anne had a moment's astonishment . . .
but it was soon lost in the pleasanter feelings which sprang from the
sight of all the ingenious contrivances and nice arrangements of Captain Harville to turn the actual space to the best possible account"

(98). As Sandra Gilbert and Susan Gubar note, Austen's role as domestic novelist parallels Captain Harville's approach to his house: both use their ingenuity to turn confining space to the best possible account.[10] Though lame and ill of health ever since receiving a severe wound in the war, Captain Harville finds "constant employment within" because of his "mind of usefulness and ingenuity" (99). Austen emphasizes his resourcefulness through a lengthy list of active verbs: "He *drew*, he *varnished*, he *carpentered*, he *glued*; he *made* toys for the children, he *fashioned* new netting-needles and pins with improvements" (99; my italics). Captain Harville makes bookshelves for the literary Captain Benwick and welcomes Captain Wentworth with brotherly warmth.

Mrs. Harville also leads a busy life. She seems eager to entertain visitors, comes to the rescue quickly after Louisa's fall, insists that Louisa stay with them, and skillfully nurses her through her recuperation. Captain and Mrs. Harville are happy, despite small rooms and the captain's physical debility, because they have warm hearts and nimble minds and fingers. As she departs from the Harvilles, Anne knows "she left great happiness behind her" (99).

Although older and less active than the Crofts or Harvilles, the parents of Charles, Henrietta, and Louisa Musgrove similarly have found great happiness by putting aside selfish ambition and working together to create a festive home. Anne knows that unlike her snobbish, vain, pretentious father, the cheerful Musgrove parents are "so totally free from all those ambitious feelings which have led to so much misconduct and misery," possessing "true parental hearts" and a sense of honor and kindness toward others (218, 182). Their house is filled with laughter, music, dancing, and a roaring Christmas fire. Austen links the Musgroves to the Crofts through the remarks of Mrs. Musgrove: "I am quite of your opinion, Mrs. Croft. . . . There is nothing so bad as a separation. I am quite of your opinion. *I* know what it is, for Mr. Musgrove always attends the assizes and I am so glad when they are over, and he is safe back again" (71). Mrs. Musgrove leads a far more limited life than Mrs. Croft (she does not know one country from another and fails to see the irony of comparing her husband's journey to the assizes to Admiral Croft's voyage to the West Indies) but shares Sophy Croft's feeling that marriages thrive on togetherness.

One need not be married to be happy or successful, however. One of the most unusual Austen characters is Mrs. Smith of *Persuasion,* a "poor, infirm, helpless widow" who has overcome incredible odds to make a new life. Her hardships are many: "She was a widow, and poor. . . . She had had difficulties of every sort to contend with, and in addition to these distresses, had been afflicted with a severe rheumatic fever, which finally settling in her legs, had made her for the present a cripple. . . . She . . . was now . . . living in a very humble way, unable even to afford herself the comfort of a servant, and of course almost excluded from society" (152–53). Sir Walter and Elizabeth Elliot scorn Anne for traveling into the bad part of town to visit her old school friend, a "mere Mrs. Smith, an every day Mrs. Smith" with "no surname of dignity" (158). In contrast, Anne recognizes that she has stumbled upon another moral lesson in how to find happiness: "She watched—observed—reflected—and finally determined . . . here was that elasticity of mind, that disposition to be comforted, that power of turning readily from evil to good, and of finding employment which carried her out of herself, which was from Nature alone. It was the choicest gift of Heaven" (154). Mrs. Smith knits both as a source of income for herself and as a charitable means of "doing a little good to one or two poor families." Her good sense, agreeable manners, and cheerful disposition keep her from letting ill health and grief ruin her spirits. Despite her hard life, Mrs. Smith has "moments only of languor and depression, to hours of occupation and enjoyment." As in the case of the lame Captain Harville, the disabled Mrs. Smith conquers adversity through her ability to work hard and think of others. Mrs. Smith's "cheerfulness and mental alacrity" enable her to adapt and survive (154–55).

The Mrs. Smith story has puzzled readers for two centuries. As Robert Liddell notes, "No part of the novel has caused greater dissatisfaction than the story of Mrs. Smith."[11] Why, one might ask, does Austen give the resilient survivor Mrs. Smith so much time near the end of the novel? Perhaps as Anne Elliot and Captain Wentworth move toward that inevitable marriage ("who can be in doubt . . . ?") Austen wishes to remind readers that if she were not bound by the conventions of courtship novels, she could have presented Anne Elliot as a chastened but fulfilled single woman making a useful and productive life for herself. Austen knew that she herself, like Mrs. Smith, had "mental alacrity" and "employment which carried her out of herself."

Another reason Austen may have included the Mrs. Smith story is to emphasize the recurring theme in this novel that people can undergo profound changes—both in outward circumstances and inner attitudes—over time. Just as she repeatedly emphasizes how many years have passed since Anne broke her engagement to Wentworth ("*Eight years*, almost *eight years* had passed. . . . What might not *eight years* do?"), so Austen persistently refers to how many years have separated Anne from her former schoolmate, Mrs. Smith née Hamilton: "*Twelve years* were gone . . . *Twelve years* had changed Anne . . . *twelve years* had transformed . . . Miss Hamilton" (60, 153). A thirty-year-old Mrs. Smith can look back at her youth and conclude, "I think differently now; time and sickness, and sorrow, have given me other notions" (201).

To a greater extent than any other Austen novel, *Persuasion* documents our capacity to learn from mistakes, to gain wisdom through suffering, to evolve into better men and women. Louisa Musgrove is "altered" after her fall, no longer the headstrong, impulsive girl who insisted on having her way (218). Despite her earlier "prejudices on the side of ancestry," Lady Russell can now admit "she had been pretty completely wrong" in severing Anne's youthful engagement to Captain Wentworth and can proclaim herself ready "to take up a new set of opinions and of hopes" (249). Anne and Captain Wentworth both feel profoundly changed from their youthful, impressionable and impulsive selves. The "so altered" Anne notes, "We are not boy and girl" (60, 221).

At the same time, Austen celebrates something constant that survives alteration. One wonders whether she repeats the word *alter* so often in *Persuasion* because she wants readers to keep in mind Shakespeare's sonnet:

> Let me not to the marriage of true minds
> Admit impediments; love is not love
> Which alters when it alteration finds,
> Or bends with the remover to remove.
> O no, it is an ever-fixed mark,
> That looks on tempests, and is never shaken;
> It is the star to every wand'ring bark,
> Whose worth's unknown, although his highth be taken.
> Love's not Time's fool, though rosy lips and cheeks
> Within his bending sickle's compass come;
>
> > (Sonnet 116)

Captain Wentworth has seen his share of tempests. Anne Elliot's rosy cheeks have paled. Both have altered during their eight years apart, yet some essential inner core will enable them to form "a marriage of true minds." As Captain Wentworth tells Anne Elliot toward the close of *Persuasion*, "to my eye you could never alter" (243).

Austen's final novel also reminds readers of Shakespeare's assertion in another sonnet that autumnal love is strongest:

> That time of year thou mayst in me behold
> When yellow leaves, or none, or few, do hang
> Upon those boughs . . .
>
> . . . .
>
> This thou perceiv'st, which makes thy love more strong

Anne Elliot and Captain Wentworth are still youthful—hardly dying trees—but the passage of time and consciousness of loss may ensure that they will "love that well, which [they] must leave ere long" (Sonnet 73).

Only those trapped in a fool's paradise of their own egotistical making—like Sir Walter Elliot in front of a mirror or looking himself up in the baronetage, Mary Musgrove malingering on a couch, or Mrs. Clay and William Elliot scheming their way to wealth and status—remain unloved, unimproved, and unredeemed. When describing Elizabeth Elliot waiting for a suitor with baronet blood, Austen again emphasizes the passing of time (*"Thirteen years* ago . . . *thirteen years* had seen . . . for *thirteen years . . . thirteen winters . . . thirteen springs"*) but suggests that nothing can change for a woman with "all selfish vanity" who believes herself perfect (6–7, 185). Throughout her works, but most particularly in *Mansfield Park* and *Persuasion,* Austen insists that selfish men and women can neither find nor give happiness.

At the end of this novel Anne understandably regrets that she has no worthy, unselfish relatives to bestow on Captain Wentworth. Anne will no doubt create a new family for herself among the warm-hearted Crofts and Harvilles. Austen reinforces the contrast by having Admiral Croft move into Kellynch Hall, former residence of Sir Walter Elliot. The outward-looking, good-natured Admiral Croft feels uncomfortable in this egotist's paradise: "We have made very few changes. . . . I have done very little besides sending away some of the large looking-glasses from my dressing-room, which was your father's. A very good man, and very much the gentleman I am sure—but I should think, Miss Elliot," (looking with serious reflection) "I should think he must be rather a dressy man for his time of life.—Such a number of looking-glasses! oh Lord! there was no getting away from oneself" (127–28). In the parenthetical description of Admiral Croft, Austen puns on a different kind of "reflection" than Sir Walter's narcissism.

One ironic moment in the novel comes when Sir Walter and Elizabeth Elliot decide to snub Admiral Croft and his wife. "We had better leave the Crofts to find their own level," they sneer (166). By this late point in the novel, Austen's readers recognize that the Crofts will indeed find their own level—with the Harvilles, Wentworths, and others with superior sense and sensibility. Austen celebrates meritocracy and action rather than aristocracy and stagnation. The very structure of the novel (from Austen's first paragraph describing Sir Walter Elliot looking himself up in the baronetage to her last paragraph describing the "national importance" of the navy) reinforces this movement.

Another radical moment in this novel is Frederick Wentworth's comment about the class system within the navy: "[The Asp was] quite worn out and broken up. I was the last man who commanded her.—Hardly fit for service then . . . so I was sent off to the West Indies. . . . The admiralty . . . entertain themselves now and then, with sending a few hundred men to sea, in a ship not fit to be employed" (64–65). One is reminded of Siegfried Sassoon's bitingly ironic poem about World War I, "Base Details":

> If I were fierce, and bald, and short of breath,
> I'd live with scarlet Majors at the Base,
> And speed glum heroes up the line to death. . . .
> And when the war is done and youth stone dead,
> I'd toddle safely home and die—in bed.[12]

But Austen does not let Wentworth's renegade comment about the admiralty stand unchallenged: Admiral Croft retorts, "Phoo, phoo! . . . what stuff these young fellows talk!" Nevertheless, Dick Musgrove's death stands as a reminder that those most likely to die are those without office or title. Not all sailors are heroic (in fact, Dick Musgrove's troublesome nature may have jeopardized the safety of the ship, and the captain would go to the bottom along with his crew), but all put their lives at risk.

Sir Walter Elliot scorns the navy because it is a "means of bringing person of obscure birth into undue distinction" and because exposure to the sea leads to weather-beaten complexions, thus making them "not fit to be seen" (19, 20). Yet Austen clearly indicates that the aristocracy has been the means of bringing people *not seen to be fit* into undue distinction. The navy is based on fraternity and duty, not hierarchy and privilege. After visiting Captain Harville and Captain Benwick in the company of Captain Wentworth, Louisa Musgrove "burst into raptures of admiration and delight on the character of the navy—their friendliness, their brotherliness, their openness, their uprightness; protesting that she was convinced of sailors having more worth and warmth than any other set of men in England; that they only knew how to live, and they only deserved to be respected and loved" (99). Like her physical actions, Louisa's remarks are extreme. With her insistence on "justice and equity," Anne Elliot offers a more balanced view: "The navy . . . have at least an equal claim with any other set of men" (19).

Bravery shown at sea gives the lie to Mary Musgrove's petulant complaint, "If there is any thing disagreeable going on, men are always sure to get out of it" (56). Mary shows neither unconventional fortitude, like Sophy Croft aboard a ship, nor conventional servitude, like Anne proclaiming "Nursing does not belong to a man, it is not his province" (56). *Both* Charles and Mary Musgrove plead sex to avoid unpleasantness: This is "quite a female case," Charles says of caring for his injured child when he instead wants his freedom, while Mary exploits feminine hysteria and sensitive nerves to defend her own right to attend a party (55). Despite its shorter length, *Persuasion* contains more battles between the sexes than any other Austen novel.

Austen posits choice for men and women. The poetical Captain Benwick may be too effeminate for Admiral Croft, but Captain Wentworth mocks neither his tenderness nor his love of reading. Benwick chooses to marry a woman more determined and resolute than himself. Sophy Croft is better at business than her husband, as was Lady Elliot. One hopes that Anne Elliot and Frederick Wentworth will not divide life into segregated male/female spheres as do the Musgroves: "The Mr. Musgroves had their own game to guard and to destroy; their own horses, dogs, and newspapers to engage them; and the females were fully occupied in all the other common subjects of housekeeping, neighbours, dress, dancing, and music" (42–43). Those who refuse to be reduced to a stereotype ("the females") have the best chance of a fulfilling life.

If Austen wished to crank out a novel quickly, she might have made Sir Walter Elliot (like Mr. Bennet or Mr. Palmer) an intelligent man whose infatuation with a beautiful but dimwitted woman condemned him to a miserable marriage. Instead, in this final novel she turns the tables and shows personal vanity and foolish infatuation to be unisex qualities: "Few women could think more of their personal appearance than he did. . . . His good looks and his rank had one fair claim on his attachment; since to them he must have owed a wife of very superior character to any thing deserved by his own. Lady Elliot had been an excellent woman, sensible and amiable; whose judgment and conduct, if they might be pardoned the youthful infatuation which made her Lady Elliot, had never required indulgence afterwards" (4). Not surprisingly, Lady Elliot's marriage leaves her unhappy. Had she lived, she might have counseled Anne in a way reminiscent of Mr. Bennet addressing Elizabeth: "My child, let me not have the grief of seeing *you* unable to respect your partner in life" (*PP*, 376).

In *Persuasion* Austen shows that both sexes are capable of folly and fortitude. She places her most extensive argument about the merits of men versus women in the mouths of two of her most resourceful and likeable people: Captain Harville for the men, and Anne Elliot for the women. Which sex is capable of the most faithful love? Does Captain Benwick's ability to overcome his grief for his fiancée, the late Fanny Harville, and marry Louisa Musgrove prove that men feel less than women? Captain Harville and Anne Elliot debate the question in a friendly, reasoned, balanced way. The exchange is so remarkable for a novel of 1816–17 that I quote it at some length. Captain Harville says,

> "Poor Fanny! she would not have forgotten him so soon!"
>
> "No," replied Anne, in a low feeling voice. . . . "It would not be the nature of any woman who truly loved. . . . We certainly do not forget you, so soon as you forget us. It is, perhaps, our fate rather than our merit. We cannot help ourselves. We live at home, quiet, confined, and our feelings prey upon us. You are forced on exertion. You have always a profession, pursuits, business of some sort or other, to take you back into the world immediately, and continual occupation and change soon weaken impressions." . . .
>
> "I will not allow it to be more man's nature than woman's to be inconstant and forget those they do love, or have loved. I believe the reverse. I believe in a true analogy between our bodily frames and our mental; and that as our bodies are the strongest, so are our feelings; capable of bearing most rough usage, and riding out the heaviest weather."
>
> "Your feelings may be the strongest," replied Anne, "but the same spirit of analogy will authorise me to assert that ours are the most tender. Man is more robust than woman, but he is not longer-lived; which exactly explains my view of the nature of their attachments. Nay, it would be too hard upon you, if it were otherwise. You have difficulties, and privations, and dangers enough to struggle with. You are always labouring and toiling, exposed to every risk and

hardship. Your home, country, friends, all quitted. Neither time, nor health, nor life, to be called your own. It would be too hard indeed" (with a faltering voice) "if woman's feelings were to be added to all this."

"We shall never agree upon this question." (232–33)

Contained within this part of the debate are key arguments raised by feminists and antifeminists. If you deny women professions, businesses, and horizons, Anne observes, you condemn them to a life of confinement and imaginary nervous complaints. Like many biological determinists, Captain Harville argues that men's stronger bodies reflect their stronger minds. Neither argues dogmatically or maliciously, however. Captain Harville acknowledges that his fellow man (Captain Benwick) seems to have gotten over his love all too quickly, and Anne is quick to praise men for the adversity they suffer during their shorter lives. Like Elizabeth sparring with Mr. Darcy or Emma with Mr. Knightley, Anne Elliot argues with intelligence. Though she speaks in a faltering voice, Anne does not waver in her purpose: to defend women without discrediting men.

As the debate continues, Captain Harville broadens their conversation to include the larger battle between the sexes; between any man and woman; between male authors and the female sex targeted by their works.

"Well, Miss Elliot," (lowering his voice) "as I was saying, we shall never agree I suppose upon this point. No man and woman would, probably. But let me observe that all histories are against you, all stories, prose and verse. . . . I do not think I ever opened a book in my life which had not something to say upon woman's inconstancy. Songs and proverbs, all talk of woman's fickleness. But perhaps you will say, these were all written by men."

"Perhaps I shall.—Yes, yes, if you please, no reference to examples in books. Men have had every advantage of us in telling their own story. Education has been theirs in so much higher a degree; the pen has been in their hands. I will not allow books to prove any thing." (234)

Anne may be gentle but her words are strong and categorical (*no* reference, *every* advantage, *not* . . . prove *any thing*).

This is not a strident argument, however, between a misogynist and a feminist. Captain Harville anticipates Anne's approach ("perhaps you will say"), and Anne goes on to acknowledge that each of them has only one perspective ("We each begin probably with a little bias towards our own sex"). In "a tone of strong feeling" Captain Harville depicts a man's emotions when separated from his family for over a year ("If I could but make you comprehend what a man suffers . . . if I could convey to you . . . If I could explain to you"), his words capturing a naval man's point of view. His words have effect, leading Anne to cry eagerly, "God forbid that I should undervalue the warm and faithful feelings of any of my fellow-creatures." Men become fellow-creatures, not merely the adversary, yet Anne continues to champion the enduring feelings of her own sex:

> "I should deserve utter contempt if I dared to suppose that true attachment and constancy were known only by woman. No, I believe you capable of every thing great and good in your married lives. . . . All the privilege I claim for my own sex (it is not a very enviable one, you need not covet it) is that of loving longest, when existence or when hope is gone." . . .
> "You are a good soul," cried Captain Harville, putting his hand on her arm quite affectionately. "There is no quarrelling with you.—And when I think of Benwick, my tongue is tied." (235–36)

Captain Harville becomes tongue-tied when faced with the example of Captain Benwick. Jane Austen must have enjoyed the irony of following a discussion of men's writings about women's inconstancy with an example *in a book by a woman* of *an inconstant man*.

Most significant is that this discussion can occur without rancor or polarization. Anne acknowledges that undervaluing all men would be contemptible. Captain Harville closes the argument with praise ("You are a good soul") and friendship ("putting his hand on her arm quite affectionately"). As Captain Wentworth listens, Anne and Captain Harville offer through their interchange a model for how men and women can have a rational, respectful, and constructive discussion.

This extraordinary discussion of men and women is missing from the early version of *Persuasion*, indicating that it was written late in Austen's career. Although it is difficult to prove anything about an author's intentions, I like to think that Austen fully enjoyed the irony of this scene in *Persuasion*. As Anne begins defending the feelings and merits of women (in effect, "telling their own story") and observes of men that "the pen has been in their hands," Captain Wentworth stops writing ("his pen had fallen down"). This calls our attention to who *is* writing: Jane Austen. As Anne Elliot insists that Captain Harville make "no reference to examples in books" by men, readers remain aware that both of them are examples in a book written by a woman.

Austen achieves additional irony through brief but pointed allusions. Although Captain Harville and Anne Elliot seem to know of no male writer who praises women's constancy ("all stories are against you, all stories, prose and verse"), Jane Austen obviously does. Earlier, Austen calls readers' attention to Matthew Prior's "Henry and Emma." The reference is fleeting and occurs after Louisa Musgrove's accident, when Anne Elliot comes forward to nurse her: "Without emulating the feelings of an Emma towards her Henry, [Anne Elliot] would have attended on Louisa with a zeal above the common claims of regard, for [Captain Wentworth's] sake" (116). What readers in search of Jane Austen might discover through this allusion is that Austen points our way directly to a long poem celebrating woman's superior faithfulness. Prior's invocation calls for an end to male disparagements of women:

> No longer Man of Woman shall complain,
> That He may love, and not be lov'd again:
> That We in vain the fickle Sex pursue,
> Who change the Constant Lover for the New.[13]

Prior celebrates a woman who is unbelievably faithful to one man. In Prior's poem, Henry tests Emma by telling her she should not love him because he has been exiled to the woods, must fight in battle, will endure hardships, and has taken a mistress. Rather than be dissuaded, Emma responds that she will be partner to his woe, help him in battle, and even care tenderly for his mistress. Your mistress will be the "happy object" I will follow and serve, a groveling Emma tells Henry: "What she demands, incessant I'll prepare: / I'll weave Her Garlands; and I'll pleat Her Hair." Throughout the poem we hear Emma's refrain, "I, of all Mankind, have lov'd but Thee alone."

Austen's allusion to this poem shows that she could have countered Captain Harville's argument that all male poets depict fickle women. At the same time, I suspect Emma's doormat approach (uttering self-effacing comments while making garlands for Henry's mistress) offended Austen's sensibility. Austen makes sure to tell us that the loyal, loving Anne Elliot could tend to Louisa's injuries faithfully but "*without* emulating the feelings of an Emma towards her Henry."

Another allusion shows us that Anne Elliot reads *women's* literature. As Anne tries to maneuver away from Mr. Elliot to an open position on a concert bench so that Captain Wentworth will have a chance to speak to her, she feels like a character in Fanny Burney's *Cecilia* (1782). In *Northanger Abbey* Austen praised *Cecilia* (and two other women's novels) as demonstrating a "thorough knowledge of human nature" with "genius, wit, and taste" (*NA*, 38). This time the thought occurs not to the narrator but to Anne herself: "by some other removals, and a little scheming of her own, Anne was enabled to place herself much nearer the end of the bench than she had been before, much more within reach of a passer-by. She could not do so, without comparing herself with Miss Larolles, the inimitable Miss Larolles—but still she did it" (189). Anne is a far cry from Burney's Miss Larolles, a voluble, illiterate, manipulative woman who schemes her way to the end of a bench in hopes of capturing Mr. Meadows, a disdainful, ungallant man: "'Do you know,' continued Miss Larolles, 'Mr. Meadows has not spoke one word to me all the evening! Though I am sure he saw me, for I sat at the outside on purpose to speak to a person or two, that I knew would be strolling about; for if one sits on the inside, there's no speaking to a creature, you know. . . . It's the shockingest thing you can conceive to be made sit in the middle of those forms; one might as well be at home, for nobody can speak to one.'" [14] Anne Elliot demonstrates the proper way to read novels: she compares herself to a character (to make sure her action would not be as unseemly and undignified as hers) before acting, but she never confuses fiction with reality, as Catherine Morland does in *Northanger Abbey*.

Though Anne compares herself to Miss Larolles, Austen invites readers through this allusion to compare Anne to the *heroine* of Burney's *Cecilia,* a woman whose talents are underestimated by her haughty male guardians. Like Anne, Cecilia favors love over hereditary privilege, virtue over fashion, generosity over selfishness. Through her allusion to *Cecilia,* Austen reminds readers that the pen is no longer exclusively in men's hands; women authors are beginning to tell their own story.

When Anne Elliot has news to tell Lady Russell of Mr. Elliot's sordid past, she delays "the explanatory visit" because of a prior engagement: "She had promised to be with the Musgroves from breakfast to dinner. Her faith was plighted, and Mr. Elliot's character, like the Sultaness Scheherazade's head, must live another day" (229). Why this fleeting and oddly placed allusion to Scheherazade, the fictitious queen of *Arabian Nights* who kept herself from being beheaded by beginning spellbinding stories? Through digressions like this one, Austen keeps readers conscious of the power of art—specifically, her own art.

Anne Elliot does not display humor (though she feels amused, suppresses smiles, and looks down to hide smiles), but Austen does. The narrator of *Persuasion* uses her dry, Mr. Bennet-like wit to attack pretense and blindness, as in her description of the Musgrove parents' denial of the shortcomings of the feckless son they lost at sea:

> The real circumstances of this pathetic piece of family history were, that the Musgroves had had the ill fortune of a very troublesome, hopeless son; and the good fortune to lose him before he reached his twentieth year; that he had been sent to sea, because he was stupid and unmanageable on shore; that he had been very little cared for at any time by his family, though quite as much as he deserved; seldom heard of, and scarcely at all regretted, when the intelligence of his death abroad had worked its way to Uppercross, two years before.
>
> He had, in fact, though his sisters were now doing all they could for him, by calling him "poor Richard," been nothing better than a thick-headed, unfeeling, unprofitable Dick Musgrove, who had never done any thing to entitle himself to more than the abbreviation of his name, living or dead. (50–51)

This passage sounds as caustic as some of the comments Austen's relatives censored from her letters, as when she noted, "Mr Waller is dead, I see;—I cannot greive about it, nor perhaps can his Widow very much" (22 June 1808). What a far cry the account of Dick Musgrove is from the sentimental deathbed scenes of a Charles Dickens. Austen had the unfeminine audacity—and realism—to propose that early death may be one way of removing an incorrigible troublemaker and allowing bereaved but relieved relatives to construct a false but pleasing memory of the dearly departed.

Austen also interrupts the novel to offer two paragraphs pertaining to Mrs. Musgrove's obesity. After noting that Mrs. Musgrove's position between Anne and Captain Wentworth on the couch presents "no insubstantial barrier" as she is "of a comfortable substantial size," the narrator then turns to considering our unfair tendency to equate beauty with feeling, size with sentiment. Captain Wentworth has to use "self command" to keep himself from laughing at Mrs. Musgrove's "large fat sighings over the destiny of a son, whom alive nobody had cared for." The narrator knows that humor (in this case, ridicule) can be unjust: "Personal size and mental sorrow have certainly no necessary proportions. A large bulky figure has as good a right to be in deep affliction, as the most graceful set of limbs in the world. But, fair or not fair, there are unbecoming conjunctions, which reason will patronize in vain,—which taste cannot tolerate,—which ridicule will seize" (68). This seems a puzzling passage. Does Austen include it to suggest that both Anne and Captain Wentworth know how to control their humor, to keep their amusement from harming anyone? Does she add the passage to remind readers that *all* of us, not just the complexion-conscious Sir Walter Elliot, judge others by their superficial appearance? The passage reminds me of a conversation in Charlotte Brontë's *Jane Eyre* (1847) about our tendency to respond more to a *beautiful* person's distress:

> Bessie, when she heard this narrative [telling that Jane Eyre's parents died of typhus fever, leaving her a penniless orphan], sighed and said, "Poor Miss Jane is to be pitied, too, Abbot."
>
> "Yes," responded Abbot, "if she were a nice, pretty child, one might compassionate her forlornness; but one really cannot care for such a little toad as that."
>
> "Not a great deal, to be sure," agreed Bessie: "at any rate, a beauty like Miss Georgiana would be more moving in the same condition."
>
> "Yes, I dote on Miss Georgiana!" cried the fervent Abbot. "Little darling!—with her long curls and her blue eyes." [15]

Like Brontë, Austen knew there was injustice in assuming beautiful people are "more moving" in affliction. In drama from Shakespeare to Dryden, Austen would have encountered fat older women invariably turned into the large butts of comedy, not figures of pathos. Austen's wry narrative voice here reminds us that she knows such stereotyping—including the amusement she herself provides in *Persuasion* through the portrait of Mrs. Musgrove's "large fat sighings"—wrongs the many Mrs. Musgroves of real life.

Perhaps because the heroine of *Persuasion* seemed "almost too good" for Austen, she offers through her blunt, hard-hitting, and acerbic narrative voice an antithesis. Anne is invariably tactful, subtle, and mild; the narrator (and, by implication, women in general) need not be so. Too often readers have equated Anne and Austen, as in acquaintance Mrs. Barrett's comment, "Anne Elliot was herself [Jane Austen]; her enthusiasm for the navy, and her perfect unselfishness, reflect her completely." [16] Similarly, Anne Thackeray wrote, "Anne Elliot must have been Jane Austen herself, speaking for the last time."[17] Austen's relatives certainly would have been pleased with this conclusion, as they hoped readers would see only the sweet side of Jane Austen. But in fact Austen goes to great lengths in *Persuasion* to separate her narrative voice from her heroine. As Elizabeth Jenkins observes, "Anne Elliot could not have written *Pride and Prejudice*."[18] Austen tells us that Anne Elliot "longed for the power of representing to them all what they were about," but only Austen herself will deliver those sorts of blows (82). Anne blushes demurely at her father's behavior but never criticizes him; the narrator skewers him with her words. To read this Austen novel is to travel the same path but with two different guides—one, a gentle heroine; the other, a not-so-polite woman author determined to use her artistic powers to shatter illusion and reflect the reality she sees.

Austen does not, however, use the same self-conscious narrative voice in *Persuasion* that she adopted in *Northanger Abbey*. Rather than stepping in as narrator to deliver a lengthy diatribe against male prose writers and their condescension toward mere novels, Austen delivers her impassioned apologia indirectly. In literary exchanges between the poetry loving Captain Benwick and Anne Elliot, Austen never mentions the word "novel":

> He was evidently a young man of considerable taste in reading, though principally in poetry; . . . and having talked of poetry, the richness of the present age, and gone through a brief comparison of opinion as to the first-rate poets, trying to ascertain whether *Marmion* or *The Lady of the Lake* were to be preferred, and how ranked the *Giaour* and *The Bride of Abydos* . . . he shewed himself so intimately acquainted with all the tenderest songs of the one poet, and all the impassioned descriptions of hopeless agony of the other; he repeated, with such tremulous feeling, the various lines which imaged a broken heart, or a mind destroyed by wretchedness, . . . that she ventured to hope that he did not always read only poetry. . . .
>
> [F]eeling in herself the right of seniority of mind, she ventured to recommend a larger allowance of prose in his daily study; and on being requested to particularize, mentioned such works of our best moralists, such collections of the finest letters, such memoirs of characters of worth and suffering, as occurred to her at the moment as calculated to rouse and fortify the mind by the highest precepts, and the

> strongest examples of moral and religious endurances. . . .
>
> When the evening was over, Anne could not but be amused . . . that, like many other great moralists and preachers, she had been eloquent on a point in which her own conduct would ill bear examination. (100–101)

Anne's list of recommended reading for Captain Benwick includes moral works, letters, and biographical memoirs, but no novels. Austen must have enjoyed the irony of this moment within her novel. Readers recognize the unstated fact that *Persuasion* itself is "calculated to rouse and fortify the mind by the highest precepts." Austen proves that a novel—a novel written by Austen, anyway—can "be of use," to echo Admiral Croft's phrase. Though fictional, a novel can be as true a representation of human character as a memoir and as edifying as a moral work. Though in prose, a novel can capture some of the themes and the lyricism of poetry.

In the passage quoted above, Austen turns her attention to contemporary romantic poetry. The four poetical examples Captain Benwick cites all offer laments for lost love (as *Persuasion* does) but without salutary prescriptions for recovery. The two Scott poems lugubriously bemoan the eternal separation between lovers:

> Where shall the lover rest,
>   Whom the fates sever
> From his true maiden's breast,
>   Parted forever? . . .
>   ("Marmion")

> Like the dew on the mountain
>   Like the foam on the river
> Like the bubble on the fountain,
>   Thou art gone, and forever. . . .
>   ("The Lady of the Lake")[19]

In Byron's "The Bride of Abydos," Zuleika dies of a broken heart. Byron's "Giaour" sounds as gothic as anything Catherine Morland read:

> But first, on earth as Vampire sent,
> Thy corse shall from its tomb be rent;
> Then ghastly haunt thy native place,
> And suck the blood of all thy race.
>
> . . . .
>
> Wet with thine own best blood shall drip
> Thy gnashing tooth and haggard lip.
>   ("Giaour")[20]

No wonder Anne Elliot tries to encourage the melancholy Captain Benwick to broaden his reading list. Anne knows that if carried to its sensational extreme ("hopeless agony," "tremulous feeling," "broken heart," "a mind destroyed by wretchedness"), romantic poetry can encourage an emotional wallowing.

Yet at the same time, Austen demonstrates in *Persuasion* that she herself could have written tremulous romantic poetry. She has Anne consider "the view of the last smiles of the year upon the tawny leaves and withered hedges" and reminds us of "the thousand poetical descriptions extant of autumn. . . . some tender sonnet, fraught with the apt analogy of the declining year, with declining happiness, and images of youth and hope and spring all gone together" (84–85). Austen's own language here almost rises to blank verse: "The images of youth and hope and spring / All gone together, blessed her memory." This is the only Austen novel employing words like *tawny* and *poetical*. By stressing the fact that there are a thousand such descriptions, Austen illustrates that romantic discourse on nature had become trite—and rather overblown. When Austen describes Anne as in a "desolate tranquility" or "grieving to forego all the influence so sweet and so sad of the autumnal months in the country," we sense that Anne is in danger of becoming as addicted to melancholy dead leaves as Marianne Dashwood in *Sense and Sensibility* (36, 33). To balance such images, Austen immediately follows her description of mournful sonnets with a matter-of-fact, tongue-in-cheek account of farmers at work in the fields: "the ploughs at work, and the fresh-made path spoke the farmer, counteracting the sweets of poetical despondence, and meaning to have spring again" (85). Austen explores nostalgia and aging, but she also chides those who carry such backward looking lamentation to such an extreme that they fail to embrace life's exciting, constantly changing possibilities.

Most striking is the balance Austen achieves between the romantic and the prosaic; the sublime and the mundane. Note two sample sentences from *Persuasion* describing Lyme Regis:

> There is nothing to admire in the buildings themselves, the remarkable situation of the town, the principal street almost hurrying into the water, the walk to the Cobb, skirting round the pleasant little bay, which in the season is animated with bathing machines and company; the Cobb itself, its old wonders and new improvements, with the very beautiful line of cliffs stretching out to the east of the town, are what the stranger's eye will seek; and a very strange stranger it must be, who does not see charms in the immediate environs of

Lyme, to make him wish to know it better. The scenes in its neighbourhood, Charmouth, with its high grounds and extensive sweeps of country, and still more its sweet retired bay, backed by dark cliffs, where fragments of low rock among the sands make it the happiest spot for watching the flow of the tide, for sitting in unwearied contemplation; the woody varieties of the cheerful village of Up Lyme; and, above all, Pinny, with its green chasms between romantic rocks, where the scattered forest trees and orchards of luxuriant growth declare that many a generation must have passed away since the first partial falling of the cliff prepared the ground for such a state, where a scene so wonderful and so lovely is exhibited, as may more than equal any of the resembling scenes of the far-famed Isle of Wight: these places must be visited, and visited again, to make the worth of Lyme understood. (95–96)

These two giant sentences are in the narrator's voice, not Anne's, and perhaps stand as a model of how to respond to the world around us. Austen insists that natural beauty can affect everyone (only "a very strange stranger" would not be charmed) and find it a source of "contemplation." We need not journey far to have such an experience: in less than a day's journey, Anne has found "a scene . . . as may more than equal any of the resembling scenes of the far-famed Isle of Wight." The narrator's description balances a romantic sensibility ("green chasms between romantic rocks") with a more down-to-earth observation of real life ("bathing machines and company"). She refuses either to be nostalgic or indifferent to the past, noting both "old wonders and new improvements." Austen argues that the sights of nature enable us to transcend the narrow limits of our own time period ("many a generation must have passed away since the first partial falling of the cliff") and contemplate something far grander than our own reflection in a looking glass. Unlike travelers thinking they "know" a place after a few minutes at a key tourist spot, Austen demonstrates a humble, careful, gradual approach to the world around her: "these places must be visited, and visited again, to make the worth of Lyme understood."

Narrative passages describing Lyme may seem tacked on—after all, what do they have to do with the central love story of Anne Elliot and Frederick Wentworth? Why not get on with the plot? Yet in fact such accounts are an integral part of Austen's larger themes in the novel. Throughout *Persuasion* Austen uses travel as a metaphor. Anne Elliot discovers that even journeying for three miles can lead to "a total change of conversation, opinions, and ideas" and teach us "the art of knowing our own nothingness beyond our own circle" (42). At each house she visits she adapts to new customs, believing that "every little social commonwealth should dictate its own matters of discourse" (43). Similarly, Admiral Croft has learned from his far-flung travels that the world is a varied place with many approaches, not just one right one. "One man's ways may be as good as another's, but we all like our own best. And so you must judge for yourself," the admiral tells Anne (127). He is speaking of her feelings at seeing her child-hood home adapted to suit the Crofts, but his remark (like so many others in the novel) illustrates a broader "universal truth."

Those who cannot travel—that is, those who cannot adapt to the ways of others or even find out what those ways might be—are hopelessly trapped. When Sir Walter and Elizabeth Elliot move to Bath, they simply transport their own limitations ("so much to be vain of in the littlenesses of a town") and focus on having their acquaintance "exceedingly sought after" rather than seeking out new perspectives from others (138, 137). Sir Walter's only sightseeing in Bath consists of tallying the number of plain women he sees (eighty-seven in a row at last count) and reveling in how many eyes he thinks are fixed upon his own exceedingly handsome countenance (141).

At the end of *Persuasion* Austen pretends she has written nothing more than a romance with no redeeming moral to offer her readers: "Who can be in doubt of what followed? When any two young people take it into their heads to marry, they are pretty sure by perseverance to carry their point, be they ever so poor, or ever so imprudent, or ever so little likely to be necessary to each other's ultimate comfort. This may be bad morality to conclude with, but I believe it to be truth; and if such parties succeed, how should a Captain Wentworth and an Anne Elliot, with the advantage of maturity of mind, con-sciousness of right, and one independent fortune between them, fail of bearing down every opposition?" (248). Austen places this mock apology at the *beginning* of the final chapter, signaling to readers that this is not really her conclusion. Instead, the final paragraphs of *Persuasion* focus on Captain Wentworth's act of friendship in helping Mrs. Smith resolve her property losses in the West Indies. We end with a sense of action and exertion. Running throughout *Persuasion* is the clear argument that happiness comes to those with patience and per-severance, a warm, unselfish generosity toward others, a desire to be useful, an awareness of other worlds, and an openness to change.

In this last of Austen's six completed novels, our guide has been a seriously comic, deeply humanistic woman boldly taking pen in hand to tell an untold story. Like Mrs. Smith's knitting or Captain Harville's woodworking, Jane Austen's writing vocation gave her a sense of purpose, "the choicest gift of Heaven."

9

Behold Me Immortal

Finding Jane Austen Today

Oh, may I join the choir invisible
Of those immortal dead who live again.
          —George Eliot, "The Choir Invisible" (1867)

Immortality is not a gift,
Immortality is an achievement;
And only those who strive mightily
Shall possess it.
          —Edgar Lee Masters, *Spoon River Anthology* (1915)

Oh! subjects rebellious! . . .
When once we are buried you think we are gone
But behold me immortal! . . .

.   .   .   .

Henceforward I'll triumph in shewing my powers
          —from Jane Austen's final poem, written three
                    days before her death

Three days before her death, a suffering, diseased Jane Austen took up the pen to write. As her brother Henry Austen put it, "She wrote whilst she could hold a pen, and with a pencil when a pen was become too laborious" (*NA*, 4). Her family members would have liked "dear Aunt Jane's" final burst of poetry to be a pious utterance. Instead, she wrote six stanzas of doggerel about a saint so hopping mad that he springs out of his shrine to berate the public for attending horse races rather than honoring him (*MW*, 451–52). Saint Swithin threatens the rebellious, dissolute public—including "satin'd and ermined" Lords and Ladies—with a month of rain. Although Henry Austen included these "stanzas replete with fancy and vigour" in the first edition of his Biographical Notice to accompany *Persuasion* and *Northanger Abbey,* relatives persuaded him to delete the poem from the next edition. Niece Caroline explained that she did not want the verses "introduced as the latest workings of her mind. . . . The joke about the dead Saint, and the Winchester races, all jumbled up together, would read badly." [1]

What do we make of the latest workings of Austen's mind? The poem in many ways captures the quintessential Jane Austen—the artist who creatively made use of her surroundings; the feisty, irreverent being who, from adolescence to her death at age forty-one, discerned the amusing discrepancy between the ideal and the real.

In May of 1817, a terminally ill Jane Austen had been moved to Winchester in order to be nearer to doctors. Just days before her death, Austen must have enjoyed the irony of reading in the *Hampshire Chronicle* that Winchester Races "for horses, mares, and geldings" would take place on July 14, the day before Saint Swithin's day. [2] She knew the old British legend that linked Saint Swithin, former bishop of Winchester (previously called Venta), to a forty-day rainfall punishing those who moved his body. Austen's doggerel explores the humorous incongruity between the divine and the mortal. Instead of a fiery, Jonathan Edwards–style "Sinners at the Hands of an Angry God," Austen describes an egotistical minor saint ("It is said the good people forgot their old saint") provoked into ordering a meteorological punishment:

> Set off for your course, I'll pursue with *my* rain.
> . . . .
> Henceforward I'll triumph in shewing my powers,
> . . . .
> The curse upon Venta is July in showers.

This is hardly Zeus with a thunderbolt. The curses of a little-known Hampshire saint lead only to incessant summer drizzle.

Yet we also may be left with questions. Does Austen choose Saint Swithin in part because of his reputation for helping the poor and for favoring natural simplicity (he was reportedly furious that his bones were moved from the open-air churchyard into a cathedral)? By selecting a specifically British saint who is annoyed by the dissolute behavior of the fashionable aristocracy, does she register an attack on her countrymen's secularism, pettiness, and class segregation?

> The races however were fix'd and determin'd
> The company came & the Weather was charming
> The Lords & the Ladies were sattin'd & ermin'd
> And nobody saw any future alarming.

Like Sir Walter Elliot of *Persuasion* admiring his own smooth appearance in a looking glass rather than concerning himself with his growing debts or with the "quick alarm" faced by his country's naval officers, so the well-dressed lords and ladies of this final poem regard their place in the world with utter complacency. There is something charming and alarming "all jumbled up together" (as niece Caroline put it) in much of Austen's writing.

Contemplating Austen's death at age forty-one, Sir Walter Scott exclaimed, "What a pity such a gifted creature died so early!"[3] Had illness not cut short her career, Austen undoubtedly would have continued to produce not just jocular verses but also more fiction. As she had written in a letter, "I have not yet—as almost every Writer of Fancy does sooner or later—overwritten myself" (31 December 1815). Had she lived to eighty, like William Wordsworth, or ninety-one, like one of her brothers, we probably would have another shelf of unforgettable, carefully crafted novels. Perhaps as she herself grew older, she would have created an increasing number of characters determined to age with dignity.

One suspects, though, that even while aging with dignity, Austen would have preserved her sense of humor. As she writes of Emma Woodhouse at the end of *Emma*, "Serious she was . . . and yet there was no preventing a laugh" (475). Just months before her death, Austen wrote a backwards letter for the amusement of her niece:

> Ym raed Yssac
>
> I hsiw uoy a yppah wen raey. Ruoy xis snisuoc emac ereh yadretsey, dna dah hcae a eceip fo ekac.—Siht si elttil Yssac's yadhtrib, dna ehs si eerht sraey dlo. . . .
>
> Ruoy Etanoitceffa Tnua
> Enaj Netsua (8 January 1817)

Other late letters contain puns or such touches as to place the word "Jackass" next to her initials, "J. A." (23 June 1816).

Some biographers believe Jane Austen may have died of Addison's disease, an adrenal gland insufficiency that causes skin discoloration, fatigue, nausea, and stomach ailments. Others speculate that she instead may have died of breast cancer, lymphoma, or tuberculosis. Without concrete evidence, we will never know for sure, nor does it seem particularly important: what is clear is that Austen died at a far too young age of a painful illness that gradually sapped her strength. How irritating that some linked her early death to her unfeminine practice of writing: in 1902 William Lyon Phelps reminded readers of Austen's meek, lowly heart and noted of her death, "May it not have been owing to the consuming flame of genius? . . . The bodily frame pays dearly for artistic creation."[4]

At the time of her death, Austen was still *enjoying* artistic creation and had begun the novel *Sanditon*. Familiar themes appear: idle ladies and gentlemen who use nervous complaints as a way to get attention, fill time, and avoid work ("He is so delicate that he can engage in no Profession"); women trained to be ornaments rather than citizens ("very accomplished and very ignorant"); and aristocrats who have done nothing to deserve their titles ("Lady Denham . . . born to Wealth but not to Education . . . talked and talked only of her own concerns") (*MW*, 385, 421, 375, 399). But, as always in Austen, *Sanditon* introduces dramatically new types of characters and themes. Austen takes a swipe at modern "progress" by showing that Mr. Parker's boosterism and commercialism will lead him to mar the pristine coast with tacky resorts. She demonstrates that men as well as women can respond to sentimental books in harmful ways: even sillier than Catherine Morland, Sir Edward Denham decides to model himself after the seductive, glamorous villains in the romances he has read.

Most striking to readers of *Sanditon* is Austen's courage in laughing at hypochondria and what she calls "Medecine" while she herself was terminally ill and at the mercy of physicians. The Parker sisters visit physician after physician for treatment (leeches, tooth extractions, and so on) of a variety of mysterious disorders: "The Sisters were perhaps driven to . . . the invention of odd complaints. . . . It should seem that they must be extremely ill themselves. Some natural delicacy of Constitution in fact, with an unfortunate turn for Medecine, especially quack Medecine, had given them an early tendency at various times, to various Disorders;—the rest of their sufferings was from Fancy, the love of Distinction & the love of the Wonderful" (*MW*, 412). Austen observes that their medical conditions "seemed more like the amusement of eager Minds in want of employment than of actual afflictions and relief" (412). Arthur professes his status as Nervous Invalid ("I am very nervous. . . . I am very subject to Perspiration, and there cannot be a surer sign of Nervousness") while downing heaping plates of food on the sly (415–16). Embracing unequal health care, Lady Denham wants no physicians in town for fear "it would be only encouraging our servants and the Poor to fancy themselves ill" (393).

If we search for Jane Austen in *Sanditon,* we find her continuing at the end of her life to celebrate the superiority of her own kind of novels to the sentimental, sensational trash of the day. She does this indirectly, by having the deluded Sir Arthur Denham praise melodramatic romances and attack novels of common life: "We have many leisure hours, and read a great deal.—I am no indiscriminate Novel-Reader. The mere Trash of the common Circulating Library, I hold in the highest contempt—. . . those vapid tissues of ordinary occurrences" (*MW*, 403). Ironically, it was precisely that charge—that they display *only* "ordinary occurrences"—that was leveled at Austen's novels by readers of her era.

Sir Edward Denham of *Sanditon* prefers "novels . . . such as display Human Nature with Grandeur" and "the Sublimity of intense Feeling" to those of everyday life (*MW*, 403). If we consider that the term *realism* in literature or any art would not enter the English language for over two decades after Austen's death, it is no wonder many readers of Austen's novels seemed to find something lacking in books about common life. Austen's own publisher confessed to Sir Walter Scott that her books lacked "incident and romance."[5] Scott insisted that Austen was a genius at "the art of copying nature as she really exists in the common walks of life, and presenting to the reader . . . a correct and striking representation of that which is daily taking place around him," and he recognized that Austen's interest in creating fiction about "ordinary life" or "real life" made her "the first . . . of a new class."[6] Others agreed but felt that novels about everyday people did not count as Literature:

> There is no story whatsoever, and the heroine is no better than other people.
>
> The authoress . . . is deficient in imagination, utterly and entirely devoid of invention. Her characters, her incidents, her sentiments, are obviously all drawn exclusively from experience.
>
> What vile creatures her parsons are! She has not a dream of the high Catholic ethos.
>
> She is capital as far as she goes: but she never goes out of the parlor.[7]

Even from the beginning, though, readers granted Austen's characters a life outside the books, beginning with family members who begged to know the fates of characters after the final chapters had ended. Did Mary Bennet ever marry? How long did Mr. Woodhouse live to plague the newlyweds? Events and places in Austen's novels seemed almost to require historical markers: "Show me the exact spot where Louisa Musgrove fell," Victorian Poet Laureate Alfred Lord Tennyson exclaimed when visiting Lyme Regis, and he placed Austen next to Shakespeare for the lifelikeness of her characters.[8] Across the Atlantic, dean of letters William Dean Howells observed in *Criticism and Fiction* (1892), "Jane Austen was the first and the last of the English novelists to treat material with entire truthfulness."[9] Reginald Farrer claimed of Austen in a centennial essay of 1917 that "The secret of her immortality is [that] . . . of all writers, she it is who pursues truth with most utter and undeniable devotion." [10]

Rudyard Kipling perceived that Austen's truthfulness to reality explained both her foes and her fans. A soldier ponders Austen's popularity in "The Janeites": "Jane? Why, she was a little old maid 'oo'd written 'alf a dozen books about a hundred years ago. 'Twasn't as if there was anythin' TO 'em either. I know I had to read 'em. They weren't adventurous, nor smutty, nor what you'd call even interestin'—all about girls o' seventeen . . . not certain 'oom they'd like to marry; an' their dances an' card-parties an' picnics. . . . I 'ad only six books to remember. . . . But, as I was sayin', what beat me was there was nothin' TO 'em nor IN 'em. . . . I mean that 'er characters was no USE! They was only just like people you run across any day." [11] Austen's fidelity to truth (not "universally acknowledged" truisms but the reality before her) makes her works perennial. R. W. Chapman, Austen's first scholarly editor, placed Austen in the company of the very greatest: "Her modernity is like Chaucer's or Shakespeare's, the effect of her truth." [12] Sir Walter Scott had also emphasized Austen's truth, praising her for possessing "the exquisite touch, which renders ordinary commonplace things and characters interesting from the truth of the description." [13]

The truth can be disconcerting. Kipling's baffled soldier concludes, "Some'ow Jane put it down all so naked it made you ashamed." [14] Truth can be overpowering, even violent, especially when combined with laughter. Satan in Twain's "Mysterious Stranger" views humor as a powerful weapon against falsity: "For your race, in its poverty, has unquestionably one really effective weapon—laughter. Power, money, persuasion, supplication, persecution—these can lift at a colossal humbug but only laughter can blow it to rags and atoms at a blast. Against the assault of laughter nothing can stand. You are always fussing and fighting with your other weapons. Do you ever use that one? No: you leave it lying rusting. As a race, do you ever use it at all? No; you lack sense and the courage." [15] Austen had the sense and the courage to use humor to attack pretense and penetrate the truth. To a great extent, we laugh at a Mr. Collins or an Aunt Norris because we recognize the traits they embody. As George Bernard Shaw put it, "My way of joking is to tell the truth. It's the funniest joke in the world." [16] Some critics spotted Austen's irony but failed to see themselves as targets, reminding one of Swift's definition of satire as "a sort of glass, wherein beholders do generally discover everybody's face but their own." [17]

Humor can be cruel. For the last two centuries Austen readers have used surprisingly violent imagery to describe her comic art. As early as 1870 Mrs. Oliphant begins describing Austen's "fine stinging yet soft-voiced contempt." [18] In 1911 an anonymous poet in the *Atlantic Monthly* envisions a warlike Jane Austen armed with the truth:

> Thou seekest truth, and when 'tis found
> Thou dost its sportive whims confound; . . .
> It dreads thy logic's bristling fence,
> Thy files of serried evidence,
> Thy panoplied, embattled in sense,
>   Irrefragable Jane! [19]

This irrefragable Jane also brandishes her "bodkin's slender steel," suggesting the image of a small but sharply pointed instrument. Lord David Cecil attributes Austen's "ruthless irony" to her "knife-edged mind." [20]

Even those like novelist Arnold Bennett who belittle Jane Austen as a little novelist with a tiny world acknowledge "Jane's lethal irony." [21] Virginia Woolf calls Austen "alarming," confesses she would not want to be alone in a room with her, and cites her ability to skewer characters with just a few words: "Sometimes it seems as if her creatures were born merely to give Jane Austen the supreme delight of slicing their heads off." [22] Noting that over the years Austen's irony has kept its bite, Eudora Welty likens each Austen novel to "a formidable engine of strategy [that] could kill us all, had she wished it to; it fires at us, all along the way, using understatements in good aim." [23] Dorothy Van Ghent describes Austen's "two inches of ivory" as "an elephant's tusk . . . a savagely probing instrument as well as a masterpiece of refinement." [24] Harold Nicolson compares Austen's mind to a very small, sharp pair of scissors. [25] Lee Siegel calls Austen "piercing" and "quietly fearsome" and wonders, "Who's Afraid of Jane Austen?" [26] Bruce Chatwin observes, "She penetrates into . . . her characters with knife-edged clearness." [27] Fay Weldon offers a brutal image of Austen:

"Something truly frightening rumbled there beneath the bubbling mirth: something capable of taking the world by its heels, and shaking it—as a mother takes a choking baby—shaking out great muddy gobbets of barbarity and incomprehension and cruelty, and setting it on its feet again, altogether better and improved. She knew too much, you see, for her own good." [28] Weldon's description reminds me of Emily Dickinson's reference to herself as "Vesuvius at home," a powerful volcano lurking beneath a deceptively calm surface. [29] One contemporary poet envisions Austen's novels as squares of fabric, a traditionally feminine and comforting image, but stresses Austen's gadfly-like power:

> Why do we turn to her sampler squares for solace?
> Nothing she saw was free of snobbery or class.
> Yet the needlework of those needle eyes. . . .
> We are pricked to tears by the justice of her violence. [30]

Atlantic Monthly illustration of Austen with fan and mallet
(Reproduced by permission of Tom Lulevitch)

We can be pricked to tears or torn to shreds: Harry Potter author J. K. Rowling concludes of her favorite writer, Jane Austen, "I think that she would be polite and quiet while pulling us to pieces in her mind's eye." [31] Film director Ang Lee *(Sense and Sensibility)* describes Austen's dry, shrewd humor as cruel and cutting and notes that he followed a natural progression in moving from the verbal sparring of Austen to women engaged in martial arts *(Crouching Tiger, Hidden Dragon)*.[32] One contemporary illustrator for the *Atlantic Monthly* draws Austen delicately fanning herself while wielding a formidable mallet behind her back. Margaret Drabble refers to Austen's comic wit as "a rapier-like attack on convention and absurdity." [33] Favorite images for Austen's violence seem to be knives and scissors, but arrows will work as well: In her recent autobiography, P. D. James describes Austen's potent "shafts of asperity, cynicism, even of malice." [34]

Potent malice was precisely what Austen's relatives worked so hard to remove from her writing and her image. Violence seemed indecorous in a maiden aunt. Comments made about Eudora Welty at the time of her death in 2001 apply equally well to Jane Austen: "Surprisingly, for one whose work is so marked by the keen double knife-edge of satire and remorseless honesty, she was treated as the genial and polite Honorary Maiden Aunt of American letters. No other maiden aunt in history can have been, in her heart, less a maiden and less like the greeting-card aunt of one's dreams. To almost the end, Eudora Welty was both a fierce observer of the wide world around her and its loving consumer." [35] Like Welty, Austen was a fierce observer, though critics and relatives worked hard to sheathe the knife-like power of her words and to create a Sweet-and-Low image for the public to swallow. "No malice lurked beneath" the surface of Austen's writing, insisted great-nephew Lord Brabourne in his preface to a bowdlerized edition of Austen's letters.[36] I like Lee Siegel's comment that saying Austen lacks malice is "like saying that no alcohol lurks in claret." [37]

The alcohol-free Jane Austen remains the dominant image in the twenty-first century. Surveying several shelves of Austen material at Border's Bookstore and Barnes & Noble, I spot lacy-bordered editions and biographies, most with the softened image of Austen's face. Barnes & Noble also sells a three-dimensional bust of Austen—with ringlets and ruffles—holding a quotation reading "Life seems but a quick succession of busy nothings." This line refers to the petty, mean-spirited Aunt Norris of *Mansfield Park*, not to Austen herself, yet a casual browser at the bookstore would deduce from the bust that

LIFE SEEMS
BUT A QUICK
SUCCESSION
OF BUSY
NOTHINGS.

Barnes & Noble bust of Austen

Austen was highly feminine and woefully trivial. Four prettified images of Austen decorate the cover of *Jane Austen: A Celebration* (2000),
while the back cover cites Kipling's remarks about "Jane." John
Halperin's 1984 biography, with its steadfast insistence that Austen
was a sex-starved spinster writing romances as a consolation prize for
her own bitter disappointments, remains in paperback on the shelves
of both bookstores. In local libraries, readers may check out illustrated editions of Austen's novels emphasizing those moments when
heroines cry, play piano, or listen in speechless admiration to the men
around them. For example, the Heritage Press edition of *Pride and
Prejudice* does not depict Elizabeth jumping over a fence but does show
her in a state of fluttering forlornness after Darcy rejects her as "not
handsome enough" to tempt him to dance. How different this visual
image is from Austen's *actual* description of a resilient Elizabeth whose
"lively, playful disposition" leaves her determined to tell the story to
friends "with great spirit" (*PP*, 12).

'*Not handsome enough*'

Heritage Press illustration of a forlorn Elizabeth Bennet,
an image not matching the text's emphasis on her wit and resilience

Care to present Jane Austen on the stage? One can still purchase *The Novelist: A Romantic Portrait of Jane Austen* by Howard Fast, first produced in New York in 1991. Fast's two-person play presents Jane Austen in 1817 conversing with Captain Thomas Crighton, an imaginary friend of Austen's brother. The two are listed as "Jane" and "Crighton." Our stage directions reassure us that at age forty, Jane Austen is "a woman still attractive" and "rather slender." Thank goodness. Crighton has come to profess his love and throw himself at her feet: "Madam, my intention, my very honorable, decent intention is to marry you."[38]

As I read *The Novelist*, I feel the way I do while watching a farcical, degrading beauty pageant that others take seriously. Like the sickly Elizabeth Barrett Browning in *The Barretts of Wimpole Street* rescued from intellectualism by love, so Fast's shuddering, smoldering "Jane" discovers in her final weeks of life that the passionate embrace of a man surpasses any previous experience she has had:

"They were the best, the sweetest, the most precious three weeks in all my life. . . . I have waited all my life for you to walk into this room. Stay with me through the night. Don't let go of me. Tired. Of too much dream and too little living. . . . I wanted to be very beautiful for your return." Argh! One wonders what the audacious author who wrote "Beware of swoons" would say if she saw these stage directions for herself: "(Suddenly SHE lets go, gives up the struggle to maintain her poise, and begins to fall forward in a faint. CRIGHTON leaps toward her, catches her, lifts her and carries her to the couch. As HE sets her down SHE opens her eyes)." "Stay with me," she murmurs to the dashing captain.

Despite the title *The Novelist*, the Austen in Fast's play would exchange her masterpieces for this brief foray into passion. She leaves Crighton a maudlin farewell letter: "I constructed a life, my dear Thomas, that was filled with sensible and reasonable explanations for who I was and what I was. Jane Austen, a middle-aged spinster, who whiled her time away writing entertainments that were a substitute for life. But at least I have this good fortune, that . . . in my love for you I found a quality that was all I had ever dreamed of." The cover illustration shows a wistful woman gazing forlornly into the flame of a candle, her quill pen lying untouched on her desk. Her hair net appears made of gauze.

Oh, if Jane Austen could but respond! Perhaps she would say of Howard Fast, as she did of Sir Edward Denham in *Sanditon*, that "he had read more sentimental Novels than agreed with him" (*MW*, 404). Maybe she would create a play in which "AUSTEN" throws "THOMAS" (and his creator, "HOWARD") out the window and resumes her writing.

It seems we have made little progress from Byron's assertion, "Man's love is of man's life a thing apart, / 'Tis woman's whole existence."[39] In fact, Howard Fast's play reminds me of an eighteenth-century poet's "Advice to a Lady" included in *Elegant Extracts*, a work Austen refers to in *Emma*:

> Nor make to dangerous wit a vain pretence,
> But wisely rest content with modest sense;
> For wit, like wine, intoxicates the brain,
> Too strong for feeble women to sustain. . . .
> To rougher Man Ambition's task resign,
> 'Tis ours in senates or in courts to shine. . . .
> One only care your gentle breasts should move,
> Th'important business of your life is love;

Cover illustration of Howard Fast's lugubrious play
The Novelist (Reproduced by permission of
Samuel French, Inc.)

To this great point direct your constant aim,
This makes your happiness, and this your fame.[40]

Fast's Jane indeed shows herself to be feeble, without wit, and obsessed by love. "There is only one medicine I need, and that's yourself," Jane moans.

Like Fast's *The Novelist,* Helen Jerome's 1936 *Pride and Prejudice* remains available today to theatre groups around the world. Jerome's dramatization has the revealing subtitle "A Sentimental Comedy" and ignores Austen's derision of the maudlin and the mawkish. Jane Bennet nearly dies, while Elizabeth utters platitudes, not barbed witticisms. In Jerome's hands, Darcy becomes a man of Byronic "dark surging passions," while Elizabeth tearfully admits, "I am abased" as she bows her head and gazes upward at her Mr. Right:

DARCY, Dare I ask you again?–Again?
ELIZABETH, (Smiles up at him through her tears) My father

277

says you are the sort of gentleman one would not dare refuse anything he condescended to ask—(Puts her head on his shoulder.)

DARCY, My cruel—my kind—oh, my lovely Elizabeth!

CURTAIN [41]

As Joseph Wiesenfarth puts it, "The play turns a novel of manners that sparkles with wit into a melodrama that drips with sentiment." [42]

In 2001, I learned that the Children's Theatre of Madison planned to stage the Jerome dramatization. The artistic director, hoping to introduce students in her summer drama school to Jane Austen, had ordered copies of the only *Pride and Prejudice* script advertised as available from Samuel French. Because I had discovered in the university library, quite by accident, that A. A. Milne had adapted the novel more faithfully, I urged the director to consider staging his version *(Miss Elizabeth Bennet)* instead. We discovered that the Milne script remains legally unavailable for production, eclipsed by the Broadway interest in Jerome's script. In his preface, a disappointed Milne observes of those who seek to adapt the "divine and incomparable Austen," "I do feel strongly that if one is bold (or impertinent) enough to force one's collaboration upon a greater writer than oneself, one must do it in the hope that one's contribution will be positive." [43] The Children's Theatre of Madison decided to create its own adaptation, as have other schools and societies seeking new ways to bring Austen, not Jane, to the stage.

Because Helen Jerome's script became the basis for Aldous Huxley's highly influential 1940 movie version of *Pride and Prejudice*, her distorted approach to Austen reached an enormous audience. "Learn how to attract men. See 'Pride and Prejudice'" read one blurb advertising the film, while another boasted, "Gossip. It tells how pretty girls t-e-a-s-e-d men into marriage!" [44] "We Want a Husband!" reads a blurb apparently spoken by all five Bennet girls in another poster. In this film Lady Catherine becomes not a despicable aristocrat but Darcy's helper. The 1940 *Pride and Prejudice* not surprisingly generated reviews arguing it appealed primarily to a female audience: "We must remember that all matrons loved it in their high school days," wrote a reviewer in *Box Office Digest*. [45]

What might Austen think of the plethora of films from 1940 to the present with some connection to her novels? *Entertainment Weekly* depicted Austen on a cell phone, lounging poolside while reading about herself in *Variety*. One suspects that Austen would enjoy sharing box office profits but would discover that, as in the case of Mary Shelley's

Poster of the 1940 movie *Pride and Prejudice* (© 1940 Turner
Entertainment Co., a Warner Bros. Company,
all rights reserved, used by permission)

Frankenstein, directors have made various kinds of cinematic monsters
of her novels. Austen would find herself a celebrity of sorts but with
much of that attention far removed from the novels themselves. In
The Five-Minute Iliad and Other Instant Classics, Greg Nagan wryly calls
Austen a screenplay writer who "languished in obscurity until the
invention of cinematography."[46]

In all fairness, many adaptations, particularly those done by the
BBC, capture Austen's sparkling dialogue and unforgettable dramatic
conflicts in brilliant ways. Yet even those films reasonably faithful to
Austen's plot and characterization have tended to focus on romance
at the expense of other themes. The 1995 *Pride and Prejudice* boasted
an "erotically enhanced Darcy" with "smoldering eyes" who fences,
extinguishes a candle with his bare hands, and "strips and dives into
a pool."[47] The Darcy parties that grew out of this film would give

Entertainment Weekly picture of Austen on a cell phone
(© 1995 Theo Westenberger, used by permission)

Austen new grist to pulverize in her mill. As if uncomfortable with
Austen's creation of complex characters, the 1995 *Sense and Sensibility*
emphasized Colonel Brandon's "soul-searching eyes," romanticism ("I
shall run mad"), and dashing horseback riding rather than his flannel
waistcoat. As he carries Marianne in his arms (a scene not in the
novel), Brandon's eyes are "full of tears." [48] Nora Nachumi notes that
the film version "actually celebrates the conventions of romance the
novel condemns." [49]

As if taking Austen back full circle to the sweet maiden aunt
portrayed by her relatives, some filmmakers have reduced her novels
to little more than sappy love stories. Male heartthrobs in frilly shirts
and leggings pursue beautiful women with cleavage showing at the
tops of their pastel-colored regency gowns. As Ruth Perry notes, in

such adaptations "most of the intellectual content gets dropped out," especially "the complicating lines, the deeply ironic ones, where the mind has a lot of play."[50] Much of Austen's power lies in her indirect assault on humbug. As Napoleon said, "Nothing is so insulting as to add irony to injury."[51] With the ironic narrator missing, many films lack Austen's original force.

The marketing of Austen films as "chick flicks" seems only to have reinforced the notion that her novels are feminine. As filmmaker Ang Lee noted, he was asked to direct *Sense and Sensibility* without having read an Austen novel: "I know her novels exist and they're there but I consider them girlie stuff and never want to read them. *Pride and Prejudice* is for girls."[52] Have we advanced much beyond H. W. Garrod's 1928 denunciation of Austen as "a mere slip of a girl"?[53] As I mentioned in my very first paragraph of this book, female students greatly outnumber males in my Jane Austen seminars at the University of Wisconsin. Teachers at Columbia report similar findings: "Shapiro began the class in his customary way. He asked the students if they liked [*Pride and Prejudice*]. He went around the room, and he quickly discovered that the girls liked it and the boys did not. . . . Their dismissals came with a frosting of contempt. Darcy himself couldn't have been any more disdainful. It was a waste of their time, this trivial girls' stuff. . . . As I paused for an instant, looking through my notes, it flashed through my mind that the men had to love this book and love Elizabeth or else they could not grow past this stage of their lives; they would remain insensible."[54] Continuing the tradition of Mark Twain, male comedians and cartoonists joke about being dragged to see Austen films when they would rather watch the Super Bowl, while popular movies depict leading men trying unsuccessfully to slug their way through *Pride and Prejudice*. "O.K., I admit it. I'm sorry. I can't stand Jane Austen," confesses a man in a recent cartoon. A mother coerces a grimacing son into reading Austen only by wielding a rolling pin.

This attitude must end. In some ways, we have moved backwards from the time when W. H. Auden could write with utter confidence of Austen's readership:

> But tell Jane Austen, that is, if you dare,
> How much her novels are beloved down here.
> She wrote them for posterity, she said;
> 'Twas rash, but by posterity she's read.[55]

Auden wrote those lines in 1937, three years before the wave of Austen films began to link her to frilly costumes. Jane Austen is no more a

"OK, I ADMIT IT. I'M SORRY. I CAN'T
STAND JANE AUSTEN."

One of many contemporary cartoons emphasizing men's
dislike of Austen (Reproduced by permission of Carole Cable)

A Mother's Persuasion
(Reproduced by permission of
Phil Cornell)

writer for women than Shakespeare is a writer for men. As Anne
Brontë insisted, "If a book is a good book it is for both men and
women."[56] I imagine that Jane Austen would have agreed with Charlotte Brontë: "I wish critics would judge me as an *author*, not as a
woman."[57]

To what extent have Jane Austen societies exacerbated the problem? Fay Weldon describes the British Jane Austen Society this way:
"I think she has been used rather unfairly here in England. She has
turned into heritage. She has become something that's associated with
cream teas and vicarage lawns and a kind of England that barely existed. . . . The Jane Austen Society rather likes to count the times
buttons are mentioned in, say, *Mansfield Park*, and like to know that
kind of detail about the novel without really being aware of the profundity of what goes on in them.[58] Not surprisingly, women far outnumber men at Jane Austen Society meetings, whether in England,
Australia, or North America.[59]

This is a shame. Society meetings do include events that might
be deemed frivolous—quizzes, contests, skits—but after all Austen herself loved charades, riddles, and theatricals. Far more time is spent
listening to talks from leading Austen scholars and biographers from
around the world than in attending regency balls or purchasing Austen
tea towels and medallions. Austen's ability to appeal simultaneously
to a popular and academic audience demonstrates the clarity, universality, and profundity of her works. Too often, newspaper coverage
of Austen meetings—whether those sponsored by literary societies or
by universities—focuses only on the fluff, not on the new ideas under
discussion.

When the *Chicago Tribune* ran a lengthy feature called "Austen's
Powers" about the Center for the Humanities's "Jane Austen in the
Twenty-first Century" festival at the University of Wisconsin, it mentioned our sponsorship of an English country dance and a game show
but not the fact that speakers included internationally acclaimed novelist and *Oxford Companion to Literature* editor Margaret Drabble, distinguished BBC screenwriter Andrew Davies, or renowned Austen scholars Claudia Johnson, Juliet McMaster, Jan Fergus, Joseph Wiesenfarth,
and others.[60] The news summary of the story noted that the festival
"will give novelist Jane Austen's admirers a chance to dance, watch
movies, compete in a game show, get behind an 'open mike,' and tour
gardens," while the illustration featured a softened "Jane" with balloons
and a party hat. No quotations were included from Austen scholars
who would be speaking at the University of Wisconsin conference,

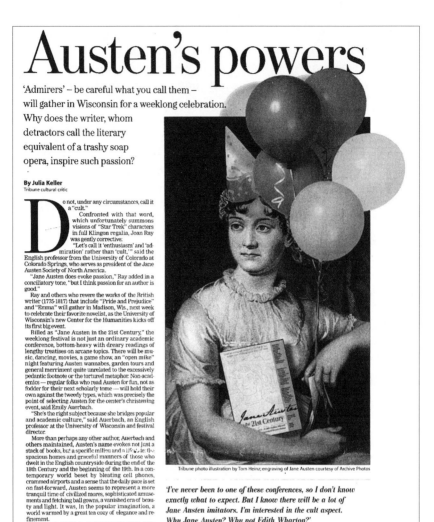

Austen's powers

'Admirers' – be careful what you call them –
will gather in Wisconsin for a weeklong celebration.
Why does the writer, whom
detractors call the literary
equivalent of a trashy soap
opera, inspire such passion?

By Julia Keller
Tribune cultural critic

Do not, under any circumstances, call it a "cult."

Confronted with that word, which unfortunately summons visions of "Star Trek" characters in full Klingon regalia, Joan Ray was gently corrective:

"Let's call it 'enthusiasm' and 'admiration' rather than 'cult,'" said the English professor from the University of Colorado at Colorado Springs, who serves as president of the Jane Austen Society of North America.

"Jane Austen does evoke passion," Ray added in a conciliatory tone, "but I think passion for an author is good."

Ray and others who revere the works of the British writer (1775-1817) that include "Pride and Prejudice" and "Emma" will gather in Madison, Wis., next week to celebrate their favorite novelist, as the University of Wisconsin's new Center for the Humanities kicks off its first big event.

Billed as "Jane Austen in the 21st Century," the weeklong festival is not just an ordinary academic conference, bottom-heavy with dreary readings of lengthy treatises on arcane topics. There will be music, dancing, movies, a game show, an "open mike" night featuring Austen wannabes, garden tours and general merriment quite unrelated to the excessively pedantic footnote or the tortured metaphor. Non-academics — regular folks who read Austen for fun, not as fodder for their next scholarly tome — will hold their own against the tweedy types, which was precisely the point of selecting Austen for the center's christening event, said Emily Auerbach.

"She's the right subject because she bridges popular and academic culture," said Auerbach, an English professor at the University of Wisconsin and festival director.

More than perhaps any other author, Auerbach and others maintained, Austen's name evokes not just a stack of books, but a specific milieu and a lifestyle: the spacious homes and graceful manners of those who dwelt in the English countryside during the end of the 18th Century and the beginning of the 19th. In a contemporary world beset by bleating cell phones, crammed airports and a sense that the daily pace is set on fast-forward, Austen seems to represent a more tranquil time of civilized mores, sophisticated amusements and fetching ball gowns, a vanished era of beauty and light. It was, in the popular imagination, a world warmed by a great tea cozy of elegance and refinement.

"That way of life is appealing for modern audi-

PLEASE SEE **AUSTEN**, PAGE 4

Tribune photo illustration by Tom Heinz; engraving of Jane Austen courtesy of Archive Photos

'I've never been to one of these conferences, so I don't know exactly what to expect. But I know there will be a lot of Jane Austen imitators. I'm interested in the cult aspect.

Why Jane Austen? Why not Edith Wharton?'

Poet Tenaya Darlington

Chicago Tribune illustration showing Austen with party hat
and balloons (*Chicago Tribune* illustration by Tom Heinz)

though the column spent several inches of ink on the thoughts of a
male college student with a website called "Jane Austen Must Die."
Another newspaper entitled its coverage of our festival "All About
Jane" and printed the portrait of Austen with a wedding ring and
ruffles.[61] Such approaches will not help draw male readers to Jane
Austen—or encourage anyone to regard her as a philosophically profound and keen-witted artist. I agree with JASNA President Joan Ray's
conclusion, "What makes Austen so popular among readers of all

Saturday, April 21, 2001 ★ ——————— Wisconsin State Journal ——————— Features Editor: Chris Juzwik, (608) 252-61

All about Jane

UW-Madison pays homage to author Jane Austen

By William R. Wineke
Wisconsin State Journal

Emily Auerbach's UW-Madison class studying the literature of Jane Austen is pretty typical.

"I have 40 students and 39 of them are women," Auerbach reports. "To me, that suggests there's something deeply wrong in our culture."

From that, one might guess that Auerbach is one of this community's many Jane Austen fanatics. One would be right.

Auerbach is coordinating the "Jane Austen in the 21st Century" festival at the UW-Madison April 23-29. The festival, sponsored by the Center for the Humanities, offers an almost bewildering array of free activities, ranging from concerts

and sermons to movies and medical lectures. More than 2,000 people have already registered, Auerbach says.

Why all this interest in an English writer who lived from 1775 to 1817? As it turns out, people aren't neutral when it comes to Austen and her work.

"What I've noticed is that she inspires either adoration or extreme detestation," Auerbach said. "When you think about it, that's pretty unusual. You find people who are really enthusiastic about William Shakespeare — but you don't find many people who really hate his work. If you don't like Shakespeare, you ignore him; but people who dislike Austen are adamant about it."

Auerbach, obviously, isn't in that category. She is busy completing work on "Searching for Jane Austen," a book the UW Press hopes to publish next year. She says the strengths

Please see JANE, Page C8

Screenwriter Davies shares his perspective

By Amanda Henry
Wisconsin State Journal

He caused an international epic of swooning with his 1995 adaptation of "Pride and Prei

author Helen Fielding on the big-screen version of "Bridget Jones's Diary."

Davies will present the talk, "Mrs. Darcy in the Bath and Other Temptations: Thoughts

Wisconsin State Journal article entitled "All About Jane"
(Reproduced by permission of *Wisconsin State Journal*)

tastes, critical approaches, and preferences is that her work is incredibly rich—richer than anything anyone can write about it." [62]

If Austen leveled her ironic gaze at academia, she might continue to find the stuff satires are made of. Titles of academic papers about her work ("The Hermeneutics of Embodied Metaphor as a Cognitive Construct in Austen's *Emma*") might remind her of Catherine Morland's observation in *Northanger Abbey* that speaking well has come to mean being unintelligible. Some scholars determined to shatter the image of Jane Austen as a prude have gone so far in the other direction that she becomes a nymphomaniac whose every word or act carries sexual connotations. Marianne Dashwood's restlessness signifies her masturbation, while Mr. Gardiner's allusion to fishing tackle has phallic significance. [63] The possibility that Jane Austen shared a bed with her sister reveals her lesbianism. [64] Carried to an extreme,

Cover illustration of *Pride and Promiscuity*

this angle of analysis leads to a spoof like *Pride and Promiscuity: The Lost Sex Scenes of Jane Austen:* "Both were in the throes of desire; and desire had outstripped sense. Elizabeth took advantage of their weakened state and pulled Mr. Darcy down to the ground. . . . She arranged him on the grass and with an unexpected gesture sat square on his middle with her muslin scattered round her knees. . . . Mr. Darcy put his hands on Elizabeth's breasts and pushed up each soft globe so that both were near escaping the rim of her chemise."[65] The cover illustration reveals Charlotte Lucas dressed up as Lady Catherine whipping Mr. Collins into a sexual frenzy. In some ways, these works express in risqué fashion the same disparaging notion of Austen as a sex-starved spinster writing fiction as a consolation for life without orgasm.

Yet the explosion of attention paid to Austen, whether in spoofs, films, scholarly books, websites, societies, detective books, musicals, or other creative extensions, has helped generate exciting new interest in Jane Austen. They also serve to prove Virginia Woolf's assertion that Jane Austen's characters "are so rounded and substantial that they have the power to move out of the scenes in which she placed them into other moods and circumstances."[66] Emma Woodhouse can become a spoiled Valley Girl *(Clueless);* Mrs. Bennet is spotted serving gherkins at Christmas parties *(Bridget Jones's Diary).* As Ezra Pound put it, "Literature is news that STAYS news."[67] Throughout two centuries of response to Austen's novels, readers have invariably found that the characters follow them back into their own lives. Detective novelist Dorothy Sayers claims that Elinor and Marianne Dashwood can even be transplanted to a henhouse:

> I have purchased two hens. In their habits they display, respectively Sense and Sensibility, and I have therefore named them Elinor and Marianne. Elinor is a round, comfortable, motherly-looking little body, who lays one steady, regular, undistinguished egg per day, and allows nothing to disturb her equanimity. . . . Marianne is leggier, timid, and liable to hysterics. Sometimes she lays a shell-less egg, sometimes a double yolk, sometimes no egg at all. On the days when she lays no egg she nevertheless goes and sits in the nest for the usual time, and seems to imagine that nothing more is required. As my gardener says: 'She just *thinks* she's laid an egg.' Too much imagination—in fact, Sensibility. But when she does lay an egg it is larger than Elinor's.[68]

If, as Robertson Davies observes at the beginning of a novel, "Readers who think that they can identify the creations of the author's fancy among their own acquaintance are paying the author an extravagant compliment," then perhaps Sayers's ability to discover avian versions of Austen's characters is the ultimate testimony, as is J. K. Rowling's discovery of a mean-spirited cat named Mrs. Norris.[69]

It is not surprising that Harold Bloom calls Austen "the most Shakespearean of all novelists."[70] In *Shakespeare: The Invention of the Human,* Bloom argues that Shakespeare did not just *reflect* humanity but actually helped to *create* it through his profound and powerful characterization; for example, not until we meet Iago and Othello do we understand jealousy. Rudyard Kipling similarly noted, "No one in the world knew what truth was till somebody had told a story."[71] Austen's characters give us a vocabulary for discussing a wide range of human possibilities and problems, be it unequal marriages, undeserving aristocrats, egotistical parents, or romantic dreamers. We can simultaneously know what it means to be a Miss Bates (an annoyingly "great talker upon little matters") and to be one too impatient to treat her with kindness (Emma). Novelist Margaret Drabble noted in an interview that Jane Austen was "one of the funniest writers who ever wrote" yet also transformed the novel into a serious art form: "Her legacy is much of fiction as we know it today. She created a kind of fiction, a kind of concentration on character, on the importance of the inner life, on the significance of domestic detail, the importance of human relationships, which really hadn't been perceived before she perceived it. It is that aspect of her that makes one realize why George Henry Lewes called her the female Shakespeare–her extraordinary insight into human relationships and small as well as large events. I think her legacy is that she made prose fiction a vehicle for very serious speculation about human behavior."[72] Put together, the heroines, heroes, and key minor figures in Austen's novels offer a penetrating study of human nature in any era as well as the particular political and social systems of Austen's day.

Eudora Welty singles out for praise Austen's "habit of seeing both sides of her own subject–of seeing it indeed in the round." Perhaps this gift explains Austen's resistance to easy labels. Clergymen can be despicable or admirable. Military men can be coarse and gross (Fanny Price's father), gallant (Frederick Wentworth), dissolute (Admiral Crawford), honest (Admiral Croft), unscrupulous (Wickham), heroic (William Price), literary (Captain Benwick), lazy and selfish (Dick Musgrove), or hardworking and generous (Captain Harville). *Both* men and women can be vain about their appearances, selfish about money, overawed by rank, and limited by parochialism; *both* men and women can function capably, think profoundly, feel deeply, create imaginatively, laugh wittily, and love faithfully. Without vindicating the rights of anyone directly, Austen posits a humanism far ahead of her time. "How really *modern* she is, after all," Welty concludes of Austen.[73]

In an essay on humorists Mark Twain observes, "Humour must not professedly teach and it must not professedly preach, but it must do both if it would live forever."[74] Austen's novels survive precisely because of this unique mixture of entertainment and instruction. Austen knew that Lydia Bennet gaped when forced to listen to Fordyce's *Sermons* and that Mr. Collins "belonged to one of the universities" yet remained "not a sensible man" (*PP*, 70). Jane Austen demonstrates through the narrative voice running throughout her novels how to combine intelligence with affection, book learning with life experience, humor with gravity. If we grant her a place among the serious philosophers—those who seek to impart wisdom—then perhaps we will quit thinking of her as "Jane." As she wrote in a letter, "Wisdom is better than wit, & in the long run will certainly have the laugh on her side" (18 November 1814).

If Abraham Lincoln could credit Harriet Beecher Stowe with power to stir a nation ("So this is the little lady who made this big war?"), then perhaps it is not hyperbolic to say that Jane Austen's novels may have changed the way men and women see themselves, whether it be within a marriage or within a class structure.[75] In the *Loiterer*, the journal they published at Oxford, Austen's brothers had argued that "of all chemical mixtures, Ink is the most dangerous," little suspecting that their sister would be the one whose ink might prove quite volatile.[76] Fay Weldon counters the image of Austen as a timid, insulated maiden aunt with a tribute to her novels as social catalysts: "Fiction . . . tends to be a subversive element in society. Elizabeth Bennet, that wayward, capricious girl, listening to the beat of feeling, rather than the pulsing urge for survival, paying attention to the subtle demands of human dignity rather than the cruder ones of established convention, must have quite upset a number of her readers, changed their minds, and with their minds, their lives, and with their lives, the society they lived in: prodding it quicker and faster along the slow, difficult road that has led us out of barbarity into civilization. . . . . Fiction stretches our sensibilities and our understanding, as mere information never can."[77] As George Crabbe wrote in his poem "The Library," "This, books can do:— . . . they give / New views to life, and teach us how to live."[78] Jane Austen's novels offer readers an expanded sense of human possibility.

What do we find, then, at the end of this search for Jane Austen? A century and a half ago, one reviewer described Austen as winning at the game of hide-and-seek: "The authoress herself is never visible, never even peeps from behind the curtain."[79] Perhaps because he is looking for a childlike peeping Jane, he ignores the self-confident woman writer standing tall behind the curtain. Austen, however, might have been pleased that the reviewer considered her invisible. Even before she had become a published novelist, she complained about writers like Samuel Egerton Brydges who inserted themselves clumsily into their fiction: "We have got 'Fitz-Albini'. . . . My father is disappointed—*I* am not, for I expected nothing better. Never did any book carry more internal evidence of its author. Every sentiment is completely Egerton's. There is very little story, and what there is told in a strange, unconnected way" (25 November 1798). In contrast, readers find very little direct "internal evidence" of Austen in her novels—only clues. Woolf finds this absence of authorial presence a sign of greatness, making Austen "as inscrutable in her small way as Shakespeare in his vast one." Woolf concludes, "The people whom we admire most as writers, then, have something elusive, enigmatic, impersonal about them."[80]

The more one searches for the enigmatic Jane Austen, the more one discovers artistry and intelligence, allusiveness and wit. At those times when I have followed a reference to Scheherazade in *Persuasion* or to Cowper in *Mansfield Park*, I have felt myself connected to Austen's smiling, knowing presence. Austen seems deliberately to have designed her ironic narrative voice so that, as Katherine Mansfield put it, "every true admirer of the novels cherishes the happy thought that he alone—reading between the lines—has become the secret friend of their author."[81] Austen invites readers to feel conspiratorial, to share with her a delight in uncovering absurdity and celebrating fairness. I agree with Wayne Booth that Jane Austen stands as the most important character in the novels: "The dramatic illusion of her presence as a character is thus fully as important as any other element in the story. . . . Only in her can we find a mind and heart that can give us clarity without oversimplification, sympathy and romance without sentimentality, and biting irony without cynicism."[82] As the titles to my chapters suggest, Jane Austen emerges from the pages of her novels as one striving for genius, wit, and taste, an excellent heart, a lively mind, the heroism of principle, the power of imagination, and the ability to mature over time.

Searching for Jane Austen uncovers a woman who, like Sophy Croft in *Persuasion*, "had no distrust of herself, and no doubt of what to do" (48). Even as a child writing spoofs Austen sensed that she had the gift to see through sentimental twaddle to human truth. Austen courageously and steadfastly made literature her business. "An artist cannot do anything slovenly," she observed in her early twenties (17 November 1798). To the end of her life she remained, like Anne Elliot in *Persuasion,* "extremely glad to be employed" (71). Austen noted just three months before her death, "I can sit up in my bed & employ myself" (22 May 1817).

At the end of this search, Jane Austen seems closer yet still out of reach—as she will always be to those of us who write about her life or her novels. She remains, in the words of Virginia Woolf, a "little aloof and inscrutable yet beautiful because of her greatness as an artist."[83] As Rudyard Kipling's Macklin says in "The Janeites," "Gawd bless 'er, whoever she was."

Appendixes
Notes
Selected Bibliography
Index

Appendix A

A Barkeeper Entering the Kingdom of Heaven
Did Mark Twain Really Hate Jane Austen?

Whenever I take up "Pride and Prejudice" or "Sense and Sensibility," I feel like a barkeeper entering the Kingdom of Heaven. . . . Jane Austen . . . makes me detest all her people, without reserve.

—from Mark Twain's "Jane Austen,"
an unpublished, incomplete fragment

Mark Twain expressed unparalleled hatred of Jane Austen, defining an ideal library as one with none of her books on its shelves. "Just that one omission alone would make a fairly good library out of a library that hadn't a book in it," Twain insisted in *Following the Equator*. Did Mark Twain genuinely detest Jane Austen? Or was the bushy-eyebrowed, irascible Twain merely posing?

In his extensive correspondence with fellow author and critic William Dean Howells, Mark Twain seemed to enjoy venting his literary spleen on Jane Austen precisely because he knew her to be Howells's favorite author. In 1909 Twain wrote that "Jane Austin" [*sic*] was "entirely impossible" and that he could not read her prose even if paid a salary to do so. Howells notes in *My Mark Twain* (1910) that in fiction Twain "had certain distinct loathings; there were certain authors whose names he seemed not so much to pronounce as to spew out of his mouth." Howells writes, "His prime abhorrence was my dear and honored prime favorite, Jane Austen. He once said to me, I suppose after he had been reading some of my unsparing praise of her—I am always praising her, '*You* seem to think that woman could write,' and he forbore withering me with his scorn, apparently because we had been friends so long and he more pitied than hated me for my bad taste." Rather than pitying Twain when he was sick, Howells threatened to come and read *Pride and Prejudice* to him.

Reprinted from *The Virginia Quarterly Review* 75 (Winter 1999) 1: 109–20.

Twain marveled that Austen had been allowed to die a natural death rather than face execution for her literary crimes. "Her books madden me so that I can't conceal my frenzy," Twain observed, apparently viewing an Austen novel as a book that "once you put it down you simply can't pick it up." Yet one becomes suspicious of Twain's supposedly frenzied loathing when he confesses that he likes to reread Jane Austen's novels just so he can hate them all over again. In a letter to Joseph Twichell in 1898, Twain fumed, "I have to stop every time I begin. Everytime I read 'Pride and Prejudice' I want to dig her up and beat her over the skull with her own shin-bone."

Twain obviously enjoyed taking verbal pot shots at "classic" authors. In his famous essay "Fenimore Cooper's Literary Offenses," Twain lambasted Cooper for scoring "114 offenses against literary art out of a possible 115" and committing "a crime against the language" through his stilted diction and sentimentalized characterizations. Perhaps Twain planned a similar essay to pillory the much-praised Jane Austen: an incomplete and unpublished fragment called "Jane Austen" is now housed in the Mark Twain papers at the University of California–Berkeley Library. Why might Twain have become uncomfortable with a vitriolic attack on the "impossible Jane Austin"? Could it be that he found too much common ground?

"Jane Austen" opens with the unforgettable image of the uncouth Twain entering the polite parlor-room society of Jane Austen's novels: "Whenever I take up 'Pride and Prejudice' or 'Sense and Sensibility,' I feel like a barkeeper entering the Kingdom of Heaven. I mean, I feel as he would probably feel, would almost certainly feel. I am quite sure I know what his sensations would be—and his private comments. He would be certain to curl his lip, as those ultra-good Presbyterians went filing self-complacently along. Because he considered himself better than they? Not at all. They would not be to his taste—*that* is all." Twain's barkeeper has no taste for the stifling, "ultra-good" (and ultra self-righteous) world of Sunday school.

Like Huckleberry Finn dying to escape the parlor and head out for the river, Twain imagines his cantankerous barkeeper unable to abide the polite ladies and gentlemen in Austen's novels. "He would not want to associate with them; he would not like their gait, their style, their ways; their talk would enrage him."

At the same time, Twain's barkeeper suspects his lack of appreciation might reveal some cultural failing. "Yet he would be secretly ashamed of himself, secretly angry with himself that this was so. Why? Because barkeepers are like everybody else—it humiliates them to find that there are fine things, great things, admirable things, which others can perceive and they can't." The barkeeper would "brace up" for another attack on Austen's novels:

> What would the barkeeper do next? Give it up and go down below, where his own kind are? No, not yet. He would wander out into the solitudes and take a long rest; then he would brace up and attack the proposition again, saying to himself, "Others have found the secret charm that is in those Presbyterians, therefore it must be a fact, and not an illusion; I will try again; what those others have found, I can find."
>
> So he tries again. Does he succeed? No. Because he has not educated his taste yet, he has not reformed his taste, his taste remains as it was before, and the thing involved is purely a matter of *taste*: he will not be able to enjoy those Presbyterians until he as learned to admire them.

Although Twain notes "Jane Austen's characters are not Presbyterians and I am not a barkeeper," he deleted that passage from the essay, perhaps not wanting to relinquish the parallels he saw between himself and his low-brow but persevering barkeeper.

Just as Twain had quipped that it is easy to quit smoking—he had done it many times—so he jokes in "Jane Austen" that Austen's novels are easier to start than to finish: "Does Jane Austen do her work too remorselessly well? For me, I mean? Maybe that is it. She makes me detest all her people, without reserve. Is that her intention? It is not believable. Then is it her purpose to make the reader detest her people up to the middle of the book and like them in the rest of the chapters? That could be. That would be high art. It would be worth while, too. Some day I will examine the other end of her books and see." Twain admits that "*All* the great critics praise her art generously" for her supposed gift of characterization. "To start with, they say she draws her characters with sharp discrimination and a sure touch. I believe that this is true, as long as the characters she is drawing are odious."

Then the essay takes a sudden turn, switching from general anti-Austen invective to a consideration of *Sense and Sensibility*—or rather, the beginning of *Sense and Sensibility!* Twain remarks, "I am doing 'Sense and Sensibility' now, and have accomplished the first third of it—not for the first time." He then parses the characters one by one, demonstrating surprising perception. He starts with Marianne Dashwood, the emotional heroine with greater sensibility than sense:

"To my mind, Marianne is not attractive; I am sure I should not care for her, in actual life. I suppose she was intended to be unattractive." Indeed, Twain and Austen share a discomfort with unbridled sentimentality. Austen describes Marianne as "eager in everything," possessing an "excess of . . . sensibility" in which "her sorrows, her joys, could have no moderation." When upset, Marianne "court[s] misery" and wallows in her grief, "seeking increase of wretchedness in every reflection that could afford it" and indulging in "melancholy remembrances." "I must feel—I must be wretched," Marianne gushes in her "effusion of sorrow" and "nourishment of grief," perhaps foreshadowing Twain's Emmeline Grangerford, the young poet of *Huckleberry Finn* who "could write about anything you choose to give her to write about, just so it was sadful." Like Twain, Austen mocked heroines too busy heaving their bosoms to act rationally. "One fatal swoon has cost me my Life," exclaims one hyperventilating heroine of a burlesque Austen wrote as a teenager. "Beware of swoons, Dear Laura. . . . Run mad as often as you chuse; but do not faint." Because Marianne of *Sense and Sensibility* waxes poetic and melancholic ("And you, ye well-known trees!"), she has little time to help others around her—or herself.

Twain then turns his withering gaze on Marianne's sensible older sister, Elinor, and the man she will eventually marry, Edward Ferrars. "Edward Ferrars has fallen in love with Elinor, and she with him; the justification of this may develop later, but thus far there is no way to account for it; for, thus far, Elinor is a wax figure and Edward a shadow, and how could such manufactures as these warm up and feel a passion." Twain correctly notes that both Edward and Elinor are reserved in nature, governing their emotions rather than wearing them openly, like Marianne. Even Elinor admits of Edward, "There was, at times, a want of spirits about him."

A comparison of a typical Edward Ferrars sentence with one of Huck Finn's may shed light on Twain's coldness toward Austen's "hero." Edward says, "You have not been able, then, to bring your sister over to your plan of general civility," while Huck states plainly, "I clumb up the shed . . . and I was dog-tired." Twain not surprisingly considered the Oxford-educated, mother-dominated Edward Ferrars a milquetoast.

Twain's essay continues his analysis of Edward and his relationships: "Edward is an unpleasant shadow, because he has discarded his harmless waxwork and engaged himself to Lucy Steele, who is coarse, ignorant, vicious, brainless, heartless, a flatterer, a sneak—and is described by the supplanted waxwork as being 'a woman superior in person and understanding to half her sex;' and 'time and habit will teach Edward to forget that he ever thought another superior to her.' Elinor knows Lucy quite well. Are those sentimental falsities put into her mouth to make us think she is a noble and magnanimous waxwork, and thus exalt her in our estimation? And do they do it?" Here suspicion turns to surmise. Although Twain had boasted earlier in "Jane Austen" that he was doing "the first third" of *Sense and Sensibility* and not for the first time, he quotes here from the *final* third of her three-volume novel.

Was Mark Twain a closet Janeite, a fake who read and appreciated far more of Jane Austen than he admitted?

Twain shows his understanding of Austen through his apt description of Lucy Steele as "coarse, ignorant, vicious, brainless, heartless, a flatterer, and a sneak." Despite his usual admiration for down-to-earth speech and manners, Twain clearly does *not* prefer the uneducated, "ignorant and illiterate" Lucy with her bad grammar and "want of real elegance" to the well-bred Dashwood sisters. Lucy's "insincerity" and "artfulness" make her vicious—for *both* Austen and Twain.

For Marianne's tormentor, the smooth-talking Willoughby who leads her on while planning marriage to an heiress, Twain has nothing but censure: "Willoughby is a frankly cruel, criminal and filthy society-gentleman." Like Austen, Twain scorned those whose gentlemanly appearance masked an inhuman, hollow core. Just as Austen had made the powerful, socially superior Lady Catherine de Bourgh the *least* admirable character in *Pride and Prejudice,* so Twain had no truck with aristocracy by birth rather than by behavior, scornfully observing that the Russian emperor sneezes just like anybody else. In *Sense and Sensibility,* the Lady Catherine equivalent is Edward's haughty and malicious mother, Mrs. Ferrars. Twain concludes, "Old Mrs. Ferrars is an execrable gentlewoman and unsurpassably coarse and offensive."

For his remaining character notes, Twain adds the label "gentleman" or "lady," followed by "coarse," as if to endorse Austen's scathing indictment of the upper classes.

> Mr. Dashwood, gentleman, is a coarse and cold-hearted money-worshipper; his Fanny is coarse and mean. Neither of them ever says or does a pleasant thing.
>
> Mr. Robert Ferrars, gentleman, is coarse, is a snob, and an all-round offensive person.

Mr. Palmer, gentleman, is coarse, brute-mannered, and probably an ass, though we cannot tell, yet, because he cloaks himself behind silences which are not often broken by speeches that contain material enough to construct an analysis out of.

His wife, lady, is coarse and silly.

Lucy Steele's sister is coarse, foolish, and disagreeable.

By this point, Twain has reiterated the word "coarse" for eight characters. One might have assumed that Twain would embrace coarseness—the rough crudeness he seemed to cultivate in remarks such as "If I can't swear in heaven I won't stay there"—but here he equates the term with general meanness and the crass money-mindedness of Austen's schemers.

Austen would hardly dispute Twain's spluttering character analyses. John and Fanny Dashwood are indeed coarse, mean, cold-hearted money-worshippers who refuse to share their inheritance with relatives. Should they give three thousand pounds away? No, they decide. They selfishly talk the initial sum down to nothing but occasional "presents of fish and game." As Fanny observes when quashing the idea of a yearly donation to her husband's widowed stepmother, "people always live forever when there is any annuity to be paid them."

Robert Ferrars possesses "emptiness and conceit," Austen tells us, and perhaps she and Twain would agree that he deserves to marry (as he does) the equally offensive Lucy Steele.

Rather than celebrating Mr. Palmer's bad manners, Twain senses his brutishness and the horror of the Palmers' loveless marriage. Austen observed of the dourly antisocial Mr. Palmer, "His temper might perhaps be a little soured by finding, like many others of his sex, that through some unaccountable bias in favour of beauty, he was the husband of a very silly woman." Mr. Palmer responds to his marriage to a brainless woman by retreating behind his newspaper, putting it down only to utter contemptuous comments about everyone, particularly his wife. Twain echoes Austen's description of Mrs. Palmer as "silly" and pronounces her husband "an ass." (Austen runs Mr. Palmer through more politely but with a sharper rapier as a man of "studied indifference, insolence, and discontent.")

Last on Twain's character list in "Jane Austen" is Lucy Steele's fawningly affected sister, dismissed as "coarse, foolish, and disagreeable" (and no lady) by *both* Twain and Austen.

And there, with his complaint about the disagreeable Miss Steele, Twain's essay abruptly ends. Did he leave the essay unfinished because, like his barkeeper, he had been defeated in his attempt to appreciate Jane Austen? Or was it (I would argue) that he could no longer reconcile his virile desire to disparage Austen with the fact that he actually "got" her? I suspect that he was afraid that admitting honestly to reaching the final parts of *Sense and Sensibility* would be unmasculine, like confessing he admired ballet or played the flute.

If Twain were alive today, would he maintain his image by grumbling malevolently about Jane Austen's status as "The Woman of the Year"? If Twain continued his anti-Austen pose, he would find plenty of company among contemporary American male humorists. While working on a series about Jane Austen for National Public Radio satellite distribution featuring Margaret Drabble and a cadre of other distinguished Austen scholars and admirers, I turned for comic relief to two institutions of American humor—Andy Rooney and Dave Barry—and heard echoes of Twain.

From his office at CBS's *60 Minutes,* Rooney made it clear to me that he had a decided Twainish prejudice against Austen: "What do I think of Jane Austen? Almost nothing, I'm afraid. I've never read anything she wrote and don't feel any great void where knowledge of her work would be. Jane Austen has not been chosen by me as someone I deliberately wish to be ignorant of; I just never got at reading *Pride and Prejudice* or *Sense and Sensibility.* They seemed to be the Bobbsey Twins for grown-ups." Rooney admitted he had not read anything by "Evelyn Brontë" either (have any of us?).

Humorist Dave Barry of the *Miami Herald* expressed sorrow at learning that Austen had not written *Wuthering Heights* ("that was my one shot at reading a Jane Austen book"). I asked him what image comes into his mind when he hears the name Jane Austen: "Well, I picture all these movies that I don't go to—that's the main image—with that all-star Emma Thompson, who I'm sure is a wonderful actress. I'm looking at the multiplex and I'm almost going to go into that movie with Emma Thompson and then right next door there's a movie where Arnold Schwarzenegger crashes a jet ski into a helicopter and I think that's probably more along my line of thinking, so I never quite get to those Jane Austen movies." Barry chastised Rooney for dismissing *Pride and Prejudice* and *Sense and Sensibility,* noting, "I don't understand why he would criticize two books he had not personally read, so I can't say I would agree with him." Instead, Barry concluded, "Everyone should read everything she ever wrote and then tell me about it so I don't personally have to." Like Twain, who boasted "I don't know anything about anything, and never did," Barry and

Rooney seem to celebrate their philistinism—particularly in regard to women writers.

How unfortunate that Jane Austen (1775–1817) died two decades before the birth of Mark Twain (1835–1910). What might she have said (ironically, no doubt) of him? What if the two had met on one of Twain's trips to Europe? Ushered into her presence in rural Hampshire, would Twain have felt like a barkeeper entering the kingdom of heaven?

Thinking of Twain, the irrepressible American riverboat pilot, and Austen, the tea-drinking maiden aunt, I'm reminded of Bogart and Hepburn in the film classic *The African Queen*. Charlie, the unshaven, boorish pilot of the *African Queen*, shares Twain's delight in cigars, alcohol, freedom, and laxity, noting "Never do today what you can put off till tomorrow" (much as Twain quipped "Do not put off till tomorrow what can be put off till day-after-tomorrow just as well"). Like Twain in the company of Austen's gentlemen and ladies, Charlie seems hilariously out of place at high tea with Rosie and her reverend brother. Both look at Charlie in pained but elegant silence as his stomach growls uncontrollably. Charlie may be natural, but as Rosie disdainfully observes, "Nature is what we're put in this world to rise above."

The dislike is mutual: Charlie scorns the "skinny old maid" Rosie and her world of propriety and sobriety. He feels much like the "cramped up" Huckleberry Finn: "The Widow Douglas . . . allowed she would sivilize me; but it was rough living in the house all the time, considering how dismal regular and decent the widow was in all her ways; and so when I couldn't stand it no longer, I lit out." But Charlie and Rosie "light out" together—and the results are surprising. Weeks together in a boat strip away layers of seemingly insurmountable cultural differences—not to mention the layers of Rosie's starched, high-necked lacy gown. Charlie and Rosie discover a common zest for life.

Could not Twain and Austen be seen as such an odd couple? I believe Jane Austen would have enjoyed Mark Twain's pair of stories called "The Good Little Boy" and "The Bad Little Boy." Overturning moralistic Sunday school stories, Twain's superhumanly, ridiculously good little boy meets with a miserable death, while his bad little boy winds up rich and with a seat in the legislature. Austen had commented in a letter, "Pictures of perfection . . . make me sick and wicked." Overturning conduct books advising girls to be pious, submissive, and ladylike, Austen wrote sketches as a teenager in which heroines get drunk, steal, lie, commit murder, and raise armies, enjoying themselves. Even in her mature works, she presented protagonists devoid of traditionally "heroic" qualities. Note her opening to *Northanger Abbey,* "No one who had ever seen Catherine Morland in her infancy would have supposed her born to be an heroine. . . . The Morlands . . . were in general very plain, and Catherine . . . as plain as any. She had a thin awkward figure, a sallow skin without colour, dark lank hair, and strong features. . . . She was moreover noisy and wild, hated confinement and cleanliness, and loved nothing so well in the world as rolling down the green slope at the back of the house." Huckleberry Finn might have enjoyed rolling down the slope with Catherine Morland, escaping "confinement and cleanliness"–or "sivilization," as Huck put it. Austen's heroines are not all "sadful," either. Elizabeth Bennet admits in *Pride and Prejudice,* "I dearly love a laugh. I never ridicule what is wise and good. Follies and nonsense, whims and inconsistencies *do* divert me, I own, and I laugh at them whenever I can."

Twain and Austen would have been hard pressed to decide who was the more irreverent of the two. Both took on clergymen, aristocrats, and "superiors" of all sorts, skewering them in just a few ironic words. Austen observed of some tedious neighbors, "I was as civil to them as their bad breath would allow" and pronounced her clergyman Mr. Collins "favoured" with stupidity. Twain noted of a clergyman, "He charged nothing for his preaching, and it was worth it too," and he quipped that doctors need but two things: ignorance and confidence.

Despite their pose as "mere" comic writers, both believed deeply in the power of their humor to reveal deeper truths about human behavior. Austen argued in *Northanger Abbey* that a work dismissed as "only a novel" was in fact "only some work in which the greatest powers of the mind are displayed, in which the most thorough knowledge of human nature, the happiest delineation of its varieties, the liveliest effusions of wit and humour are conveyed to the world in the best chosen language." But her voice would remain comic, she insisted when a clergyman asked her to change her style: "My dear Sir, You are very very kind in your hints . . . [but] I could not sit seriously down to write . . . under any other motive than to save my life; and if it were indispensable for me to keep it up and never relax into laughing at myself or other people, I am sure I should be hung before I had finished the first chapter." Austen ends the letter by asserting, "No, I must keep to my own style and go on in my own way."

As Satan observes about the human race in Mark Twain's "The Mysterious Stranger," laughter may not only be its best medicine but also its best weapon: "For your race, in its poverty, has unquestionably one really effective weapon—laughter. Power, money, persuasion, supplication, persecution—these can lift at a colossal humbug but only laughter can blow it to rags and atoms at a blast. Against the assault of laughter nothing can stand. You are always fussing and fighting with your other weapons. Do you ever use that one? No; you leave it lying rusting. As a race, do you ever use it at all? No; you lack sense and the courage." Both Twain and Austen had the "sense and the courage" to use humor to attack the "colossal humbug" they observed around them.

Twain noted, "We keep losing all the world's great authors. Chaucer is dead, so is Shakespeare, so is Milton. And I'm not feeling very well myself." Twain and Austen both belong in that pantheon of the world's great authors, perhaps winking at each other when they think no one is looking.

Since publishing this essay several years ago, I have been informed by Professor James Flavin of Shawnee State University that he suspects Twain stole Austen's idea of people who talk themselves out of having to give away a large amount of money. Twain uses this process in a conversation between men in chapter 32 of *Life on the Mississippi*. Rather than returning ten thousand dollars (as opposed to Austen's three thousand pounds) to its rightful owner, Twain's men convince themselves to keep the money and give away only a gift. Like Austen's Dashwoods, Twain's men use Catch-22 reasoning, arguing that the rightful owner is so poor that he would not know what to do with money anyway. This link suggests that Twain not only liked Austen but found her useful for his own fictional purposes! I am grateful to Professor Flavin for pointing out this connection.

Mark Twain
(Reproduced by permission of
Barry Carlsen)

Appendix B

Full Text of Mark Twain's
"Jane Austen"

BRACKETS INDICATE MATERIAL DELETED FROM THE MANUSCRIPT BY
MARK TWAIN. BRACKETS WITHIN BRACKETS INDICATE MATERIAL
DELETED BY MARK TWAIN BEFORE HE STRUCK OUT THE ENTIRE PASSAGE.

Whenever I take up "Pride and Prejudice" or "Sense and Sensibility," I feel like a barkeeper entering the Kingdom of Heaven. I mean, I feel as he would probably feel, would almost certainly feel. I am quite sure I know what his sensations would be—and his private comments. He would be certain to curl his lip, as those ultra-good Presbyterians went filing self-complacently along. Because he considered himself better than they? Not at all. They would not be to his *taste*—that is all.

He would not want to associate with them; he would not like their gait, their style, their ways; their talk would enrage him. Yet he would be secretly ashamed of himself, secretly angry with himself that this was so. Why? Because barkeepers are like everybody else—it humiliates them to find that there [are fine things which] are fine things, great things, admirable things, which others can perceive and they can't.

What would the barkeeper do next? Give it up and go down below, where his own kind are? No, not yet. He would wander out into the solitudes and take a long rest; then he would brace up and attack the proposition again, saying to himself, "Others have found the secret charm that is in those Presbyterians, therefore it must be a fact, and not an illusion; I will try again; what those others have found, I can find."

So he tries again. Does he succeed? No. Because he has not educated his taste yet, he has not reformed his taste, his taste remains as it was before, and the thing involved is purely a matter of *taste*: [these are Presbyterians, he has never been used to their kind, [he has a petrified] there was a strong prejudice against them in the Bowery, he brought that prejudice away with him] he will not be able to enjoy those Presbyterians until he as learned to admire them.

[Jane Austen's characters are not Presbyterians and I am not a barkeeper.]

Does Jane Austen do her work too remorselessly well? For me, I mean? Maybe that is it. She makes me detest all her people, without reserve. Is that her intention? It is not believable. Then is it her purpose to make the reader detest her people up to the middle of the book and like them in the rest of the chapters? That could be. That would be high art. It would be worth while, too. Some day I will examine the other end of her books and see.

All the great critics praise her art generously. To start with, they say she draws her characters with sharp discrimination and a sure touch. I believe that this is true, as long as the characters she is drawing are odious. I am doing "Sense and Sensibility" now, and have accomplished the first third of it—not for the first time. To my mind, Marianne is not attractive; I am sure I should not care for her, in actual life. I suppose she was intended to be unattractive. Edward Ferrars has fallen in love with Elinor, and she with him; the justification of this may develop later, but thus far there is no way to account for it; for, thus far, Elinor is a wax figure and Edward a shadow, and how could such manufactures as these warm up and feel a passion. Edward is an unpleasant shadow, because he has discarded his harmless [wax] waxwork and engaged himself to Lucy Steele, who is coarse, ignorant, vicious, brainless, heartless, a flatterer, a sneak—and is described [in these following words] by the supplanted waxwork as being "a woman superior in person and understanding to half her sex;" and "time and habit will teach Edward to forget that he ever thought another superior to her." Elinor knows Lucy quite well. Are those sentimental falsities put into her mouth to make us think she is a noble and magnanimous waxwork, and thus exalt her in our estimation? And do they do it?

Willoughby is a frankly cruel, criminal and filthy society-gentleman.

Old Mrs. Ferrars is an execrable gentlewoman and unsurpassably coarse and offensive.

Mr. Dashwood, gentleman, is a coarse and cold-hearted money-worshipper; his Fanny is coarse and mean. Neither of them ever says or does a pleasant thing.

Mr. Robert Ferrars, gentleman, is coarse, is a snob, and an all-round offensive person.

Mr. Palmer, gentleman, is coarse, brute-mannered, and probably an ass, though we cannot tell, yet, because he cloaks himself behind silences which are not often broken by speeches that contain material enough to construct an analysis out of.

His wife, lady, is coarse and silly.

Lucy Steele's sister is coarse, foolish, and disagreeable.

Notes

Chapter 1. Dear Aunt Jane

1. Ang Lee, interview by Steve Paulson, *To the Best of Our Knowledge,* Wisconsin Public Radio, 24 December 2000.

2. *The Wisconsin State Journal,* 21 April 2001, used the large headline "All About Jane" on the front page of the Daybreak section for its coverage of "Jane Austen in the Twenty-first Century," a University of Wisconsin Center for the Humanities festival featuring internationally known Austen scholars. Would the headline for a Twain event have read "All About Mark"?

3. Robert Southey to Charlotte Brontë, March 1837, in *The Life and Correspondence of Robert Southey,* ed. Charles Cuthbert Southey (New York: Harpers, 1851), 547.

4. Poem J. 1129, *The Complete Poems of Emily Dickinson,* ed. Thomas Johnson (Boston: Little, Brown, 1951), 506.

5. Virginia Woolf, "Jane Austen at Sixty," *Athenaeum,* 15 December 1923, reprinted in *Jane Austen: The Critical Heritage,* ed. B. C. Southam (London: Routledge & Kegan Paul, 1968), 2: 301.

6. "The Beautifull Cassandra," *MW,* 47. See Abbreviations for full publishing information for Austen quotations.

7. *NA,* 3–9. Henry Austen's brief Biographical Notice (written for the first volume of the posthumously published *Northanger Abbey* and *Persuasion*) is included in the fifth volume of R. W. Chapman's standard edition of Austen's novels.

8. Contrast the full letter of 20 November 1800 as printed in *Jane Austen's Letters: New Edition,* ed. Deirdre Le Faye (Oxford: Oxford University Press, 1995), 61, with the censored version the public first encountered in 1884 when it was printed in *The Letters of Jane Austen,* ed. Lord Edward Brabourne (London: Bentley & Son, 1884), 1: 243.

9. Jan Fergus, *Jane Austen: A Literary Life* (New York: St. Martin's Press, 1991).

10. Deirdre Le Faye, ed., *Jane Austen: A Family Record* (London: British Library, 1989), 232.

11. James Edward Austen-Leigh, *Memoir of Jane Austen,* 2d ed. (London: Bentley, 1871), 2, 165, 130, 141.

12. P. D. James, *Time to Be in Earnest: A Fragment of Autobiography* (New York: Knopf, 2000), 79.

13. See Le Faye, *Jane Austen,* 7, 9, 15, and Austen-Leigh, *Memoir,* 11.

14. Austen-Leigh, *Memoir,* 96.

15. Contrast Austen-Leigh, *Memoir,* 130, with Austen's letter of 5 April 1809 and discussion of novels in *NA,* 37–38.

16. Margaret Drabble, introduction to *Jane Austen's Beginnings: The Juvenilia and Lady Susan,* ed. J. David Grey (Ann Arbor: University of Michigan Press, 1989), xiv.

17. Juliet McMaster, letter to author, 2001.

18. Caroline Austen, *My Aunt Jane Austen: A Memoir* (1867; reprint, Jane Austen Society, 1952), 9.

19. Austen-Leigh, *Memoir,* 54.

20. Ibid., 14, 165.

21. Ibid., 60. In the next three paragraphs, the examples of Austen-Leigh's censorship refer to his cut or altered versions of letters of 12 November 1800, 14 September 1805, and 8 April 1805.

22. Barbara Seeber, *General Consent in Jane Austen: A Study in Dialogism* (Montreal: McGill-Queen's University Press, 2000), 140–41.

23. Austen-Leigh, *Memoir*, 87. Austen-Leigh quotes from Caroline Austen, *My Aunt Jane Austen*, 8.

24. Letters of 28 October 1798, 19 December 1798, and 20 June 1808. This will be the last time I insert *sic* for Austen's unorthodox spelling and grammar ("beautifull," "friendship," "ancle," "I shall be hanged," and so forth). I will instead trust that the reader will recognize Austen's "wonderfull" originals.

25. "Personalities," *Collected Essays of Virginia Woolf* (London: Hogarth Press, 1966), 2: 276.

26. Letters referred to in this paragraph are from 26 May 1801, 21 April 1805, 8 April 1805, 6 May 1801, 28 September 1814, 2 March 1814, 20 May 1813, and 2 March 1814.

27. Austen-Leigh, *Memoir*, 114.

28. Ibid., 116.

29. Ibid., 119.

30. Carol Shields, *Jane Austen: A Penguin Life* (New York: Viking, 2001), 88.

31. Austen-Leigh, *Memoir*, 127, 141, 130, 160.

32. Virginia Woolf, "Jane Austen," *The Essays of Virginia Woolf*, ed. Andrew McNeillie (London: Hogarth Press, 1986), 2: 9; Le Faye, *Jane Austen*, 255; Shields, *Jane Austen*, 183.

33. Cited in Southam, *Critical Heritage*, 2: 12.

34. Caroline Austen, *My Aunt Jane Austen*, 5, 16.

35. *The Autobiography of Margaret Oliphant: The Complete Text*, ed. Elisabeth Jay (Oxford: Oxford University Press, 1990), 30.

36. Southam, *Critical Heritage*, 2: 4; Park Honan, *Jane Austen: Her Life* (New York: St. Martin's, 1987), 291.

37. Helen Denman, "The Portraits," in *Jane Austen Companion*, ed. J. David Grey (New York: Macmillan, 1986), 342.

38. Cassandra-Estes Austen to James Edward Austen-Leigh, 18 December 1869, in Le Faye, *Jane Austen*, 253.

39. Le Faye, *Jane Austen*, 254.

40. Deirdre Le Faye, "A Literary Portrait Re-Examined: Jane Austen and Mary Anne Campion," *The Book Collector* (Winter 1996), 524.

41. May Becker, *Presenting Miss Jane Austen* (New York: Dodd Mead, 1952), with Edward Price's "Conjectural portrait derived from Cassandra's sketch and contemporary descriptions."

42. Claudia Johnson, "Fair Maid of Kent," *Times Literary Supplement*, 13 March 1998, 15.

43. Valerie Myer, *Jane Austen: Obstinate Heart* (New York: Arcade, 1997), 1.

44. R. W. B. Lewis, *Edith Wharton: A Biography* (New York: Harper & Row, 1975), 272.

45. John Woodbridge, preface to *The Tenth Muse* by Anne Bradstreet, 2d ed. (Boston: John Foster, 1678), iii–iv.

46. Edward Fuller, preface to *Woman in the Nineteenth Century* by Margaret Fuller (Boston: Jewett, 1855; reprint, New York: Norton, 1971), 6–7.

47. Johanna Johnston, *Runaway to Heaven: The Story of Harriet Beecher Stowe* (New York: Doubleday, 1963), 275.

48. Alice King, *The Argosy*, cited in Southam, *Critical Heritage*, 2: 38.

49. *The Letters and Journals of Thomas Wentworth Higginson*, 1846, ed. Mary Thacher Higginson (Boston: Houghton Mifflin, 1921), 268; also see Thomas H. Johnson, introduction to *Complete Poems of Emily Dickinson*, vi.

50. Martha Bianchi Dickinson, preface to *The Complete Poems of Emily Dickinson* (New York: Barnes & Noble, 1996), 8.

51. Austen-Leigh, *Memoir*, 1.

52. Mary Austen-Leigh, cited in Southam, *Critical Heritage,* 2: 2.
53. Oliver Elton, *Survey of Literature, 1780–1830* (London: Edward Arnold, 1912), 1: 191–92.
54. John Bailey, *Introductions to Jane Austen* (London: Oxford University Press, 1931), 1, 2, 6, 22.
55. *Benet's Reader's Encyclopedia,* 4th ed. (New York: Harper & Row, 1965), 65.
56. Juliet McMaster, interview by the author, *Jane Austen and the Courage to Write,* a series of Wisconsin Public Radio documentaries on women writers, 1995, www.dcs.wisc.edu/lsa/courage.htm.
57. E. V. Lucas, introduction to *Pride and Prejudice* (London: Methuen, 1900), xiii.
58. Cardinal John Newman, *Letters* (1891), cited in Southam, *Critical Heritage,* 1: 117; Adolphus Jack, *Essays on the Novel, as Illustrated by Scott and Miss Austen* (London and New York: Macmillan, 1897), 282; Leslie Stephen, "Humour," *Cornhill Magazine* 33 (1876): 325, cited in Southam, *Critical Heritage,* 2: 174.
59. Eudora Welty, "Finding a Voice," *One Writer's Beginnings* (Cambridge, Mass.: Harvard University Press, 1983), 104.
60. Thomas Wentworth Higginson, *Women and Men* (New York: Harper & Brothers, 1888), 156; Alexander Woolcott, "A Treat for Janeites," *McCall's Magazine* (December 1933), cited in Southam, *Critical Heritage,* 2: 119; H. G. Wells, character in *The Brothers* (New York: Viking, 1938), 26–27; D. H. Lawrence, *A Propos of Lady Chatterley's Lover* (London: Mandrake Press, 1930), 58; second D. H. Lawrence quotation ("narrow-gutted spinster") cited without documentation in B. C. Southam, *Jane Austen* (London: Longman, 1975), 14; Ralph Waldo Emerson, *The Journals of Ralph Waldo Emerson: 1856–63,* ed. E. W. Emerson and W. E. Forbes (Boston: Houghton Mifflin, 1913), 9: 336.
61. Ezra Pound, review of Robert Frost's *North of Boston, Poetry* (December 1914), cited in Southam, *Critical Heritage,* 2: 84.
62. Virginia Woolf, *A Room of One's Own* (New York: Harcourt, Brace, 1929), 128.
63. Thomas Carlyle's disparagement of Austen is reported in Francis Espinasse, *Literary Recollections and Sketches* (London: Hodder and Stoughton, 1893), 261.
64. Anonymous critic cited in Mary Austen-Leigh, *Personal Aspects of Jane Austen* (New York: Dutton, 1920), 6.
65. Letter to R. W. Chapman, 20 November 1936, in *The Letters of Virginia Woolf,* ed. Nigel Nicolsen and Joanne Traumann (New York: Harcourt Brace Jovanovich, 1975–80), 6: 87.
66. In order, the five quotations are from the following sources: George Sampson, *Bookman,* January 1924, cited in Southam, *Critical Heritage,* 2: 101; Arnold Bennett, "Books and Persons," *Evening Standard,* 21 July 1927, cited in Southam, *Critical Heritage,* 2: 288; Lord David Cecil, *Jane Austen* (Cambridge: Cambridge University Press, 1935), 5; Richard Aldington, *Jane Austen* (Pasadena: Ampersand Press, 1948), 3–4; John Leonard, "Novel Colonies," review of *Culture and Imperialism* by Edward Said, *Nation* (22 March 1993), 383.
67. R. W. Chapman, *Jane Austen: Facts and Problems* (Oxford: Clarendon Press, 1948), 1.
68. Letter to Miyeko Kamiya, 1 June 1967, *The Letters of Leonard Woolf,* ed. Frederick Spotts (New York: Harcourt Brace Jovanovich, 1989), 557.
69. *Writing in Prose and Verse of Rudyard Kipling* (New York: Scribners, 1897–1937), 31: 190–91.
70. The three quotations are in this order: Myer, *Jane Austen,* 64, 41; John Halperin, *The Life of Jane Austen* (Baltimore: Johns Hopkins University Press, 1984), 108, 110; Martin Amis, "Miss Jane's Prime," *Atlantic Monthly* (February 1990), 101.
71. Kenneth Turan, "Pride and Prejudice: An Informal History of the Garson-Olivier Motion Picture," *Persuasions* 11 (1989): 142.
72. *The Selected Poems of Anne Stevenson, 1956–86* (Oxford and New York: Oxford University Press, 1987), 130.

73. Brian Wilks, *Jane Austen* (Maplewood, N.J.: Hamlyn, 1978).
74. David Nokes, *Jane Austen: A Life* (New York: Farrar Straus & Giroux, 2000); M. C. Hammond, *Relating to Jane* (London: Minerva Press, 1998); Audrey Hawkbridge, *Jane and Her Gentlemen* (London: Peter Owen, 2000).
75. Myer, *Jane Austen*, 1.
76. Katherine Mansfield, review of *Personal Aspects of Jane Austen* by Mary Austen-Leigh, 3 December 1920, in *Novels and Novelists*, ed. J. M. Murry (New York: Knopf, 1930), 314.
77. John Middleton Murry, *Katherine Mansfield and Other Literary Studies* (London: Constable, 1959), 90, and *Between Two Worlds* (London: Jonathan Cape, 1935), 194. Ian Gordon notes in his introduction to Katherine Mansfield's *Urewera Notebook* (Oxford: Oxford University Press, 1978), 16, that Murry "discarded, suppressed, edited, and manipulated" his wife's works.
78. *The Journals of Katherine Mansfield*, ed. J. M. Murry (London: Constable, 1927), 102; letter of 12 December 1920, *The Collected Letters of Katherine Mansfield*, ed. Vincent O'Sullivan and Margaret Scott (Oxford: Clarendon, 1996), 4: 149.
79. Katherine Anne Porter, "The Art of Katherine Mansfield," *Nation* 145 (23 October 1937): 435, in *The Critical Response to Katherine Mansfield*, ed. J. Pilditch (Westport, Conn.: Greenwood Press, 1996), 45.
80. Letter of 17 January 1921, *Collected Letters of Katherine Mansfield*, 4: 165.
81. Porter, *Critical Response to Katherine Mansfield*, 47.
82. Lord David Cecil, *Jane Austen*, 5
83. G. K. Chesterton, preface to *Love and Freindship and Other Early Works* (London: Chatto & Winders, 1922), xv.
84. See, for example, excerpts from *Pen Portraits of Literary Women* (1887), Mrs. Malden's *Jane Austen* (1889), and an introduction to a 1912 edition of *Pride and Prejudice* by Chapman's wife, Katherine Metcalfe, cited in Southam, *Critical Heritage*, 2: 38, 80, 42.
85. William Lyon Phelps, introduction to *The Novels and Letters of Jane Austen* (New York: Holby, 1906), x.
86. Henry James, "Gustave Flaubert, 1902" and "Lesson of Balzac, 1907," in *The House of Fiction*, ed. Leon Edel (London: Rupert Hart-Davis, 1957), 207, 62–63.
87. Helen Bevinton, "A Few More Oddities," *When Found, Make a Verse Of* (New York: Simon & Schuster, 1961), 117.
88. James, *Time to Be in Earnest*, 228.
89. Letter of 7 May 1850, *The Letters of Emily Dickinson*, ed. Thomas H. Johnson (Cambridge, Mass.: Harvard University Press, 1958), 1: 99.
90. *Essays of Virginia Woolf*, ed. McNeillie, 3: 270.
91. Woolf, *A Room of One's Own*, 129–30.

Chapter 2. Beware of Swoons

1. Brian Southam, "Juvenilia," in Grey, *Jane Austen Companion*, 245.
2. Ibid.
3. Drabble, foreword to *Jane Austen's Beginnings*, ed. J. David Grey, xiii.
4. Agnes Bennett, *Agnes De-Courci: A Domestic Tale*, 4: 192, cited in Margaret Anne Doody, "Jane Austen's Reading," in Grey, *Jane Austen Companion*, 361. The full text of Bennett's potboiler is available online through the Chawton House web site at http://www.chawton.org/novels/agnes/.
5. William Collins, *Odes on Several Descriptive and Allegorical Subjects* (London: A. Millar, 1747), 1–2. Collins's poem continues with references to deserted streams, lutes, myrtles and turtles, dreams, and a "buskined Muse."
6. Deborah Kaplan, *Jane Austen among Women* (Baltimore: Johns Hopkins University Press, 1992), 17. Kaplan's work offers an excellent source of quotations from conduct books of Austen's day. In addition, a sampling of quotations from

conduct books in the collection of Yale's Bienecke Library is offered online at www.muohio.ed/~mclainjl/beinecke.htm.

7. Dr. John Gregory, *A Father's Legacy to His Daughters* (1774; reprint, Boston: James Dow, 1834), 24, 25–26, 27, 32, 35.

8. *Wisdom in Miniature; or the Young Gentleman and Lady's Pleasing Instructor* (Worcester: Isaiah Thomas, 1795), 126; Jane West, *Letters to a Young Lady in which the Duties and Character of Women Are Considered* (Troy: O. Penniman, 1806), 31, 50, in Kaplan, *Jane Austen among Women*, 81–82; Hester Chapone, *Letters on the Improvement of the Mind* (1773; reprint, Boston: James B. Dow, 1834), 94, in Kaplan, *Jane Austen among Women*, 42; James Fordyce, *Sermons to Young Women*, 1766; 11th ed. (London: Cadell, 1792), 2: 10, 11; Chase Amos, *The Excellent Female* (Litchfield: Collier and Buel, 1792), 11; Thomas Gisborne, *An Enquiry into the Duties of the Female Sex* (1797; reprint, New York: Garland, 1974), 251, 317.

9. *The Complete Short Stories of Mark Twain* (New York: Doubleday, 1957), 67–68.

10. Ibid., 6–8.

11. "Fenimore Cooper's Literary Offenses," *The Great Short Works of Mark Twain* (New York: Harper & Row, 1967), 181.

12. Halperin, *Life of Jane Austen*, 50.

13. Mark Twain, *The Adventures of Huckleberry Finn* (Boston: Houghton Mifflin, 1958), 86.

14. Doody notes in "Jane Austen's Reading," in Grey, *Jane Austen Companion*, 358, that from "Jack and Alice" onward, "Sir Charles Grandison . . . is an almost-constant presence in Austen's fiction."

15. West, *Letters to a Young Lady*, 376, in Kaplan, *Jane Austen among Women*, 42.

16. Karen Hartnick, introduction to *Henry and Eliza* (Alberta: Juvenilia Press, 1996), xiii.

17. Virginia Woolf, *The Common Reader: First Series,* ed. Andrew McNeillie (1925; reprint, New York: Harcourt Brace & Jovanovich, 1984), 136. These same remarks also appear in "Jane Austen Practising," *Essays of Virginia Woolf,* ed. McNeillie, 3: 334.

18. Devoney Looser, *British Women Writers and the Writing of History* (Baltimore: Johns Hopkins University Press, 2000). See my review of Looser's book in *JASNA News: The Newsletter of the Jane Austen Society of North America* 17 (Summer 2001): 26–27.

19. West, *Letters to a Young Lady*, 376, in Kaplan, *Jane Austen among Women*, 20.

20. *Essays of Virginia Woolf,* ed. McNeillie, 3: 333 (here Woolf notes, "The girl of seventeen is laughing, in her corner, at the world") or 4: 147 ("The girl of fifteen is laughing, in her corner, at the world"). I hope scholars in the future will create a volume collecting all Woolf's comments on Austen ("Jane Austen Practising," "Jane Austen and the Geese," "Jane Austen at Sixty," "Jane Austen," numerous references throughout the letters, diaries, and *A Room of One's Own*).

21. Brownstein, preface to *Henry and Eliza*, ed. Hartnick, viii.

22. Halperin, *Life of Jane Austen*, 39, 36.

23. Claudia Johnson, *Jane Austen: Women, Politics, and the Novel* (Chicago: University of Chicago Press, 1988), 28.

24. James Austen, *Loiterer* 1, no. 9 (28 March 1789): 4–7. Li-Ping Geng's introduction to this two-volume facsimile set highlights some of the parallels between the *Loiterer* and Austen's juvenilia. I am indebted to Valerie Fritche for her work on *The Loiterer* as part of a student thesis.

25. Ibid., 2: 11.

26. Margaret Doody, introduction to *Catharine and Other Writings* (Oxford: Oxford University Press, 1993), xvi.

27. Juliet McMaster, interview by the author, *Jane Austen and the Courage to Write,* Wisconsin Public Radio, October 1995.
28. Austen-Leigh, *Memoir,* 87.
29. Doody, introduction to *Catharine and Other Writings,* xxiii.
30. Ibid., xviii. Doody notes that Austen originally used the "impudently collo-quial word" *cockylorum* in *A History of England.*

Chapter 3. Only Genius, Wit, and Taste

1. Wilde's alleged remark is repeated in many biographies, including Barbara Belford's *Oscar Wilde: A Certain Genius* (New York: Random House, 2000), 93.
2. A. Walton Litz, *Jane Austen: A Study of Her Artistic Development* (New York: Oxford University Press, 1965), 69; Honan, *Jane Austen,* 141.
3. Alexander Pope, *Selected Poetry and Prose* (New York: Rinehart, 1951), 114.
4. *The Complete Poems of Thomas Gray* (Oxford: Clarendon Press, 1999), 38–39.
5. *The Complete Poetical Works of James Thomson* (London: Oxford University Press, 1908), 14.
6. William Dean Howells, *Heroines of Fiction* (New York: Harper & Brothers, 1901), 1: 58.
7. Dr. Gregory, *A Father's Legacy to His Daughters,* 26.
8. Paul Morrison, "Enclosed in Openness: *Northanger Abbey* and the Domestic Carceral," *Texas Studies in Literature and Language* 33 (Spring 1991): 2–3.
9. Mary Astell, *The Christian Religion, as Profes'd by a Daughter of the Church of England* (London: R. Wilkins, 1717), 206–7. See a full discussion of Austen's place among women historians in Looser, *British Women Writers and the Writing of History,* particularly her discussion of Elinor Tilney's way of merging history and fiction.
10. Horace Walpole, *Castle of Otranto* (London: J. M. Dent, 1993), 23–24.
11. Matthew Lewis, *The Monk: A Romance* (London: Penguin, 1998), 325.
12. In his introduction to the Oxford World Classics edition of *Mysteries of Udolpho,* Terry Castle notes that Radcliffe based her descriptions of southern Europe on travel books, paintings, and her imagination, not actual trips.
13. Claudia Johnson, interview by the author, *Jane Austen and the Courage to Write,* Wisconsin Public Radio, October 1995; Morrison, "Enclosed in Openness," 21.
14. See www.pemberley.com/janeinfo/nhabgoth.
15. Quotations are from "Advice to Ladies on Exercise and Education," "On Ladies' Dress," and "False Exaltation of Women," in *Essays of Richard Steele,* edited by L. E. Steele. (London: Macmillan, 1923), 236, 163–66, 280.
16. James Austen, *Loiterer* 1, no. 9 (28 March 1789): 9.
17. Halperin, *Life of Jane Austen,* 110.

Chapter 4. An Excellent Heart

1. Shields, *Jane Austen,* 48.
2. Eva Brann, "Whose Sense? Whose Sensibility?" *Persuasions* 12 (1990): 131.
3. Stuart Tave, *Some Words of Jane Austen* (Chicago: University of Chicago Press, 1973), 96.
4. John Hardy, *Jane Austen's Heroines: Intimacy in Human Relationships* (London: Routledge, Kegan & Paul, 1984).
5. Marvin Mudrick, *Jane Austen: Irony as Defense and Discovery* (Princeton: Princeton University Press, 1952), 93.
6. Eliza Hancock to Philadelphia Hancock, 3 May 1797, in Richard Austen-Leigh, *Austen Papers* (London, 1942), 159, cited in Le Faye, *Family Record,* 94.
7. *Englishwoman's Domestic Magazine,* 1866, cited in Southam, *Critical Heritage,* 1: 206.
8. Marilyn Butler, *Jane Austen and the War of Ideas* (Oxford: Clarendon Press, 1975), 196; Lawrence Lerner, "*Sense and Sensibility*: A Mixed-Up Book," in *The Truthtellers:*

Jane Austen, George Eliot, and D. H. Lawrence (London: Chatto & Windus, 1967), 166.

9. George Moore, *Avowals* (1919; reprint, London: Heinemann, 1924), 39–40.

10. See Tony Tanner, *Jane Austen* (Cambridge, Mass.: Harvard University Press, 1986), 91.

11. Le Faye, *Jane Austen,* 178.

12. Maurice Agulhon, *Marianne into Battle: Republican Imagery and Symbolism in France, 1789–1880,* trans. Janet Lloyd (Cambridge: Cambridge University Press, 1981), 16. Also see the discussion of Marianne's dangerous name in Margaret Anne Doody's introduction to *Sense and Sensibility* (Oxford: Oxford World Classics, 1990), xvii.

13. Lynn Hunt, *Politics, Culture, and Class in the French Revolution* (Berkeley: University of California Press, 1984), 62.

14. See Honan, *Jane Austen,* 98.

15. George Moore, "Turgueneff," *Fortnightly Review,* February 1888, cited in Southam, *Critical Heritage,* 2: 188.

16. Marat-Mauger's remarks are cited in Hunt, *Politics, Culture, and Class in the French Revolution,* 27.

17. Steele Gibbons, introduction to *Sense and Sensibility* (New York: Heritage Press, 1957), x.

18. For the complete text of Twain's remarks in "Jane Austen," an unpublished essay about *Sense and Sensibility,* see my appendix.

19. Susan Morgan, "Polite Lies: The Veiled Heroine of *Sense and Sensibility,*" *Nineteenth-Century Fiction* 31 (September 1976): 191.

20. Blaise Pascal, *Pensées,* section 4, line 277 (New York: Dutton, 1958), 79.

21. See the discussion of Ang Lee's *Sense and Sensibility* in *Jane Austen in Hollywood,* ed. Linda Troost and Sayre Greenfield (Lexington: University Press of Kentucky, 1998). For example, Cheryl Nixon notes that "the film remakes Brandon into a standard-bearer of true emotion" and "a courtship hero" (39), and Nora Nachumi observes that "the movie works hard to create the impression that Brandon is the perfect romantic hero for Marianne" (133).

22. William Cowper, *The Task,* book 4, line 560, in *Poetical Works,* ed. H. S. Milford (London: Oxford University Press, 1967), 231.

23. Honan, *Jane Austen,* 275, 278; Marvin Mudrick, *Jane Austen,* 88; Louis Menand, "What Jane Austen Doesn't Tell Us," *New York Review of Books* (1 February 1996), 14.

24. *Nabobs* were wealthy, important colonists; *mohrs* were coins used in British India; *palanquins* were closed litters on which several natives would transport VIPs.

25. Mary Wollstonecraft, *Vindication of the Rights of Woman* (1792; reprint, London: Penguin, 1985), 151–52.

26. Ibid., 158.

27. Ibid., 154.

28. John Bennett, *Letters to a Young Lady* (Warrington: W. Eyres, 1789), 7.

29. "The Princess," 5: 439–41, in *The Poems of Tennyson,* ed. Christopher Ricks (London: Longmans, 1969), 815.

30. Halperin, *Life of Jane Austen,* 91.

31. Joan Ray, "Code Word Jane Austen, or How a Chinese Film About Martial Arts Teaches Life Arts," *Persuasions* 22 (2000): 10.

32. Joseph Wiesenfarth, *The Errand of Form: An Assay of Jane Austen's Art* (New York: Fordham University Press, 1967), 55.

33. W. H. Auden, "Letter to Lord Byron, Part 1," in *Letters from Iceland* (London: Faber & Faber, 1937), 21.

34. Isobel Armstrong, *Sense and Sensibility* (London and New York: Penguin Books, 1994), 81.

35. "Willoughby is a stage villain," notes William Lyon Phelps in his introduction to the 1906 New York Holby edition of *Sense and Sensibility* (xxxvii).
36. See, for instance, Halperin's description of *Sense and Sensibility* as "bleak and black and nasty" in *Life of Jane Austen*, 84.
37. Eudora Welty, "The Radiance of Jane Austen" (1969), in *The Eye of the Story: Selected Essays and Reviews* (New York: Random House, 1978), 8–9.

Chapter 5. The Liveliness of Your Mind

1. Johnson, *Jane Austen*, 73.
2. Caroline Austen, *My Aunt Jane Austen*, 5, 16.
3. Honan, *Jane Austen*, 184.
4. Myer, *Jane Austen*, 1.
5. Hannah More, *Essays on Various Subjects, Principally Designed for Young Ladies* (1775; reprint, London: Wilkie & Cadell, 1777), 145. See a discussion of Austen and More in Armstrong, *Sense and Sensibility*, 61.
6. More, *Essays on Various Subjects*, 145.
7. Samuel Johnson, *A Dictionary of the English Language* (1755; reprint, London: Reeves & Turner, 1877), 504.
8. Wollstonecraft, *Vindication of the Rights of Woman*, 144–45.
9. Johnson, *Jane Austen*, 76–77.
10. Hester Chapone, letter 4 (On the Regulation of the Heart and Affections), *Letters on the Improvement of the Mind*, cited in Frank Bradbrook's explanatory notes in the Oxford World Classics edition of *Pride and Prejudice* (Oxford, 1990), 348.
11. Compare *PP*, 289, and vol. 2, letter 8 of Fanny Burney's *Evelina* (Oxford: Oxford World Classics, 1982), 164.
12. Honan, *Jane Austen*, 186.
13. I am indebted for this idea to Ruth Perry's "Home at Last: Biographical Background to *Pride and Prejudice*," in *Approaches to Teaching Pride and Prejudice*, ed. Marcia Folsom (New York: Modern Language Association, 1993), 46–56.
14. Letter of December 1814 to Sir William Elford, *The Letters of Mary Russell Mitford*, ed. R. Brimley Johnson (New York: Dial Press, 1925), 121–22.
15. Penny Gay, *Jane Austen's Pride and Prejudice* (Sydney: Sydney University Press, 1990), 27.
16. Edward Copeland, "The Economic Realities of Jane Austen's Darcy," in Folsom, *Approaches to Teaching Pride and Prejudice*, 43–45.
17. Pierre de Beaumarchais, *The Marriage of Figaro*, 5.3, in *The Three Figaro Plays*, trans. David Edney (Ottawa: Dovehouse, 2000), 324.
18. *The Complete Plays of Gilbert and Sullivan* (New York: Norton, 1941), 303.
19. Charlotte-Maria Middleton in Le Faye, *Jane Austen*, 178.
20. Lord David Cecil, *A Portrait of Jane Austen* (New York: Hill, 1978), 62.
21. James Fordyce, "On Female Virtue," in *Sermons to Young Women* (1766; reprint, London: T. Cadell, 1792), 1: 148–49.
22. Richard Brinsley Sheridan, *The Rivals*, 2.2, in *Masterpieces of the Drama*, ed. Allison, Carr, and Eastman (New York: Macmillan, 1957), 289. I am indebted for the link between Lydia Bennet and Lydia Languish to Honan, *Jane Austen*, 34. Honan reminds us that Austen's brothers acted out *The Rivals*.
23. Le Faye, *Jane Austen*, 175.
24. Fanny Burney, *Cecilia: or Memoirs of an Heiress* (London: Virago, 1986), 908.
25. Letter to Orion and May Clemens, 19–20 October 1865, in *Mark Twain's Letters* (Berkeley: University of California Press, 1988), 1: 323.

Chapter 6. All the Heroism of Principle

1. Kingsley Amis, "What Became of Jane Austen?" (1957), in *What Became of Jane Austen? And Other Questions* (New York: Harcourt Brace Jovanovich, 1970), 16.
2. Reginald Farrar, "Jane Austen, ob. July 18, 1817," *Quarterly Review* (July 1917), in Southam, *Critical Heritage*, 2: 264; Nina Auerbach, "Jane Austen's Dangerous Charm: Feeling as One Ought About Fanny Price," *Persuasions* 2 (16 December 1980): 9; Karen Joy Fowler, *The Jane Austen Book Club* (New York: Putnam's, 2004), 83.
3. Lionel Trilling, introduction to *Emma* (Boston: Houghton Mifflin, 1957), viii.
4. Honan, *Jane Austen*, 34.
5. Ibid., 354.
6. *Wisdom in Miniature; or the Young Gentleman and Lady's Pleasing Instructor*, 126.
7. Chase Amos, *On Female Excellence, or, A discourse: in which good character in women is described* (Litchfield: Collier & Buel, 1792), 11.
8. Fordyce, *Sermons to Young Women*, 2: 10–11.
9. Dr. Gregory, *A Father's Legacy to His Daughters*, 24.
10. Wordsworth, "Lines Composed a Few Miles above Tintern Abbey," *Selected Poems and Prefaces*, ed. Jack Stillinger (New York: Riverside, 1965), 110.
11. Isaac Hawkins Browne, *A Pipe of Tobacco: In Imitation of Six Several Authors*, ed. H. F. B. Brett-Smith (Oxford: Blackwell, 1923), 2.
12. Honan, *Jane Austen*, 56.
13. Ibid., 340.
14. See for instance Glenda Hudson, *Sibling Love and Incest in Jane Austen's Fiction* (New York: St. Martin's Press, 1999).
15. Halperin, *Life of Jane Austen*, 249.
16. *The Poetical Works of William Cowper* (London: Macmillan, 1924), 183. See also "The Negro's Complaint" and "Pity for Poor Africans," 361–63.
17. Cited in Honan, *Jane Austen*, 3.
18. Virginia Woolf, *Times Literary Supplement*, 8 May 1913, in Southam, *Critical Heritage*, 2: 241.
19. *Poetical Works of William Cowper*, 297.
20. Charlotte Brontë, *Jane Eyre* (Middlesex: Penguin, 1966), 141.
21. *Poetical Works of Sir Walter Scott* (London: Macmillan, 1890), 11–49.
22. Honan, *Jane Austen*, 337.
23. George Crabbe, "The Parish Register II," in *The Complete Poetical Works*, ed. Norma Dalrymple-Champneys and Arthur Pollard (Oxford: Clarendon Press, 1988), 1: 251–52.
24. Le Faye, *Jane Austen*, 158.
25. Samuel Johnson, *Rasselas*, ed. George Birkbeck (Oxford: Clarendon Press, 1927), 99.
26. Joseph Wiesenfarth, *Errand of Form*, 95. The reference is to Marvell's "To his Coy Mistress," lines 41–46.
27. Honan, *Jane Austen*, 333.
28. Wiesenfarth, *Errand of Form*, 90.
29. Harriet Byron in *Sir Charles Grandison*, 9: 24, 131, cited in Wiesenfarth, *Errand of Form*, 87–88.
30. Honan, *Jane Austen*, 334.
31. Le Faye, *Jane Austen*, 175.
32. Woolf, "Jane Austen," in *Common Reader*, ed. McNeillie, 130.

Chapter 7. An Imaginist Like Herself

1. Honan, *Jane Austen*, 364; Reginald Farrar, "Jane Austen, ob. July 18, 1817," in Southam, *Critical Heritage*, 2: 265–66; A. C. Bradley, "Jane Austen," *Essays and*

Studies (1911), in Southam, *Critical Heritage,* 2: 237; Edith Wharton, *The Writing of Fiction* (New York and London: Scribners, 1925), 128–30; Chapman, *Jane Austen,* 201; Ronald Blythe, introduction to *Emma* (Middlesex: Penguin, 1966), 7.

2. John J. McAleer, introduction to *Death Times Three* by Rex Stout (New York: Bantam, 1985), vii.
3. Le Faye, *Jane Austen,* 187.
4. Tanner, *Jane Austen,* 176.
5. Honan, *Jane Austen,* 373; Sandra Gilbert and Susan Gubar, *The Madwoman in the Attic: The Woman Writer and the Nineteenth-Century Literary Imagination* (New Haven: Yale University Press, 1979), 158.
6. Cowper, *The Task,* book 4, "The Winter Evening," line 290, in *Poetical Works,* ed. Milford.
7. Shields, *Jane Austen,* 160.
8. Caroline Austen, *My Aunt Jane Austen,* 5.
9. Sheilah Graham and Gerold Frank, *Beloved Infidel: The Education of a Woman* (New York: Holt, 1959), 215.
10. Michael Korda, "The Third Man," *New Yorker* (25 March 1996), 45.
11. John Murray to Walter Scott, 25 December 1815, cited in Honan, *Jane Austen,* 372.
12. Ann Radcliffe, *The Romance of the Forest* (Oxford: Oxford University Press, 1986), 166.
13. Oliver Goldsmith, "The Deserted Village," in *The Poetical Works of Oliver Goldsmith* (London: Oxford University Press, 1927), 25.
14. Edward Young, "Various Effects of Pride," in *Elegant Extracts,* ed. V. Knox (London: John Sharpe, n.d.), 2: 36.
15. See Colleen Sheedan's conclusion that Austen is a "rakish trickster" with a "tinge of mischief" in her ink in "The Riddles of *Emma,*" *Persuasions* 22 (2000): 50.
16. Edward Gibbon, *Decline and Fall of the Roman Empire* (Philadelphia: Porter & Coates, 1845), 6: 518.
17. *Lady's Magazine,* November 1802, 563, in Edward Copeland, "Money" in *The Cambridge Companion to Jane Austen,* ed. Edward Copeland and Juliet McMaster (Cambridge: Cambridge University Press, 1997), 142.
18. E. M. Forster, "Notes on the English Character," in *Abinger Harvest* (New York: Harcourt Brace & Jovanovich, 1936), 5.
19. Robert McCrum et al., *The Story of English* (New York: Viking, 1986), 62.
20. Kathryn L. Shanks Libin, "Music, Character, and Social Standing in Jane Austen's *Emma,*" *Persuasions* 22 (2000): 18.
21. See my discussion of this in *Maestros, Dilettantes, and Philistines: The Musician in the Victorian Novel* (New York: Peter Lang, 1989) and Phyllis Weliver's *Women Musicians in Victorian Fiction, 1860–1900* (Burlington, Vt.: Ashgate, 2000).
22. James Austen, *Loiterer* 1, no. 10 (4 April 1789): 6, 12.
23. Camille Paglia, *Sexual Personae: Art and Decadence from Nefertiti to Emily Dickinson* (New Haven: Yale University Press, 1990), 199, 441.
24. Wislawa Szymborska, *No End of Fun* (1967), in *View with a Grain of Sand: Selected Poems,* trans. Stanislaw Branczak and Clare Cavanagh (New York: Harcourt Brace, 1995), 36.
25. Chapman, *Jane Austen,* 202–3.

Chapter 8. The Advantage of Maturity of Mind

1. Howells, *Heroines of Fiction,* 1: 52.
2. Tyler, *Friendly Jane Austen,* 201.
3. Barbara McLean, "Professional Persuasion: Dr. Anne Elliot," *Persuasions* 15 (16 December 1993): 170–77.

4. Marvin Mudrick, afterword to *Persuasion* (New York: New American Library, 1964), 248.
5. Wollstonecraft, *Vindication of the Rights of Woman*, 147.
6. Cited in *A New Dictionary of Quotations on Historical Principles from Ancient and Modern Sources*, ed. H. L. Mencken (1942; reprint, New York: Knopf, 1991), 765.
7. Byron, *Don Juan*, canto 3, stanza 8 in *Poetical Works*, ed. Frederick Page (London: Oxford University Press, 1970), 686.
8. Fordyce, *Sermons to Young Women*, 1: 104.
9. John Stuart Mill, *The Subjection of Women* (New York: Appleton & Co., 1869), 177.
10. Gilbert and Gubar, *Madwoman in the Attic*, 180.
11. Robert Liddell, *The Novels of Jane Austen* (London: Longmans, 1963), 119.
12. Siegfried Sassoon, *Collected Poems, 1908–1956* (London: Faber & Faber, 1984), 75.
13. "Henry and Emma, a Poem Upon the Model of the Nut-brown Maid" in *The Literary Works of Matthew Prior,* ed. H. Bunker Wright and Monroe K. Spears(Oxford: Clarendon Press, 1959), 1: 279, 295 (lines 13–16; 605–6).
14. Burney, *Cecilia*, 278.
15. Brontë, *Jane Eyre*, 58.
16. Chapman, *Jane Austen*, 98.
17. Anne Thackeray, "Jane Austen," *Cornhill Magazine* (1871), xxiv, cited in Southam, *Critical Heritage,* 2: 167.
18. Elizabeth Jenkins, *Jane Austen* (New York: Pellegrini, 1949), 356.
19. See *Poetical Works of Sir Walter Scott,* 56–126; 133–91.
20. For the two cited poems, see Byron's *Poetical Works,* ed. Page, 252–76.

Chapter 9. Behold Me Immortal

1. Letter of July 1871 from Caroline Austen to James Edward Austen-Leigh, cited in Doody, introduction to *Catharine and Other Writings,* xxii.
2. Honan, *Jane Austen,* 401.
3. Entry of 14 March 1826, *The Journal of Walter Scott, 1825–26,* ed. J. G. Tait (Edinburgh, 1939), 135.
4. William Lyon Phelps, introduction to *The Novels and Letters of Jane Austen* (New York: Holby, 1906), 1: xx.
5. Cited in Southam, *Critical Heritage,* 1: 13.
6. Ibid., 1: 58.
7. Susan Ferrier's comment cited in Le Faye, *Jane Austen,* 208; *British Critic,* March 1818, cited in Southam, *Critical Heritage,* 1: 80; Cardinal Newman, letter of 1891, cited in Southam, *Critical Heritage,* 1: 117; Fitzgerald's letter of 24 December 1871 to W. F. Pollock, *Letters of Edward Fitzgerald* (1894), 2: 131, reprinted in Southam, *Critical Heritage,* 2: 300.
8. Tennyson's remark at Lyme cited in Sarah Chauncey Woolsey, preface to *The Letters of Jane Austen* (Boston: Little Brown, 1903), x; Tennyson's comments about Austen's lifelikeness reprinted in Southam, *Critical Heritage,* 1: 24.
9. Howells, *Criticism and Fiction,* cited in Southam, *Critical Heritage,* 2: 203.
10. Reginald Farrer, "Jane Austen, *ob.* July 18, 1817," in Southam, *Critical Heritage,* 2: 254.
11. "The Janeites," in *Writings in Prose and Verse of Rudyard Kipling,* 31: 169–72.
12. Chapman, *Jane Austen,* 210.
13. Diary entry of 14 March 1826, *Journal of Walter Scott,* ed. Tait, 135.
14. "The Janeites," in *Writings in Prose and Verse of Rudyard Kipling,* 31: 173.
15. "Mysterious Stranger," in *Great Short Works of Mark Twain,* 360.
16. George Bernard Shaw, *John Bull's Other Island* (1907; reprint, London: Constable, 1947), 101.

17. Preface to *The Battle of the Books* (1704), in *The Prose Works of Jonathan Swift*, ed. Temple Scott (London: George Bell, 1907), 1: 160.
18. Mrs. Margaret Oliphant, "Miss Austen and Miss Mitford," *Blackwood's Edinburgh Magazine* 107 (March 1870), 294, in Judith O'Neill, *Critics on Jane Austen* (Coral Gables, Fla.: University of Miami Press, 1970), 13.
19. Anonymous, "To Jane Austen," *Atlantic Monthly* 108 (1911): 572–73. I tracked down this poem after seeing a portion of it quoted in Claudia Johnson's *Janeites* (Princeton: Princeton University Press, 2000), 185.
20. Lord David Cecil, *Jane Austen*, 17, 24.
21. Arnold Bennett, "Books and Persons," *Evening Standard*, 21 July 1927, in *Jane Austen: A Celebration*, ed. Maggie Lane and David Selwyn (Manchester: Carcanet, 2000), 11.
22. Woolf, "Jane Austen," in *Common Reader*, ed. McNeillie, 140.
23. Eudora Welty, "The Radiance of Jane Austen," in *The Eye of the Story*, 4–5.
24. Dorothy Van Ghent, *The English Novel: Form and Function* (New York: Holt, Rinehart & Winston, 1953), 100.
25. Cited in Chapman, *Jane Austen*, 93.
26. Lee Siegel, "A Writer Who Is Good for You," *Atlantic Monthly* 281(January 1998): 93–98.
27. Bruce Chatwin, cited in *Jane Austen*, ed. Lane and Selwyn, 27.
28. Fay Weldon, *Letters to Alice on First Reading Jane Austen* (London: Rainbird, 1984), 97–98.
29. J. 1705, *Complete Poems of Emily Dickinson*, 694.
30. *Selected Poems of Anne Stevenson*, 130.
31. J. K. Rowling, interview with *Bon Appétit*, cited in *The Wire: JASNA-Wisconsin Newsletter* 15 (Spring 2002): 13.
32. Ang Lee, interview by Steve Paulson, *To the Best of Our Knowledge*, Wisconsin Public Radio, 24 December 2000.
33. Margaret Drabble, interview by the author, *Jane Austen and the Courage to Write*, Wisconsin Public Radio, February 1997.
34. James, *Time to Be in Earnest*, 79.
35. Reynolds Price, "One Writer's Place in Fiction," *New York Times*, Op-Ed Page, 27 July 2001, A21.
36. Brabourne, preface to *Letters of Jane Austen*, 1: 47.
37. Siegel, "A Writer Who Is Good for You."
38. Howard Fast, *The Novelist: A Romantic Portrait of Jane Austen* (New York: Samuel French, 1976; 1992), 65, 67. Subsequent quotations are from this edition of Howard Fast's play.
39. Byron, *Don Juan*, stanza 194, in *Poetical Works*, ed. Page, 658.
40. Lyttelton, "Advice to a Lady," in Knox, *Elegant Extracts*, 2: 49–50.
41. Helen Jerome, *Pride and Prejudice: A Sentimental Comedy in Three Acts*, acting edition (New York: French, 1936), 108.
42. Joseph Wiesenfarth, "The Garson-Olivier *Pride and Prejudice:* A Hollywood Story," *Text und Ton im Film*, ed. Paul Goetsch and Dietrich Scheunemann (Tübingen: Gunter Narr, 1997), 84.
43. A. A. Milne, preface to *Miss Elizabeth Bennet: A Play from Pride and Prejudice*, (London: Chatto & Windus, 1936), xii.
44. Rachel Brownstein, "Out of the Drawing Room, Onto the Lawn," in *Jane Austen in Hollywood*, ed. Troost and Greenfield, 14.
45. *Box Office Digest*, 20 July 1940, cited in Wiesenfarth, "The Garson-Olivier *Pride and Prejudice*," 90.
46. Greg Nagan, *The Five-Minute Iliad and Other Instant Classics: Great Books for the Short Attention Span* (New York: Simon & Schuster, 2000), 65.

47. See Menand, "What Jane Austen Doesn't Tell Us," 13.
48. Emma Thompson, *The Sense and Sensibility Screenplay and Diaries: Bringing Jane Austen's Novel to Film* (New York: Newmarket Press, 1996), 179, 186.
49. Nora Nachumi, "'As If!' Translating Austen's Ironic Narrator to Film," in *Jane Austen in Hollywood,* ed. Troost and Greenfield, 132.
50. Peter Monaghan, "With Sex and Sensibility, Scholars Redefine Jane Austen," *The Chronicle of Higher Education* 47 (17 August 2001): A10.
51. Letter of 3 December 1816 to Barry E. O'Meara at St. Helena, in *A New Dictionary of Quotations on Historical Principles from Ancient and Modern Sources,* ed. Mencken, 601.
52. Ang Lee, interview.
53. H. W. Garrod, "Jane Austen: A Depreciation," *Essays by Divers Hands: Transactions of the Royal Society of Literature* 8 (1928): 40, cited in Southam, *Critical Heritage,* 2: 105.
54. David Denby, *Great Books: My Adventures with Homer, Rousseau, Woolf, and Other Indestructible Writers* (New York: Simon & Schuster, 1996), 332–33.
55. Auden, "Letter to Lord Byron, Part 1," in *Letters from Iceland* (London: Faber & Faber, 1937), 21.
56. Anne Brontë, preface to the second edition of *The Tenant of Wildfell Hall* (22 July 1848; reprint, Oxford: Oxford World Classics, 1992), 5.
57. Letter to George Henry Lewes, 19 January 1850, *The Letters of Charlotte Brontë,* ed. Margaret Smith (Oxford: Clarendon Press, 2000), 2: 332.
58. Fay Weldon, interview by the author, *Jane Austen and the Courage to Write,* Wisconsin Public Radio, September 1996.
59. For example, Susannah Fullerton, President of the Jane Austen Society of Australia, notes a 91 percent female membership (private correspondence, 5 March 2002).
60. Julia Keller, "Austen's Powers," *Chicago Tribune,* 17 April 2001, section 2 (Tempo), 1, 4.
61. William Wineke, "All About Jane," *Wisconsin State Journal,* 21 April 2001, section C (Daybreak), 1, 8.
62. Joan Ray, "Deflating the JASNA Myth," *JASNA News* 17 (Winter 2001): 4.
63. See Eve Sedgewick, "Jane Austen and the Masturbating Girl," *Critical Inquiry* 17 (Summer 1991): 818–37. A sample sentence reads, "Elinor's pupils, those lens tractable sphincters of the soul, won't close against the hapless hemorrhaging of her visual attention-flow toward Marianne . . . her completely visual fixation on her sister's specularized, desired, envied, and punished autoeroticism." Douglas Bush's reference to the phallic implications of Mr. Gardiner's fishing tackle is in "Mrs. Bennet and the Dark Gods," *Twentieth-Century Interpretations of Pride and Prejudice,* ed. E. Rubinstein (Englewood Cliffs, N.J.: Prentice-Hall, 1969), 114.
64. Terry Castle, "Was Jane Austen Gay?" *London Review of Books,* 1995, cited in Johnson, "The Divine Miss Jane: Jane Austen, Janeites, and the Discipline of Novel Studies," in *Janeites,* 27.
65. Arielle Eckstut and Dennis Ashton, eds., *Pride and Promiscuity: The Lost Sex Scenes of Jane Austen* (New York: Fireside, 2001), 25.
66. Virginia Woolf, *Times Literary Supplement,* 8 May 1913, in Southam, *Critical Heritage,* 2: 244.
67. Ezra Pound, *ABC of Reading* (New York: New Directions, 1960), 29.
68. Dorothy Sayers, letter to C. S. Lewis, cited in *Jane Austen,* ed. Lane and Selwyn, 74.
69. Robertson Davies, *Tempest-tost* (Toronto: Clarke Irwin, 1951), v.
70. Harold Bloom, ed., *Jane Austen* (Philadelphia: Chelsea House Publishers, 2000), 7.

71. "Fiction," in *A Book of Words*, in *The Writings in Prose and Verse of Rudyard Kipling*, 32: 300.

72. Drabble, interview by the author, *Jane Austen and the Courage to Write,* Wisconsin Public Radio, February 1997.

73. Eudora Welty, "The Radiance of Jane Austen," 12.

74. Twain, "Humorists" (31 July 1906), in *Mark Twain in Eruption,* ed. Bernard DeVoto (New York: Harper & Brothers, 1940), 202.

75. Johanna Johnston, *Runaway to Heaven: The Story of Harriet Beecher Stowe* (New York: Doubleday, 1963), 357.

76. James Austen, *Loiterer* 1, no. 1 (31 January 1789): 7.

77. Weldon, *Letters to Alice on First Reading Jane Austen,* 81–82.

78. Crabbe, "The Library," lines 41–42, in *Complete Poetical Works,* ed. Dalrymple-Champneys and Pollard, 118.

79. J. F. Kirk, 1853 essay on Thackeray, cited in D. Michael Kramp, "The Purity of Jane; or Austen's Cultural Importance in Nineteenth-Century America," *Persuasions* 22 (2000): 34.80. "Personalities," *Collected Essays of Virginia Woolf,* 2: 275.

81. Katherine Mansfield, *Athenaeum*, 3 December 1920, 758–59, in Southam, *Critical Heritage,* 2: 97.

82. Wayne Booth, *The Rhetoric of Fiction* (Chicago: University of Chicago Press, 1961), 266.

83. Woolf, *Times Literary Supplement*, 8 May 1913, in Southam, *Critical Heritage,* 2: 245.

Selected Bibliography

Agulhon, Maurice. *Marianne into Battle: Republican Imagery and Symbolism in France, 1789–1880.* Translated by Janet Lloyd. Cambridge: Cambridge University Press, 1981.

Aldington, Richard. *Jane Austen.* Pasadena: Ampersand Press, 1948.

Amis, Kingsley. *What Became of Jane Austen? And Other Questions.* New York: Harcourt Brace Jovanovich, 1970.

Amos, Chase. *On Female Excellence, or, A discourse: in which good character in women is described.* Litchfield: Collier & Buel, 1792.

Armstrong, Isobel. *Sense and Sensibility.* London and New York: Penguin, 1994.

Auden, W. H. *Letters from Iceland.* London: Faber & Faber, 1937.

Auerbach, Emily. *Maestros, Dilettantes, and Philistines: The Musician in the Victorian Novel.* New York: Peter Lang, 1989.

Austen, Caroline. *My Aunt Jane Austen: A Memoir.* London: Spottiswoode, 1867; reprint, London: Jane Austen Society, 1952.

Austen, James, ed. *The Loiterer.* Oxford: 1789–1790; facsimile edition with an introduction edited by Li-Ping Geng. Ann Arbor: Scholars' Facsimiles and Reprints, 2000.

Austen-Leigh, James Edward. *Memoir of Jane Austen.* Second edition. London: Bentley, 1871.

Austen-Leigh, Mary. *Personal Aspects of Jane Austen.* New York: Dutton, 1920.

Bailey, John. *Introductions to Jane Austen.* London: Oxford University Press, 1931.

Becker, May. *Presenting Miss Jane Austen.* New York: Dodd Mead, 1952.

Bloom, Harold, ed. *Jane Austen.* Philadelphia: Chelsea House Publishers, 2000.

_____. *Shakespeare: The Invention of the Human.* New York: Riverhead, 1998.

Booth, Wayne. *The Rhetoric of Fiction.* Chicago: University of Chicago Press, 1961.

Brabourne, Lord Edward, ed. *Letters of Jane Austen.* London: Bentley & Son, 1884.

Brontë, Charlotte. *Jane Eyre.* Middlesex: Penguin, 1966.

Burney, Fanny. *Evelina.* Oxford: Oxford World Classics, 1982.

_____. *Cecilia: Or Memoirs of an Heiress.* London: Virago, 1986.

Butler, Marilyn. *Jane Austen and the War of Ideas.* Oxford: Clarendon Press, 1975.

Cecil, Lord David. *Jane Austen.* Cambridge: Cambridge University Press, 1935.

———. *A Portrait of Jane Austen.* New York: Hill, 1978.

Chapman, R. W. *Jane Austen: Facts and Problems.* Oxford: Clarendon Press, 1948.

Copeland, Edward, and Juliet McMaster. *Cambridge Companion to Jane Austen.* Cambridge: Cambridge University Press, 1997.

Dickinson, Emily. *The Complete Poems of Emily Dickinson.* Edited by Thomas Johnson. Boston: Little, Brown, 1951.

Doody, Margaret. Introduction to *Catharine and Other Writings.* Oxford: Oxford University Press, 1993.

Eckstut, Arielle, and Dennis Ashton. *Pride and Promiscuity: The Lost Sex Scenes of Jane Austen.* New York: Fireside, 2001.

Fast, Howard. *The Novelist: A Romantic Portrait of Jane Austen.* New York: Samuel French, 1976.

Fergus, Jan. *Jane Austen: A Literary Life.* New York: St. Martin's Press, 1991.

Folsom, Marcia, ed. *Approaches to Teaching Pride and Prejudice.* New York: Modern Language Association, 1993.

Fordyce, James. *Sermons to Young Women.* 1766; reprint, London: T. Cadell, 1792.

Fowler, Karen Joy. *The Jane Austen Book Club.* New York: Putnam's, 2004.

Gay, Penny. *Jane Austen's Pride and Prejudice.* Sydney: Sydney University Press, 1990.

Gilbert, Sandra M., and Susan Gubar. *The Madwoman in the Attic: The Woman Writer and the Nineteenth-Century Literary Imagination.* New Haven: Yale University Press, 1979.

Gregory, Dr. John. *A Father's Legacy to His Daughters.* 1774; reprint, Boston: James Dow, 1834.

Grey, J. David, ed. *Jane Austen's Beginnings: The Juvenilia and Lady Susan.* Ann Arbor: University of Michigan Press, 1989.

———. *The Jane Austen Companion.* New York: Macmillan, 1986.

Halperin, John. *The Life of Jane Austen.* Baltimore: Johns Hopkins University Press, 1984.

Hammond, M. C. *Relating to Jane.* London: Minerva Press, 1998.

Hardy, John. *Jane Austen's Heroines: Intimacy in Human Relationships.* London: Routledge, Kegan & Paul, 1984.

Hartnick, Karen, ed. *Henry and Eliza.* Alberta: Juvenilia Press, 1996.

Hawkbridge, Audrey. *Jane and Her Gentlemen.* London: Peter Owen, 2000.

Honan, Park. *Jane Austen: Her Life.* New York: St. Martin's Press, 1987.

Howells, William Dean. *Heroines of Fiction.* New York: Harper & Brothers, 1901.

Hudson, Glenda. *Sibling Love and Incest in Jane Austen's Fiction.* New York: St. Martin's Press, 1999.

Hunt, Lynn. *Politics, Culture, and Class in the French Revolution.* Berkeley: University of California Press, 1984.

James, P. D. *Time to Be in Earnest: A Fragment of Autobiography.* New York: Knopf, 2000.

Jenkins, Elizabeth. *Jane Austen.* New York: Pellegrini, 1949.

Jerome, Helen. *Pride and Prejudice: A Sentimental Comedy in Three Acts.* New York: French, 1936.

Johnson, Claudia. *Jane Austen: Women, Politics, and the Novel.* Chicago: University of Chicago Press, 1988.

———. *Janeites.* Princeton: Princeton University Press, 2000.

Kaplan, Deborah. *Jane Austen among Women.* Baltimore: Johns Hopkins University Press, 1992.

Kipling, Rudyard. *Writings in Prose and Verse of Rudyard Kipling.* New York: Scribners, 1898–1937.

Knox, V., ed. *Elegant Extracts.* London: John Sharpe, n.d.

Lane, Maggie, and David Selwyn, eds. *Jane Austen: A Celebration.* Manchester: Carcanet, 2000.

Le Faye, Deirdre, ed., *Jane Austen: A Family Record.* London: British Library, 1989.

Lerner, Lawrence. *The Truthtellers: Jane Austen, George Eliot, and D. H. Lawrence.* London: Chatto & Sindus, 1967.

Lewis, Matthew. *The Monk: A Romance.* London: Penguin, 1998.

Liddell, Robert. *The Novels of Jane Austen.* London: Longmans, 1963.

Litz, A. Walton. *Jane Austen: A Study of Her Artistic Development.* New York: Oxford University Press, 1965.

Looser, Devoney. *British Women Writers and the Writing of History, 1670–1820.* Baltimore: Johns Hopkins University Press, 2000.

Mansfield, Katherine. *Novels and Novelists.* Edited by J. M. Murry. New York: Knopf, 1930.

Milne, A. A. *Miss Elizabeth Bennet: A Play from Pride and Prejudice.* London: Chatto & Windus, 1936.

Moore, George. *Avowals.* 1919; reprint, London: Heinemann, 1924.

More, Hannah. *Essays on Various Subjects, Principally Designed for Young Ladies.* 1775; reprint, London: Wilkie & Cadell, 1777.

Mudrick, Marvin. *Jane Austen: Irony as Defense and Discovery.* Princeton: Princeton University Press, 1952.

Myer, Valerie. *Jane Austen: Obstinate Heart.* New York: Arcade, 1997.

Nokes, David. *Jane Austen: A Life.* New York: Farrar Straus & Giroux, 2000.

O'Neill, Judith. *Critics on Jane Austen*. Coral Gables, Fla.: University of Miami Press, 1970.

Pool, Daniel. *What Jane Austen Ate and Charles Dickens Knew*. New York: Touchstone, 1993.

Radcliffe, Ann. *Mysteries of Udolpho*. Oxford: Oxford World Classics, 1998.

Roche, Regina. *The Romance of the Forest*. Oxford: Oxford University Press, 1986.

Rubinstein, E., ed. *Twentieth-Century Interpretations of Pride and Prejudice*. Englewood Cliffs, N.J.: Prentice-Hall, 1969.

Seeber, Barbara. *General Consent in Jane Austen: A Study in Dialogism*. Montreal: McGill-Queen's University Press, 2000.

Shields, Carol. *Jane Austen: A Penguin Life*. New York: Viking, 2001.

Southam, B. C., ed. *Jane Austen: The Critical Heritage*. 2 vols. London: Routledge & Kegan Paul, 1968.

Tanner, Tony. *Jane Austen*. Cambridge, Mass.: Harvard University Press, 1986.

Tave, Stuart. *Some Words of Jane Austen*. Chicago: University of Chicago Press, 1973.

Thompson, Emma. *The Sense and Sensibility Screenplay and Diaries: Bringing Jane Austen's Novel to Film*. New York: Newmarket Press, 1996.

Troost, Linda, and Sayre Greenfield, eds. *Jane Austen in Hollywood*. Lexington: University Press of Kentucky, 1998.

Twain, Mark. *The Complete Short Stories of Mark Twain*. New York: Doubleday, 1957.

_____. *The Adventures of Huckleberry Finn*. Boston: Houghton Mifflin, 1958.

_____. *The Great Short Works of Mark Twain*. New York: Harper & Row, 1967.

Tyler, Natalie. *The Friendly Jane Austen*. New York: Viking, 1999.

Van Ghent, Dorothy. *The English Novel: Form and Function*. New York: Holt, Rinehart & Winston, 1953.

Walpole, Horace. *Castle of Otranto*. London: J. M. Dent, 1993.

Weldon, Fay. *Letters to Alice on First Reading Jane Austen*. London: Rainbird, 1984.

Weliver, Phyllis. *Women Musicians in Victorian Fiction, 1860–1900*. Burlington, Vt.: Ashgate, 2000.

Welty, Eudora. *One Writer's Beginnings*. Cambridge, Mass.: Harvard University Press, 1983.

_____. *The Eye of the Story: Selected Essays and Reviews*. New York: Random House, 1978.

Wiesenfarth, Joseph. *The Errand of Form: An Assay of Jane Austen's Art*. New York: Fordham University Press, 1967.

Wilks, Brian. *Jane Austen.* Maplewood, N.J.: Hamlyn, 1978.

Wollstonecraft, Mary. *Vindication of the Rights of Woman.* 1792; reprint, London: Penguin, 1985.

Woolf, Virginia. *Collected Essays of Virginia Woolf.* London: Hogarth Press, 1966.

_____. *The Essays of Virginia Woolf.* Edited by Andrew McNeillie. London: Hogarth Press, 1986.

_____. *A Room of One's Own.* New York: Harcourt, Brace, 1929.

Index

Adams, Charles (fictional character), 51–52
Addison, Joseph, 94, 95–96
adolescence, 93, 168–69, 179
adolescent works. *See* juvenilia
adventure: in juvenilia, 53–54; in *Northanger Abbey,* 73
"Advice to a Lady" (Lyttelton), 276–77
The African Queen (film), 302
age: adolescence, 93, 168–69, 179; gender and aging, 239; heroines as mature women, 233, 239; maturation as transformative process, 111, 248; nostalgia and, 261; as subject in juvenilia, 62–63
Agulhon, Maurice, 104
Aldington, Richard, 30
Allen, Mrs. (fictional character), 81–83
allusions. *See* literary allusions
Amis, Kingsley, 167
Amos, Chase, 172
Anglo Saxon terms, 224
Anne Elliot. *See* Elliot, Anne (fictional character)
anonymity, women writers and, 4
appearance: aging and, 239; of Anne Elliot, 233; beauty, 122, 133, 144; biographers' preoccupation with, 34; first impressions and prejudice, 152–53; in *Mansfield Park,* 175; parallels between descriptions of Austen and Elizabeth Bennet, 133; in *Persuasion,* 233, 239, 257–58; in *Pride and Prejudice,* 152–53, 156; in *Sense and Sensibility,* 115–16; vanity, 51, 115–16, 249, 251–52
Arabian Nights, 256
argument: in *Emma,* 214; in *Persuasion,* 252–54; in *Pride and Prejudice,* 155–56
aristocracy. *See* class system
artistic talent: in *Emma,* 210–11, 218–19, 225; feminine tasks as limiting to, 211, 214; Mary Bennet and, 142, 143; misdirected, 210–11; in *Persuasion,* 234; in *Pride and Prejudice,* 142, 143, 162; in *Sense and Sensibility,* 104, 109

Ashton, Dennis, 286
Astell, Mary, 85
athleticism and vigor: in *Mansfield Park,* 179–80; in *Northanger Abbey,* 71; in *Persuasion,* 242–43; in *Pride and Prejudice,* 135
Auden, W. H., 118, 281
"Aunt Jane," 7–12, 17, 19–20, 24, 27, 30, 38, 67
Austen, Caroline (niece), 17, 67
Austen, Cassandra (sister): Anne Elliot compared to, 236; as Austen's audience, 42; correspondence with, 9–10, 68; drawing of niece by, *207;* illustrations for "The History of England," *59;* on *Mansfield Park,* 187; portraits of Austen by, *18, 20; Pride and Prejudice* linked to, 144; *Sense and Sensibility* linked to, 102
Austen, Cassy (niece), 19–20
Austen, Charles (brother), gifts to sisters, *172*
Austen, Frank (brother), 170, 194
Austen, Henry (brother), 38; on Austen's last days, 265; as biographer, 4–6, 27, 67; the *Loiterer,* 65, 96, 225–26; novels disparaged by, 96; publication of Austen's works and, 38, 65
Austen, James (brother): the *Loiterer,* 65, 96, 225–26; novels disparaged by, 96
Austen, Jane: Cassandra Austen and, 144; on critics, 5; death of, 265, 267–68; on genius in *Northanger Abbey,* 70; health of, 233, 265, 267; on heroines, 129, 146, 219, 232–33; life and talent belittled, 5, 8, 10, 14, 16–17, 27, 28–31, 32, 36, 271 (*see also* "Aunt Jane"; "Jane"); physical appearance of, 34, 133–34, 163–64; as political, 36, 57, 104–5, 115, 124, 128, 174–75, 185; on *Pride and Prejudice,* 128; publication history, 4, 212; as reader, 48–49, 67, 86–87, 104, 200 (*see also* literary allusions); religion and, 170–71, *172;* self-concept of, 39, 65, 68–69, 84–85, 93, 290. *See also* authorship;

329

Elliot, Anne (fictional character): as artistically talented, 234; as avatar of Austen, 234–35, 258–59; Fanny Price compared to, 233; as heroine, 232–33, 235; intelligence of, 235; Lady Russell and, 239–40; as motherless, 152; physical description of, 234; as useful and resourceful, 235–36

Elliot, Elizabeth (fictional character), 249, 251–52

Elliot, Sir Walter (fictional character), 249–50, 251–52

Elton, Mr. (fictional character), 203, 206, 210, 213, 217, 222–23, 224, 227

Elton, Mrs. (fictional character), 209–10, 225, 227, 231

Emerson, Ralph Waldo, 128

Emma: argument in, 214; authorship in, 213, 230–31; celibacy in, 228; change and stasis in, 214–17, 229–30; character development in, 208–10; class system in, 222–23; critics on, 201, 203; education in, 211–12; gender role reversal in, 229; gentlemanliness in, 221–24; gossip in, 217; independence in, 227, 229; irony in, 213, 221, 230, 250; as *kunstlerroman*, 213; literary allusions in, 202, 212–13, 229, 276–77; love in, 226–27; marriage in, 202–3, 215, 226–29; as masterpiece, 201; matchmaking in, 202–3, 210, 213–14; narrator in, 210, 213, 218; novels as subject in, 212–13; patterns of habit in, 214–17; possible sources of plot, 217; prejudice in, 222; selfishness in, 211, 230; suffering in, 219, 220

Emma Woodhouse. *See* Woodhouse, Emma (fictional character)

emotions: control of, 177; English character and, 223; excess feeling as flaw, 108; Fanny Price as empathetic, 177; gender roles and, 101, 252–53; in *Sense and Sensibility*, 103, 108, 119, 124–25; Woolf on Austen and, 200

encyclopedias: on Austen, 27–28; portraits used in, 21, *22*

endings: critics on, 192–93; in *Emma*, 228–29; in *Mansfield Park*, 184; in

Northanger Abbey, 97–98; in *Persuasion*, 263; in *Sense and Sensibility*, 127

England: Anglo Saxon terms, 224; British imperialism in *Sense and Sensibility*, 116; defense of English life in *Northanger Abbey*, 89–90; Elinor Dashwood as exemplar of British character, 109; "John Bull" and fictional characters, 119; as "land without music," 225; national character of British men, 223–24, 225–26

epistolary novels, mocked in juvenilia, 54–55, 61–62

epitaph, 6

Essays on Various Subjects, Principally Designed for Young Ladies (More), 136

fainting: Austen described as, 276; hysteria in *Persuasion*, 237; in juvenilia, 41, 61–62

Fairfax, Jane (fictional character), 207, 218–20, 225

Fanny Price. *See* Price, Fanny (fictional character)

Farrer, Reginald, 270

fathers: Austen's father, 66, 103, 166, 194; Mr. Bennet in *Pride and Prejudice*, 132, 155, 161–62, 163; conventional characterizations of, 73; Cowper and role of, 195–96; Sir Elliot in *Persuasion*, 249–50, 251–52; Emma as assuming fatherly control of others, 229; Fanny Price's father as absent, 169; General Tilney as villain in *Northanger Abbey*, 89, 91; in juvenilia, 51, 54, 62, 66, 105–6; Mr. Musgrove in *Persuasion*, 246; in *Northanger Abbey*, 71; in "Plan of a Novel," 15–16, 219; in *Sense and Sensibility*, 109, 161–64; Sir Thomas Bertram as father figure in *Mansfield Park*, 173–74, 183–86; Mr. Woodhouse in *Emma*, 214–15, 217, 222, 227. *See also* orphans

A Father's Legacy to His Daughters (Gregory), 44–45, 172

Faulkner, William, 204

"The female philosopher: A Letter," 55–56

femininity: artistic talent and, 211, 214; blushing modesty and, 172–73; education as unfeminine, 82, 164;